PRACTICAL GARDENING
AND
FOOD PRODUCTION
IN PICTURES

A garden points the way to health and heart's content.

PRACTICAL GARDENING

AND

FOOD PRODUCTION

IN PICTURES

BY

RICHARD SUDELL, F.I.L.A.

ODHAMS PRESS LIMITED
LONG ACRE, LONDON, W.C.2

MADE AND PRINTED IN GREAT BRITAIN
BY ODHAMS (WATFORD) LTD., WATFORD

CONTENTS

5

FOREWORD

THIS book is built on an entirely new principle. Every aspect of the art and science of gardening is presented through the medium of pictures and diagrams, so as to enable the veriest novice to undertake with confidence the cultivation of fruit, flowers and vegetables, the care of poultry, bees and rabbits. It has been said that one good picture is worth ten thousand words; this book is proof of the truth of that statement. With it at his elbow, the gardener cannot go wrong, for he is not merely told, but also shown, what to do in every conceivable circumstance.

ACKNOWLEDGMENTS

Thanks are due to the following for permission to use illustrations : The Ministry of Agriculture and the Controller of His Majesty's Stationery Office ; The Ilford Allotment Society ; The *Feathered World* ; Carter's Tested Seeds, Ltd., Raynes Park; George Fowler Lee & Co., Ltd., Reading ; Laxton Bros. (Bedford), Ltd.; Plant Protection, Ltd., Yalding ; Messrs. George Pyne, Topsham, Devon ; Sutton & Sons, Ltd., Reading.

A new front plot before work has been started.

PIONEER WORK

TACKLING A NEW GARDEN PLOT

A new garden plot is like the canvas of a painter, a space whereon a picture will be made. It is a thrilling moment when you have secured your house and then turn to the garden. I have shared many of these exciting moments with the beginner in garden making. You look at the unsightly plot, just as the builder has left it. "What shall I do first?" you ask.

First take a walk round the boundary. Remember a tree or a hedge in your neighbour's plot is *part of your picture*. Note the views, if any. See what is grown in the gardens around. All these neighbouring details will help you in your own garden making. Take a note pad with you. Check up the fences, positions of trees on your own and in nearby gardens. A tree in the next plot may cast a shadow or roots may penetrate. It helps a lot to begin by clearing away rubbish. Make a heap of old bricks, stones, etc. Cut down brambles or tree suckers. Often a new plot looks entirely different when tidied up. Peg out possible paths, lawn areas and beds. During this preliminary work you will get some rough idea of the first layout. Never cut a tree down until you are sure that it is necessary—better live with it awhile. There is no harm in cutting out dead wood from a tree and a few branches could be thinned out. Overhanging branches may have to be lopped.

Then in the evening after a busy day you can make a few trial sketch layouts. Remember every detail noted on your note pad will assist you in making the final plan—the position of manhole

9

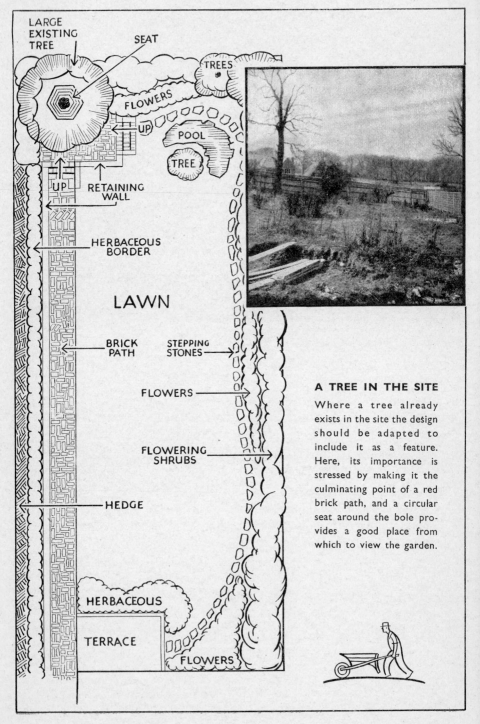

LARGE EXISTING TREE

SEAT

TREES

FLOWERS

UP

POOL

TREE

UP

RETAINING WALL

HERBACEOUS BORDER

LAWN

BRICK PATH

STEPPING STONES

FLOWERS

FLOWERING SHRUBS

HEDGE

HERBACEOUS

TERRACE

FLOWERS

A TREE IN THE SITE

Where a tree already exists in the site the design should be adapted to include it as a feature. Here, its importance is stressed by making it the culminating point of a red brick path, and a circular seat around the bole provides a good place from which to view the garden.

THE PROBLEM OF THE NEW PLOT

The prospect is most discouraging at first sight. Just a dull strip of ground with a little coarse meadow grass and all the rubbish left by the builders lying on the surface. Over the low fence the washing lines and coal sheds, though useful to their owners, are not ornamental.

covers, drains, dumps of soil and levels. On paper put the areas you desire—lawn, vegetable garden, essential paths, flower borders, and shrubberies. The initial creation cannot be done hurriedly. Soon an idea will occur and then you can proceed with the design of your garden.

WHAT IS SOIL?

Soil is the term we use to describe the surface layer of the earth's crust. Briefly there are two types of soil :—

(*a*) Soil that has been under cultivation for a year or more, that is, under the plough, or kept open by hand digging.

(*b*) Soil that has been under grass, in meadow or pasture, or laid down as a lawn.

As gardeners we are not concerned with the unbroken rocks that protrude from the soil in various parts, except when we use them for ornamental purposes, as for instance when we make rock gardens and paths. These rocks are the basis of the various soils, the soils themselves being the rocks crushed

or broken by weather action and by the growth of vegetation through the ages. Naturally, as the rocks vary from district to district, so also do the soils of different localities vary, but for the gardener the golden rule is that " There is no *bad* soil." Every variety of soil has some virtue, and every variety of soil can be so prepared that it will yield good crops. Naturally the soil varies in the amount of hard work needed to bring it into good condition, but there may be some consolation to those who find the task difficult in the fact that the difficult soil is sometimes more fertile than easy soil when it is once in " good heart."

TYPES OF SOIL

Beginners often ask " What is light soil? " The answer is that " light " means light in weight on the spade, not light in colour. The difference between light and heavy soils is due to the size of the soil particles of which they are composed. Heavy soils are composed of very fine particles, which pack closely together. They also hold moisture readily, and very quickly become caked and sticky, or when dried out set into a cement-like lump. Light soils are composed of large soil particles, sand chiefly, and these do not readily adhere to each other, so that when you tread over light soil it shifts under the foot. Light soils also allow water to pass very readily through them, and so become dry rather rapidly in periods of drought.

LIGHT SOILS

The difference between these two extremes is soon discovered by the cultivator, and he must adapt his soil treatment accordingly. Light soils, which quickly lose their moisture, need very heavy dressings of heavy, sticky manure —cow or pig manure is ideal—leaves, and other moisture-holding materials. In addition, any artificial fertilizers that

are applied should be given in spring or during the active growing season of summer. If they are given in autumn they will probably disappear through the soil and be below the part reached by plant roots when they are required.

HEAVY SOILS

Heavy soils, on the other hand, need gritty matter, sand, strawy manure— horse manure if possible—and any other materials that will keep the texture of the soil more open. Artificial fertilizers are often applied in autumn in order that they can work on the soil itself during winter, breaking down the lumps, and gradually penetrating the top spit.

Some soils are very chalky; they may perhaps lie over chalk deposits, which are near enough to the surface to be brought up during digging. These are called calcareous or chalky soils, and their treatment is a little different from

PROTECTIVE PLANTING

Before undertaking any planting the height of the fence has been increased by a simple treillage on which climbers can be trained. This overcomes the difficulty of the immediate surroundings, and the more distant washing and sheds can be screened by careful planting and an attractive little summer house. Flowering standard trees are particularly useful because, not only do they serve this purpose, but also flowers can be grown beneath them.

soils which are deficient in lime. Some soils are composed chiefly of decomposing plant fibres, and free from any trace of lime. Such soils are slightly acid, and although they are ideal for the cultivation of certain flowering plants, they are only a good home for food crops after they have been well limed to counteract the acidity. These soils are generally known as peaty soils. The finest potato growing soils of Lancashire are on the sites of old peat beds.

Old woodland soils, where many seasons' fall of leaves constitutes the top layer, will also have this slight acidity which must be counteracted by additions of lime, but woodland soils are, when first cultivated, rather richer in plant food (and in pests) than peaty moors.

What may be regarded as ideal soils are the marly soils found in many parts of the country, which are very fertile and contain a proportion of lime, and also the cultivated " medium loam " that gardeners produce by deep digging and adequate manuring of any other soil type.

No matter what type of soil the garden has there are sure to be some disadvantages, so adopt methods to improve the soil and where possible, cultivate the plants most suited to the conditions.

TABLE OF SOILS

The following table of soils shows the chief characteristic of each soil type, according to its composition. Soil can be analysed to discover its place in this table, but it is not at all necessary for the amateur gardener to know any more of this matter than he can find out easily by noting how the soil responds to the use of the spade. As before stated, when soil sticks to the spade and is heavy on it, it is *heavy* soil that needs strawy manure and grit and ash in it to improve it. If it shifts under the feet and is light and sandy on the spade it is *light* soil that needs plenty of heavy manure to hold moisture. Probably it is something between these two extremes, and then it can be treated by really deep double digging, adding whatever manure is available.

COMPOSITION OF SOILS

Vegetable or peaty soils contain above 5 per cent humus or decayed vegetable matter.

Chalky or calcareous soil contains above 20 per cent lime or chalk.

Marly soil contains 5 to 20 per cent lime or chalk.

Sandy soil contains over 90 per cent sand.

Loamy soil contains over 30 per cent clay.

Clay loam contains 30 to 50 per cent clay.

Clay soil contains above 50 per cent clay.

TESTING A SITE

No two garden sites are alike; each possesses some local character which makes it different from all other plots. Even on a new housing estate, in surveying sites which on the plan look alike, one finds on closer inspection that they are different. It is, however, just this difference in character that makes garden planning so fascinating; it calls for invention and adaptation to local conditions.

There are three things that I do on visiting the site for a new garden: first I dig a few trial holes about a foot square and 18 in. deep in half a dozen places. This enables me to inspect the nature of the soil. Secondly, I note the kind of vegetation growing on the plot as this is also a guide to the type of soil; for instance, corn spurrey is indicative of a poor soil; rushes of a sour, marshy soil; and rich, luscious grass shows a fertile soil. Thirdly, I note the amount of sunshine and the aspect of the plot.

It is always advisable to check up the boundary measurements with those given on the plan; I have known a variation of 5 ft. in quite a small garden. Recently I opened a trench on a new site to connect a water point. The trench was about 3 ft. deep and I noticed that water accumulated at the lower end revealing a hidden spring. Unexpected discoveries such as this are best exposed right at the start so that full use can be

A NEGLECTED GARDEN

No matter how well kept a garden has been it becomes very wild and overgrown if neglected for a couple of years. Borders get swamped with coarse-growing plants and the choicest flowers are smothered. Overgrown hedges hide a good view with a dense barrier of leaves.

made of them or the necessary steps taken.

If the soil is waterlogged, holes dug here and there will quickly fill with water and from this can easily be seen the amount of drainage required. Trees often occur on a garden site and these should never be destroyed without careful consideration. Sometimes there are far too many trees which must be considerably thinned out, but one or two should always be preserved as they can, with care, be introduced into the layout scheme with delightful effect.

SCREEN PLANTING

A problem which has to be faced at an early stage in garden planning is that of the views obtained from the garden to the surrounding country. If there are ugly buildings they will call for screen planting—one of the first essentials in permanent planting. It may be, on the other hand, that a view can be opened up through a high hedge or a belt of trees. I have seen gardens near the

seaside where the vegetation has been allowed to grow 30 or 40 ft. high and completely shut out the view of the sea. Opportunities should not be missed in this way, but each garden planned according to its surroundings.

IDEAL SITE

Let me say a word or two about selecting the site for a new garden. This is often determined by the house being already built, but if there is a free choice the ideal site should be not too overlooked by the surrounding plots, have a slope away from the house, preferably to the south, have a deep soil and subsoil that retains moisture. The average good soil is about 8 in. to a foot in depth with a subsoil of marl or clay, but we have to be content with the plot as we find it, and this ideal is not always attainable.

Before anything is attempted in the way of a layout, an accurate plan of the site is necessary. This is usually obtainable either from the estate agent or by a survey, and it is then quite easy, with the help of tracing paper, to indicate the various areas. For example, the flower garden and lawns should occupy the area nearest the house ; the vegetable and fruit garden being in a less conspicuous part of the plot. An area would also be required for service in connexion with the house itself. The front section of the garden is usually treated in an ornamental fashion.

TYPE OF GARDEN

There is another point to consider, and that is the use to which the garden is going to be put. Is it to be a pleasure garden entirely with gay borders and beds of flowers, trees and shrubs, plenty of lawn for games or leisure? Is it to be a gardener's garden with beds and borders for the cultivation of special flowers and plants? Is an area to be devoted to food production, vegetables, salads and fruit? Is a large section of it to be occupied by a rock garden? There are a hundred and one possible combinations of these different types of garden which can only be made by the person responsible for the care and maintenance. Garden planning is essentially individualistic and before it is finally settled a consensus of opinion of the members of the household should be taken to ensure a mutually satisfactory decision.

Do not consider your plan only from the point of view of the garden. Remember that a large proportion of the day is spent indoors and it is important that the principal windows should have a pleasant outlook.

TAKE YOUR TIME

To many amateurs the first sight of a new garden plot is a little formidable, and I am afraid many abandon the attempt to create a garden. The task is, however, made much easier by adopting some plan that can be carried out over a period of two or three years. I have seen so many gardeners acquire an ideal garden plot

A FINE VIEW DISCLOSED

The borders are well planted with gay flowers. The paths laid with crazy paving and a sundial set on an enlarged portion at the end. Some of the trees have been removed completely and the remainder trimmed. The hedge has been clipped and thus a charming view disclosed.

Remember the children; don't have a " keep off the grass " garde. .

and start off with too ambitious a scheme which, owing to drought or some other factor, they have had to abandon. Avoid this disappointment by tackling the work in easy stages. Each section of the work can have the individual attention of the owner and the finished garden is a personal achievement. I always begin with the parts nearest the house ; there may be a terrace to be built, and the necessary service paths must be constructed. Then the lawn and flower borders can be laid out to be followed by the vegetable and fruit garden. Where there is a plot of about 40 ft. by 60 ft. to be dealt with, an amateur, by working in the weekends and long evenings, could complete the work in about a couple of years. If it is possible to afford to have certain parts of the work done by contractors, such as the terrace, paths, lawns, digging, leaving only the planting to be done by the owner himself, the same garden could, of course, be made in a single season. But there is a great satisfaction about doing all the work oneself, and there are

very few constructional jobs which are beyond the scope of the amateur, provided the operation is thoroughly understood beforehand and the work is not done too hurriedly. This section of the book is intended to help those who wish to design and make a garden. Each part of the garden is dealt with separately, and varied possibilities shown for each feature.

Those who have no time to do all the preliminary heavy work, yet cannot afford to employ a contractor, will find that a man employed by the hour, even if he has had no previous experience of such work, will be able to help a great deal in levelling sites for lawns, laying the foundation for paths and do rough digging provided the work is first explained clearly. I like a garden that is growing and I think most amateurs feel the same ; when it is finished we look round for fresh fields to conquer, and a programme spread over three years is the best policy and gives the most satisfaction.

SMALL GARDEN ON A SLOPE

Variations of level add considerable interest to the garden. Banks can be treated informally as in this garden where supporting rocks are covered with easily grown plants. The second rise is treated in the same way, and all the steps are made of the same stone as the path.

VALUE OF FLOWER BORDERS

The borders of this front garden are filled with colourful summer flowers. Note the treatment of the trellis fence which slopes up at the house wall; this gives added privacy between two bow windows, and could be used to provide support for some choice variety of climbing plant.

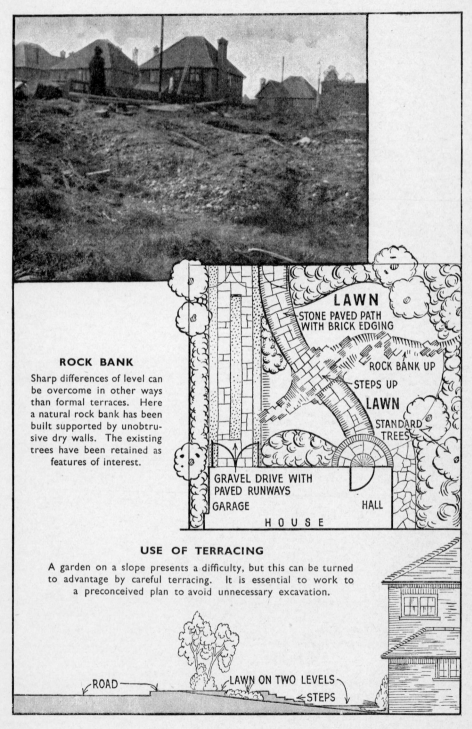

ROCK BANK

Sharp differences of level can be overcome in other ways than formal terraces. Here a natural rock bank has been built supported by unobtrusive dry walls. The existing trees have been retained as features of interest.

LAWN
STONE PAVED PATH
WITH BRICK EDGING

ROCK BANK UP

STEPS UP

LAWN

STANDARD
TREES

GRAVEL DRIVE WITH
PAVED RUNWAYS

GARAGE   HALL

H O U S E

USE OF TERRACING

A garden on a slope presents a difficulty, but this can be turned to advantage by careful terracing. It is essential to work to a preconceived plan to avoid unnecessary excavation.

ROAD   LAWN ON TWO LEVELS
STEPS

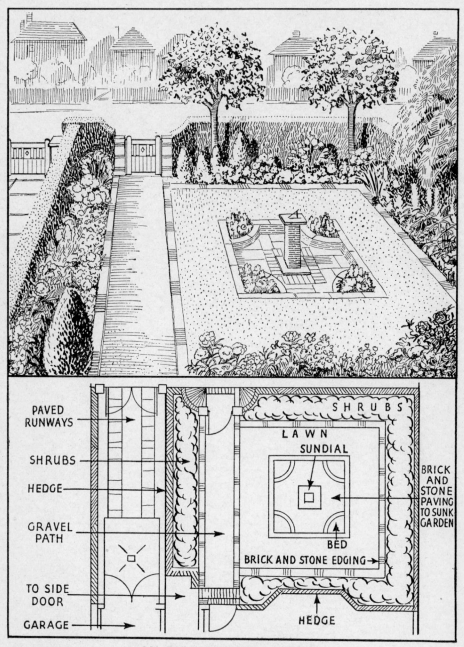

Labels on the diagram:
PAVED RUNWAYS
SHRUBS
HEDGE
GRAVEL PATH
TO SIDE DOOR
GARAGE
SHRUBS
LAWN
SUNDIAL
BED
BRICK AND STONE EDGING
BRICK AND STONE PAVING TO SUNK GARDEN
HEDGE

AN EASILY TENDED GARDEN

The maintenance of this front garden has been minimized by the introduction of a stone-paved sunk garden and flowering shrubs. A narrow strip of brick and stone paving makes a neat and effective edging to the lawn. The sketch shows the view that would be obtained from the windows of the house, if the garden were laid out as detailed in the diagram given here.

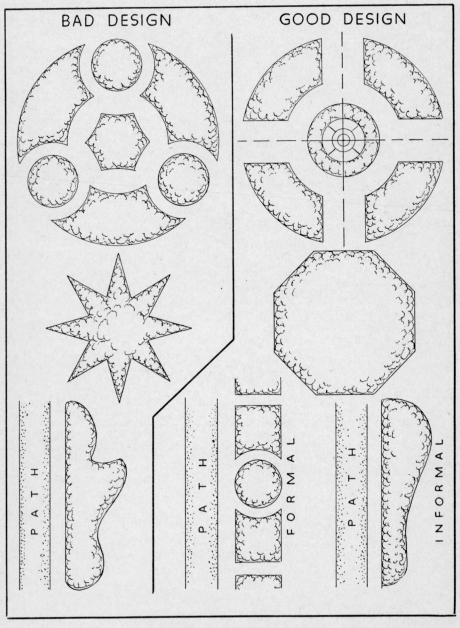

DESIGNS FOR FORMAL BEDS

Cut-out beds in the lawn can look most attractive, but the design must be simple. Not only are elaborate schemes difficult to construct, but they tend soon to lose their shapes by constant edge clipping. On the right are seen simplified forms of the ideas on the left. Formal beds demand considerable care and must never be allowed to get untidy. Regular weeding, hoeing and edge clipping are essential if the design is to retain a clean and neat appearance.

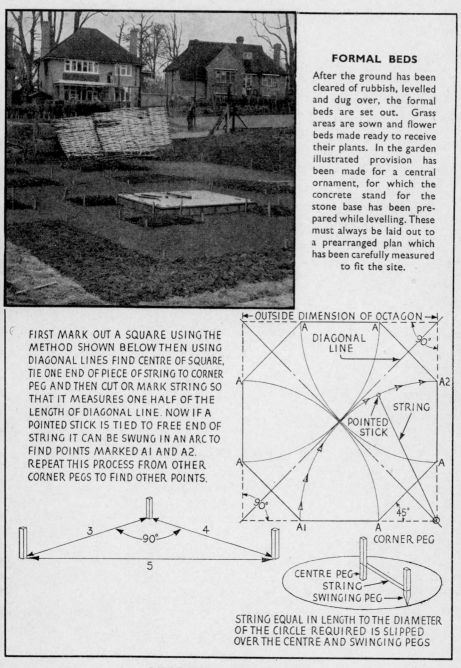

FORMAL BEDS

After the ground has been cleared of rubbish, levelled and dug over, the formal beds are set out. Grass areas are sown and flower beds made ready to receive their plants. In the garden illustrated provision has been made for a central ornament, for which the concrete stand for the stone base has been prepared while levelling. These must always be laid out to a prearranged plan which has been carefully measured to fit the site.

FIRST MARK OUT A SQUARE USING THE METHOD SHOWN BELOW THEN USING DIAGONAL LINES FIND CENTRE OF SQUARE, TIE ONE END OF PIECE OF STRING TO CORNER PEG AND THEN CUT OR MARK STRING SO THAT IT MEASURES ONE HALF OF THE LENGTH OF DIAGONAL LINE. NOW IF A POINTED STICK IS TIED TO FREE END OF STRING IT CAN BE SWUNG IN AN ARC TO FIND POINTS MARKED A1 AND A2. REPEAT THIS PROCESS FROM OTHER CORNER PEGS TO FIND OTHER POINTS.

OUTSIDE DIMENSION OF OCTAGON

DIAGONAL LINE

STRING

POINTED STICK

CORNER PEG

CENTRE PEG
STRING
SWINGING PEG

STRING EQUAL IN LENGTH TO THE DIAMETER OF THE CIRCLE REQUIRED IS SLIPPED OVER THE CENTRE AND SWINGING PEGS

DIRECTIONS FOR LAYOUT

The equipment required to lay out the garden areas consists of a few pointed sticks, some sharpened pegs, a tape measure and a cord. Right angles are secured by triangulation.

LAWN

HEDGE

CRAZY PAVED PATH

KITCHEN
YARD

LAVENDER HEDGE

HOUSE

THE L-SHAPED HOUSE

Many semi-detached houses are built with a kitchen block projecting beyond the main structure, leaving a rectangular space behind half the house. This can charmingly be filled by a small formal garden with patterned paving and surrounded by a lavender hedge.

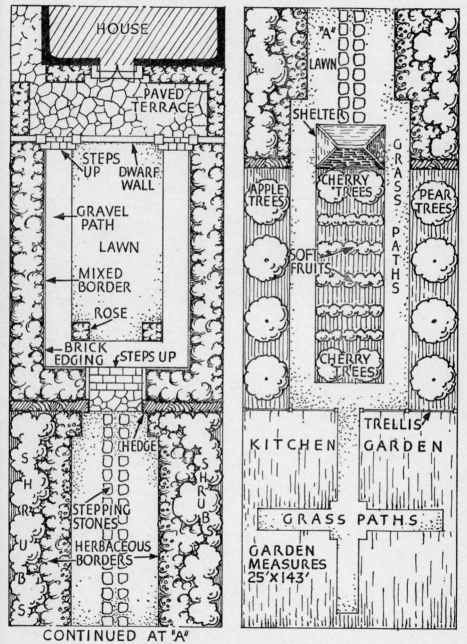

HOUSE

PAVED TERRACE

STEPS UP

DWARF WALL

GRAVEL PATH

LAWN

MIXED BORDER

ROSE

BRICK EDGING

STEPS UP

HEDGE

STEPPING STONES

HERBACEOUS BORDERS

SHRUBS

SHRUBS

"A" LAWN

SHELTER

GRASS PATHS

APPLE TREES

CHERRY TREES

PEAR TREES

SOFT FRUITS

CHERRY TREES

KITCHEN GARDEN

TRELLIS

GRASS PATHS

GARDEN MEASURES 25'x143'

CONTINUED AT "A"

UTILIZING A LONG NARROW SITE

The simplest way of dealing with a long narrow site is to divide it into separate areas. Near the house is the main lawn leading from the terrace and surrounded by herbaceous borders.

From this there is a less formal garden of herbaceous plants backed by shrubs with a summer house at one end. Beyond this is the fruit garden and then the kitchen garden.

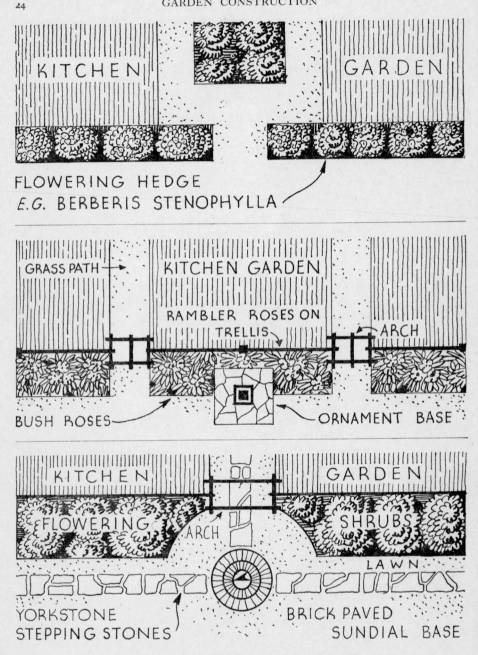

KITCHEN   GARDEN

FLOWERING HEDGE
E.G. BERBERIS STENOPHYLLA

GRASS PATH →   KITCHEN GARDEN

RAMBLER ROSES ON
TRELLIS   ARCH

BUSH ROSES   ORNAMENT BASE

KITCHEN   GARDEN

FLOWERING   SHRUBS

ARCH

LAWN

YORKSTONE
STEPPING STONES   BRICK PAVED
SUNDIAL BASE

HEDGE PARTITIONS IN THE GARDEN

The use of hedges to divide the kitchen from the pleasure garden has much to recommend it. If evergreen shrubs are used, these act as a windbreak in addition to being ornamental.

Spring flowering shrubs afford welcome colour at a time when it is most needed, and roses form an exquisite summer background for lawn, flower beds or vegetable patch.

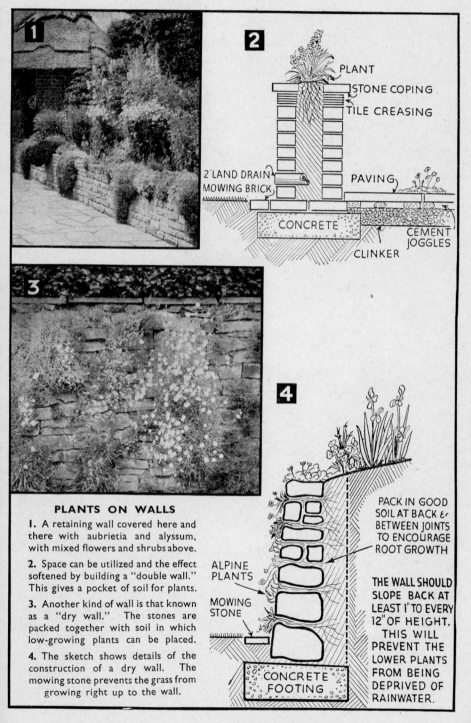

1

2

PLANT

STONE COPING

TILE CREASING

2' LAND DRAIN
MOWING BRICK

PAVING

CONCRETE

CEMENT
JOGGLES

CLINKER

3

4

PACK IN GOOD
SOIL AT BACK &
BETWEEN JOINTS
TO ENCOURAGE
ROOT GROWTH

ALPINE
PLANTS

MOWING
STONE

THE WALL SHOULD
SLOPE BACK AT
LEAST 1" TO EVERY
12" OF HEIGHT.
THIS WILL
PREVENT THE
LOWER PLANTS
FROM BEING
DEPRIVED OF
RAINWATER.

CONCRETE
FOOTING

PLANTS ON WALLS

1. A retaining wall covered here and there with aubrietia and alyssum, with mixed flowers and shrubs above.

2. Space can be utilized and the effect softened by building a "double wall." This gives a pocket of soil for plants.

3. Another kind of wall is that known as a "dry wall." The stones are packed together with soil in which low-growing plants can be placed.

4. The sketch shows details of the construction of a dry wall. The mowing stone prevents the grass from growing right up to the wall.

CRAZY PAVING

2. A charming effect is here produced by an artistic curving of the crazy paving path leading to a small paved area in the lawn. Both path and area are lined with edging plants, some of which are allowed to encroach.

GRASS PATH

1. A broad grass path is an admirable foil to the bright colours of the double mixed flower border. Although not so serviceable as the harder wearing materials, careful maintenance will ensure a long life for such a path.

VISTA EFFECT

4. The trees at the end of this grass path have been carefully thinned to allow a view of the countryside beyond the garden. The twin borders give an impression of spaciousness.

CONCRETE WALK

3. A concrete walk bordered by flowers to soften the effect. This material is very serviceable and soon weathers to an unobtrusive grey tone. Such a path could be widened by adding grass verges at either edge of the concrete.

MAKING A GRAVEL PATH

1. Clean dry paths are essential in a garden. One of the most economical materials to use is gravel. Where the subsoil is inclined to be heavy the foundation of the path should be made up of five inches, at least, of broken brick or large stones, and three inches of hard clinker. If the subsoil is light four inches of clinker alone will be sufficient. This is roughly levelled, rolled and rammed before the gravel is put on. The latter must be evenly distributed, and it is wiser to tip the heaps at the side of the proposed footway rather than in the centre to ensure this. The surface must be consolidated by ramming and then rolled.

STEPPING STONES

3. To provide easy walking in all weathers without spoiling the effect of a broad expanse of grass, stepping stones can be laid in the lawn. They should be laid flush with the grass to avoid interference with mowing. For this purpose use large rectangular slabs of stone placed at even distances spaced for comfortable strides. This idea can be used in many parts of the garden as it is equally suitable for inclusion in a formal layout or in the informal section and as an approach to the rock garden.

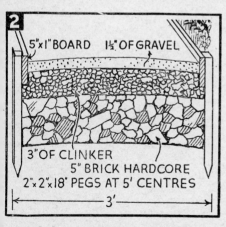

2. Section through a gravel path.

CRAZY PAVING

4. A happy compromise between formal and informal can be obtained by the use of crazy paving laid as a path with straight edges. If the paving is laid on soil the effect is soon softened by the growth of moss in the crevices. The steps in this picture are of brick and lead to a paved terrace similar to the path.

LAYING PAVING

1. The stones are laid on joggles of cement as shown, or bedded into sand.

2. The stones are cut to fit in a certain area, and a line of string across the paved area assists in keeping the longitudinal lines parallel.

3. The stones are bedded down to the required level by lightly tapping with the butt end of a 7-lb. hammer.

4. When it is intended to set plants in the joints, these are lightly raked out and a mixture of sand and soil brushed in to provide a root-hold for alpines.

5. The finished work should not show any signs of a straight joint. All the stones are keyed together into a strong mosaic.

GOOD IDEAS FOR GARDEN STEPS

1. A delightfully informal effect can be obtained by a flight of steps constructed in Somerset ripple-faced stone.   Note how the alpine planting has been kept away from the tread, providing a clear space for easy walking.

2. Details of the construction of a short flight of steps in crazy paving on concrete foundation.

3. Old red roofing tiles make an admirable riser for a flight of steps; they are easy to lay and their dark colour contrasts with the more sombre shade of the stone tread.

4. Steps built of Westmorland rock are unobtrusive and reliable to walk upon.   The whole effect is softened by judicious planting.

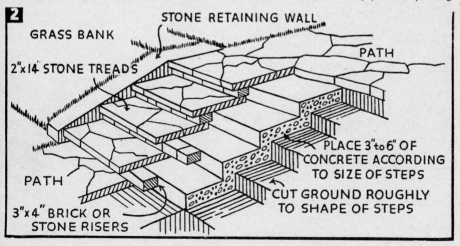

STONE RETAINING WALL

GRASS BANK

PATH

2"x14" STONE TREADS

PLACE 3"to 6" OF CONCRETE ACCORDING TO SIZE OF STEPS

CUT GROUND ROUGHLY TO SHAPE OF STEPS

PATH

3"x4" BRICK OR STONE RISERS

SMALL GARDENS

Even the smallest plot can be made colourful by careful planning and skilful utilization of all available space.

HOW TO UTILIZE SPACE

1. Gay borders of bright flowers, geraniums in a hanging basket and wired pots on the trellis.

2. Tomatoes placed against the walls, hanging pots by the window and a neat miniature fence.

3. Wire netting protects the plot from dogs and footballs, boards the beds from careless feet.

4. Brick walls with ramblers, stone vases and seats, steps and terracing in a formal layout.

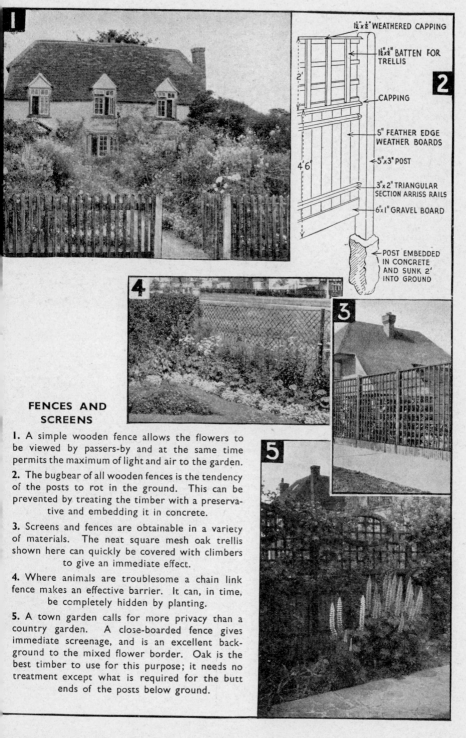

Diagram labels:
- 1¾"x⅝" WEATHERED CAPPING
- 1¾"x⅞" BATTEN FOR TRELLIS
- CAPPING
- 5" FEATHER EDGE WEATHER BOARDS
- 5"x3" POST
- 3"x2" TRIANGULAR SECTION ARRISS RAILS
- 6"x1" GRAVEL BOARD
- POST EMBEDDED IN CONCRETE AND SUNK 2' INTO GROUND

FENCES AND SCREENS

1. A simple wooden fence allows the flowers to be viewed by passers-by and at the same time permits the maximum of light and air to the garden.

2. The bugbear of all wooden fences is the tendency of the posts to rot in the ground. This can be prevented by treating the timber with a preservative and embedding it in concrete.

3. Screens and fences are obtainable in a variety of materials. The neat square mesh oak trellis shown here can quickly be covered with climbers to give an immediate effect.

4. Where animals are troublesome a chain link fence makes an effective barrier. It can, in time, be completely hidden by planting.

5. A town garden calls for more privacy than a country garden. A close-boarded fence gives immediate screenage, and is an excellent background to the mixed flower border. Oak is the best timber to use for this purpose; it needs no treatment except what is required for the butt ends of the posts below ground.

CLOTHING A DEAD TREE

1. A dead tree makes an excellent climbing post for Virginian creeper or clematis and can thus be turned from an eyesore to an asset.

HIDING A GULLY

2. A gully can be effectively hidden by growing Cotoneaster horizontalis over it. This shrub bears bright scarlet berries in the autumn

CONCEALING A DRAINPIPE

3. A sheltered corner of the house with sunny aspect provides an ideal place for Abutilon vitifolium, which will eventually completely screen the drainpipe on the house wall

DISGUISING A SHELTER

4. A concrete or steel air-raid shelter is an ugly structure. Usually it is partly buried below ground; in that case the roof and sides can be built up to form a rock garden

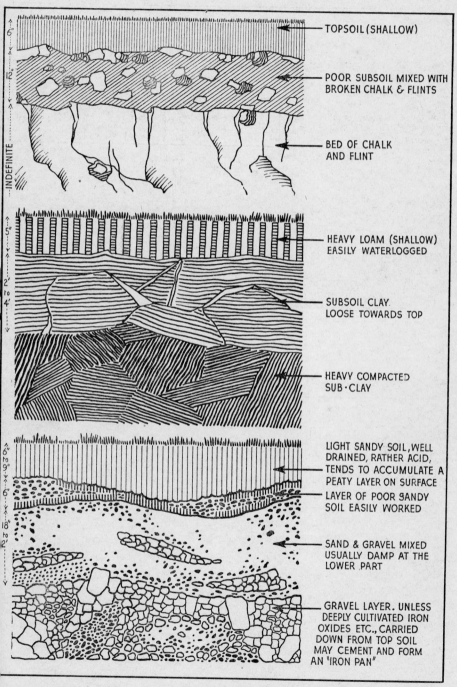

DIAGRAM SHOWING VARIETIES OF TOPSOIL AND SUBSOIL

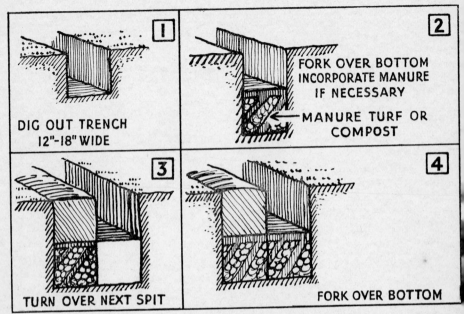

DIAGRAM ILLUSTRATING DOUBLE DIGGING

The most fertile soil is in the top layer, but to improve drainage and fertility it is necessary to break up the subsoil. This is done by double digging or bastard trenching. The soil is moved from the first trench and left in a heap for filling in the last trench when the digging is completed. The subsoil is broken up with a stout digging fork but left where it is, and into it is worked manure, stones if they are not too large, grass clippings and vegetable matter.

DIAGRAM ILLUSTRATING RIDGING

Ridging is carried out in three operations. Mark the ground to be dug in strips three spades wide. Start at the far end of the first and take out a trench 1 ft. wide. Then turn spit A into the centre of the trench, followed by spit B also into the centre and finally spit C on top of the first two. When the whole is completed there will be a series of ridges parallel to each other. This method of ridging is especially beneficial for heavy clay soils.

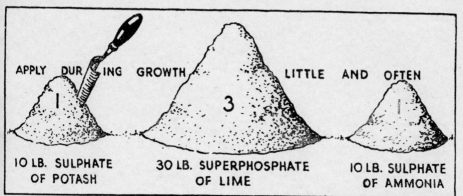

APPLY DURING GROWTH

LITTLE AND OFTEN

1

3

10 LB. SULPHATE OF POTASH

30 LB. SUPERPHOSPHATE OF LIME

10 LB. SULPHATE OF AMMONIA

For a 10 rod plot, one to two tons of animal manure with the above quantities of fertilizers should be sufficient to keep the ground in good heart.

FERTILIZERS AND MANURES

A garden is usually made on ground that has previously been cultivated, and so the soil is assumed to be sufficiently fertile for vegetable production. But vegetables take a lot out of the soil. Many are greedy feeders; the vegetation is nearly all taken away instead of being allowed to die down and decay into the ground, and the soil is not enriched, as is pasture, by animal droppings. So the gardener must constantly feed the soil with animal manures and artificial fertilizers if he desires good results.

FOUR FERTILIZERS

Plants need a considerable number of chemical substances with which to build up their stems, leaves, flowers and fruits, but from the practical gardener's viewpoint only four need be considered. The other substances are usually present in any soil, and certainly in all soils reasonably well worked and well supplied with decaying organic manure.

The four substances that are of vital importance are :—

Nitrogen. This makes plants grow to a large size, increasing the length of stems, the size of leaves, flowers and fruits. Without nitrogen plants are stunted, and the foliage may become prematurely yellow.

Potash. A general stimulant, increasing the depth of colour in leaves and flowers, and maintaining health and vigour.

Phosphorus. This encourages the growth of flowers and fruits.

Lime. This acts on soil particles in such a way that plant food is made soluble, so that the roots can absorb it.

One might think that if these four chemical substances are the essentials, the gardener need only apply them generously to be quite sure of good crops from his garden. Soil fertility is hardly so simple an affair as that. It is, in fact, so complicated that scientists are still trying to solve its mysteries, and the more they explore them the more complex the subject appears. However, the practical food gardener will not go far wrong if he keeps more or less to these four fertilizers, provided he understands how they should be balanced one against the other.

HUMUS NEEDED

The first consideration when dealing with the question of fertilizers is the texture of the soil. This must be got right before anything else is done. If soil has not enough decaying organic matter, or " humus," in its composition to take hold of, and hold on to, the plant

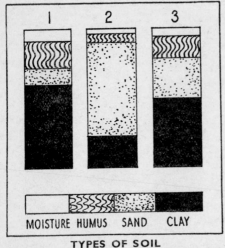

TYPES OF SOIL

The proportions of humus, sand and clay determine the type of soil, as shown. **1.** Clay soil. **2.** Sandy soil. **3.** Loam.

foods, it is just a waste of labour and cash to use fertilizers. Plants can absorb only soluble food. The reason why they do not grow in desert sand is that water passes down through the soil into the subsoil so rapidly that the plant roots have no time to take in the plant food that is in solution. If your garden soil is too sandy, you can keep on for ever giving it soluble fertilizer and still have poor crops. By burying grass, weeds or manure, you add humus to the soil, and it is this humus which holds on to moisture even during drought. You have only to turn over a deep pile of old leaves in the height of summer to realize how moisture is held by them.

THE COMPOST PIT

Other vegetable matter—decaying plant tops, parings, and so on—are similar in this respect to leaves, and so are the various farm and stable manures. It is up to every cultivator, therefore, to turn his attention to the provision of humus, and the best way for the average householder to accumulate stores of this valuable material is for him to construct a compost pit, the construction of which is shown in the accompanying illustration.

All kinds of vegetable refuse from the house should be thrown into the compost pit and there allowed to decay, or at least to begin to decay. As each layer becomes about 6 in. thick, a little calcium cyanamide, or sulphate of ammonia (1 oz. to the square yard), is sprinkled on the refuse. This assists decomposition and makes the contents of the pit more quickly available as plant food.

ALWAYS COVER MANURE

A dusting of soil should be spread over the layer of refuse and the cyanamide: this will not only minimize the odour arising from the pit, but the soil will absorb the ammonia that is given off during decomposition. This is important, because ammonia is a form of soluble nitrogenous fertilizer. While the heap is decomposing, it should be turned over occasionally to admit air ; this hastens decomposition.

It is not absolutely necessary for vegetation to be decomposed before it is dug into the soil, but experiments have shown that the most value is added to the land when partly decomposed organic refuse is incorporated. There is an old saying that the proper place for manure to decay is in the soil. This would seem to contradict the statement that manure should be partially decayed before it is used. The true meaning of the phrase is that manure should not be allowed to lie uncovered on the soil surface, or even in a heap. If stable manure is stacked temporarily in a heap, it should always be covered with a layer of soil 3 in. or 4 in. thick, which will absorb the ammonia that the manure gives off. As it is the ammonia of the manure heap that makes it offensive, the soil covering will be appreciated by neighbours!

Mulches of old decayed manure are sometimes recommended. The manure used for these should be in dry crumbly condition, not wet and odorous. If manure is in warm moist condition, and is used to mulch soil surfaces, it should be turned in under about 3 in. of soil.

In the average garden, large enough to supply the bulk of the vegetables needed by the household, the supply of available refuse from the house, from grass clippings (where a lawn exists) and from the sweeping up of leaves, is quite sufficient to form enough compost to meet the needs of the vegetable plot. This does not mean that *food* sufficient for the needs of the plants grown has been supplied, but only that sufficient organic matter, or humus, is in this way put back into the soil. Plant food is also necessary.

VALUE OF MANURE

Generally speaking, the chief value of manure is its power to hold plant food in solution. The best place for it, therefore, is where plant roots are likely to be ; that is, in or just below the top fertile soil. As small seedlings and a good many older plants are damaged if their roots come into actual contact with fresh manure, the best practice is to fork manure lightly into the trenches dug when preparing the ground for the crop.

Although the contents of the compost pit are not very rich in actual food, animal droppings, which contain other waste products, do actually feed the plants, for they contain all the three vital plant foods—nitrates, phosphates and potash. Very rarely, however, are the quantities of stable manure available sufficient to supply all the plant food that the crops need. The best way to supplement the supply is to use a dressing of a general fertilizer that contains all three foods.

Those who prefer to mix this up for themselves can use the following :—

Seven lb. sulphate of ammonia (a form of nitrate), 14 lb. sulphate of potash (a form of potash), 28 lb. superphosphate of lime (a form of phosphate).

Note particularly : Though we speak of superphosphate of *lime*, this does not mean that there is any free lime in the chemical ; as a matter of fact, there is no available lime in it at all, and lime has to be added to the plot after digging, whether a general fertilizer is used or not. The three ingredients, the proportions of which can vary a little according to the plants that are being treated, can be mixed freely and stored ready for use as and

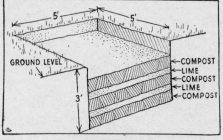

COMPOST PIT

The sides of the pit made for the compost heap can be lined with bricks or cemented.

when required. The mixture recommended can be used at the rate of 1 oz. or 2 oz. per square yard among growing crops, or over soil that is to be forked over in summer or autumn to receive a fresh crop. Not all common fertilizers are suitable for mixing. Nitrate of soda, for instance, is a useful form of nitrogenous fertilizer, but it must be applied by itself and only during the growing season. Do not try to mix it.

OTHER FERTILIZERS

There are, in addition to general fertilizers, various other substances commonly used by gardeners. Each has a definite use and a definite position in horticultural practice. Some are best on light soils, some on heavy, some best for autumn use, some for spring. Some are impure and to be used with extreme caution, some are concentrated and suitable for use in very small quantities on very special plants. It is to make these points clear that these fertilizers are here described, but I want first to emphasize this point : *If you dig well, use organic matter as manure in the trenches, and supplement this with a general fertilizer*, you can grow most crops very well indeed, and it is not worth while to do anything more than this on a small vegetable garden.

NITROGENOUS FERTILIZERS

Sulphate of ammonia. Suitable for use on all soils except acid ones. Can be used in spring and summer at the rate of ½ oz. per square yard. Should not be mixed with basic slag or lime, but can be mixed with sand for even distribution. Use as top dressing.

Nitrate of soda. Suitable for any soils, but specially valuable if applied to light soil at frequent intervals during active growth. Use in liquid form, or water in well after applying top dressing. Rate about ½ oz. per square yard.

Calcium cyanamide. Suitable for lime-free soils. Apply to vacant ground only, at least seven days before it is sown or planted, at ½ oz. to the square yard if used in conjunction with organic refuse.

Nitro-chalk. Two oz. per square yard can be advantageously used on heavy soils and acid soils in spring and summer. Mix into the surface layer while digging or hoeing.

Soot. Of slight food value only; its chief value lies in its power to raise the soil temperature by darkening its colour. Sprinkle until soil surface is black. Also useful, with lime, as an insecticide.

Dried blood. From ½ oz. to 1 oz. of this used in spring is a good dressing, suitable for any soils. Supplies nitrogen.

PHOSPHATIC FERTILIZERS
Superphosphate of lime. It should be regarded as an acid manure, and where the soil of a food garden is naturally acid, superphosphate should be used in spring only after heavy winter dressings of lime. Two oz. per square yard is an average dressing.

Basic slag. A very valuable form of phosphate for use in the vegetable garden. Suitable for all soils, so long as they contain humus, and slow acting; therefore long lasting in effect. Use in autumn or winter at the rate of 2 oz. to 4 oz. per square yard.

Bonemeal or boneflour. Up to 3 oz. per square yard is a good dressing suitable for soils that are not too well supplied with humus. Can be applied in spring, but is slow acting, and its effect is felt over the second season.

Dissolved bones. Use as boneflour. Best for use on chalky soil.

N.B.—*As a general rule all fertilizers are best applied to the surface, hoed in or washed in by rain.*

POTASH FERTILIZERS
Sulphate of potash. Very useful on heavy soils. Up to 1 oz. per square yard mixed with other fertilizers and applied in spring or autumn.

Kainit. Less pure than sulphate of potash, but equally useful except on a few crops such as strawberries, where the purer form is needed. Can be used at 2 oz. per square yard in autumn.

Nitrate of potash. Useful for all soils. Can be applied in spring or autumn at ½ oz. to 1 oz. per square yard.

LIME
Slaked lime (i.e., the ordinary lime supplied by any local builder) is the most usual form in which to apply the necessary lime to a food plot. Any quantity up to ¾ lb. per square yard can be used,

HOP MANURE

Hop manure, which is clean and odourless can be used in place of stable manure.

but for an average plot 4 oz. the first season and an annual dressing of 2 oz. to 3 oz. subsequently is about right. Dress over the surface immediately after digging. There is a common superstition that lime and manure should not both be used on the same ground. Actually, lime hastens the decay of organic refuse, and can be used in the compost pit for this purpose. On the open ground the manure is dug in during digging, and the lime added as a surface dressing immediately the digging is complete. It gets washed down to the manure, aids in its decomposition, and the released plant food which results is absorbed by the surrounding soil and retained for use by the plant. **Powdered chalk.** Use exactly as lime, but more freely, on light soils.

Gas lime. To be used only on vacant soils in autumn, where land can lie idle until the spring. It is an insecticide and very useful on soils where club root has been troublesome. Use about 4 oz. per square yard.

ORGANIC MANURES

Farmyard drainings. Use diluted with about three times the amount of water. Such liquid manure is rich in nitrogen, but not in phosphates.

Poultry manure. One pint of dry droppings in 2 gal. of water makes enough liquid fertilizer for two-thirds of a square yard of food garden.

Cow or sheep manure. Use in the same way as poultry manure.

Stable manure. This is a variable manure, and must be judged by its appearance. Good samples are " sweet," and the straw will be well rotted or " short." In 1 ton of stable and other animal manure there may be about 10 lb. of nitrogen, 10 lb. of potash and 5 lb. of phosphates. Two loads of stable manure would be a very good dressing for a 10 rod plot, but a smaller dressing supplemented by artificials would suffice.

Green manure. This is the only form of organic manure possible to some gardeners. It is obtained as follows : When the plot is left vacant in summer or autumn, sow it thinly with mustard,

lucerne or other quick-growing greenstuff, and allow the plants to grow until they are nearly ready to flower. Then dig them in as you would surface weeds. Green manuring is only practicable where the land can be left uncropped for a few months.

There are many other artificial fertilizers, but those mentioned above are the most common and the most profitable. The important points to remember in connexion with all these fertilizers are as follows :—

1. Never mix fertilizers unless you are quite sure they will mix satisfactorily. Some will make unwelcome chemical changes if they are mixed before use.

2. Always apply artificial fertilizers sparingly. Crush all large lumps before you begin, divide up the fertilizer into small quantities each sufficient for a given strip of land, scatter thinly and evenly with a sweep of the hand.

3. Never allow fertilizers, whether applied dry or watered on with the watering can, to go on to plant foliage. If they do, wash them off immediately with clean water.

4. Never apply liquid fertilizer to very dry soils. Always use the hose or watering can first.

5. Never use fertilizers on small seedlings that have not yet taken hold of the ground, or on sickly plants. It is like overfeeding babies and invalids!

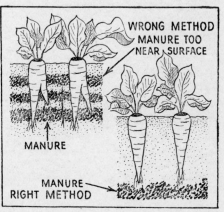

Manure must be deep in the soil or root vegetables will become forked.

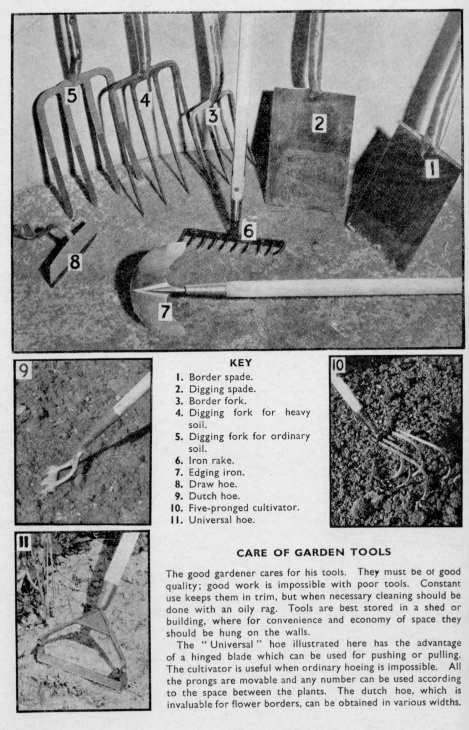

KEY

1. Border spade.
2. Digging spade.
3. Border fork.
4. Digging fork for heavy soil.
5. Digging fork for ordinary soil.
6. Iron rake.
7. Edging iron.
8. Draw hoe.
9. Dutch hoe.
10. Five-pronged cultivator.
11. Universal hoe.

CARE OF GARDEN TOOLS

The good gardener cares for his tools. They must be of good quality; good work is impossible with poor tools. Constant use keeps them in trim, but when necessary cleaning should be done with an oily rag. Tools are best stored in a shed or building, where for convenience and economy of space they should be hung on the walls.

The "Universal" hoe illustrated here has the advantage of a hinged blade which can be used for pushing or pulling. The cultivator is useful when ordinary hoeing is impossible. All the prongs are movable and any number can be used according to the space between the plants. The dutch hoe, which is invaluable for flower borders, can be obtained in various widths.

SMALL HAND TOOLS

1. A basket on wheels is very handy when weeding. It is light and easy to move, and holds a considerable quantity of rubbish.

2. The choice of the long- or short-handled trowel depends on personal taste, but most people find the shorter the easier to manage.

3. When planting bulbs in grass, use a bulb planter to remove the piece of turf for inserting the bulb. Afterwards the turf is replaced to leave the lawn unmarked.

4. A hand-fork is a very useful tool when working in the rock garden or among small plants. Always keep it scrupulously clean.

GARDEN SHEARS

2. Keep shears sharp. Sharpen frequently on the stone, and always after use dry the blades and smear with an oily rag.

SECATEUR

1. The Rolcut type of secateur makes a clean, straight cut without fear of bruising the bark. Worn parts can be renewed. Always cut just above a joint or close back to the main branch.

HAND ROLLER

4. To maintain lawns and gravel paths in good condition a roller is necessary. For small gardens one weighing about 2 cwt. is advisable. Rolling should be done after rain but not when the ground is sodden. This caution applies more particularly to heavy soils.

A HOSE EXTENSION

3. An ideal way to water the garden. The fine misty spray penetrates the soil without beating down the surface, and the whole apparatus can easily be moved from place to place. Many hours of labour are saved thus.

STAKING GARDEN PLANTS

Staking is one of the most important operations in the garden and varies with the type of plant under consideration. Whatever method is employed it should be done early in May.

1. The most usual method employed is to place three bamboo canes at equal distances round each clump and twist tarred string from cane to cane. Insert the canes at least 9 in. in the soil to withstand strong winds and rain.

2. Pea boughs pushed in among herbaceous perennials and smaller twigs among annuals is the least unsightly and best method. As will be seen from the illustration, when the plants are in flower the supporting twigs are almost invisible.

3. There are many patented stakes on the market, of which the type illustrated is most suitable for delphiniums and other tall perennials. Different sized rings are available for single stems or whole clumps.

4. Yet another simple method for the coarser perennials, such as Michaelmas daisies, is shown here. A circular piece of wire netting and a stout stake are all that is required. As the plants grow taller the wire is gently raised. Many flowering plants need stakes to support their heavy blooms. Give them the required support early, or a sudden storm of wind or rain may ruin all the flowers. Other plants, e.g., Montbretias and even gladioli if planted deeply, need no staking.

PROTECTION FROM WEATHER

I. Late frosts play havoc with early blossoms, particularly fruit. Fish netting can be draped over the trees or, better still, supported on a light wooden frame. In colder districts a double or treble layer of netting may be necessary to give the plants complete protection.

2. In Britain winter dampness takes toll of more plants than frost. Particularly is this so in the case of alpines which in their natural haunts are protected by snow and thus kept dry. When growth begins in the spring the melting snow provides abundant moisture. It is impossible to reproduce these conditions in the garden except by means of artificial protection from rain. In the rock garden specially susceptible subjects can be sheltered beneath small sheets of glass supported on notched pegs. Woolly leaved cushion plants suffer most.

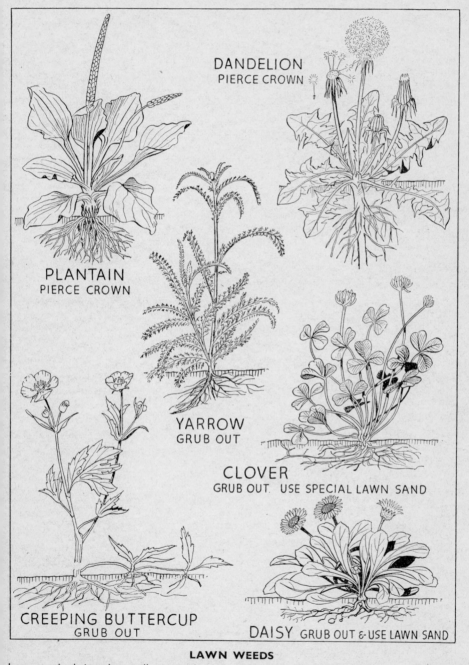

DANDELION
PIERCE CROWN

PLANTAIN
PIERCE CROWN

YARROW
GRUB OUT

CLOVER
GRUB OUT. USE SPECIAL LAWN SAND

CREEPING BUTTERCUP
GRUB OUT

DAISY GRUB OUT & USE LAWN SAND

LAWN WEEDS

Lawn weeds, being almost all perennials, are usually of a persistent character, and although they can be controlled to a certain extent with lawn sand, hand eradication is often the most effective. Use the daisy grubber illustrated on page 95. Once a lawn is free of weeds, dust occasionally with sulphate of ammonia, $\frac{1}{4}$ oz. per square yard, and add compost lightly in autumn.

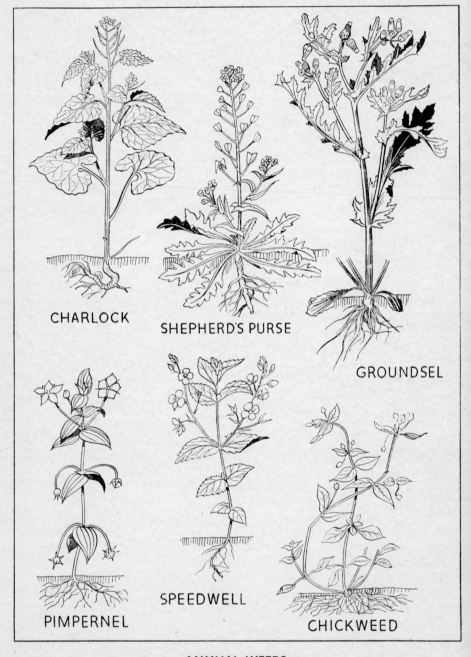

CHARLOCK

SHEPHERD'S PURSE

GROUNDSEL

PIMPERNEL

SPEEDWELL

CHICKWEED

ANNUAL WEEDS

Annual weeds are the easiest to get rid of, provided they are not allowed to seed. In the very young stages they can be hoed off, but otherwise they must be hand pulled. Being shallow rooted they can be dug in when turning over ground. They are worst in wet seasons.

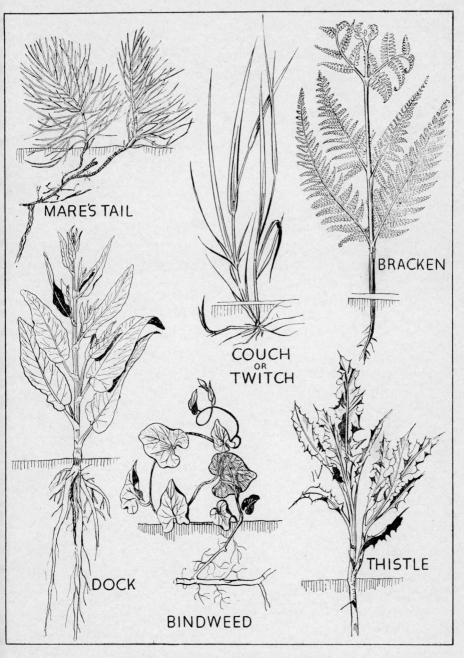

MARE'S TAIL

BRACKEN

COUCH
OR
TWITCH

DOCK

BINDWEED

THISTLE

DEEP ROOTED PERENNIAL WEEDS

Deep rooted perennial weeds can only be eradicated by deep digging. As any small portion of the root left in or on the soil is able to grow and form a new plant, the gardener should be careful to put all such weeds on the bonfire. They must not be dug into the ground.

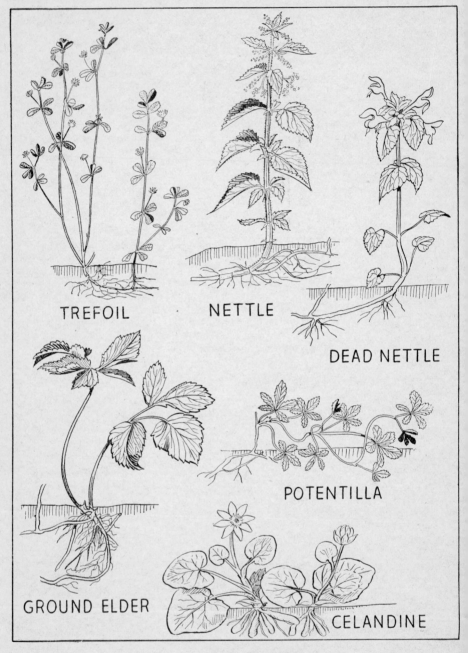

TREFOIL

NETTLE

DEAD NETTLE

POTENTILLA

GROUND ELDER

CELANDINE

CREEPING WEEDS

Many perennial weeds have spreading roots or underground stems. These assist rapid growth, so action must be taken immediately such weeds appear in the garden. Grub up every portion of root and burn. Any one of the above weeds can, if neglected, quickly overrun a garden.

GARDEN PESTS AND DISEASES
GENERAL PRECAUTIONS

In all parts of the garden, pests can play havoc with the crops, whether flower, fruit or vegetable. These insect pests are divided into three classes according to the type of destruction they do and the necessary control. Those that live in the soil can only be destroyed by the use of a soil fumigant or soil sterilization. Insects that eat foliage can be killed by poison, which is usually sprayed on to the foliage and adheres as a thin film, which the insects eventually consume. The third type are those that suck plant sap and therefore cannot be killed by poisoning their food. A spray of insecticide that comes in actual contact with their bodies is the only remedy in this case.

The following are among the most common insect pests :—

Soil Pests

Carrot fly	Onion fly
Celery fly	Slugs
Millepede	Wireworms

Leaf-eating Pests

Apple sawfly	Gooseberry sawfly
Cabbage butterfly	Winter moth

Sucking Pests

Aphides	Pea and bean
Apple sucker	weevil
Big bud	Woolly aphis

COMMON GARDEN PESTS

Aphis (1). On broad beans.
Damage : The tips of the beans become smothered with small black flies, causing distortion of the plants.
Control : Pinch out the tops of the beans and burn them. If this is done at the first sign of trouble, no other treatment will be necessary ; but if the infestation has become serious, the plants must be sprayed with a nicotine solution or a derris spray.
Aphis (2). On crops other than broad beans.
Damage : These flies are not so readily

seen as they are the green variety, but they cause a curling of the leaves and usually attack the growing tips of the plants first. They infest roses, and are found also on plums, dahlias and chrysanthemums.
Control : They can be destroyed in the same way as the black variety, with nicotine solution or derris spray.
Ants. Ants will usually be found where green fly (aphis) is present.
Damage : No serious damage is done to plants. Ant nests disturb lawn surfaces and the ants themselves are a nuisance to humans.
Control : A good ant destroyer is borax mixed with plaster of paris, or sawdust soaked in paraffin. Sprinkle the mixture over the ground wherever ants are troublesome. If possible, the nest should be dug up and burnt.

BLACK FLY

A broad bean leaf, showing characteristic attack of black aphis.

Birds. *Damage :* They eat the seeds.
Control : No spraying will prevent birds from eating newly-sown seeds ; preventatives must be of a mechanical nature. The cheapest and simplest device is illustrated on page 50. For each row you require two pieces of wood 1 ft. wide by 6 in. to 9 in. high, two pegs made

from 1 in. by ½ in. wood and 9 in. to 12 in. long, and three to four dozen nails. Stud the largest piece of wood with the nails on three edges. Set each board in position at the end of the row and thread from end to end with black thread, starting with the lowest nail and moving up one at a time until the whole board is covered. Give the cotton a twist round each nail to prevent it slipping. When finished, the row will be covered with a black thread " tent." An alternative is to use small-mesh wire netting, 15 in. to 18 in. wide, arched over the rows. It is necessary to place a small piece at either end to prevent birds from getting under the arch. Otherwise netting is almost useless.

Damage : They are particularly harmful to young plants, of which in time they will eat the entire roots.

Control : Lay baits made of paris green and bran.

Millepedes. These have long cylindrical brownish bodies with two pairs of legs on each segment and should be distinguished from centipedes, which have only one pair of legs on each segment, as the latter are of benefit to the garden. They move very fast, but curl up when disturbed.

Damage : Millepedes eat the roots of bulbs, potatoes and almost any form of vegetable beneath the soil. They bore into the flesh and ruin it for the table.

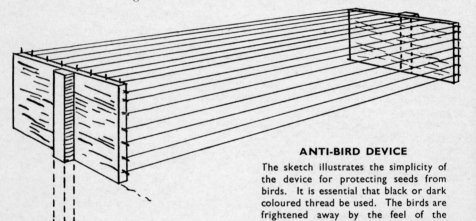

ANTI-BIRD DEVICE

The sketch illustrates the simplicity of the device for protecting seeds from birds. It is essential that black or dark coloured thread be used. The birds are frightened away by the feel of the *unseen* threads, and white or light coloured thread would be easily visible.

Cutworms or soil caterpillars. These are dull green or brown in colour. When fully grown they pupate, or form a chrysalis, and turn into owlet and yellow underwing moths.

Damage : They do much by eating the seedlings off at ground level and also by eating the roots of plants.

Control : Lay baits made of paris green and bran.

Leather-jackets. The larvae of the crane fly or daddy-long-legs are about 1 in. to 1½ in. long and legless, with very tough skins. In colour they are a dark brownish grey and are therefore not easily detected in the soil.

Control : The soil should be well limed and sprinkled with naphthalene. Millepedes can also be trapped in hollowed-out swedes or turnips buried just below the surface of the soil.

Slugs and snails. *Damage :* They eat the leaves of lettuces and other tender growth. They can frequently be traced by the slimy trail they leave behind them.

Control : Inspection at dusk will reveal them coming out of hiding, since they only feed at night and particularly in damp weather. Thickly sprinkle lime in a ring round the plants so as to prevent slugs reaching them. Another method is to trap them in hollowed-out orange or

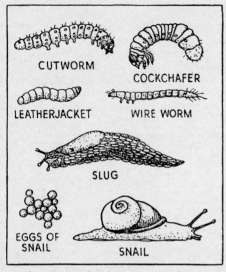

CUTWORM

COCKCHAFER

LEATHERJACKET

WIRE WORM

SLUG

EGGS OF SNAIL

SNAIL

Common garden enemies, natural size.

grapefruit skins. Take the empty skin of half an orange or grapefruit, remove a very small portion at one edge to make an entrance and place it inverted on the ground among the crops. The skins should be inspected daily, preferably in the mornings. An effective bait is meta and bran. Crush half a meta tablet and mix with a handful of bran. Set little heaps among the crops. Still a further method is to put down little heaps of paris green mixed with bran. This mixture attracts the slugs and is poisonous. Care should be exercised when handling the mixture, especially if domestic pets are about. Snails' eggs are white and semi-transparent, about the size of a sweet pea seed, and are often found when digging. Destroy them by burning.

Wireworms. These are yellow, with a brown head and have three pairs of legs near the head.

Damage : Wireworms are usually present on newly broken land, in which case they are likely to be very numerous. They attack crops of potatoes and carrots, by eating into the flesh of the roots and tubers.

Control : The soil should be turned frequently, as they dislike aerated soil, and this also exposes them to the ravages

of birds. Lime and whizzed (i.e., finely flaked) naphthalene should also be used as against wireworms, or a trap may be employed. Bury a piece of carrot attached to a stick just under the soil and pull it up frequently, destroying all the wireworms which have collected on it.

Woodlice. These are about ½ in. long, brownish grey, and curl up into a ball when touched. They like damp, dark situations and therefore hide under pots and boxes. They may also be found in rubbish of any kind which has been left about.

Damage : They are usually only troublesome in cold frames and greenhouses.

Control : A greenhouse kept quite clear of all rubbish is less likely to attract woodlice. They may be trapped in a hollowed-out apple and then collected and destroyed. They are also attracted by a mixture of paris green and bran.

Caterpillars. *Damage :* Small holes will appear in the middle and at the edges of leaves of the cabbage tribe. If no measures are taken, these holes will gradually increase in size until many of the leaves are completely eaten away. In bad seasons they will destroy the crop.

Control : Early in the season the small yellow eggs of the caterpillar are to be found on the underside of the leaves. You can expect these when you see the

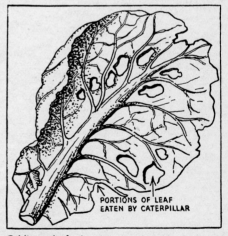

PORTIONS OF LEAF EATEN BY CATERPILLAR

Cabbage leaf showing results of attack by caterpillars.

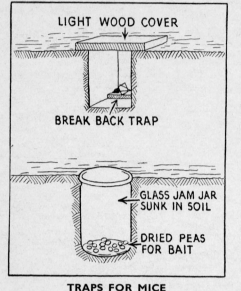

TRAPS FOR MICE

Alternative methods of trapping mice which cannot harm small birds. The mice from the jam jar must be drowned.

round with wire netting, burying it at least 1 ft. underground. An even better method is to allow 2 ft. underground, and bend the extra foot outwards away from the plot. An effective smear for trees can be made as follows : Heat raw linseed oil in a container five times the volume of the oil to be heated, and do this in the open. When it gives off a slightly bluish smoke, add 3 oz. of powdered sulphur for each quart of oil, adding only a *little* at a time and then allow to get cold. It is ready for use when cold. While mixing keep it off all clothing.

PESTS OF SPECIAL CROPS

Cabbage root fly. *Damage :* The fly lays its eggs on the soil near the base of cabbages, sprouts and cauliflowers. These hatch out into maggots which burrow into the roots.

Control : Dissolve $\frac{1}{4}$ oz. mercuric chloride in 2 gal. of water. This solution should be used when planting cabbages,

white butterflies about. If you can find them remove them and burn, otherwise spray the plants with derris.

Mice. *Damage :* These pests are very troublesome in some country districts, eating the seeds of peas and beans as soon as they have been sown.

Control : Before sowing, rub the peas or beans in red lead and a few drops of paraffin. Only a thin film of red lead is required. The paraffin evaporates, leaving the seed coated. Another method is to soak the seed in a mixture of red lead and paraffin mixed to a very thin paste, and a third to put the peas in tepid water, leave them to soak overnight, put them on paper next morning, sprinkle over them a few drops of paraffin, roll well, and then roll in red lead, using a teaspoonful of red lead to a pint of peas.

Rabbits. *Damage:* The havoc wrought in a garden by these pests cannot be overestimated. They will eat the green leaves of practically all plants and destroy a whole crop of seedlings in a few hours.

Control : Wire the plot all the way

The ring of lime round cabbages prevents attack by slugs and snails.

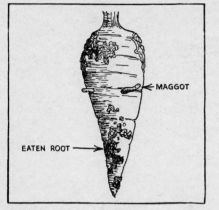

Carrot attacked by carrot fly maggots.

Celery fly. *Damage :* The fly lays its eggs in the leaf and these hatch out into maggots which burrow between the upper and lower skin of the leaf, giving it the appearance of white blisters.

Control : Celery fly attacks the plant in the seed bed stage. Regular spraying with nicotine is necessary.

Onion fly. *Damage :* The onion fly acts in the same way as the carrot fly and the maggots do much damage by burrowing into the bulb of the onion.

Control : A light dusting with whizzed naphthalene is one method of counteracting attacks and should be used just before the seedlings are thinned out. A second application should be made about

etc., ¼ pt. being poured into each hole as planting proceeds. If in previous years attacks have been severe a second watering should be made ten days later. Watering the seed bed with this solution at the time of sowing is also helpful.

Carrot fly. *Damage :* The fly lays its eggs near the roots and the maggots burrow in and feed on the carrot.

Control : The flies are attracted to the plant by the smell, and if this is counteracted attacks are less likely. Whizzed naphthalene is the simplest method and should be used immediately before thinning the seedlings and again ten days later. Do not leave the thinnings lying about, but burn them.

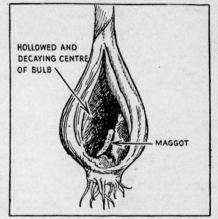

Section of onion rendered useless by attack of onion fly maggot.

ten days later. Another method is to sprinkle with creosote mixed with sand. All seedlings removed from the crop by thinning should be burnt immediately in the compost pit.

Pea thrip. *Damage :* The grubs feed on the surface of the young leaves, making them turn a silvery colour. They also feed on the flowers, and as the pods develop these become twisted and turn the same silvery green colour. The affected pods are always small and misshapen. Pea thrip is more prevalent on light soils than on heavy ones and is most troublesome during May and June.

Control : As pea thrip hibernates in the soil, a soil fumigant is the most useful

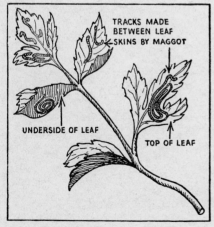

Celery fly maggots in the leaf.

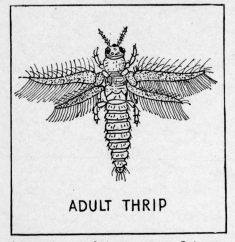

ADULT THRIP

Adult thrip, magnified thirty times. Only seen on close inspection.

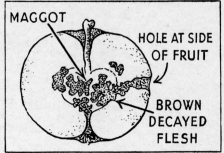

Section of apple with sawfly maggot.

means of counteracting it. The plants may also be sprayed with nicotine or derris wash.

Turnip flea beetle. *Damage :* These very minute beetles, which hop a considerable height when touched, eat the seedlings as soon as they appear and make lots of little holes in turnip leaves. They lay their eggs in spring.

Control : No real remedy is known. Sow the seeds thickly to allow a reasonable number of plants getting through the attack. If a rag smeared with tree-banding grease is dragged over the rows, the beetles will stick to it and can then be destroyed.

Turnip gall weevil. *Damage:* The eggs are laid in the spring on the roots. The grubs hatch out and feed on the plant, causing a gall to grow in which they live. When fully fed they emerge from the gall.

Control : Strong growing plants are less likely to attack. Rotation of crops helps to overcome the gall weevil. All infected roots must be burnt.

Apple capsid. *Damage:* Causes distortion of the fruit and leaves corky scars on the skin. Young growth stunted and whole crop may be lost.

Control: Nicotine spray before flower buds open and at petal fall. Grease banding.

Apple sawfly. *Damage:* Fruit destroyed by burrowing maggot.

Control: Spray with nicotine before petal fall.

Gooseberry sawfly. *Damage:* Bushes often defoliated.

Control : Spray with lead arsenate, or non-poisonous wash if fruit is formed.

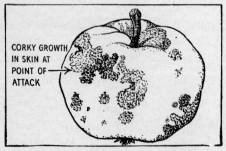

Mature apple disfigured by capsid bug.

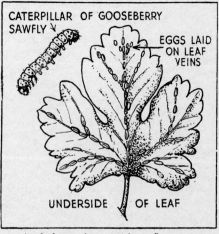

Leaf of gooseberry with sawfly eggs.

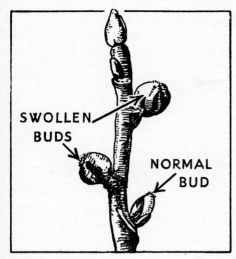

Winter shoot of black currant attacked by big bud mite.

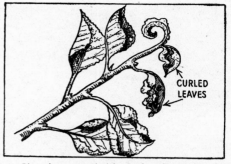

Plum leaves curled by leaf curling aphis.

Big bud mite. *Damage :* Infested buds dry up, or produce distorted leaves. Fruit crop greatly reduced.

Control : Hand pick big buds before March. Spray lime sulphur 1:13 when leaves are the size of a florin.

Plum aphis. *Damage :* Leaves tightly curled, and later fall. Growth stopped and young fruits fall.

Control : Winter spraying, five to seven per cent tar oil to kill the eggs. Spray with nicotine in spring before the leaves curl.

Woolly aphis or **American blight.** *Damage :* Leaves, shoots and branches attacked. The irritation of the insects' sucking causes swellings which crack and form a "canker." Roots also attacked.

Control : Spray winter oil wash. Grease banding. Paint colonies of blight with paraffin emulsion.

Winter moth. *Damage :* Young shoots and flower clusters eaten by caterpillars.

Control : Grease banding in autumn. Spray before and after blossoming with lead arsenate to poison young caterpillars. Female moths have no proper wings, so must *crawl* up the trunk. Keeps bands tacky.

The greenhouse has some troublesome pests, aphis being the most common. Conditions in the greenhouse are under the gardener's control so that he can use fumigation as well as the more usual methods of pest control.

Red spider. *Damage :* The insects sucking the leaves cause pale patches.

Control : The insect only thrives under dry conditions, so regular spraying with water and thorough damping down is generally sufficient. In severe cases nicotine spray can be used. Be sure to

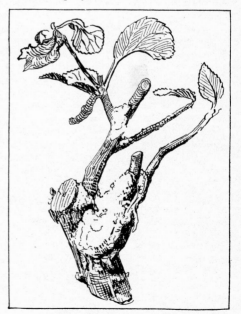

Woolly aphis on old and young wood.

Greatly enlarged photo of white fly on underside of tomato leaf.

Apple and pear scab. *Damage :* The two diseases are caused by different fungi, but the damage and control are the same. Dark spots on the leaves which spread to large patches. The disease spreads to the fruit producing scabs, spots and cracks which render the fruit unsaleable.

Control : Burn fallen leaves. Remove and burn diseased fruit. In winter cut out and burn all diseased wood. Spray with bordeaux mixture or lime sulphur. Care must be taken with bordeaux as it burns some varieties.

Apple canker. *Damage :* Spreading cracks on the young bark. The disease gradually eats into the wood, eventually killing off whole branches.

Control : The spores of the fungus always enter the tree through existing wounds, thus by keeping down insect pests and scab the trees have more chance of avoiding infection. All dead wood must be removed and burned.

wet under the leaves as it is there that the insects lodge.

Scale. *Damage :* In severe cases the growth may be stunted. On palms and hard leaved plants leaves are made unsightly.

Control : Wash with nicotine and soft soap. Scrape off scales with a blunt wooden label. Once removed from the host the insect dies. Found mostly on the underside of the leaves.

White fly. *Damage :* Leaves much weakened by the extraction of sap.

Control : Fumigate with tetrachlorethane ; the house must be airtight.

PLANT DISEASES

Silver leaf disease. *Damage:* This disease attacks plums and cherries. Infected branches show silvery foliage and wood a brown stain. It is caused by infection through wounds. It will destroy the tree if left neglected.

Control : Remove all dead wood and burn before mid-July. Cut back to healthy wood. Paint over sear with white lead paint. Give the tree a tonic of potash.

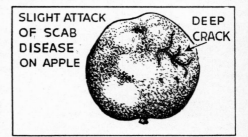

Apple showing scab damage.

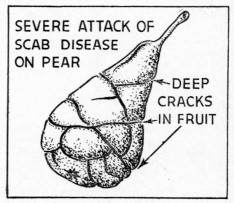

Pear showing scab damage.

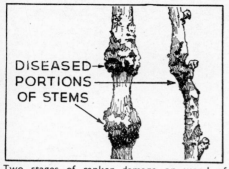

Two stages of canker damage on wood of apple tree.

Gooseberry mildew. *Damage :* A white film over the leaves and fruit which gradually turns mealy. This is followed by a brown " felt " which also attacks the tips of the shoots.

Control : The disease thrives in moist atmospheres. Give bushes plenty of space when planting and keep them open by careful pruning. Young shoots should be tipped in September and the diseased wood burnt. Spray with lime sulphur 1:30 when the disease first appears.

Black spot on roses. *Damage:* Dark spots on the full grown leaves in mid-summer. In severe cases the wood is affected. Leaves fall off and the whole bush is weakened.

Control : Burn fallen leaves. Prune away and burn diseased wood. Spray in spring with bordeaux mixture or liver of sulphur.

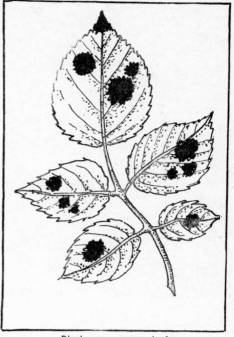

Black spot on rose leaf.

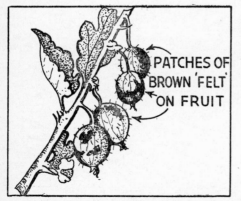

PATCHES OF BROWN 'FELT' ON FRUIT

Gooseberries ruined by mildew.

Rust on chrysanthemum leaf.

ROSE MILDEW

Leaf of rose disfigured and curled by mildew.

DISEASES OF SPECIAL CROPS

Chrysanthemum rust. *Damage:* Small reddish circles on the leaves turning darker as they spread. The whole plant is rendered unsightly and is unfit for sale.

Control : Burn diseased leaves. Spray with potassium sulphide or weak lime sulphur. Dust with flowers of sulphur. The disease attacks thistles and hawkweeds so keep the garden free from such weeds. Vigorous spraying with water spreads the disease spores, so keep spraying down to the minimum until the disease is under control.

Rose mildew. *Damage:* Young leaves, shoots and flower buds covered with the familiar white powder.

Control : Spray with lime sulphur as soon as the leaves expand. Do not wait for the disease to start, especially in damp districts where the disease is prevalent. Varieties with glossy leaves are less susceptible to the disease than others. Strong, vigorous growth should be encouraged to help the bushes to resist the disease.

Club root. *Symptoms :* This disease is also known as "finger and toe." It causes a malformation of the roots of all members of the Brassica family, which includes cabbages, sprouts, etc., and attacks turnips and radishes. The infection is carried in the soil and is very contagious.

Control : Heavy dressings of lime help to counteract the trouble, also good drainage and rotation of crops. A chemical now marketed under the name "Brassisan" has proved very effective, and if used according to the makers' instructions it is non-poisonous. Seed beds should also be treated with this powder. Mercuric chloride, a poison, is an alternative remedy. Where it is known that club root is in the soil, dissolve 1 oz. in $12\frac{1}{2}$ gal. of water, and before seed sowing water the drills with this solution, using 1 pt. to every 5 ft. When transplanting, pour $\frac{1}{2}$ pt. into each hole. Destroy all infected plants.

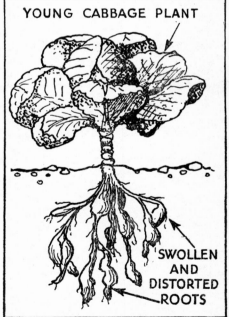

YOUNG CABBAGE PLANT

SWOLLEN AND DISTORTED ROOTS

Diagram showing the typical "finger and toe" distortion of a cabbage root.

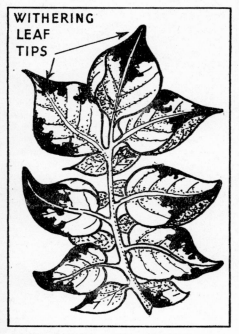

Potato leaf tips withered by blight.

Mint rust. *Symptoms :* Orange-coloured patches appear on the leaves and stems of mint, causing distortion. Eventually the plants die down early in the season.

Control : There is little hope of curing the disease once it has made an appearance. The mint should be taken up and burnt, and a new stock started in a different part of the garden or allotment. Spray the vacated ground with a solution of copper sulphide and follow this with a dressing of lime.

Pea mildew. *Symptoms :* A white downy mildew appears on the leaves, pods and stems, causing growth to cease prematurely. It does not usually appear until the summer is well advanced.

Control : Spray the plants with liver of sulphur.

Potato blight. *Symptoms :* Brown patches appear on the leaves and stems which, if left unchecked, increase in size, become dark in colour and gradually cause the leaves to curl up until finally the whole plant is affected, tubers and all.

Control : Success is obtained by thorough spraying with bordeaux mixture at the end of June and three weeks later. In a wet season a third spraying will be necessary. The undersides of the leaves must be wetted as well as the tops. Keeping the tubers well covered with soil prevents the spores from reaching the tubers when washed from the leaves The rotation of crops helps.

Potato scab. *Symptoms :* This fungus affects the tubers, causing brown corky spots and patches. It is more prevalent on limy and sandy soils.

Control : There are no means of discerning the trouble until the tubers are lifted. Therefore, if it is known that there is potato scab in the soil, precautions should be taken before planting. Soak the seed for two hours in a solution of formalin made by dissolving $\frac{1}{2}$ pt. in 15 gal. of water.

Potato wart disease. *Symptoms* This disease is more likely to appear when potatoes are grown on the same land year after year. It first attacks the tubers near the eyes, causing wrinkles and warts to appear. These gradually increase in size until the tubers become a brown spongy mass.

Control : Once the disease appears there is no remedy. The simplest means to prevent the trouble is to plant immune varieties. If wart disease does appear, it must be notified to the local horticultural superintendent.

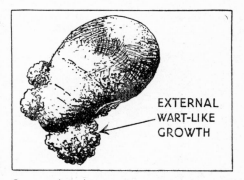

Potato tuber showing damage caused by wart disease. Any attack is notifiable.

TOMATO
LEAF
MOULD

Tomato leaf showing mould or rust.

Tomato leaf rust. *Damage :* Young leaves become covered with small brown spots which spread over the underside of the leaf. In bad cases the fruit is attacked.

Control : Spray with potassium sulphide ¼ oz. per gallon of water as soon as the disease appears. Keep the house well ventilated and a dry atmosphere. The plants must not be in any way overcrowded.

Tomato sleepy disease. *Damage :* Leaves become discoloured and droop and the plant collapses.

Control : Remove and burn diseased plants. The infection takes place in the soil. Dig in quicklime and leave bare. Plant next crop in different soil.

Damping-off disease of seedlings. *Damage :* This is a very troublesome disease which can fortunately be prevented. It attacks young plants in the seed pan, causing them to shrivel at the soil level and fall over.

Control : Water seed pans with cheshunt compound. Give as much light and air as possible. Transplant seedlings before they get overcrowded.

FINAL HINTS

Soil fumigant. Naphthalene dusted along the rows of young crops will keep away soil pests of the fly type. Those pests which live their entire life in the soil can be destroyed by the use of a patent soil fumigant obtainable from a horticultural sundriesman.

Sprays. The most common insecticides used against leaf-eating insects are lead arsenate, and against sucking insects nicotine, derris and tar oil winter washes. The first and last are mixed with soft soap, which acts as a spreader.

Never leave rubbish lying about. Remember the old gardener's motto : *Get it clean and keep it clean.* The moment ground becomes vacant, dig it well, turning in all annual weeds. Then leave it exposed so that birds can find the insects.

Do not delay seed sowing. Weak plants are always more susceptible to both pests and diseases. A healthy plant can resist disease better than a sickly specimen, therefore cultivate well. Keep up the supply of potash, which helps all plants to resist disease ; but avoid excessive nitrogenous fertilizing. If you see leaves turning yellow, remove them before decay sets in. Remember that sunlight and air are two of the best germ destroyers, so do not overcrowd. Grow the plants at their proper distances and avoid coddling them when they are still in the frame or greenhouse.

Keep a watchful eye for disease on any plants that come to you from friends or nurserymen ; one plant carrying a trace of infectious disease will quickly spread the trouble to every plant of its kind in the garden. Remember that organic manure is often a source of disease entering a garden. Some varieties of a plant are more susceptible than others, so ask for immune varieties.

PREPARATION OF INSECTICIDES

Derris. This can be had in powder or liquid form. To make the liquid spray, dissolve ¼ lb. of derris in 12 gal. of water, and if there is no soap included in the bought preparation, stir in ½ lb. of soft soap. As with all insecticides and fungicides, the soap acts as a spreader. There are many proprietary insecticides on the market with a derris basis, all of which are equally effective.

Lime. Slaked lime is preferable to quicklime for use as an insecticide. If not obtained already slaked, it may be treated in the following way : Add just sufficient water to wet the lumps of quicklime, but no more. A great heat will be produced and the lumps will quickly break up into a fine powder. If an excess of water is used, the result will be a sloppy paste instead of a fine powder that can easily be handled.

Nicotine. A solution of nicotine may be bought ; it should contain 98 per cent nicotine. Dissolve 1 oz. of this, together with 1 lb. of soft soap, in 10 gal. of water.

Paris green. This can be obtained in powder form. One oz. should be mixed with 2 lb. of bran and sprinkled with water to moisten. If possible, sweeten the water with a little treacle or sugar before adding. This poison bait may be laid about in small heaps where required. It should be remembered that paris green is poisonous to animals.

Meta. Crush half a tablet of meta and mix with bran. The mixture should be laid about in heaps.

GREASE BANDING

A method of controlling winter moth on standard and half-standard fruit trees, it is a valuable control for many fruit pests. Insects falling off the trees and attempting to climb up again by the trunk are caught in the grease. The bands should be applied by the middle of October to catch the earliest insects ascending to lay eggs. A periodic removal of dead leaves, etc., from the bands should be carried out through the winter, and the grease re-combed or fresh bands applied in spring.

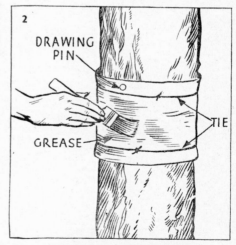

GREASE BANDS TRAP PESTS

The paper being tied in position for grease banding. Note the handy method of hanging the roll of paper round the neck, leaving both hands free for tying. When only a few trees are to be banded, it is better to buy the small cartons of bands ready greased.

APPLYING THE GREASE

The band is now fixed and the grease applied. Use a stiff brush or a flat piece of wood. Where the trunk is not even a drawing pin can be used to fix the paper in a hollow. This prevents insects from passing under the band.

PREPARATION OF FUNGICIDES

Bordeaux mixture. Use 1 lb. of copper sulphate and 1 lb. quicklime to 12½ gal. of water. Lime water is made by mixing the lime with a gallon of water. The copper sulphate is mixed with the remaining water in a non-metal container. When it has completely dissolved, pour the solution into the lime water. If necessary the two solutions should be left to stand overnight before mixing to make sure that the crystals are well dissolved. Bordeaux mixture can be bought ready for use.

Cheshunt compound. Two parts finely divided copper sulphate, eleven parts *fresh* ammonium carbonate; mix together and store for twenty-four hours in a tightly stoppered bottle. Use 1 oz. of the mixture to 2 gal. of water.

Lime sulphur. A valuable fungicide for both winter and summer use. It is purchased in concentrated form and should be used according to the instructions given by the maker.

Liver of sulphur. This is purchased in the dry form. To make a liquid for spraying, dissolve 1 oz. in 2 gal. of water. Must be used freshly mixed. Keep the undissolved stock in a tightly sealed vessel.

Flowers of sulphur. Used as a dry powder when a sulphur wash is not required. Sprinkled finely over the plant, or spread with a special blower which can be purchased for the purpose.

Warning. Care should be taken with all sprays containing copper salts as they corrode metal vessels. All spraying apparatus and syringes should be thoroughly washed with clear water before being put away.

For small orchards a small knapsack sprayer such as the one shown above is useful for spraying insecticide or fungicide washes. Choose a calm day and wear old clothes.

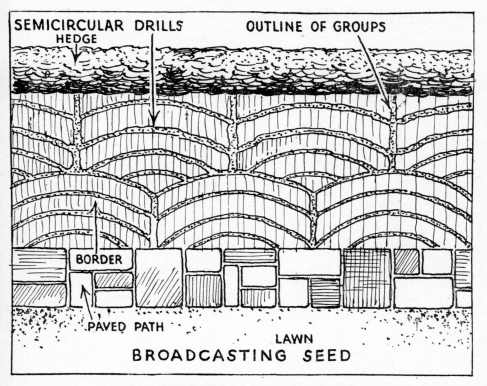

SEMICIRCULAR DRILLS   OUTLINE OF GROUPS

HEDGE

BORDER

PAVED PATH   LAWN

BROADCASTING SEED

PLAN FOR SOWING ANNUAL BORDER

The best method of sowing a border of annuals is to mark out the areas for each variety. Inside each block sow the seed in curved drills. This way ugly straight lines are avoided, and an artistic blending of the different flowers obtained. Very fine seeds need no covering.

PLANT PROPAGATION
RAISING CROPS FROM SEED

Raising plants from seed is a simple matter if the ground is carefully prepared beforehand and the seedlings given a little attention in the way of thinning, weeding and hoeing. It is essential that the ground should be in what is termed a good tilth ; that is to say, the particles of soil should be broken down to a fine state so that the seeds are not lost in rough ground. The earlier the ground is dug prior to seed sowing the easier it will be to break down with fork and rake. When crops are removed in the autumn, dig deep, at the same time incorporating organic manure where required. Leave the ground in a rough state, or in ridges, to be weathered by the frost and rain. Early in the New Year it should be possible to break down the ridges. When ready to sow, rake the ground, removing all stones and other coarse material from the surface so that the young seedlings will have no difficulty in pushing their way through the soil. Soil that is on the heavy side will be made more porous and better suited to seed germination if sand is added to a depth of from 2 in. to 3 in. To light soil add plenty of humus.

SOWING SEED

When sowing seeds in a drill keep hand near the soil and the line will be straight and even.

METHODS OF SOWING

Aim at neatness in the vegetable plot. It makes hoeing and fertilizing easier, and the garden a more pleasant sight. All crops should be grown in straight rows. When taking out drills for seed sowing, use a taut line and the draw hoe.

Seeds vary considerably in size, and on this depends the method of sowing. To sow large seeds, such as peas or beans, take out a small trench 3 in. deep, using a spade or draw hoe, and set the seeds at the bottom in a staggered double or triple row. Sow a few extra seeds at the ends of the rows. These plants may be transferred later into any spare spaces.

Finer seed is sown in drills $\frac{1}{2}$ in. to 1 in. deep, made by drawing the corner of a draw hoe along the ground. It is important to sow really thinly, as the final distance between the plants of all root crops is at least 6 in. If sown thickly, there is unnecessary wastage. To ensure thin sowing, tear off a small portion of the packet at one corner so that seed can only pass a little at a time. To cover the seeds, use the back of the rake. This avoids disturbing the seeds.

Do not make the mistake of burying seeds too deeply. A useful rough and ready gardeners rule is : Cover the seeds with twice their own depth of soil.

NURSERY SEED BED

There are some vegetables—notably the Brassicas (i.e., cabbage, brussels sprouts, cauliflower, broccoli and kale)—which, unlike root crops and legumes (peas and beans), are easily transplanted while they are seedlings. Therefore, in order to take up as little room in the garden as possible, they are sown all together on a small, specially prepared bed. This nursery seed bed is prepared in the same way as the rest of the kitchen garden, but the rows of seeds may be sown as close together as 6 in. Although the seeds should be put in fairly thinly, they can be sown thicker than ordinary crops as they will be lifted and transplanted before they begin to overcrowd each other. The plants will be ready for transplanting when they are about 4 in. high. The ground so vacated can be forked over and a further sowing made for successive crops. After a year a fresh site will be advisable for the nursery seed bed, otherwise all the plant food necessary for this particular crop will be exhausted. Ground where peas and beans have been grown is good.

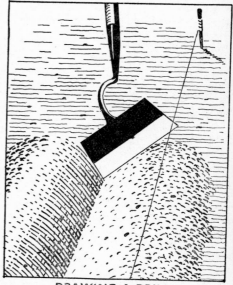

DRAWING A DRILL

Make the drills with a draw hoe. Be careful to keep an even depth the whole length of the line.

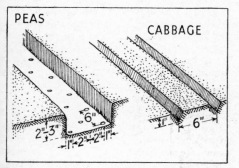

PEAS
CABBAGE

Peas are sown in shallow trenches, cabbage seed in continuous narrow drills.

SOWING AT STATIONS

Some root crops, such as parsnips, which have seeds that are large enough to handle individually, are sown at "stations." This reduces the amount of thinning and is therefore much more economical in seed. For this method, sow the seed at the required final distances, placing three seeds at each of these points. When the seedlings appear the strongest is left and the other two, if they have both germinated, pulled up.

In stony ground, gardeners find it difficult to prevent roots from forking. Although a little more work is entailed, it is possible to replace the soil with a specially prepared compost. To do this a crowbar or stout piece of wood is used to make holes about 1 ft. deep, which are filled with the prepared mixture. The three seeds are sown as before on these specially prepared spots an inch below the surface of the ground.

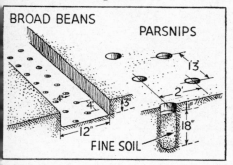

BROAD BEANS
PARSNIPS
FINE SOIL

Beans are sown in trenches. Parsnips are sown at "stations" to avoid transplanting.

SOWING IN BOXES

Some of our vegetables, such as onions, leeks and celery, are half-hardy plants and therefore cannot be sown with safety outside until April or May, which means that the crops will not mature until late in the season. In order to secure them earlier, gardeners resort to seed sowing in boxes under glass. Where a heated glasshouse is available, this should be used ; but a frame placed over a hot bed will do equally well. In this latter case the boxes should be stood on the hot bed.

The boxes are filled with a specially prepared mixture made of two parts loam, one part leaf-mould and a little sand.

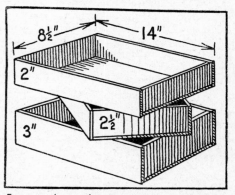

Frame and greenhouse space is economized if the seed boxes are all the same size. Above are shown boxes of handy dimensions.

This is put over broken crocks (pieces of flower pot) placed concave side down in the bottom of the box for drainage and the mixture made firm by pressing with a piece of wood. Seed is scattered thinly on the surface and covered by sifting fine soil over it. Cover the box with a sheet of glass, if you have any handy, and a piece of brown paper until the seeds have germinated. Keeping them in the dark in this way makes germination more rapid. The compost used for filling the boxes should be moist, and if covered with glass and paper should require no further watering until the seedlings are through. If, however, the boxes have to be watered, use a very fine rose on the can.

When the seeds have germinated the boxes should be transferred to a light position in the greenhouse, as near the glass as possible, so that they do not become drawn and leggy. Each day the sheet of glass should be turned and have surplus moisture wiped from it.

When the seedlings are large enough to handle, they should be pricked out into further boxes of similar soil, being placed about 1 in. apart. A small pointed stick (dibber) is useful for this work.

Towards the end of April the boxes of young plants should be gradually hardened off so that they may be ready for planting out during May and June.

TIME FOR SEED SOWING

Although the major portion of outdoor seed sowing is carried out in March and April, practically every month of the year sees the sowing of one or other of the vegetable crops. Succession of crops is all important and it is possible to secure this by sowing a particular vegetable at intervals varying from a fortnight to three months. With the introduction of new varieties, strains that will withstand cold damp winters have been produced and therefore, when ordering your seeds, include a few of these varieties. These may be sown any time from July to early October. It is well known that broad beans are perfectly hardy, provided a longpod type is grown, and sowings should not be made until November.

With a cold frame or greenhouse, salads can be raised all the year round. Seed may be sown at any season, the only point to be considered being the variety As with autumn sowings outside, hardy varieties need to be selected. Where the frame is over a hotbed, the reverse applies ; sow tender varieties.

Seedsmen's catalogues generally give a good selection of varieties of each type of crop for different purposes, and the grower can choose which seeds will best suit his requirements. The best season for all gardening operations varies slightly in different districts. The grower will always find a gardening neighbour who can advise him as to the local peculiarities of that variable factor—the weather

SEEDLINGS IN THE GREENHOUSE

An open staging in a light, airy greenhouse is the best place to put the boxes of pricked-out seedlings. To avoid all possibility of confusion each box and variety should be clearly named a wooden label and a special gardening penc being used. Keep boxes clear of weed

FOR EARLY CROPS USE CLOCHES OR A COLD FRAME

CAREFUL HANDLING OF YOUNG SEED-INGS ENSURES STURDY PLANTS AND PROFITABLE CROPS

A SIMPLE PLANT NURSERY

Seedlings can be raised early in the year if given the protection of a cold frame or cloche.

Bedding plants should be transferred to boxes which are prepared as follows: Cover the drainage holes with broken crocks, concave side down, and over this place a layer of rough material, such as decaying leaves.

Fill the box with a compost made of two parts loam, one part leaf-mould and half part sand, passed through ¼-in. sieve.

4. When the soil in the box has been pressed firm the seedlings may be pricked out one or two inches apart.

Newly transplanted seedlings need plenty of moisture, fresh air, and shade from bright sunshine. Keep the seed boxes free from weeds.

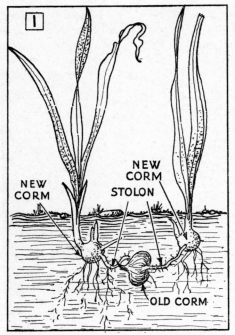

Natural reproduction of montbretia.

ROOT PROPAGATION

There are a few vegetables that are raised other than by seed. Crops of potatoes and Jerusalem artichokes are raised from tubers planted in the soil during March and April. To get a small supply of asparagus for the following year, three-year-old crowns should be purchased and planted during the spring in the usual way with the crown just below the surface. Crowns of rhubarb may also be purchased for spring

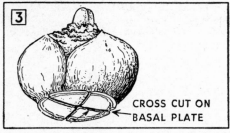

Hyacinth bulb slit to encourage growth of bulbils, i.e., small bulbous growths.

planting. When planting them, keep the crown just above the surface of the soil.

Later, rhubarb roots will need dividing —they can be lifted in spring or autumn, cut into small pieces with a sharp knife and replanted. Each portion must, of course, have a crown attached.

The treatment of sea-kale is rather different from that of all other vegetables. Propagation is carried out by means of thongs. These are pieces of root 4 in. to

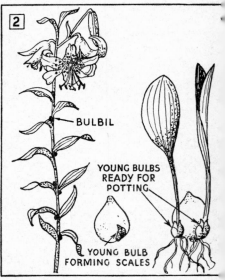

Lily reproduction by means of bulbils.

6 in. long and as thick as a finger, cut from the fleshy roots of a plant when it has been lifted. They are planted in April with the thicker end uppermost, but as it is not always easy to determine this, they are cut straight across at the top and slanting at the bottom. These pieces should be planted vertically with the top a few inches below the surface. In the case of sea-kale, no crown is necessary.

Shallots are a vegetable unique in their method of growth. Individual bulbs are half pushed into the soil during the early spring and by midsummer six or more bulbs are produced round the one originally planted.

POTTING-ON A GREENHOUSE PLANT

Greenhouse plants are potted-on several times before they are established in their final pots. The stages in this operation are shown above. At each potting-on a pot one size larger is used.

1. Place a crock over the drainage hole, concave side down, and cover this with rough decaying leaves. Place a little compost over this and ram gently.

2. To remove the plant from the old pot tap the rim carefully on wood, holding the left hand over the soil to prevent it falling out.

3. Place the ball of soil in the new pot and shake compost in the space between the two. Ram this firm, but do not ram the ball of old soil, otherwise root injury will result.

4. Finally, smooth the surface with a little fresh compost. After potting water the plants carefully until their roots are running freely in the new soil. No liquid manure should be given for a few weeks. Never use old soil, and keep the atmosphere in the house moist.

REPRODUCTION BY DIVISION

One of the simplest ways of increasing the stock of a plant is by dividing the old clumps. Most herbaceous plants can be dealt with in this manner. Delphiniums, Michaelmas daisies and phloxes are all easily divided

1. An old clump of iris lifted for division

2. When you lift an old clump and examine it carefully, round the edges will be seen young rooted shoots which can be separated from the parent plant without damage. Here the new rhizomes, or root-like underground stems, can be seen well furnished with young roots.

3. To divide very old and matted clumps it is advisable to insert a fork or trowel into the centre and gently divide the clump.

The best times to divide clumps are—when growth begins in spring or while the soil is still warm in September. Never plant roots showing any sign of disease.

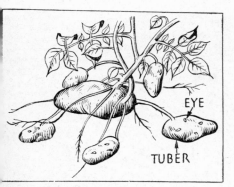

BY TUBERS

Potatoes are reproduced by underground tubers, which will grow even if cut in pieces provided there is an eye on each portion.

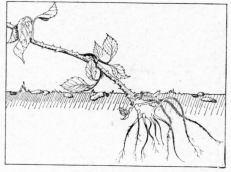

BY LAYERS

Loganberries will produce roots at the tips of the shoots if these are buried in the soil.

BY CUTTINGS

Many plants can be increased by means of cuttings. These can be made in various ways, according to the type of plant. The diagram below shows:—

1. A cutting of dahlia pulled from the old stem with a heel.

2. A piece of berberis cut from a shoot just below a leaf joint.

3. A piece of clematis shoot cut midway between two joints.

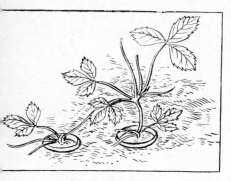

BY RUNNERS

Strawberries produce runners which can be pegged down to pots of soil and later cut from the parent plant. Each plant sends out many runners, but these should be reduced to two or three stronger ones.

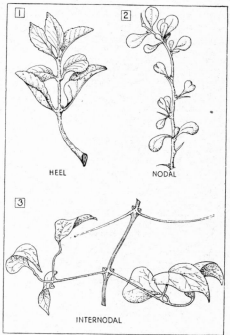

BY OFFSETS

Sempervivums, or house leeks, send out little rosettes on wiry stems. These later form roots.

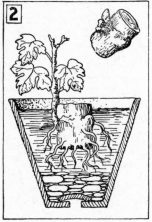

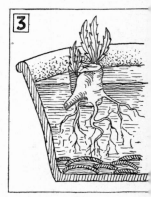

CUTTINGS FOR POTTING-UP

1. Carnation cuttings removed for cutting, free and ready for potting-up. The foliage is shortened to prevent loss of moisture until roots are formed.

2. Vine eye ready for placing in a pot and with the young shoot rooted.

3. Oriental poppy root sending out young roots and leaf shoots.

When shoots are 3 in. high the cuttings can be planted out-door.

HOW TO TREAT CUTTINGS

Cuttings need a close atmosphere while rooting, and a form of sand is ideal for the purpose, but while sand is an excellent rooting medium, it has little food value, so all cuttings should be potted into soil as soon as possible after the roots are formed. Care should be taken when removing the rooted cuttings from the sand, as the new roots are often very brittle. Best times to take cuttings are September and March.

1. The modern method of rooting difficult cuttings is to use a root-forming chemical. These are untreated cuttings.

2. These are cuttings planted at the same time, but treated with Hortomone A.

3. Small batches of cuttings can be put in a pot and covered with a bell jar. Lift the latter off each day, and wipe moisture from it.

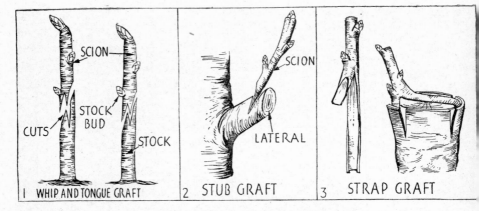

WHIP, STUB AND STRAP GRAFTING

Most fruit trees, named varieties of rho-dodendrons and many other trees and shrubs are increased by grafting. This is a delicate operation and requires a great deal of practice before it can be performed successfully. The growing tissue of a tree is just beneath the bark; the object of grafting is to unite the two cambium layers.

1. Whip grafting is used for joining a stock and scion of the same thickness.

2. Stub grafting and **3,** strap grafting are both used when the stock is thicker than the scion.

In all cases the completed graft is covered with grafting wax. When the stock is the same size as the scion the two are bound with raffia under the wax. The purpose of the wax is to exclude air and excessive damp from the join, and help the parts to unite as quickly as possible.

CLEFT GRAFTING

Cleft grafting is used for renewing old trees. The branches are cut off below the twigs and a scion of young wood inserted, as shown in the diagrams. Use a sharp knife

BEAUTY IN GATES

1. Gates are a necessary evil, but by careful choice they can be made to look as pleasing as any other part of the garden furniture. A simple oak gate looks well.

2. A painted gate hung between brick pillars gives privacy.

FRAME FOR VISTAS

3. A solid wooden gate not only gives absolute security against dogs and other trespassers, but when it is open it makes a delightful frame for the garden beyond.

4. Wrought iron makes an attractive entrance gate because it affords protection but at the same time allows passers-by to have a glimpse of the garden. It should be hung between stone or brick piers which can be softened, as here, by ivies, or by other creepers.

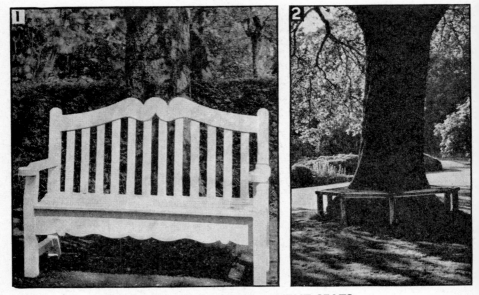

MOVABLE AND PERMANENT SEATS

1. A small occasional seat which can very easily be moved. Beneath a shady tree is an ideal setting. Store indoors during bad weather.

2. A permanent seat can be fixed round the bole of a tree to give an all round view. Oak or teak untreated are the best woods.

FOR FORMAL AND INFORMAL SETTINGS

3. A simple elm-wood seat on a raised concrete base is suitable for any garden. Face it south.

4. A portable garden hammock should be as carefully placed as the permanent furniture.

PLACING A SEAT

1. The placing of a garden seat is as important as the seat itself. The end of a grass path running between twin flower borders is an admirable position.

A SOLID BASE

2. The garden seat which is to be a permanent feature of the garden should be set on a solid base. Flag stones can be laid flush with the grass and surrounding flower beds; these prevent damage to the turf, which otherwise is worn bare, and enables the seat to be used after heavy falls of rain.

USE OF WOOD AND STONE

3. A quiet rose garden is an excellent place for contemplation, and here a plain wooden seat is set back in a recess made by clipped hedges to avoid draughts. In large or formal gardens stone seats are an impressive feature. They are made more comfortable by fitting a framework of wooden slats to the seat. Make use of weathered oak, as the colour is inconspicuous.

SIMPLE ARCH DESIGN
2. The arch shown in (1) before being covered by climbers. Note the extreme simplicity.

ARCHES FOR LINKS
1. Arches form useful links between one part of the garden and another. Here is seen what can be done with rambler roses on a plain arch.

TRELLISES GIVE PRIVACY
3. A plain squared trellis used to screen off a corner of a garden for a quiet retreat.

TWO GARDENS IN ONE
4. A square arch is employed as the central feature of a barrier of plants and shrubs dividing the garden into two self-contained gardens.

HIDING UGLY WALLS

1. Climbers, except the self-clinging kinds, cannot be grown against a wall without support. The easiest and most decorative means is provided by a neat trellis which can be carried round the buttresses. The wood used is untreated oak, which quickly weathers to a soft silvery grey and yet lasts many years. Suitable climbers are *Vitis Henryii*, wistaria, and climbing knotweed. *Polygonum baldschuanicum*. Use either honeysuckle or clematis.

DIAMOND TRELLIS

2. Diamond trellis can be made of common yellow deal laths which can be creosoted or painted as desired. It gives an immediate screen.

RUSTIC TREILLAGE

3. A less formal effect can be obtained by the use of rustic treillage. This is particularly suitable for roses, clematis and honeysuckles.

LIGHT PERGOLAS

1. Light types of pergolas can be constructed of wood, chains, rope or steel rods. The last-named, seen here, effectively supports roses.

USE OF BAMBOO

2. Pergolas should not be so dense as to shut out the sunshine. Bamboos, which are light and strong, are used here with success.

SCREEN AND WALK

3. Here the purpose of the pergola is twofold: a shady walk and a screen. It is covered over with *Vitis coignetiæ*, the Himalayan vine.

FLANKING STEPS

4. The path beneath the pergola must lead somewhere. An unusual and attractive method of flanking a flight of steps is here adopted.

A SMALL GARDEN FULL OF LOVELY FEATURES

1. Here are two pictures of the same garden showing an attractive use of a variety of garden features. The greenhouse is a lean-to, from which one emerges to discover a small lily pool crossed by a rustic bridge, which is seen close up in the picture below, taken from the house.

2. Beyond this a low wall of ornamental bricks is crowned at the ends with stone jars bearing flowering shrubs, a motif which is repeated the length of the garden. Between the low walls a sundial is built into a flagged path. A winding path such as is seen above gives a garden a sense of variety and size, which is enhanced by the use of crazy paving.

A SECLUDED BOWER OF FLOWERS

Here is a very simple design for secluding a tiny bower of flowers round an ornamental pool. A gateway, up the posts of which will be trained ramblers, gives entry. On either side are trellises, on which japonica or other flowering subjects can be trained. Between gateway and trellises evergreen shrubs are planted, and on either side of the pool flowers are massed.

AN OLD WELL BEAUTIFIED

Too often the well is an unsightly feature of a cottage garden. It need not be, as the illustration here shows. Round the bricked mouth of the well alpines grow in a crazy paving; a simple wooden well-head crowns the well, and the earthenware jug adds a homely touch. Rough elm boards are used as roofing material, supported on square oak posts.

MANY BIRDS ARE GARDENERS' FRIENDS

1. Many gardeners regard birds as their friends. By placing a dovecot near the summer-house in a quiet part of the garden pleasant hours can be passed in watching the antics of the birds.

2. Where there is no danger from cats a bird bath can be placed attractively on the ground.
3. A design which gives birds a firm foothold.
4. A bird bath raised on a decorated column.

MINIATURE SUNK GARDEN

1. A raised bird bath may be placed in a small sunken garden. Rock plants growing between the stones and scrambling over the foot of the pedestal add colour to the picture. Even if the birds are absent the bath is a feature of perennial interest, particularly if attractively sited in a lawn or paved courtyard.

MERMAID'S POOL

2. Another garden ornament is seen on the right. A small stone mermaid is seated on a rock in the little pool. This sunken garden is a sheltered spot where the plants in the crevices of the retaining wall will open early in the season, giving a multi-coloured setting for the rings of green grass and grey paving stones.

SUNDIAL VISTAS

3. The sundial seems to demand an old-world setting. Here it is seen charmingly placed in a circle of crazy paving which breaks the straight line of the garden path. Sweet smelling herbs are especially suitable for planting round the sundial. They flourish in warm dry soil, and low-growing thymes clothe the stones with a fragrant carpet.

HIDING UGLINESS

I. Here a low wall of thin bricks has been built round an angle to provide a corner gay with rock plants, flowering shrubs and creepers.

JAPANESE GARDEN

2. For those who like formal ornaments, the wooden pillar supporting a miniature garden will prove attractive. The massing of flowers round its base adds to its charm.

ITALIAN OIL JAR

4. An antique stone jar fits exquisitely at the end of a low cottage wall along which runs a crazy paving fringed with rock plants and lavender. Its primary purpose is to hide drains and soften hard wall outlines.

FLOWERS IN TUBS

3. Tubs are a feature in many gardens. They can take either annuals or perennials. The square box in the background adds a touch of novelty. Creosote wood to preserve it.

A sundial can be admirably sited at the intersection of two paths.

TABLE FOR SETTING A SUNDIAL

EQUATION TABLE—**FAST** means that the watch should be ahead of the dial and **SLOW**, behind it.

1. The longitude of the district must be ascertained, i.e., the number of degrees it is east or west of the Greenwich meridian. This can be found by referring to a map. If east of Greenwich, four minutes must be added, and if west, the same number must be subtracted from the watch time, for each degree of longitude.
2. The sundial must be set by the sun ; summer time cannot be shown.
3. The sundial must be set in full sunshine.

JANUARY		FEBRUARY		MARCH		APRIL		MAY		JUNE	
Days	**Mins.**	**Days**	**Mins.**	**Days**	**Mins.**	**Days**	**Mins.**	**Days**	**Mins.**	**Days**	**Mins.**
2	Fast 4	3	Fast 12	4	Fast 12	1	Fast 4	2	Slow 3	4	Slow 2
4	,, 5	20	,, 14	8	,, 11	5	,, 3	15	,, 4	10	,, 1
7	,, 6	27	,, 13	12	,, 10	8	,, 2	28	,, 3	14	,, 0
9	,, 7			16	,, 9	12	,, 1			20	Fast 1
11	,, 8			19	,, 8	15	,, 0			24	,, 2
14	,, 9			23	,, 7	20	Slow 1			29	,, 3
17	,, 10			26	,, 6	25	,, 2				
20	,, 11			29	,, 5						
24	,, 12										
28	,, 13										

JULY		AUGUST		SEPTEMBER		OCTOBER		NOVEMBER		DECEMBER	
Days	**Mins.**	**Days**	**Mins.**	**Days**	**Mins.**	**Days**	**Mins.**	**Days**	**Mins.**	**Days**	**Mins.**
4	Fast 4	4	Fast 6	1	Fast 0	1	Slow 10	11	Slow 16	1	Slow 11
10	,, 5	12	,, 5	5	Slow 1	4	,, 11	17	,, 15	4	,, 10
19	,, 6	17	,, 4	8	,, 2	7	,, 12	22	,, 14	6	,, 9
		22	,, 3	11	,, 3	11	,, 13	25	,, 13	6	,, 8
		26	,, 2	13	,, 4	15	,, 14	29	,, 12	11	,, 7
		29	,, 1	16	,, 5	20	,, 15			13	,, 6
				19	,, 6	27	,, 16			15	,, 3
				22	,, 7					17	,, 4
				25	,, 8					19	,, 3
				28	,, 9					23	,, 2
										23	,, 1
										25	,, 0
										27	Fast 1
										29	,, 2
										31	,, 3

A simply designed little lawn which gives an air of prosperity to the garden. Set flush with the formal paving it provides a perfect foil for the massed flower borders on either side.

MAKING A GOOD LAWN

The first essential to remember in making a lawn is that grass is a plant like a rose or a marigold ; it needs a constant supply of food and a reasonable depth of soil. The first step, therefore, in making a lawn is thoroughly to prepare the soil. It pays to give as much time as possible to this part of the work because in later years the appearance of the turf will be considerably improved. If the site is covered with builder's clay and brickbats it should be trenched so that the rubbish is buried and the good fertile soil brought to the top. Take care to dig out perennial weeds such as clover, daisies and dandelions, otherwise these will give untold trouble after the lawn is made.

There is no need to remove bricks or stones unless these are very numerous ; in fact, rough material of this kind buried underneath assists in draining the lawn and provides a drier surface in wet weather. Unless water is held up and makes the grass " soggy," it is not necessary to lay a drain ; grass, especially during the growing season, takes up a remarkable amount of water and most lawns suffer from lack of moisture in drought rather than the reverse.

There are two ways of raising a lawn : from turf, or seed. The latter method is the more economical, and if a little care is given to the cultivation of the grass and the preparation of the seed bed, the best possible lawn will result. Turf is more suitable for town gardens where it is difficult to obtain good soil, as in this case there is already a 2 in. layer of soil

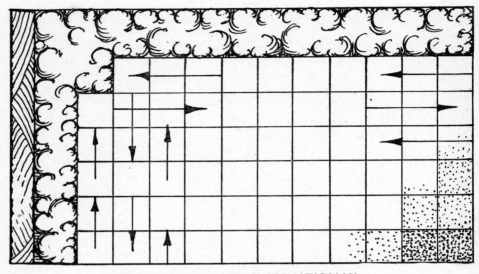

SOW YOUR LAWN SYSTEMATICALLY

In sowing a lawn the seed must be evenly distributed. The best results are obtained by using the method illustrated. With half the seed, sow up and down the lawn over even marked spaces. Then repeat with the rest of the seed, sowing from side to side. If the lawn is required for immediate use apply seed at the rate of 2 oz. per square yard. Where larger areas are sown 1 oz. to 1½ oz. per square yard may be sufficient, but the lawn could not be used for six months after sowing. Deal ruthlessly with the weeds that are certain to appear.

with the turf which is a valuable asset. The advantage of this method is that the lawn can be used a few weeks after laying. Always inspect the turf before purchasing and see that it is reasonably free from weeds ; no field turf is entirely free. As far as possible, pull out what weeds are there as the lawn is being laid. I have found it a good practice to dress the surface of the prepared soil with bone-flour before the turves are laid. This causes the roots to run freely and the grass to catch hold of the new soil more quickly.

MAINTAINING THE LAWN

A good lawn can soon go wrong ; chemical changes in the soil create conditions under which weeds develop and the grass suffers. To keep turf in perfect condition needs just as much care and attention as do flowers in the borders. A lawn that is cut once a week, for example, over a period of thirty weeks would give an output of 30 in. of grass.

This means the removal of considerable nourishment from the soil, and it is obvious that it must be replaced at least once a year.

TOP-DRESSING WITH COMPOST

The time-honoured method of keeping a lawn up to concert pitch is to dress the surface with compost. This is a mixture of various materials such as old potting soil or soil from hotbeds, rotted leaves passed through a ¼ in. sieve and mixed with well decayed manure, sharp sand or bonfire ash, or even fine coal ash can be used. The whole should be thoroughly well mixed together and sifted before using. The best time to use such a compost is autumn or winter, applied at the rate of 5 lb. per square yard. It should be applied evenly and well brushed in.

The leaves which fall on the lawn in autumn should be at once swept up ; left there, they rot the grass. Lop branches of overhanging trees and shrubs.

HOW TO LAY TURVES

Turves are supplied either in strips 3 ft. long by 1 ft. wide or 1 ft. squares. In either case they should be bonded, that is to say, laid like bricks in a wall, with no two vertical joints in line. If the turf varies in thickness this can be adjusted by underpacking or removing some of the soil before laying the turf in position. On poor soil a dusting of boneflour helps.

BEATING INTO POSITION

After being laid, the turf is beaten into position. A beater is easily made out of a heavy piece of wood with a long handle as shown. The back of a heavy spade can be used but this is not so effective and is more back-aching! Apply a dusting of sandy soil and brush into cracks.

LEVELLING THE GROUND FOR A LAWN

To make a successful lawn the ground must be even, whether sloping or level. For games, it must be levelled; for this use pegs, straight-edge and spirit level as illustrated. For sowing, the soil should be flush with the top of the pegs. Consolidate newly dug soil by rolling several times. Repeated raking is necessary to obtain the fine crumbly surface essential for sowing.

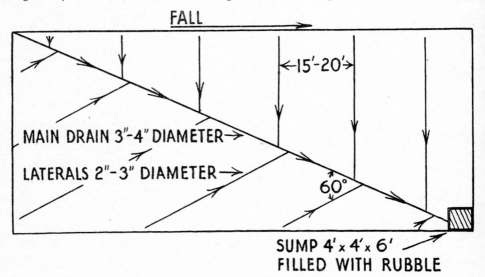

PLAN OF LAWN DRAINAGE SYSTEM

Drainage is of first importance for a lawn. The diagram shows how drain pipes should be laid. Note that the main drain needs a pipe of larger gauge. Place a piece of tile over each junction and fill the trench with clinkers or stones, cover with 9 in. of sand for good results.

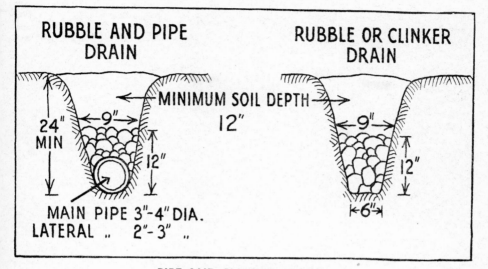

PIPE AND CLINKER DRAINS

On heavy clay soils a pipe drain is needed and should be laid as shown in the left-hand drawing. The clinker drain as illustrated in the right-hand drawing is sufficient for many places, but it has the grave disadvantage of silting up more quickly than the more expensive pipe drain.

IMPROVING DAMP LAWNS

First, see that the drainage is right. If surface water accumulates and remains for several hours after heavy rain, it is an indication that drainage is required. In a small lawn this can quite often be carried out by means of clinker drains. There is usually a fall from one end to the other and the easiest method is to open a trench across the lawn 1 ft. wide and 2 ft. deep, fill in the bottom of the trench with rough clinker, broken bricks or stones to the depth of 12 in. and over this replace the soil. Several such drains may be necessary; place them at intervals of 15 ft. to 20 ft.

FOR CLAY SOILS

An alternative method where the water does not remain too long is to brush into the grass sharp sand, fine gritty ashes, or fine coke breeze. On clay soils, through constant rolling and mowing, the top layer of the soil tends to cake hard and if this can be penetrated with gritty material, after piercing with a fork, any surface dampness will be removed. Clay soils are particularly liable to pools of water, which often stand for long periods.

USE OF FERTILIZERS

Recent research has shown that the effect of lime is to encourage worm casts and also the growth of certain weeds. Its application should only take place in exceptional circumstances. Fertilizers are applied to lawns during the growing season, April to September. Their use is two-fold: they discourage weeds and encourage grass. At first this might seem bewildering until the two sorts of crops are compared; grass has fine, thin leaves on which the fertilizer does not settle but goes straight to the roots to feed them, whereas most weeds have broader leaves which are burnt by the fertilizer. The same fertilizer, therefore, has a different effect on the two types of plants. Mowing, too, encourages thicker and more luscious turf, but discourages the growth of weeds.

Use lawn sand for removing weeds from the lawn.

can be purchased for controlling weeds in lawns. It is also possible to make up a good lawn sand at home :—

> 56 lb. fine silver sand.
> 4 lb. nitrate of soda.
> 4 lb. sulphate of ammonia.
> 3 lb. fine ground sulphate of iron.

A cheaper mixture can also be made from :—

> 1 lb. sulphate of iron.
> 3 lb. sulphate of ammonia.
> 30 lb. fine sand.

USEFUL LAWN FERTILIZERS

For autumn application.

(*a*) Fine ground bonemeal—3 oz. per square yard for general use.

(*b*) Kainit—3 oz. per square yard, for use on patches of coarse grass to encourage growth of the finer leaved varieties.

For spring application.

Superphosphate—four parts.
Sulphate of potash—one part.
Sulphate of ammonia—one part.
The mixture applied at the rate of 1 oz. per square yard.

For spring and summer application.

Frequent light dressings of a nitrogenous manure are beneficial during spring and summer, especially on light, impoverished soils. For this purpose either of the following can be used :—

Sulphate of ammonia.
Peruvian guano.

Even distribution of small quantities is easier if the fertilizer is mixed with equal quantities of finely sieved soil or sand.

Lawn sand.

A variety of ready-made lawn sand

When applying lawn sand it must be remembered that dry conditions are essential. The longer the chemical lies on the broad leaves of the weeds and burns them the more rapid will be the result, rain will soon wash the leaves clean. The action of lawn sand is two-fold, destroying weeds and feeding the fine grasses : the inclusion of sulphate of iron gives the lawn a good rich colour.

LAWN SEED MIXTURES

Seedsmen generally supply a variety of lawn seed mixtures for various purposes. The following lists give suitable grasses for difficult situations :—

For dry, sandy soils, a mixture includes :—

Festuca duriuscula.
Festuca elation.
Festuca ovina.

For shady sites.

Poa nemoralis.
Festuca ovina.

For acid soils and by the sea.

Festuca rubra.

For city gardens.

Poa annua.
Poa nemoralis.

LAWN MOWERS

1. The precision machine, with blades removed for cleaning.

2. The same ready for mowing.

3. Small petrol-driven mower. Economical for large areas.

4. Light hand machine, for small lawns, with 10-in or 12-in. blades.

5. Larger hand machine, with roomy grass box.

FOR THE DIFFICULT LAWN

1. Lawn edges need trimming weekly. This is done easily with long-handled edging shears.

2. A small power machine worked on the same principle as the vacuum cleaner. It is attached to the electricity supply in the house by means of a long flex. These machines have been much reduced in price during recent years.

3. Grass banks are very attractive if well kept, but are not easily cut with an ordinary mower. A special light machine on a long handle can be had, which makes this work simple.

ROLL WITH CARE

1. Rolling the lawn should be done with care. A light soil requires more attention in this way; a heavy soil should never be rolled in wet weather. Use a 1½ to 2 cwt. hand roller.

ROOTS NEED AIR

2. Pricking over the surface in the autumn with a sharp-tined fork is an important operation as it helps to aerate the turf. This should be done before applying compost.

TO CLEAR MOSS

3. Scarifying the lawn is important where moss is prevalent. Sometimes this raking is sufficient, but in more severe cases the moss should be treated first with a special preparation.

FOR WEEDS

4. Deep-rooted weeds such as daisies and dandelions can be most easily grubbed out with this special daisy grubber, which can be purchased for a few pence at any ironmonger's.

TO REMOVE HOLLOWS

1. Hollows in the lawn can be removed in the following way. Tools needed are straight-edge, spirit level, half moon, spade, rake, turf lifter.

CUT OUT TURF

2. Cut out a square of turf with a half moon. Make the square larger than the area of the hollow and cut the turf from 2 in. to $2\frac{1}{2}$ in. thick.

ROLL IT BACK

3. Lift the turf and roll it back beyond the sunken part. Look for any cause of subsidence. If the lawn is dry, it should be soaked with water a few hours earlier.

ADD FINE SOIL

4. Stamp the subsoil firm and fill the hollow with some fine soil from the wheelbarrow. These soils should be moist, but not so wet as to become sticky when sodden.

RAKE AND TREAD

5. Rake the soil down to make a perfectly even surface. Tread it to make sure there is enough soil to raise the turf sufficiently.

PUT BACK TURF

6. Replace the turf and press it down firmly The finished patch should be slightly highe than the surrounding level to allow for settling

BEAT DOWN TURF

Beat the turf with the back of pade to make it firm, so that no holes or spaces are left.

TEST WITH SPIRIT LEVEL

8. Test the patch with the spirit level, to make sure that the hollow has been completely removed. Work finely sifted soil into any crevices or slight hollows.

RE-SOW BARE PATCHES

Bare patches should be scarified h a sharp-tined rake and sown with grass seed mixed with fine soil.

PROTECT FROM BIRDS

10. After sowing, it is wise to protect the seed from birds by placing some branches over it. This work is best done in the lawn sowing seasons.

—D

REPAIRING EDGES

When an edge of the lawn gets patchy an down-trodden, it can be repaired by liftin out a square of turf and relaying it so that th clean edge is outermost. The poor patc can then be re-sown.

1. The turf is cut first of all with a ha moon as shown. If a board is put down an steadied by the foot, it will be easier to mak a straight cut.

2. With a turfing-iron or spade cut unde the turf.

3. Lift the square out without breaking i

4. Turn the turf round.

5. Replace with the good edge outermost an make firm. Check levels with straight-edg

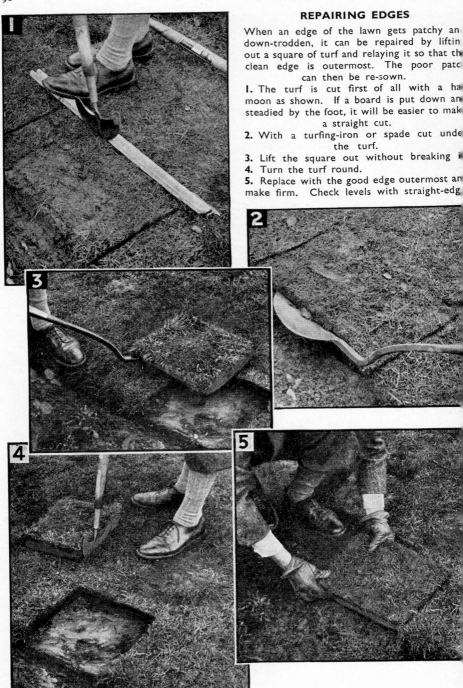

rees will break the force of wind. Suitable bjects for this purpose are: black and white poplars, cypresses, sycamores, Scotch elms, ilex, holly, yew, and, near the sea, Holm oak.

lt winds play havoc with most plants for everal miles inland around all our coasts. A attle hurdle gives excellent protection and can have a hedge planted on the garden side, thus giving a pleasant view from the house. Tamarix, Cupressus and sea buckthorn do well.

SHRUBS FOR BOUNDARY HEDGES

As boundary hedges must be kept from over-hanging the footway, it is usual to plant a shrub that can be clipped. Although privet has been used extensively in the past, it impoverishes any border that may be alongside and therefore *Lonicera nitida* is more suitabl Holly, as shown here, is a good alternativ although considerably slower in growth makes an excellent thick hedge of lasting valu Keep all hedges clear of weeds at the bottor

HEDGES OF FLOWERING SHRUBS

How attractive our streets would look with informal hedges such as this. The three subjects used are *Forsythia intermedia*, *Berberis stenophylla* and *Cotoneaster horizontalis*. These give colour during spring and autumn and, in spite severe pruning to keep them within boun flower and berry freely. Rambler roses train along the fence would be another alternativ

HEDGES TO DIVIDE THE GARDEN

terior hedges can serve two purposes: to nclose separate parts of the garden and to ovide a green setting for lawns and borders. the garden shown above their use on a large scale is shown, but hedges of beech, lonicera, or box can be used to advantage in quite small gardens. Dwarf hedges can be made of lavender, box, or *Lonicera nitida*.

USE OF INFORMAL HEDGES

ll use can be made of the informal hedge here parts of the garden are to be divided e from the other. The pendant branches *Berberis stenophylla* wreathed with golden ossom in the early spring are but one of the many possibilities. Note the strong contrast in both form and colour by the introduction of fastigiate Irish yews at the entrance between the two parts of the garden. The berberis is secateur-pruned immediately after flowering.

SHRUBS NEED LITTLE ATTENTION

1. For the busy gardener shrubs are ideal; they require little attention and quickly give the new garden a furnished look. The seat in the above picture is sheltered by flowering trees which will fill the garden with colour in spring. After the trees have finished blooming they provide a cool and restful background for the roses planted round the seat. A little pruning for shape is all that is required, and should be done annually

VARIETY OF COLOUR AND FORM

2. As much variation of colour and form can be provided by trees and shrubs in the garden as by mixed flowers. Here, rounded dark green yews, delicate silver variegated maple, bronze Japanese maple, and brilliant-flowered azaleas are full of interest all the year round

FOR SCREENING

. Flowering trees are here used
s an attractive screen between
he tennis court and the rest of the
arden. The tree flowering on the
eft is *Prunus serrulata albo pleno*, with
lusters of large double flowers.

FOR EFFECT

2. A very fine forsythia in bloom in
a corner of a small front garden.

FOR SHADE

3. The slender pendulous branches of
the weeping birch provide a shady
spot on the lawn. The network
of wiry twigs is lovely in winter,
especially in very cold weather when
they are covered with frost. Purple
and white crocuses naturalized in the
grass under birches make a fine show.

FOR HEIGHT

2. The creamy flowers of pyracantha borne i
May are followed by brilliant orange berri
which give rise to the popular name of firethor
It is a vigorous grower and is often seen coverir
the side of a three-storied house. Branche
of the berries cut in the autumn last very we
in water and are a useful house decoratio

USE UNDER WINDOWS

1. *Cotoneaster horizontalis* is a good subject for
furnishing walls beneath windows where the
fan-like branches and brilliant autumn colours
show particularly well against a cream background. The berries are a lovely bright red,
and stay on the branches for many months.
The branches press against the wall and need
little support. The bush can also be used on
the ground where the branches follow the line
of the soil, covering mounds, rocks or steps.

TO COVER UGLINESS

4. The attraction of old man's beard (*Clema*
vitalba) is familiar to all. The fluffy seed hea
are a feature in the winter hedgerows. In tl
garden it can be used to cover an ugly she
Owing to its rampant growth a look out mu
be kept lest it smother nearby treasure

AN OLD FAVOURITE

3. Virginian creeper is well known for its
autumn brilliance and it has the advantage of
being self-clinging. Try *Vitis inconstans Veitchii*
(*Ampelopsis Veitchii*) or *Vitis inconstans Lowii.*

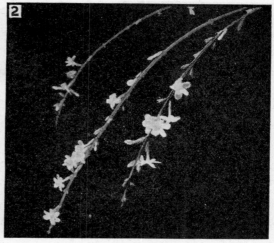

JAPANESE QUINCE

Before the winter days are gone
ne Japanese quince, *Cydonia japonica*,
making a good show. It thrives well
in a sunny position on a wall.

WINTER JASMINE

2. The easiest climber for a house wall of any aspect
is the winter jasmine, *Jasminum nudiflorum*. The golden
yellow flowers appear before the leaves. After flowering, remove all wood that has carried bloom.

EARLIEST FLOWERING HONEYSUCKLE

The earliest flowering honeysuckle is
nicera fragrantissima. If planted in the
elter of a wall it retains its foliage during
e winter so that the cream flowers are seen
to advantage. This is one of the shrubby
loniceras which are less common in gardens
than the climbing types. Planted near a window,
its sweet-smelling flowers cheer wintry days.

;—D*

BIGNONIA
1. The bright orange and scarlet trumpets of *Tecoma* (*Bignonia*) *radicans* are produced freely in August and September on a sunny south wall or in a sheltered corner.

ABUTILON
2. For a sheltered garden the pale mauve *Abutilon vitifolium* and its white variety are attractive trees with mallow-like flowers borne in large loose clusters in June.

CEANOTHUS
3. The hardiest ceanothus is the evergreen *C. rigidus*, although it, too, likes the protection of a wall. The dark blue flowers appear in April and cover the whole tree.

WISTARIA
4. One of the most adaptable spring-flowering climbers is the mauve wistaria. It requires sunshine and on a light well-drained soil will quickly cover pergolas, walls, bridges or trellises with dainty leaves.

TO HIDE FENCES

. Climbers planted to hide fences should be
f a type that does not interfere with the
order plants. Rambler roses are ideal for
he purpose. The shoots should be tied in
ccasionally and pruned after flowering. The
ose shown in the picture is American Pillar.

AGAINST A VERANDA

. Beautifying the supports of a veranda is
ften a problem. Here a wistaria is trained
ound the post, and instead of being an eyesore
becomes an attractive feature of the view.
ut out whole branches if the growth becomes
o rampant and obscures view or light.

FOR WINTER COLOUR

2. Colourful shrubs will grow on house
walls in every season. This winter-berried
Pyracantha Gibbsii, thrives in any aspect.

4. Cheer the winter with golden jasmin
blossom. It thrives on a cold north wall
and needs drastic thinning after flowering.

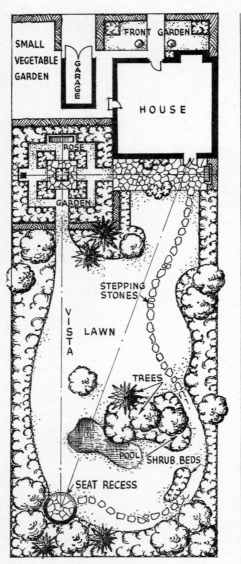

PLAN A SHRUB GARDEN

Here is a delightful garden combining formal and informal features, but at the same time planted practically entirely with trees and shrubs for economy in labour. There are no herbaceous borders or bedding plants; even the formal garden is planted with roses. Conifers are introduced here and there to give contrast of colour and form and one or two standard trees in the lawn to give a natural appearance.

KEYS TO PLANS
ON
PAGE 109

A   SHRUB   No.

1. Cupressus Allumii	2
2. Senecio Greyii	6
3. Syringa, President Carnot (2), Mdme. Lemoine (2)	4
4. Philadelphus virginal	2
5. Buddleia variabilis magnifica	2
6. Olearia Haastii	6
7. Cotoneaster horizontalis	1
8. Ribes atrosanguineum	4
9. Viburnum Carlesii	2
10. Acer palmatum dissectum atropurpureum	1
11. Hydrangea hortensis	2
12. Erica mediterranea alba hybrida	14
13. Prunus lusitanica	4
14. Forsythia intermedia spectabilis	2
15. Cytisus Burkwoodii	2
16. Cytisus Dallimorei	2
17. Rhododendron Hugh Wormald	1
18. Fuchsia corallina	4
19. Rhododendron Cynthia	1
20. Viburnum opulus	2

B   SHRUB   No.

1. Hypericum calycinum	3
2. Genista hispanica	3
3. Buddleia variabilis magnifica	3
4. Cupressus Lawsoniana Allumii	2
5. Rhododendron Pink Pearl	3
6. Rhododendron Britannia	3
7. Spiræa arguta	2
8. Olearia Haastii	2
9. Acer palmatum dissectum	2
10. Berberis aggregata	3
11. Viburnum Carlesii	2
12. Azalea Anthony Waterer	2
13. Cytisus Enchantress	3
14. Hydrangea paniculata grandiflora	2
15. Helianthemum formosum	3
16. Arundinaria japonica	2
17. Lavendula spica	4
18. Acer negundo albo variegatum	2
19. Prunus cerasus avium flora pleno	1

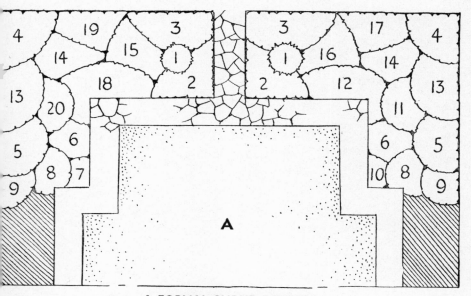

A FORMAL SHRUB BORDER

This shrub border is formal in character and planted with shrubs that will give continuity of interest throughout the year. In addition to the attractive flowering varieties, evergreens have been introduced so that the border is not bare in winter. Note the pair of *Cupressus Lawsoniana Allumii* at either side of the entrance to a farther part of the garden. These grey-green conifers should form the framework to a vista beyond as well as offering a contrast.

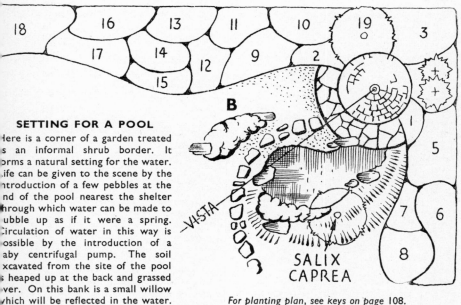

SETTING FOR A POOL

Here is a corner of a garden treated as an informal shrub border. It forms a natural setting for the water. Life can be given to the scene by the introduction of a few pebbles at the end of the pool nearest the shelter through which water can be made to bubble up as if it were a spring. Circulation of water in this way is possible by the introduction of a baby centrifugal pump. The soil excavated from the site of the pool is heaped up at the back and grassed over. On this bank is a small willow which will be reflected in the water.

For planting plan, see keys on page 108.

HONEYSUCKLE

1. Honeysuckle prefers a fairly moist soil in semi-shade. This is *Lonicera periclymenum*.

CLEMATIS

2. There are a great many named varieties o the Jackmanni type of clematis in shades of white blue, purple and crimson. They all require a cool root run with plenty of mortar-rubble in the soil, but the rest of the plant needs full sunshine for the flowers to open well. The commonest form—the purple one—is lovely on the wall o a house, especially if planted alongside the strong-growing yellow rose Gloire de Dijon

FLANKING STEPS

3. When choosing plants to place round steps don't forget that shrubs are very beautiful if well selected. At the top of the flight is a strong growing plant of *Cistus salvifolius* just starting to open its white blooms. Later on the buddleia at the foot of the steps will give its contribution of long purple spikes, so much beloved b butterflies which enhance its beauty on a sunny day The beauty of individual shrubs is most fully appreciated when they are placed in suitable an dignified relationship to their surroundings. Each shrub in this picture has a role to play—the flower at different seasons, thus providing sub ordinate accompaniment to the other in turn And they are not overcrowded, each having good position relative to the steps they adorn

LABURNUM

1. Flowering trees in the front garden help to give the house a more mature look. One of the brightest and best is laburnum; choose the variety Vossii for long sprays of flowers.

BIRD CHERRY

2. One of the most attractive small trees that blooms in April and early May is the bird cherry, *Prunus Padus*, with spikes of fragrant white flowers in clusters on the branch tips.

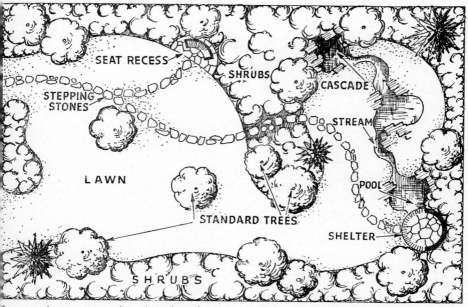

Few people seem to realize the value of our ornamental flowering and fruiting trees. They are not very expensive to buy and give an excellent return for little labour. Among those most easily grown are the flowering cherries, crab apples, laburnums and almonds.

MAGNOLIA

2. The hardiest and easiest magnolia to grow is *M. Soulangeana*. The white flowers are stained with purple on the reverse. Dress annually with leaf-mould. A dark evergreen background shows it up to perfection.

SPRING FLOWERING TREES

1. Spring flowering trees grown as specimens in the lawn are even more attractive if bulbs are grouped beneath in natural drifts. All suggestion of formality of planting must be avoided. Here is *Prunus serrulata*.

MAPLES

4. Few trees are as decorative at all seasons of the year as maples, ranging in size from dwarf bushes to quite large standard trees. They can be had in a variety of types with red, bronze or purple leaves. The variety shown below, *Acer palmatum dissectum atropurpureum*, has finely cut bronze leaves.

TREE POPPY

3. The tree poppy, *Romneya Coulteri*, is a lovely semi-shrubby plant for a well-drained, sunny border. The large satiny-white flowers with a mass of golden stamens in the centre appear in July. The branches are of a herbaceous nature and die down each year.

BERBERIS

The berberis family is invaluable: there are tall and dwarf forms, both evergreen and deciduous suitable for specimens, grouping or hedges, and the flowers, foliage and fruits of the different species give interest throughout all seasons of the year.

I. *Berberis japonica Bealei* has handsome evergreen foliage and a solid mass of yellow fragrant flowers in February. It is very slow growing and the lower parts of the branches become bare and unsightly with age.

2. *Berberis Darwinii* is smothered with orange flower clusters in April. This evergreen is suitable for informal hedges. When grown as single bushes it must be thinned ruthlessly. Wear heavy gloves; the spikes are very sharp and can give nasty wounds.

3. *Berberis Wilsonae*, which has a dwarf habit, makes a striking mass of colour in the autumn with its coral fruits and tinted foliage. Planted in bold groups it is a pleasing feature in the garden demanding the minimum of care and attention.

RHODODENDRON BORDER
1. In a garden on sandy or leafy lime-free soil a border devoted entirely to rhododendrons is always attractive.

MODERN HYBRIDS
2. Modern hybrids are brilliant in their colouring. Good choices are: Pink Pearl, Hugh Koster (crimson), and John Waterer (vivid carmine).

RHODODENDRONS GROUPED NEAR TREES
3. Rhododendrons grow successfully when grouped near trees; the roots are kept cool and moist by the natural mulch supplied by the falling leaves and the dappled shade prevents scorching of the blooms. Lilies do well planted in the same bed, as do meconopsis and gentians.

MAGNOLIA

1. *Magnolia stellata* is the earliest of the magnolias, producing its white, starry, fragrant flowers in March and April before the leaves appear.

ERICA

2. On light soils the difficulty of soil erosion can often be overcome by planting the shrub border with ericas, which prevent evaporation.

IRISH YEW

3. Irish yews can be used in the formal garden or the avenue.

WYCH-HAZEL

4. Before winter is over the wych-hazel displays its golden blossoms.

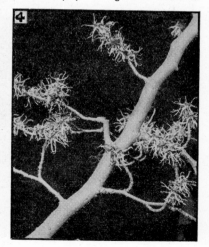

SHRUBS FOR SUMMER

1. The snowball tree is an effective large shrub with foliage that changes colour in the autumn. *Viburnum opulus sterile* is one of the easiest to grow. When planting allow plenty of space as it grows quickly.

FLOWERING CURRANT

2. No garden should be without a flowering currant; it will grow in any soil and covers itself with blossom every spring. The variety *Ribes sanguineum carneum* is deep flesh pink; other varieties have red or white flowers.

3. Lilac needs no description. Many shades are available ranging from purple to white in single and double flowered forms. The best results are obtained by removing all the dead flower heads, and cutting out suckers annually. It cannot be pruned without sacrificing next year's bloom.
4. Allowed to spread, *Spiræa bracteata* makes a lovely show in May and June.

LATE SUMMER
AND AUTUMN EFFECTS

1. *Parrotia persica* used for autumn colour effect. It is grown for its beautiful flaming foliage; the inconspicuous yellow flowers appear in February. Grows up to 40 ft. high.

2. It is very rare to find such a beautiful shrub in full flower in the autumn as *Hibiscus syriacus elegantissima*, the tree hollyhock. Given a sheltered position and full sun it will produce magnificent double white flowers with a maroon centre from August to November. Other colours are also available.

CRAB APPLES

3. Crab apples give a brilliant display of orange and red fruits in early autumn. *Malus Toringo* (*M. Sieboldii*) forms a small tree 12 ft. high of slightly pendulous habit. All the crabs make excellent jelly. That of *Pyrus Eleyi* is wine-coloured and more full-flavoured than most.

Few gardeners take advantage of the coloured stems of shrubs to give interest in the dull winter months. *Cornus sibirica* stems are crimson, and these should be cut to the ground each February, as the brightest colouring is on the new wood. Varieties of Salix (willows) have yellow or red wood. The foliage of a number of evergreens is coloured, examples being the golden and silver Hollies, and many others have brightly coloured berries.

1. A bush of *Cornus sibirica* pruned for winter colour.

2. *Symphoricarpus racemosus lævigatus* is notable for its large, white berries which weigh down the branches in autumn. So adaptable is this shrub that it will even grow beneath pine trees. It is suitable for an uncultivated corner.

3. *Pyracantha Gibbsii* is the variety which carries the heaviest clusters of most brilliant orange berries. Birds are sometimes troublesome, but the tree can be sprayed with a solution made from quassia chips, which discourages their attention. Do not grow against a red wall.

UNUSUAL SHRUBS

A note of character and distinction is added to the garden by the planting of a number of varieties of the less well-known types of shrubs. Here are three which merit consideration for the beauty of their flowers.

1. A less well-known shrub is *Plagianthus Lyalli*. As it is not so hardy as some it enjoys full sun. It bears fragile, almost transparent, white flowers in great profusion.

2. An unusual tree that will thrive on chalk soils is the Judas tree, *Cercis siliquastrum*. Its rosy-lilac, pea-shaped flowers are borne on the old wood before the leaves are fully formed. It prefers a sheltered spot.

3. Brooms thrive in a hot, dry situation, and there are now many brightly coloured modern varieties which are distinct improvements on the original yellow *Cytisus scoparius* which is easily raised from seed.

A DAINTY BUDDLEIA

1. A less common and more dainty buddleia is *B. alternifolia*. The delicate pendulous branches are wreathed in pale blossoms in early summer. The tree needs drastic pruning of old wood to keep it shapely, but light trimming of the flowering shoots only prevents its flowering next year. Annual pruning is not advisable.

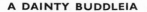

SUMMER FLOWERING

2. Summer flowering dwarf evergreen shrubs are not easy to find, but *Cistus crispus* will brighten the shrub border with its vivid magenta flowers in early June.

3. A semi-evergreen broom is *Cytisus monspessulanus*. It does particularly well on a chalky soil, growing 10 ft. high bearing bright yellow flowers. It is a useful shrub for planting in the rock garden as it does not mind dry positions. Another cytisus suitable for the rock garden is *Cytisus kewensis*

PERNETTYAS

1. The showiest of all dwarf evergreen berried shrubs are the pernettyas. They have clusters of white, pink, deep purple and crimson fruits in the autumn. They must be planted in groups; single specimens are usually infertile.

STRAWBERRY TREE

2. Both flowers and fruits of *Arbutus unedo*, the strawberry tree, appear in November. Although like small strawberries to look at, these fruits are not edible. The tree looks best grown in a lawn.

AZALEAS

3. For brilliance of flower and autumnal foliage, plant azaleas. They require little attention.

LILY OF THE VALLEY TREE

4. *Pieris floribunda* bears spikes of white flowers, resembling lily of the valley, during March and April. It makes a neat, dense, evergreen shrub

MOVING EVERGREENS

1. Evergreen shrubs should be moved in April or September when the sap has begun to rise after the winter dormancy, or before it ceases in the autumn. Large-leaved evergreens, such as laurels, should have the half leaves clipped off to decrease the amount of water lost by evaporation.

DECIDUOUS SHRUBS

2. Deciduous shrubs and trees should be moved any time from late autumn to early spring when the leaves have fallen. Climbers planted against a wall will require watering periodically as they do not get so much rain as those growing in the open. Also where they are planted in paved areas, leave the soil immediately round the stem clear so that water can penetrate to the roots.

PRUNING OF SHRUBS

Shrubs that bloom in the spring need attention immediately after flowering. This consists of the removal of old and weak wood. Many shrubs need no pruning unless odd branches grow out of shape. Let a shrub display its characteristic form.

Those which require drastic thinning are :—

Buddleia variabilis
Forsythia
Hypericum calycinum
Jasminum nudiflorum
Kerria japonica
Prunus triloba
Tamarix pentandra

Those which require no pruning other than the removal of exhausted wood and dead heads are :—

Buddleia alternifolia
Cytisus
Diervilla
Escallonia
Lilacs
Philadelphus
Rhododendrons
Ribes
Spiræas

Flowering shrubs, such as forsythia, that are used for indoor decoration, if cut in long arching sprays, require less pruning later.

1. The wood that bore last year's flowers being cut right back on *Buddleia variabilis*. It flowers on the new wood, therefore no amount of pruning is too drastic.

2. Flower of *Buddleia variabilis*.

TREES AND SHRUBS FOR ALL-THE-YEAR-ROUND

Name	Attractive for	Height	Colour	Remarks
● JANUARY				
Berberis japonica Bealei	Flowers	3 ft. to 5 ft.	Yellow	Evergreen, fragrant
Chimonanthus fragrans	Flowers	7 ft. to 9 ft	Yellow	Sweetly scented, wall protection
Erica carnea	Flowers	9 in.	Deep pink	Will grow on chalk
Garrya elliptica	Catkins	8 ft. to 12 ft.	Green	Graceful catkins
Jasminum nudiflorum	Flowers	8 ft. to 10 ft.	Yellow	Climber
● FEBRUARY				
Cornus Mas	Flowers	15 ft. to 20 ft.	Yellow	Very hardy
Erica Darleyensis	Flowers	1½ ft. to 2 ft.	Pink	Useful in a mass
Hamamelis mollis	Flowers	7 ft. to 9 ft.	Yellow	Plant near evergreen
Viburnum Tinus	Flowers	7 ft. to 10 ft.	White	Evergreen
● MARCH				
Prunus amygdalus (almond)	Flowers	Small tree	Pink	Plant in group
Cydonia japonica	Flowers	6 ft. to 8 ft.	Red	Climber
Daphne mezereum	Flowers	3 ft. to 5 ft.	Pinkish purple	Needs no pruning
Forsythia	Flowers	8 ft. to 10 ft.	Yellow	Easy to grow
Magnolia stellata	Flowers	12 ft. to 15 ft.	White	Shelter
Ulex europaeus (gorse)	Flowers	5 ft. to 6 ft.	Yellow	Light soil
● APRIL				
Berberis Darwinii	Flowers	8 ft. to 10 ft.	Orange	Evergreen
Cytisus praecox	Flowers	5 ft. to 7 ft.	Sulphur yellow	Looks well massed
Kerria japonica	Flowers	4 ft. to 6 ft.	Yellow	Sheltered corner
Prunus Pissardii (purple-leaved plum)	Flowers and foliage	Medium tree	White bronze	Division tree
Ribes sanguineum (flowering currant)	Flowers	6 ft. to 9 ft.	Pink or red	Good for towns
Salix caprea (willow)	Catkins	15 ft. to 18 ft.	Silver	Moist soil
● MAY				
Azaleas	Flowers	2 ft. to 6 ft.	Various—red or yellow	Acid soil
Berberis stenophylla	Flowers	8 ft. to 10 ft.	Yellow	Good hedge
Ceanothus rigidus	Flowers	8 ft. to 10 ft.	Blue	Evergreen
Clematis montana	Flowers		White	Rampant climber
Cytisus hybrids	Flowers	6 ft. to 7 ft.	Various	Sandy soil
Laburnum	Flowers	Small tree	Yellow	Give lime
Prunus cerasus (flowering cherry)	Flowers	Small tree	Pink or white	Mass of bloom
Pyrus floribunda (flowering crab)	Flowers	Small tree	Pink	Good lawn tree
Syringa (lilac)	Flowers	15 ft. to 18 ft.	Various	Likes clay
Wistaria	Flowers		Mauve	Climber
● JUNE				
Buddleia alternifolia	Flowers	15 ft. to 20 ft.	Mauve	Very fragrant
Cistus	Flowers	2 ft. to 8 ft.	White or pink	Sandy soil
Diervilla (weigelia)	Flowers	6 ft. to 7 ft.	Pink	Likes town
Genista hispanica	Flowers	2 ft. to 3 ft.	Yellow	Sandy soil
Viburnum various	Flowers	7 ft. to 10 ft.	White	Autumn foliage

Name	Attractive for	Height	Colour	Remarks
● JULY				
Buddleia variabilis	Flowers	10 ft. to 15 ft.	Mauve	Rampant grower
Ceanothus various	Flowers	6 ft. to 10 ft.	Blue	Shelter
Escallonia	Flowers	6 ft. to 9 ft.	Pink	Evergreen
Hypericum	Flowers	2 ft. to 6 ft.	Yellow	Can grow in shade
Jasminum officinale	Flowers	10 ft. to 20 ft.	White	Fragrant climber
Romneya Coulteri	Flowers	4 ft. to 5 ft.	White	Satin blooms
Spiræa various	Flowers	3 ft. to 8 ft.	Pink or cream	Good for towns
Yucca	Flowers and foliage	3 ft. to 7 ft.	Cream	Evergreen
● AUGUST				
Fuchsia Riccartonii	Flowers	4 ft. to 8 ft.	Red and purple	For hedges in south
Hydrangea	Flowers	3 ft. to 4 ft.	Pink or blue	Protect from frost
Leycesteria formosa	Flowers	4 ft. to 6 ft.	Green and maroon	Quick grower
Ceratostigma Willmottianum	Flowers	2 ft. to 4 ft.	Blue	Tender, south wall
Pyrus aucuparia (mountain ash)	Berries	Small tree	Scarlet	Chalky soils
● SEPTEMBER				
Hippophae rhamnoides	Berries	Small tree	Orange	Seaside
Pyrus malus	Fruits	Small tree	Crimson or scarlet	Used for preserving
Veronica hybrids	Flowers	4 ft. to 7 ft.	Various	Evergreen
Viburnum Lantana	Berries	6 ft. to 8 ft.	Scarlet	Rich colour
Pyracantha	Berries	10 ft. to 18 ft.	Orange-scarlet	Evergreen climber
Rhus Cotinus	Seed heads	6 ft. to 8 ft.	Smoky	Lovely foliage
Symphoricarpus racemosus	Berries	7 ft. to 9 ft.	White	Likes shade of trees
● OCTOBER				
Acer various	Foliage	4 ft. to 20 ft.	Crimson shades	Dwarfs in rockery
Ampelopsis	Foliage		Crimson shades	Climber
Berberis various	Foliage and berries	3 ft. to 10 ft.	Autumnal tints	Best shrub family
Cotoneaster various	Berries	2 ft. to 12 ft.	Red	Good on walls
Crataegus	Berries	Small tree	Red	Plant in hedge
Prunus Sargentii	Foliage	Small tree	Orange shades	Use in shrubbery
● NOVEMBER				
Arbutus unedo	Fruits and flowers	Medium tree	Red and white	Flowers and fruits together
Aucuba japonica	Foliage and berries	5 ft. to 8 ft.	Variegated red	Evergreen
Golden privet	Foliage	6 ft. to 10 ft.	Golden	Evergreen
Golden yew	Foliage	12 ft. to 16 ft.	Golden	Evergreen
Prunus subhirtella	Flowers	Small tree	White	Topsy-turvy tree
Senecio Greyii	Foliage	4 ft. to 6 ft.	Grey	Evergreen
Viburnum fragrans	Flowers		Pink and white	The best winter flower, very hardy
● DECEMBER				
Cornus sibirica	Stems	4 ft. to 6 ft.	Crimson	Best in masses
Cornus stolonifera	Stems	3 ft. to 5 ft.	Yellow	Leave alone
Gaultheria procumbens	Berries		Red	Creeping evergreen
Holly	Berries and foliage	Small tree	Red or yellow	Evergreen
Rubus	Stems	8 ft. to 8 ft.	Variegated white	Wild garden
Salix v. britzensis	Stems	10 ft. to 15 ft. if cut	Orange-scarlet	Water side
Skimmia japonica	Berries	3 ft. to 5 ft.	Red	Evergreen

PLANT SHRUBS CAREFULLY

The planting of trees and shrubs is permanent, therefore it should be done thoroughly. Each hole must be made sufficiently large to accommodate every root well spread out, over which fine soil is sprinkled. A common error is to plant too deep. This often leads to trouble later, as the bark of the tree is damaged by the contact with damp soil. It is easy to see at what depth the tree was previously planted and to see that it is the same in its new position. Watering is often essential after planting. Should shrubs arrive from the nursery garden during frosty weather, heel them in, and give protection with straw or sacking until the soil is frost-free.

TABLE SHOWING THE DISTANCE TO SET HEDGE PLANTS

FORMAL HEDGES

	Planting	Distance	Foliage	When to Trim
Box	12–15 in.	Staggered	Evergreen	Clip in May and August.
Beech	10 in.	,,	Deciduous	Clip in August.
Hornbeam	10 in.	,,	,,	Clip in August.
Cupressus macrocarpa ..	24 in.	Single row	Evergreen	Trim with knife, May and August.
Privet	10 in.	Staggered	,,	Clip frequently when straggly.
Lonicera nitida	12–18 in.	,,	,,	Clip in June and August.
Thorn	15–18 in.	,,	Deciduous	Clip in April and August.
Holly	12–15 in.	Single row	Evergreen	Clip in May and August.
Yew	12–18 in.	,, ,,	,,	Clip in May and August.

INFORMAL HEDGES

Berberis stenophylla ..	24 in.	Single row	Evergreen	Remove whole branches if too thick; after flowering
Cotoneaster Simonsii ..	18 in.	,, ,,	,,	Trim straggling shoots in August or February.
Escallonia	18 in.	,, ,,	,,	Trim after flowering.
Forsythia	18 in.	,, ,,	,,	Cut back in May.
Lavender	12 in.	,, ,,	,,	Trim lightly and remove dead flowers after flowering.
Briar rose	18 in.	,, ,,	Deciduous	Trim in March and August.
Gorse	18 in.	,, ,,	Evergreen	Trim after flowering.
Laurestinus	18 in.	,, ,,	,,	Trim in spring.

PEONIES RESENT DISTURBANCE

1. Although most herbaceous plants can be moved in spring or autumn a few either resent disturbance or require moving at a certain season to be sure that they will live. Peonies resent being disturbed, and if the herbaceous border has to be remade it is best to dig around the clumps without lifting them. Otherwise they require little care.

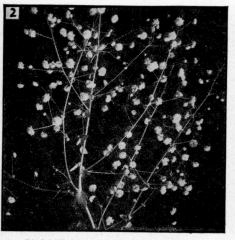

PLANT THALICTRUM DEEPLY

2. Avoid shallow planting of thalictrum roots. If too near the surface they will fail to grow strongly. Once planted they should be disturbed as little as possible. The variety shown is *Thalictrum dipterocarpum*, and sends up tall branching stems of mauve flowers. The buds are " drumsticks," attractive in themselves.

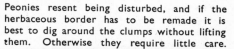

MOVE IN SPRING

3. Asters of the *Amellus* section should be moved in the spring, when planted in autumn they frequently die during the winter.

CONTRASTS IN FORM AND COLOUR

1. Hemerocallis, or day lily, is a useful plant requiring little attention. There are varieties with orange flowers as well as shades of yellow; some of the newer types are double. There is also one with variegated leaves, but with rather poor flowers.

2. *Centranthus ruber*, or valerian, seeds freely and the young plants can be collected in the autumn and planted in groups where they are required. Red, pink, and white forms are obtainable.

3. One of the earliest herbaceous plants is the oriental poppy. In addition to the well-known crimson variety there are pale pink and orange red shades, there are single and double flowered types.

4. The globe thistle, *Echinops ritro*, is a stately plant with its metal blue flower heads for the back of the border. It blooms in late July. A strong grower, clumps of echinops can thrive in rough grass in the wild garden, where they make a handsome group.

SCABIOUS

2. There are several varieties of *Scabiosa caucasica*, and one of the best is Clive Greaves. The pale mauve flowers are produced in June and grow to a height of 18 in. This is another of the plants best moved in spring, especially on cold or heavy soils.

BRISTOL FAIRY

. The best form of *Gypsophila aniculata* is Bristol Fairy. The umerous double white flowers give cloud-like appearance in the border n August. It grows to a height of ft. and the stem should be supported by short twigs. Keep a watch in the spring for slugs, the ew shoots are liable to be eaten nless protected against this pest.

BLUE FLAX

. The blue flax, *Linum perenne*, is ne of the daintiest pale blue flowers or the front of the border. It can asily be raised from seed sown outde in early summer. Another variety num narbonense, has deeper blue owers and opens a succession of owers over a long period; this num does not come true to colour om seed, so plants should be rocured. All the plants shown on is page do best on chalky soils.

CAMPANULA

1. *Campanula lactiflora* is a free flowering blue bellflower growing 3 ft. to 4 ft. high.

HEUCHERAS

2. Heucheras are useful in a mixed border, the flower spikes being sent up over a long period. The variety *Heuchera sanguinea* is shown here

DWARF MICHAELMAS DAISIES

3. The dwarf race of Michaelmas daisies ar charming little plants, very useful for the from of a border or in the rock garden. The bloom at the same time as the tall varieties

HELENIUMS

4. Heleniums are valuable plants in the autum border giving bold patches of yellow, deep re and brown. They range from 18 in. to 6 ft. hig

Flowering Seasons of Herbaceous Plants

Anchusa italica	June–Sept.
Anemone japonica	July–Oct.
Aster amellus	Aug.–Oct.
,, novae angliae	Sept.–Nov.
Campanula lactiflora	June–Sept.
Coreopsis lanceolate	Aug.–Sept.
Delphiniums	June–July
Dicentra spectabilis	May–June
Doronicum plantagineum	May–June
Echinops ritro	July–Aug.
Erigeron speciosum	June–July
Gaillardia	Aug.–Sept.
Geranium armenium	June–July
Geum, Mrs. Bradshaw	July–Aug.
Gypsophila paniculata	July–Sept.
Helenium autumnale	Aug.–Sept.
Helianthus rigidus	July–Sept.
Hemerocallis	June–July
Heuchera brizoides	July–Aug.
Iris (bearded varieties)	May–July
Kniphofia	Aug.
Liatris pycnostachya	July–Sept.
Linum perenne	May–July
Lupin (polyphyllus varieties)	May–July
Lychnis chalcedonica	July–Aug.
Monarda didyma	July–Sept.
Papaver orientalis	May–July
Phlox (suffruticosa varieties)	June–July
Rudbeckia laciniata	July–Aug.
Sidalcea malvaeflora	July–Aug.
Solidago	Aug.–Oct.
Veronica spicata	July–Aug.

ASTILBES

1. Although astilbes are usually associated with waterside planting, they are equally effective in the moist herbaceous border. The plumes of pink, crimson and white flowers are borne in summer, and most varieties reach a height of 3 ft. They can also be forced in pots.

stilbe chinensis is a very effective plant with luish flowers tinged with rose; Astilbe pumila dwarf, 9 in. high, with erect lilac rose flower spikes.

BLAZING STAR

2. Liatris pycnostachya has rosy-purple spikes in August. It grows 4 ft. high. It appreciates a place in a moist border. Where a lower grow-ing plant is wanted the variety Liatris spicata will be found useful. Also called Kansas Feather.

ALSTRŒMERIA

. Alstrœmeria, a Peruvian lily, likes a cool oot run. A well-drained sandy soil contain-g leaf-mould suits it best. The flowers appear July, and continue to bloom for a long eriod. The colour range includes a lovely lection of flames, yellows and reds. During ard winters it is wise to protect the plants covering them with a layer of cinders.

LOOSESTRIFE

4. Lythrum salicaria has purplish-rose flower spikes that grow 4 ft. high, and open from July to September. Large groups should be planted for the best effect. The variety Rose Queen is lower growing and has very fine spikes of flowers. They do well near water.

JAPANESE WIND FLOWER

2. The Japanese Wind Flower, *Anemone japonica* is one of the easiest plants to grow in shade. Both pink and white forms, which grow 3 ft. high, should be grown. Do not lift the plants more often than necessary as they resent disturbance. Blooms late in summer.

FERNS FOR SHADY CORNERS

1. In every garden there is some corner or border which is dull and shady. Even for these spots there are plants which will provide colour and interest. For damp situations ferns are suitable and not hard to grow. Here the male fern and the ribbon fern form a pleasing combination in a corner by a flight of steps.

LUPINS

4. Lupins, though usually considered border plants, will flower in the half shade. Beds of mixed coloured seedlings are very effective and the plants can be easily and cheaply raised. New strains known as " Russell lupins " have compact spikes in many good colours.

SAXIFRAGE

3. The herbaceous saxifrage, *Megasea cordifolia*, is a very accommodating plant for a position with little sun. The large leathery leaves are always clean and tidy and the deep pink flower heads, which appear very early in the year, are one of the first to appear in the border.

1. *Achillea filipendulina* has large flat heads of yellow flowers which grow 4 ft. high and provide a showy patch of colour in the border in August.

2. *Helianthus rigidus* is another useful yellow flower for the border. Being a quick grower it must be divided frequently or the size of the bloom deteriorates.

3. The variety Helianthus Monarch has fine bright yellow semi-double flowers.

4. Pentstemons are valuable herbaceous border plants although not perfectly hardy. Cuttings should be taken in September and wintered in a cold frame. They will be ready for planting out next spring to give a show the same year. In mild districts the old plants will survive the winter. Named varieties can be procured in shades of pink, red and purple, or mixed kinds can be raised from seed.

5. *Rudbeckia mollis* is one of the earliest cone flowers to bloom. The yellow flowers have a dark central cone. The plant grows 2 ft. high. Other varieties can be planted to give a succession of bloom.

BLUE MICHAELMAS DAISY

2. The most popular blue Michaelmas daisy of medium height is Little Boy Blue. It is of rather stiff habit and bears dark blue flowers

WHITE MICHAELMAS DAISY

I. The purest white Michaelmas daisy is Mount Everest, which grows to a height of 4 ft. When selecting flowers for a white border this is the best aster to choose; many of the whites get a pink or mauve tinge as the flowers fade, giving the whole spray a coloured appearance. Be sure to stake these plants early; so much of their charm is lost if the stems are allowed to fall over and grow bent or bedraggled.

FLOWERS AND FOLIAGE

4. Easily grown and attractive foliage subject are iris, megasea and yucca. The first two will succeed in sun or shade. They all repay the grower for their inclusion in the garden scheme by having beautiful flowers as well as distinctive foliage. Do not plant a yucca too near a pathway, because of the pointed leaves

PAMPAS FOR EFFECT

3. For wilder parts of the garden interest can be introduced by one or two plants of pampas grass. It needs plenty of room and should be away from overhanging trees.

RED AND GOLD IN THE BORDER

1. Red-hot pokers give a touch of brilliant red and orange colouring to the border in early autumn. Royal standard is a good variety growing to a height of 3 ft. 6 in.
2. The many forms of golden rod will succeed on heavy soils. The variety Goldstrahl is here shown.

3. Phlox require plenty of moisture and in dry summers should be watered very freely.

ERIGERONS

I. Erigerons produce their numerous mauve, shaggy blossoms on 2 ft. high plants. They closely resemble the Michaelmas daisy. One of the best is the variety called Quakeress.

VERONICA

2. A useful dwarf blue perennial is *Veronica spicata*, growing 1½ ft. high. There is also a pink flowered form called *Veronica spicata rosea*, which is useful for the front of a border.

PHYSOSTEGIA

3. Physostegia Vivid is an attractive plant, holding its heads of bright purple-crimson flowers erect on stiff stems. It spreads quickly by underground shoots. Can be divided in spring.

BUPHTHALMUM

4. The yellow flowers of *Buphthalmum salic folium* come at a time when this colour is scarce in the border, and continue to bloom until late in the autumn. Grows 2 ft. high.

THE HERBACEOUS BORDER

. The herbaceous border is a lovely feature n a garden, giving colour from early spring until late autumn. The border shown above has been specially planted for autumn display, and has a large proportion of rudbeckia, helenium, golden rod and Michaelmas daisies. Borders for the different seasons are very beautiful, but in the small garden planting for continuous bloom is generally the most satisfactory plan to adopt for reasons of space.

LATE SUMMER FLOWERS

. *Anemone japonica*, in shades of pink and white, planted with the early dwarf blue Michaelmas daisy, make a pleasant group, blooming together in late summer and autumn.

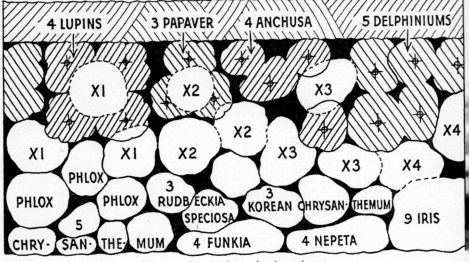

Diagram showing interplanting scheme

THE ART OF INTERPLANTING

Interplanting should be practised in herbaceous borders so that as much blossom and as few bare patches as possible are present throughout summer and autumn. Early flowering subjects, such as oriental poppy, anchusa and lupins, have very untidy growth when the flowering is past, and if a plant that blooms much later in the season is planted among these, these dull patches will be avoided. Useful flowers for this purpose are border chrysanthemums and dwarf Michaelmas daisies. Delphiniums, too, present difficulty, and a satisfactory scheme for hiding their bare stems is to plant the cloud-like *Gypsophila paniculata* alongside and the spreading growth can be arranged as a screen. Another method that may be adopted for plants at the front of the border that have passed their best is to have groups of irises, funkia and montbretia in front of them. Although the flowering period of these subjects is short, their foliage is attractive throughout the spring and summer and will successfully hide bare stems.

The art of interplanting is to combine plants of different flowering seasons so that a continuous show is obtained, and at the same time the bare stems of the early flowering subjects are hidden as the season advances by those that flower later. In the diagram the spaces marked X can be planted with gypsophila, *Statice latifolia* or tall branching annuals to cover the space left when the back plants are cut down. The second crop flowers then give a background to the front part of the border which is of late flowering plants.

Although the plants will obtain a considerable amount of food from the manure dug into the soil, each spring and early summer they should be given a few dressings of artificials. Early in the growing season, apply some sulphate of ammonia at the rate of 1 oz. per square yard and follow this in May and June with a general fertilizer. A good mixture can be made as follows: one part of sulphate of ammonia, three parts of superphosphate and one part of sulphate of potash dusted on to the surface at the rate of 2 oz. per square yard. This can be given at intervals of two or three weeks until the buds appear.

After several years herbaceous borders are apt to become less floriferous owing to the decrease in quantity of the nourishment available for the roots and the general overcrowding of the plants. Before this occurs you should find time to remake the border.

During the previous summers you will have noticed where past planning had been particularly satisfactory, or, of course, where failures have occurred, such as bare patches with no flowers for weeks on end or a bad combination of height or colour. Such deficiencies should be carefully noted so that you can avoid them on planning the new scheme. Time devoted to the working out of a plan on paper is worth the extra trouble it entails and in this way you can be sure of obtaining equal proportions of early summer, midsummer and autumn flowers.

Having worked out a plan on paper, the next step is to transfer these ideas to the border. The border should be emptied of plants, and these may be heeled in on spare ground. Although most plants should be removed, a few such as peonies and anemone japonica resent disturbance and if they are well established

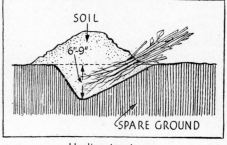

Heeling in plants.

it would be best to dig round them.

If the soil is light, double dig the border ; but where it is of a heavy clay nature, dig as deeply as possible, but do not bring the yellow clay to the surface. Break the soil down with the back of a fork as work proceeds so that it is in a fit condition to replant when the work is completed.

Now take the plan, which should have been marked out into yard squares, and having marked out the border into similar yard squares by means of sticks it will be possible to determine the allotted space for each group of flowers. Planting may then be done.

Plan for marking out border.

verbascums, asters and solidago being planted 3 ft. apart. Those of medium height, such as phlox, lupins, chrysanthemums and gypsophila should be set 2 ft. apart, and anything smaller from 1 ft. to 1½ ft.

DEPTH

1. To plant, take out a hole sufficiently large to take the roots well spread out. Lower the plant into position, and make sure that the crown is neither buried nor above the surface of the soil.

SOIL

2. Soil should then be placed round it and the whole trodden firmly. If the soil is at all dry soak it with water.

PLANTING

A herbaceous border can be planted in autumn or spring. Once planted it should remain thus for at least three years before any lifting or dividing will be necessary. It is therefore important to dig in plenty of vegetable matter or manure, if available, to keep the plants in good condition over this period. Such a border should be planned before planting so that all you have to do when the plants arrive is to mark out their allotted positions on the border with a label to each and then set out the plants, spacing them equally to cover the necessary space. The distance between the plants varies according to the height to which they grow, the tallest such as delphiniums,

COTTAGE GARDEN EFFECT

Here is a distinctive type of herbaceous border in which the plants are allowed to merge with the path, giving the cottage garden effect. Erigeron, irises, geraniums and peonies are the chief foreground plants, with bushes of buddleia at intervals to give height, and a background of rambling roses. Such an arrangement is treated as a separate feature in this garden.

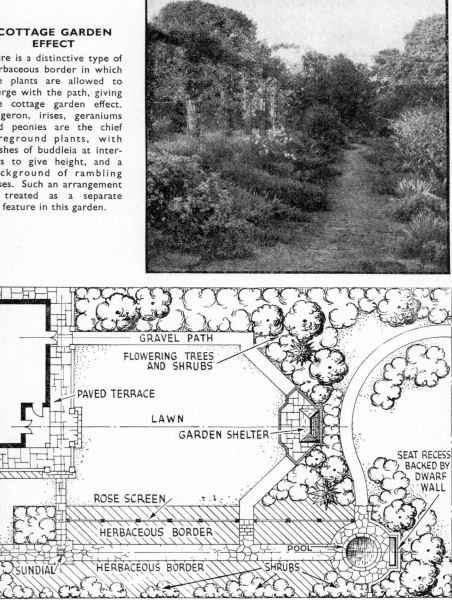

TWIN HERBACEOUS BORDERS

The introduction of twin herbaceous borders as a separate unit of the garden is shown in the plan above in relation to the rest of the lay-out. Compare the plan with the photograph, where the rose screen bordering the lawn can be seen on the left.

USE OF BOLD GROUPS

A lovely well-furnished border, each variety planted in bold groups. Notice the placing of a medium-height group of coreopsis in the front row: this breaks the line of lower growing plants and relieves the monotony of even lines, yet does not conceal the flowers behind it. The border at this point is about 12 ft. wide and allows for the inclusion of some very tall plants which would be out of place in narrower border but look spectacular here.

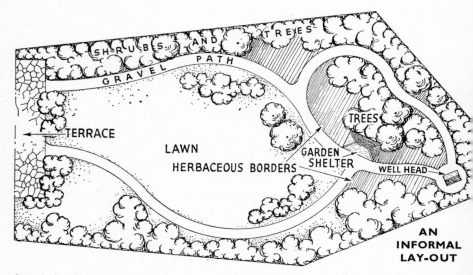

AN INFORMAL LAY-OUT

Straight borders of a set width are not essential for herbaceous plants. These may be introduced in the garden in bold groups against a background of trees and shrubs. The introduction of this style of planting in a completely informal lay-out is shown in this diagram.

PLANTS FOR A MIXED FLOWER BORDER

In a very small garden it is seldom possible to plant a herbaceous border proper. It is more usual to have a mixed flower border in which annuals and bulbs find a home with the herbaceous plants. Here dahlias, antirrhinums and calceolarias are introduced in groups amongst the helenium, phlox and *Chrysanthemum maximum*, and here and there a bush rose is introduced.

1. *Chrysanthemum maximum.*
2. Dwarf bedding dahlia.
3. Calceolaria.
4. Helenium.
5. Dahlia.
6. Phlox.
7. Helenium.
8. Dahlia.
9. Antirrhinum.
10. Calceolaria.

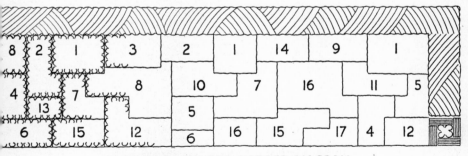

PLANTING KEY FOR BORDER DIAGRAM

The whole border is 10 ft. wide and 40 ft. long.

1. Delphiniums (three different shades of blue).
2. Aster Climax.
3. Solidago.
4. Oenothera Youngii.
5. Helenium Crimson Beauty.
6. Alyssum saxatile.
7. Aster Dick Ballard.
8. Helenium Riverton Gem.
9. Aster Barr's Pink.
10. Lupin (pale pink).
11. Lupin (deep pink).
12. Erigeron Quakeress.
13. Gypsophila paniculata.
14. Helenium Gartensonne.
15. Viola gracilis.
16. Iris Souvenir de Mme. Gaudichaud.
17. Geum Borisii.

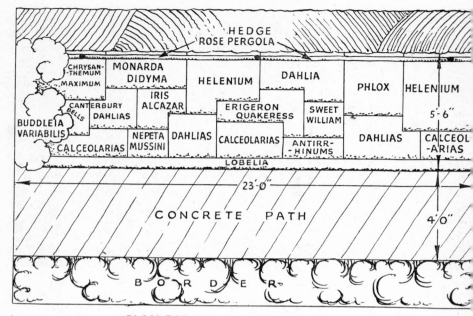

PLAN FOR SUMMER FLOWER BORDER

The plan shown above gives details of planting for a summer flower border. Making use of a mixture of herbaceous plants with biennials such as antirrhinums and Canterbury bells, and tender subjects like dahlias and calceolaria, the border will give a full display of colour during the summer and early autumn months. When planting the dahlia patches attention must be paid to the height of the varieties as well as the colour. There is space here for one tall, one medium, and two low growing varieties. Note general use of contrast.

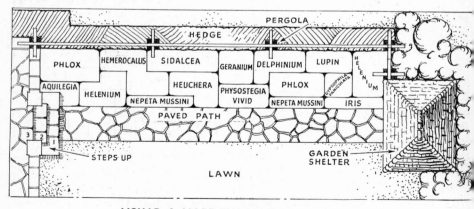

USING A NARROW STRIP OF GROUND

A narrow strip of ground can be used for herbaceous plants, though care must be taken to avoid the error of using too many different types of plants and making a "fussy" border. The diagram shows a suitable lay-out for a 4 ft. wide strip by a paved path. The border is backed by a hedge and pergola to show up the flowers.

YARROW IN A CORNER BACKED BY SHRUBS

1. Where a border ends beside a thick tree or shrubs large blocks of strong growing plants must be planted. Here *Achillea eupatorium* is used very successfully, showing no tendency to fall away from the rhododendron beside it. in spite of the heavy shade cast by the bush.

ROSEMARY OR LAVENDER FOR A BORDER END

2. Where a border stops abruptly, special care should be paid to the planting on the corner. A plant that is attractive all the year round should be placed here, such as lavender or rosemary. Although not a herbaceous plant, the grey-green foliage and blue flower heads of lavender blend well with other flowers. In this illustration the end of the border is seen in silhouette, which shows how well the nicely rounded form of the lavender bush appears.

COLOUR EFFECTS

1. In this mixed flower border bushes of hydrangea give a bright patch of colour. On the edge of the border are dwarf plants on rocks.

FOREGROUND PLANTING

2. Foreground planting in the border is important; aim at placing early flowering subjects behind those that will flower later.

ALONG A PATH

3. When the herbaceous border is placed alongside a path that is frequently used, the plants should not overhang. A grass verge gives a neat finish, and protects edging plants.

BESIDE THE LAWN

4. One of the most pleasant positions in the garden for the herbaceous border is alongside the main lawn, where the grass acts as a foil to the brilliant colours of the flowers.

ANNUAL FLOWERS

Annuals are plants which are sown, flower and set seed all in the one season. They form an extensive class which includes many of the most showy flowers. China asters, sweet peas and godetias are typical examples of true annuals.

To give the best results annuals require a deeply dug, well manured soil. There are a few exceptions to this rule, nasturtiums and mesembryanthemum giving a better show of flowers if starved.

The soil should be thoroughly dry in autumn, and a good dressing of well-rotted manure turned into the soil. Leave the surface rough to allow the frost to get well down. In spring, fork the patch over again and sprinkle on a light dressing of a general fertilizer.

Annuals are divided into two classes, hardy and half-hardy. The cultural methods of the two groups are slightly different.

Hardy annuals are able to stand the vagaries of our climate and can be sown direct into the open ground. In some cases it is most convenient to sow on a seed bed and transplant the young seedlings to their permanent quarters as space is ready for them. This way the seed may be sown quite thickly, either broadcast or in drills. Where the ground is vacant and ready, the seeds may be sown where the plants are to flower. In this case the seed must be sown very thinly ; it is merely a waste to sow too much seed, as the plants must be thinned later. As a guide for the final distances to leave between the plants it may be reckoned that the

mature plant needs to be its own height away from its neighbour to come to perfection. The weak and scrappy appearance of some annual borders is nearly always due to overcrowding.

Hardy annuals may be sown from March onwards. Marigolds, love-in-a-mist, larkspur, candytuft and lavatera are all hardy. Consult a good seed catalogue when doubtful about the hardiness of the flower you wish to sow.

The use of annuals as stop gaps in a flower border is sometimes overlooked. The busy gardener will find them invaluable for filling gaps left by the failure of a permanent plant.

Annuals pricked out into pots when young, and plunged into the ground to reduce the labour of watering, can be moved at any time. Keep a few plants of each of a range of colours in reserve for replacements, and you need fear no bare patches. For this purpose eschscholtzias, white, yellow and tangerine will be found useful for low patches. Lavatera can be used for tall groups of white or pink. Godetia and clarkia supply pinks and mauves of medium height.

Nasturtiums can be used for this purpose, but must not remain too long in their pots, or they tend to become stunted from overcrowding of the roots. The best scarlet annual for the mixed border is linum, or scarlet flax. Where blue is needed phacelia is a pretty low growing annual, and larkspur if grown in fairly large pots will reach nearly full height before they suffer from lack of space.

East Lothian Stock

MIGNONETTE

A fine flower head of the sweet-scented
Reseda odorata, variety Crimson Giant.

HALF-HARDY ANNUALS

Half-hardy annuals are plants which
cannot stand the amount of frost we so
often have in late spring. These are
sown under glass, either in frames or in
boxes and pans in a greenhouse. Before
the seedlings become crowded prick
them out 2 in. apart into fresh boxes.
Keep these boxes as near to the glass
as possible to prevent the young plants
from becoming leggy.

The time for sowing half-hardy annuals
varies, April being the most usual month.
Too early sowing is no advantage as the
plants cannot be put out of doors until
May, and harm is done if the boxes
have to remain crowded in a house after
the plants are ready to be moved.

As the time for planting out approaches
the seedlings must be gradually hardened
off. This is done by giving the greenhouse more ventilation than previously,
and in the case of frames the lights are
propped up a little farther every few
days until at last they are removed
altogether and the plants totally exposed.
This hardening off is important, as it

prevents the plants getting the double
shock of change of temperature and root
disturbance at the same time.

Some of the most usually grown half-
hardy annuals are : asters, cosmeas,
mesembryanthemums, French marigolds,
nemesias. Here again a seed catalogue
will give guidance on this matter.

The use of annuals in the rock garden
must be restrained ; only those of dwarf
or wiry habit may find a place among
the alpines. Nothing is more out of
place in the rock garden than a clump of
rampant fleshy annuals.

Sedum cœruleum is an annual stonecrop
with pale blue flowers ; when once
established it will come up every year
from self-sown seed. The dwarf poppy,
Papaver alpinum, in shades of orange,
yellow, pink and white, is another plant
suitable for a gritty bed in the sun where
it makes a brave show with its little
flowers on 3-in. stems. *Leptosiphon* is a
low growing annual with flowers of many
colours which looks well near a pathway.
Portulaca grandiflora has deep crimson-
purple flowers on 6-in. stems and should
be grown in a sunny spot.

NICOTIANA

The tobacco plant is well known for the fragrance
of its flowers, very noticeable in the evening.

Sweet Pea. Sutton's Rosita.

THE BEST CUT BLOOM

An annual that deserves special attention is the sweet pea. It is the finest of all cut blooms. Given proper cultural treatment it will continue to bloom from early summer until late autumn.

To get good results it is important to give attention to the preparation of the soil. Begin in October by opening out a trench 18 in. wide and deep. Heap the soil along one side of the trench. This will be required for filling in just before planting time in spring. Get into the bottom of the trench with a stout fork and break up the subsoil 12 in. deep. Into this dig old manure or rotted material from the compost pit, and then give the bottom of the trench and the sides a liberal dusting of lime.

Leave the trench as rough as possible throughout the winter. Fork over the subsoil again a few weeks before planting, because the sweet pea more than all other plants benefits from a well aerated soil. The little nodules which are peculiar to the sweet pea thrive better and so do the plants.

For early flowers and rich blooms sweet peas should be sown in October in small pots of rich soil and wintered in the cold frame. When the seedlings are above the soil plenty of air should be admitted on all favourable days, and they should be within 12 in. of the glass in the cold frame. Otherwise they become drawn.

The seedlings are planted out where they are to bloom 6 in. apart in two rows staggered, and should be staked immediately with a few twigs as a protection from cold winds. The row should run from north to south if possible and is best sheltered from high winds by means of a tall wall, hedge or trees. On no account should sweet peas be grown in a shady position; they like plenty of sunshine and fresh air.

Sweet peas may also be sown in March on the ground where they are to bloom.

TRAINING SWEET PEAS

There are two ways of training sweet peas : the cordon method in which the plant is grown as a single stem, or by allowing it to grow in its own sweet way with the support of pea boughs or very large mesh wire netting.

Should sweet peas be desired for exhibition they are grown on the cordon method and all side shoots are pinched out as soon as they are large enough to handle. In this way sturdy spikes of flowers, four to seven on a stem, are produced with thick stems which stand erect in the vase.

Given good cultural conditions, sweet peas are not subject to many troubles. Change the soil each year if possible. Use lime and a little potash regularly and your peas will be free of disease.

Some good varieties. *Ascot*, clear deep pink ; *Avalanche*, large pure white ; *Charm*, glowing red cerise ; *Debutante*, soft peach pink ; *Flamingo*, orange scarlet : *Loch Lomond*, rich mahogany ; *Powerscourt*, pure lavender ; *Veronica*, true mid-blue.

LAVATERA

1. Lavatera Loveliness takes its place towards the back of the border, growing 2½ ft. to 3 ft. It is a deep rose. Another variety has pure white flowers and is very beautiful.

NIGELLA

2. Love - in - a - mist needs no introduction; the little pale blue flowers in their "mist" of green are familiar to us all. Save a few of the seed pods for sowing the following year. The variety shown is nigella Miss Jekyll.

ESCHSCHOLTZIA

3. Eschscholtzias give a rich blaze of colour the whole summer. Named varieties include white, yellow, orange and flame. When special colours are needed it is best to buy new each year; otherwise use home saved seed.

SHIRLEY POPPY

4. The double Shirley poppies are very fine, and easily grown. These forms do not drop their petals so soon as the single-flowered kinds.

SALPIGLOSSIS

1. The half-hardy annual salpiglossis is particularly useful to give height to the annual border. The velvety petals are veined gold.

TAGETES

2. Tagetes are much used in summer bedding schemes and can be grown in a variety of shades of yellow and orange, some with dark markings. The French marigold, grows 1 ft. to 2 ft.

HELIPTERUM

3. *Helipterum* (*rhodanthe*) is a delicate everlasting flower, the rose-pink variety being particularly attractive. Hang upside-down in a cool, airy place away to dry for winter decoration. Can be grown from seeds or cuttings.

PETUNIAS

4. Petunia, rich pink bedder, here shown, is a lovely half-hardy annual suitable for summer bedding. The double-flowered mixtures are excellent plants for window boxes and ornamental vases, giving a display of blooms over a long period. Good also as greenhouse plants.

ZINNIAS

1. Zinnias need to be raised from seed under glass and planted out when frosts are over. When bushy plants are required, nip out the first flower bud as soon as it forms.

CHINA ASTER

2. All types of China aster make a good display in August and September. Raise them in boxes under glass and water the seedlings with cheshunt compound to prevent wilt.

ANTIRRHINUMS

3. Antirrhinums are a great standby in the flower garden as bedding, or for filling gaps in the flower border. There is a great range of colour, and dwarf, medium and tall kinds.

SWEET ALYSSUM

4. The annual alyssum is invaluable as an edging plant, with its neat little tufts covered with flowers. The usual practice is to buy them from the nurseryman planted out into boxes.

PHLOX

1. *Phlox Drummondii* is available in many colours: red, purple, mauve, pink, buff, white and salmon. The shoots should be pegged down so that the whole surface of the bed is covered. It is a half-hardy annual which must be sown under cover if early blooms are desired. Flowers from July to October.

STOCKS

2. Stocks are among the loveliest of the half-hardy annuals. The many colours blend well together and the rich perfume of the flowers is an added attraction, especially in the evening. When purchasing seed of double-flowering forms, be sure to buy the best quality, as cheap seeds produce a large percentage of singles.

NEMESIAS

3. Nemesias make a brilliant display while they last, but unfortunately their season is soon over. The shades include pink, scarlet, yellow, white, blue, buff and orange. They flower best in full sun.

VERBENAS

4. Verbenas, like phlox, can be pegged down to fill the bed. They send down shoots at intervals along the stems. The soft green foliage is a perfect foil to the reds, purples, pinks, buffs, whites and mauves.

ANNUAL CHRYSANTHEMUM

1. *Chrysanthemum segetum* is a fine annual for cutting. The seed of many named varieties can be bought. The colour range includes red, yellow, orange, fawn and white.

ANNUAL CONE FLOWER

2. The annual rudbeckia has the same cone-like centre as some of the perennials of the family, though not in such an exaggerated form. Purple, russet, red, orange, yellow and primrose shades can be grown. Excellent as cut flowers.

GODETIA

3. Godetias with shades of red, pink, mauve or white flowers can be grown. The variety shown here is Firelight. Godetias have single or double flowers, and are good pot plants.

ANNUAL FLAX

4. The annual *Linum grandiflorum rubrum* is a free flowerer and invaluable where a large clump of red is needed in a border or a rock garden.

URSINIA

I. This compact, free-flowering little plant is ursinia special hybrid. The flowers are a rich orange yellow, and many of the hybrids have purple black rings on the flowers.

TAGETES

3. A clump of *Tagetes nana*, variety Golden Gleam. Notice the finely divided foliage; the leaves are a clean green and show off the golden blooms to perfection. Much used for bedding.

SWAN RIVER DAISY

2. A half-hardy annual growing about 12 in. high. The flowers are purple, mauve or clear blue. The plant is a native of Australia, and cannot be put out of doors until the risk of spring frosts is over

ICE PLANT

4. *Mesembryanthemum criniflorum* is a colourful little annual with succulent leaves. Wait until April for sowing, unless you raise it under glass, as it will not stand any frost.

SUNFLOWER

1. The sunflower Stella red hybrids are handsome plants, and of such sturdy habit that they give the appearance of perennial plants.

COREOPSIS DRUMMONDII

2. *Coreopsis Drummondii* is an excellent flower for cutting. This variety is very free flowering, producing masses of large yellow flowers with chestnut centres, held erect on slender stems.

COREOPSIS CRIMSON KING

3. Another attractive variety of coreopsis is Crimson King. The flowers have a large area of deep red in the centre with an edging of clear yellow. Remove the flowers as soon as they fade, and the season of bloom is prolonged.

MARIGOLDS

4. What garden is complete without marigolds? The full flowered kinds in shades of yellow and orange are lovely to behold. There are also the single-flowered varieties with or without black centres. Attend to removal of dead blooms and they flower late into autumn.

BORDERS AND BEDS

1. A small garden with paved path and sundial. The border by the path is planted with antirrhinums and sweet alyssum. In the lawn are antirrhinums of contrasting colours.

A CORNER PLOT

2. A corner plot made beautiful. Sweet alyssum, antirrhinums and moon daisies are backed with herbaceous plants. A well-kept miniature lawn makes a frame to the picture.

CONTRASTS OF COLOUR

3. Beds of herbaceous plants are edged with sweet alyssum alternated with lobelia, giving a line of colour by the lawn. In the distance a bed of bright-coloured antirrhinums catches the eye and gives length to the whole garden.

COLOUR AND FRAGRANCE COMBINED

This small garden is very gay. The bed at the end of the lawn is planted with border carnations and edged with sweet alyssum. The border on the right of the picture has perennial phloxes at the back, while the front is full of Mrs. Sinkins pinks and ten-week stocks in shades of pink and mauve. A garden planted in this way can be relied upon to supply small bunches of mixed flowers for the house throughout all the summer and autumn months.

FORMAL DESIGN FOR SMALL FRONT GARDEN

A formal design for a small front garden. The small, round beds have a central standard geranium surrounded with lobelia. The other plants used are tall antirrhinums edged with deep blue lobelia, and for later flowering a bed of pentstemon edged with sweet alyssum.

USING PATH AND WALL

1. A brick path and low stone wall are the permanent features of this pleasing arrangement of beds. The square bed is planted with scarlet salvia, and the long border has polyantha roses and variegated bush geraniums with a border of blue lobelia and white sweet alyssum.

MASSED EFFECT

2. Pink hydrangeas massed against the house, and a long bed of mixed dahlias of the Coltness hybrid type with emerald green lawn as a foil.

ROCKERY AND BORDER

3. A small rockery of dianthus, achillea and sedums separated from a border of red and white antirrhinums and orange marigolds by a narrow grass path. When the rockery has finished blooming, the border of bedding plants will continue to give colour to the garden.

BEDS OF MIXED COLOURS

2. Beds may also be planted with mixed flowers. Here is a section of a round bed of this type. A continuous edging of sweet alyssum encloses border carnations, African marigolds and petunias.

SINGLE COLOUR BEDS

1. A bed of antirrhinums can be relied upon to give a good block of colour in a bedding scheme. Here the whole bed is of one variety; where desired several colours may be planted to form patterns, or taller varieties as a central line surrounded by lower growing types.

A FLOWER GARDEN PLANNED AS A WHOLE

3. A well clipped hedge and closely mown lawn make an admirable setting for flower beds. Round the edge of the garden is a mixed flower border in full bloom. The bed on the left is planted with dwarf dahlias, and the two round beds have red bush geraniums in the centre with a line of tagetes round them. All three beds are edged with alternate clumps of sweet alyssum and sky blue lobelia, giving a pleasing air of unity to the whole scheme.

CANTERBURY BELLS

CANTERBURY BELLS

Sow in the open ground in early summer, prick out when large enough, allowing 2 in. to 3 in. for each seedling. The plants should be ready for their permanent quarters in September. Allow 2 ft. for each plant to obtain fine plants.

WALLFLOWERS

Wallflowers (*Cheiranthus*) are one of the most useful plants for spring bedding. They can be had in many shades of red, bronze, yellow and orange. Tall varieties grow about 18 in. high and the dwarfs are from 9 in. to 12 in. high.

Sow the seed out of doors in May in drills about 6 in. apart. When the young plants are large enough, prick them out 6 in. apart each way. To encourage bushy growth, pinch the tip of the long tap-root. Give a thorough watering and keep the ground hoed.

The plants will be ready for their winter quarters, where they will flower, by September. Allow 12 in. between the plants. If for any reason planting has to be delayed till later, the plants should be put less than 12 in. apart.

G—F

PENTSTEMONS

Pentstemons for bedding are generally raised from cuttings put in a cold frame in autumn and kept covered from the frost all winter. In spring, nip out the central shoot to make the plants bushy.

Plants can also be raised from seed sown indoors in early spring ; these plants bloom a little later than those from cuttings and are not true to colour.

ANTIRRHINUMS

The ever popular snapdragon is much used for summer bedding. Nearly all shades of pink, red, flame, yellow and white can be grown, also particoloured varieties. Heights range from 2 ft. to 3 ft. for the tall types, 12 in. to 18 in. the intermediate, and 6 in. for the dwarf varieties.

Sow the seed in a frame or cool greenhouse in August. When large enough, prick the seedlings out into boxes and winter under glass. Keep the boxes as near the glass as possible to prevent the plants becoming leggy. Where a heated greenhouse is available, sowing may be delayed until February.

ANTIRRHINUM ST. GEORGE

1. Dwarf bush nasturtiums owing to their compact habit can be used in formal bedding schemes for complete beds or as edging plants.

2. Climbing nasturtiums used as an informal border at the top of a low stone wall show up to advantage against the grey of the stone.

SUGGESTIONS FOR BEDDING SCHEMES

SPRING BEDDING

Wallflower (tall), Blood Red.
     ,,   (dwarf), Blood Red.
Edging: White arabis or viola, Moseley Perfection (yellow).

Wallflower, Ruby Gem.
Narcissus poeticus.

Wallflower (tall), Golden.
     ,,   (dwarf), Vulcan.
Edging: Forget-me-not.

Tulip, Clara Butt.
Carpet: Forget-me-not or viola, Maggie Mott (mauve).

Tulip, Pride of Harlem.
Carpet: Double daisies or alyssum, Saxatile compactum.

Tulip, Prince of Austria.
Carpet: Viola, Archie Grant (blue), or yellow polyanthus.

Daffodil, King Alfred.
Carpet: Mixed polyanthus.

SUMMER BEDDING

Pentstemon, Chester Scarlet.
Edging: Alyssum, Snow Carpet.

Canterbury bell, pink and mauve.
Edging: Ageratum, Blue Ball.

Scarlet gladioli.
Antirrhinum, White Wonder.
Edging: Lobelia, Compact Dark Blue.

Antirrhinum, The King (tall orange and scarlet).
Antirrhinum, Golden Monarch (intermediate).
Edging: Dwarf nasturtiums or Calceolaria multiflora nana.

Cheiranthus, Allionii.
Calendula, Apricot Queen.
Edging: Alyssum, Little Dorrit.

Antirrhinum, Malmaison.
Petunia (mixed).
Edging: Lobelia, Compact Light Blue or alyssum, Lilac Queen.

IN THE HERB GARDEN

A well laid out and well stocked herb garden can be a thing of beauty as well as a useful addition to the kitchen economy.

In these days we are very conservative in our choice of pot herbs, and seldom venture beyond the well-known parsley, thyme, sage and mint. The imaginative housewife will find that she can vary the flavours of simple dishes by making use of many of the herbs which were well known to our grandmothers. Try chervil, fennel or sorrel as a change from the usual parsley. Marjoram and lemon thyme add a new flavour to stews, and mint sauce made with some balm in it is excellent.

Herbs are not hard to grow and need very little care. The herb garden should be in a sunny spot and most of the plants do best in a rather poor soil. The perennial herbs need to be cut back once

CHAMOMILE

KEY TO HERB GARDEN PLAN

1. Rosemary	5. Aconite	9. Wormwood	13. Borage	17. Thyme	21. Horehound
2. Rosemary	6. Sorrel	10. Monarda	14. Hyssop	18. Chamomile	22. Valerian
3. Lavender	7. Marigold	11. Sage	15. Tansy	19. Marjoram	23. Balm
4. Fennel	8. Peppermint	12. Arnica	16. Mint	20. Rue	

a year ; generally the cutting of sprigs to dry for winter use is sufficient. Annual herbs are sown in spring, and subsequent small sowings during the season will keep a good supply of young plants.

The majority of herbs have greyish foliage which gives a restful air to the herb garden and shows up the bright-flowered ones to advantage. If your herb garden has a paved walk, plant *Thymus Serpyllum* in the cracks and the bruised leaves will scent the air as you walk.

PLANTS FOR THE HERB GARDEN

Name	Propagation	Time	Use	Remarks
ACONITE	Division	Autumn	Medicinal	—
AGRIMONY	Seed	April	,,	—
AMERICAN CRESS	,,	August	Culinary	Biennial
ANGELICA	,,	March	,,	—
ARNICA	Division	,,	Medicinal	—
BALM	Cutting or division	April	Culinary	Likes moisture
BASIL, SWEET and BUSH	Seed	March	,,	Annual. Plant out early June
BORAGE	,,		,,	Annual
CARAWAY	,,	April	,,	,,
CHAMOMILE ...	Seed and division	,,	Medicinal	—
CHERVIL	Seed	March	Culinary	Annual. Sow in succession
CLARY	,,	April	,,	Biennial
CRESS	,,	All summer	,,	Young seedlings eaten
DANDELION ...	Seed and root cuttings	Spring	Culinary	Blanched leaves for salads
FENNEL, BITTER ...	Seed	March	,,	—
FENNEL, SWEET ...	,,	April–August	,,	Annual. Thin and earth up as celery
HOREHOUND ...	Cuttings or division	August	Medicinal	Plant out following spring 18 in. apart
HYSSOP	Cuttings	,,	,,	—
LAVENDER	,,	,,	Perfume	Likes warm, well drained position
MARIGOLD	Seed	March	Culinary	—
MARJORAM	Seed and division	,,	,,	—
MINT	Root-cutting	Autumn–Spring	,,	—
MONARDA	Division	Spring	,,	—
MUSTARD	Seed	All summer	,,	Eaten with cress
PENNYROYAL ...	Division	March	,,	Flavour like mint, moist position
PEPPERMINT ...	,,	,,	,,	
ROSEMARY	Cuttings	August	Medicinal	Likes warm, well drained position
RUE	Seed and cuttings	April–August	,,	—
SAGE	Seed and cuttings	April–May	Culinary	Shade cuttings
SAVORY (summer) ...	Seed	April	,,	Annual
SAVORY (winter) ...	Division	March	,,	—
SORREL	Seed	April–August	,,	Annual
TANSY	Division	March	,,	—
TARRAGON ...	Seed and division	April	,,	Warm border
THYME, LEMON and BLACK	Cuttings and division	Autumn	,,	Plant out in autumn
VALERIAN	Division	,,	,,	—
WORMWOOD ...	,,	March	Medicinal	—

DAFFODILS IN FORMAL AND INFORMAL SETTINGS

Nothing looks gayer or is more welcome after the dull days of winter than a garden filled with spring flowers, of which the most spectacular are bulbs. Daffodils look equally well massed in beds in a formal garden, planted among shrubs, on lawns or in rough grass.

DAFFODILS IN THE ORCHARD

This and the opposite page show by vivid contrast effective use of bulbs. Here a corner devoted to fruit trees has been left in grass which has been thickly planted with daffodils. Violets, primroses, bluebells or wood anemones along the hedge will add to the effect.

TULIPS FORMALLY MASSED

The essence of tulips is stateliness; they look doubly attractive if planted with a carpet of some low-growing plant. Here, large masses of tall Clara Butt pink tulips are delightfully associated with blue forget-me-nots. They can also be interplanted with dwarf antirrhinums.

EARLIEST TO BLOOM

1. The earliest of all hyacinths to bloom are the white Romans. As can be seen in the picture the flower spikes are slender, and each bulb sends up several spikes in succession.

INTERPLANTING

2. Pink hyacinths interplanted with golden polyanthus give a succession of bloom. Such magnificent blooms are only obtained by manuring the bed with rotted vegetable matter.

HYACINTHS MASSED FOR EFFECT

3. For massed effect in a bed set in grass hyacinths are unequalled. Here a pale blue variety is interplanted with cheeky little pansies which peep out beneath the blooms. The variety used is Grand Maître of uniform habit. Use pansies in shades of chocolate and gold.

LILIES AND RHODODENDRONS

Most lilies thrive in a leafy, cool, well-drained soil, and are most suitable for interplanting in beds of azaleas or rhododendrons. The varieties used above are the dwarf types *regale* and *croceum*, the orange lily, and at the back of the border the taller types *testaceum* and *Henryi*. Before planting some subsoil was removed for each clump and replaced with clinker

LILIES WITH HERBACEOUS PLANTS

Madonna lilies are one of the easiest to grow and will succeed on chalk. They associate well with other plants such as delphiniums and campanulas; the white and blue making a pleasing contrast. These lilies are planted in August and like to be at soil level, and the soil around them should not be loosened by forking. Established clumps are best left undisturbed

G—F*

THERAPIA

Narcissi are classified into groups according to the colour and relative lengths of the perianth (ring of petals), and the cup (or trumpet).

1. The variety Therapia belongs to the Poeticus group, the perianth being white and the short cup strong flame colour edged with deeper red.

YELLOW POPPY

2. The lower bloom, Yellow Poppy, belong to the Incomparabilis group; these have yellow or white perianth, yellow or red cup the cup longer than one-third but not so lon as the whole perianth. See also picture 3

TRESSERVE

3. The variety Tresserve, one of the trumpet group. These narcissi have the cup as long as or longer than the perianth. King Alfred, seen left in picture **2**, is another trumpet variety.

VAN WAREREN'S GIANT

4. The great size to which the modern daffodi has been developed is shown in this typica example of a trumpet-flowered variety. The extent of the petals is almost 6 in. in diameter the variety is Van Wareren's Giant.

NARCISSUS TYPES

1. Two fine blooms of narcissus: the upper is of the Barri group, showing clearly the short cup—less than one-third of the length of the perianth, or petal ring. The lower is the Poeticus group—the perianth is always white and the small cup is edged with a line of red.

2. An example of the Trumpet group, showing the large cup which is as long as or longer than the perianth. Daffodils of this class are best for naturalizing in grass.

3. Two beautiful blooms of the double-flowered group.

4. The Poetaz group is the result of a cross between the Poeticus and Tazetta groups. Tazetta narcissi have several narrow-petalled flowers on one stem. The hybrid has combined the good points of both parents.

NARCISSI FOR THE ROCK GARDEN

The dwarf species of narcissus are becoming better known among the owners of small gardens. These tiny daffodils are particularly suitable for planting in the rock garden, where their dainty flowers are seen to advantage when placed among the lower growing alpines. Most of them need well-drained soil.

1. *Narcissus cyclamineus*, so named from its suggestion of a cyclamen in bloom. Here it is seen amongst polyposium ferns in a cool, shady spot such as it loves.

2. *Narcissus pulchellus* is a dainty plant bearing two pendulous flowers on each stem. It thrives in a rock garden pocket, planted shallowly on well-drained soil.

3. *Narcissus canaliculatus* is a flower of the polyanthus type, more than one being borne on one stem. The plant grows about 6 in. high and flourishes in full sun in the rock garden.

4. *Narcissus bulbocodium*, with grass-like foliage and ballet-girl-like flowers, is most distinctive. The flowers are primrose-yellow and make a dainty patch of colour in the rock garden.

TULIP SPECIES

There is a growing interest in tulip species; these are distinctive wild types collected from various parts of southern Europe. They are excellent for adding colour and interest to the spring rock garden. They prefer well-drained soils and are best lifted after the foliage has died down and stored in a cool position until planting time in the autumn. Named varieties of some of these tulips have been bred, but these tend to lose the characteristic simplicity of form of the natural species.

VARIETIES SHOWN

1. *Tulip præstans* has brilliant orange-scarlet flowers and is unusual in that it bears more than one flower on a stem.

2. *Tulip Eichleri* has large brilliant crimson flowers with a yellow and black centre.

3. *Tulip Clusiana*, the Lady tulip, has white globular flowers, the outside of which is streaked with crimson up the centre.

4. *Tulip Kaufmanniana*, the water-lily tulip, is one of the earliest to bloom in March. The flowers are a mixture of colours, being creamy white with pinkish-red margins outside and a deep yellow inside.

5. *Tulip saxatilis* is a somewhat rare species with rosy-pink flowers with a yellow centre

EARLY FLOWERING

1. The variety Murillo has charming double flowers of delicate rose and white; it is a great favourite for forcing either as cut blooms or in bowls.

DUTCH BREEDER

2. Dutch Breeder tulips are somewhat similar to Darwins, having long stems, but the flower colours differ, the predominant shades being bronze, brown, violet and purple; the petals have a bloom on them like a ripe plum.

MAY FLOWERING

4. May-flowering tulips have slender pointed flowers. The variety shown is John Ruskin, which is apricot rose flushed with canary yellow.

DARWIN TULIPS

3. Darwin tulips are deservedly popular; they grow to a good height on graceful erect stems and the large flowers can be obtained in a very large range of colours and shades. The variety shown is Dream, which has heliotrope flowers shaded with deep purple. The base of the petals of Darwin tulips where they join the stem is generally blue or white, but changes after a short distance to the main petal colour.

1. Rose Gris-de-lin, delicate rose.

2. Prince of Austria, brick red shaded buff orange.

3. Proserpine, carmine.

4. Thomas Moore, deep golden shaded terra-cotta.

EARLY FLOWERING TULIPS

These tulips are very suitable for growing in bowls; the double-flowered varieties are used for forcing with heat, while the single ones follow on with gentle heat and are also very useful as bedding tulips. There is a much greater variety of colour in the single-flowered species, and most people consider the form is better. Those people who have not got a heated greenhouse will find it almost impossible to rear bowls of tulips to flower early in the year, as these flowers require more heat than hyacinths for the production of early blooms. But tulips are very accommodating about being moved after growth has started, and nurserymen will sell bulbs from boxes which have been forced in a hot-house. Put these into bowls when showing buds, and the flowers will open naturally in the cooler temperature of a living-room.

1. Spikes of the variety Desmond Blake Amos.

2. J. C. White is one of the primulinus gladioli; these have smaller dainty flowers and are distinguished by the hooded upper petal.

3. Top-sized corms will produce spikes of eighteen flowers. Here a spike of Star of the West is starting to open, the lower blooms first.

GLADIOLI

Gladioli have many uses in the garden: they can be used as clumps in the mixed flower borders, for whole beds in a bedding scheme or planted in rows in the kitchen garden for cut blooms. Large-flowered gladioli can be planted as early as January in light sandy soils, although March is the recognized time. The early planted corms should be protected from frost by a covering of litter. When the flowers are open the plant becomes top heavy and is liable to fall over; early staking is advisable, especially with the large-flowered varieties. The corms are lifted in autumn when the leaves wither, are cleaned of soil and dead roots, and stored in a dry frost-proof shed. Market growers produce blooms earlier by starting the corms in a warm house and planting out in April.

ROCK GARDEN POCKETS

The Heavenly Blue muscari makes a brave show in a rock garden pocket. It contrasts well with the grey stone behind it and if left alone it soon makes a large group. Above is seen a bold group of *Crocus chrysanthus* which has been left undisturbed to form a colony.

CROCUSES IN SPRING

Hybridists have worked on crocuses to increase the size of the blooms, and these are now obtainable in various colours. They are most suited to a narrow border where they can be naturalized as shown here. After a few years the corms should be lifted and divided in this way varieties are easily increased. White and purple varieties have the largest flowers

AUTUMN CROCUS

The autumn flowering colchicums, or autumn crocus, bloom before the foliage appears. They prefer a sandy loam enriched with decayed leaves. They can also be planted in grass banks where they can grow undisturbed. They are easily naturalized and are here shown growing in conjunction with violets. The leaves of the violets cover ground which would otherwise be bare. The colchicum leaves, which are large and rather ugly, appear in spring

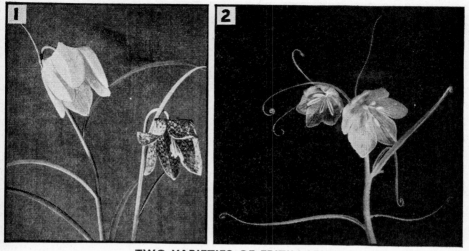

TWO VARIETIES OF FRITILLARY

1. When planting your rock garden, remember some of the more unusual bulbs. For naturalizing in grass the fritillaries or chequer-board flowers are a novelty. Allow the tops to die down. This is *Fritillaria Meleagris*, white and purple.

2. *Fritillaria verticillata* variety Thunbergii has greenish yellow flowers borne in pairs on a slender stem; as with the Snake's Head fritillary, it can be used in wild parts of the garden. The Crown Imperial is also a fritillary; it grows 30 in. high and is best grown in a flower border.

TRILLIUM

3. You can easily identify trillium by the fact that all the parts of the flower are in threes. It makes a distinctive group in the rock garden, but prefers a well-drained light soil in semi-shade. The variety *Trillium grandiflorum* has white flowers and is a very suitable plant for a shady bed of leafy soil in the wild garden.

STAR OF BETHLEHEM

4. Star of Bethlehem or *Ornithogalum* bears a mass of starry white flowers in umbrella fashion. Once planted, the bulbs come up year after year and can either be grown in the rock garden or in groups in the front of the mixed flower border. The variety *Ornithogalum umbellatum Splendens* has larger, pure white flowers.

ALLIUM

1. An unusual plant for the mixed border is *Allium neapolitanum*. It is a close cousin of the onion and bears a ball-like mass of white flowers 1½ ft. high. It is perennial and once planted requires little attention. Other varieties of allium, with blue, purple and white flowers, can be grown; many of them are only 4 in. to 6 in. high and are suitable subjects for a corner of the rock garden.

CYCLAMEN

2. There is no more delightful plant for the edge of the woodland or shady rockery than cyclamen. It is planted from little corms which are left undisturbed. It prefers plenty of leaf-mould and sand in the soil, and weeds and other encroaching plants should be pulled out. The varieties most usually grown are *Cyclamen europaeum* and *Cyclamen neapolitanum*, autumn-flowering, and *Cyclamen Coum*, spring-flowering.

FREEZIAS

3. Freezias are most suited to pot culture, but do not need placing in the dark like ordinary bulbs. They can also be grown in a very sheltered place facing south on a light, well-drained soil. There are many varieties but the old *Freezia refracta alba* is the most fragrant.

BELLADONNA LILY

4. It is a surprise to see a mass of blooms without any foliage, but this happens to be the habit of *Amaryllis belladonna*, the Belladonna lily. The flowers appear in the autumn and the foliage in early spring. It likes a southerly, sunny position in fairly rich well-drained soil.

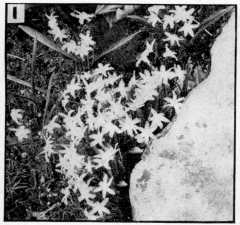

CHIONODOXA

1. The pale blue chionodoxa thrives in a position where it can be left undisturbed. Here it is protected by two rocks where it can complete its growth out of the way of the foliage of late blooming rock plants.

GRAPE HYACINTH

2. The blue muscari, or grape hyacinth, growing together with anemones makes a pleasing picture. All the attention such a group requires is keeping down the weeds and top-dressing the whole clump occasionally with decayed leaves.

WINTER ACONITE

3. Often peeping from the snow, the golden winter aconite is the earliest of spring flowers. It does best on the edge of the shrubbery or on a mossy bank in a shady place in a position facing east or west, not too dry, where it can come up quite undisturbed year after year

GIANT CAEN ANEMONES

1. The Giant Caen anemones are large single poppy-like anemones renowned for their wide range of soft colourings. They make effective groups in the front of the mixed border.

SNOWDROPS

2. Snowdrops are ideal for the shady garden or the shrubbery where they can be allowed to remain unmolested year after year. They also show to advantage in the rock garden.

ST. BRIGID ANEMONE

3. The St. Brigid anemone, which is so colourful in the cut bloom market in spring, is easily raised from seeds. They should be sown where they are to bloom, the seedlings being thinned.

BLUE WINDFLOWER

4. The delicate blue windflower, *Anemone apennina*, is a pretty subject for the rock garden. It needs a pocket to itself where it can grow undisturbed. Plant the bulbs in the autumn.

TEST THE BULBS

1. Bulbs in bowls are generally planted in a specially prepared fibre which contains some shell and ground charcoal; it can be purchased at any garden shop. Test the bulbs to see that they are sound; they should be heavy and solid. Have some water handy to moisten the fibre.

2. The fibre should be rendered sufficiently moist to bind together easily without being sticky

PLACE IN DARK

4. Place the bowls in a dark, airy cupboard, leaving the door slightly ajar to allow ventilation. After about six weeks good roots will have been made and the shoots will be about 1 in. high, when the bowls should be removed into the living-room or greenhouse. Bring them gradually nearer the light and finally as near a sunny window as possible.

PLANT NEAR SURFACE

3. Half fill the bowl with fibre and place the bulbs (hyacinths in this case, so the tops should just show) in it, pressing the fibre firmly round them. An 8 in. bowl will hold about six bulbs. The planting depths given for outdoor planting do not apply here. Bulbs in bowls for forcing are grown under artificial conditions, and should always be planted quite near the surface.

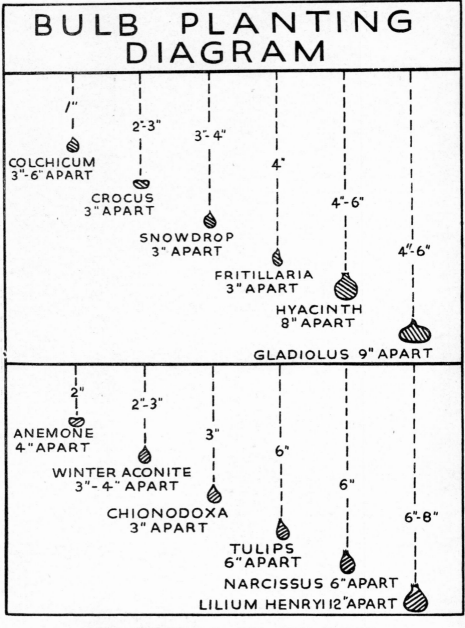

BULB PLANTING DIAGRAM

1"
COLCHICUM
3"-6" APART

2"-3"
CROCUS
3" APART

3"-4"
SNOWDROP
3" APART

4"
FRITILLARIA
3" APART

4"-6"
HYACINTH
8" APART

4"-6"
GLADIOLUS 9" APART

2"
ANEMONE
4" APART

2"-3"
WINTER ACONITE
3"-4" APART

3"
CHIONODOXA
3" APART

6"
TULIPS
6" APART

6"
NARCISSUS 6" APART

6"-8"
LILIUM HENRYI 12" APART

BULB PLANTING IN THE OPEN GROUND

This chart will be found useful when planting bulbs. The numbers on the dotted lines tell the depth below the soil surface the bulb should be placed, and printed below the name is the distance to allow between each bulb. In damp heavy soil put sand under each bulb.

PILLARS AND CHAINS

quat pillars and chains covered with flowering hoots of roses provide an attractive division between different parts of the garden. The chain should hang loosely between the pillars.

ROSES AND THEIR CULTURE

There are many reasons why roses are ɔ popular. They bloom the first year fter planting ; they keep on blooming ntil the frosts come and the more you ut them the better they seem to thrive. hey are excellent for cut blooms, and, erhaps most of all, they are popular ecause of their fragrance. They display est in small beds cut out in grass, where he green lawn serves as a foil to the aily coloured flowers.

Roses need a good, well-dug loam ontaining plenty of decaying humus nd preferably manured with bonemeal. ɔood soil can be produced in any garden ' you are willing to use the spade onstantly for a few months or weeks rior to planting.

Turn over the top spit and break up he under layer to a depth of 18 in. Tix in the subsoil all the old vegetation

you have at your disposal, old leaves, grass clippings, and so on, and use 4 oz. of coarse bonemeal to the square yard in the top layer.

Finish by dusting lime over the beds at the rate of 2 oz. to 4 oz. per square yard—the heavier dressing on the heaviest soil and on town soils where soot falls.

When you plan a complete rose garden, the beds generally group themselves round a centre ornament or a central bed, and form, perhaps a circle of concentric beds or a square or rectangle, according to the site and the wishes of the owner.

Beds intended to be of even size, and cut badly so that they are not perfectly regular in outline, are to be avoided at all costs. Beds made intentionally irregular and informal can be delightful.

Measure up the beds accurately and

SOME USES FOR RAMBLER ROSES

1. An old tree stump can be quickly and attractive disguised by planting two varieties of roses of differer shades around the bole.

2. In place of the weeping standard rambler ros supported on stout poles make attractive specimen

3. Rambler roses trained over a rustic arch are her used at the entrance to the kitchen garden. Th dark foliage of the evergreen hedge makes a goo background for the pale clusters of bloom.

estimate carefully how many roses you wi need. Distances for planting vary, bot according to the type and according to th variety, for some bush roses grow much mo vigorously than others. A rough guide is t set ordinary bush roses 2 ft. apart (som varieties a little closer), leaving a margin o 12 in. at the sides of the bed.

A bed 4 ft. wide would take two rows o bushes, while a bed 5 ft. wide might take thre rows, the roses being set so that the plants i the middle row alternate with those at th edges.

SUMMER EFFECTS

1. For clothing a bower, roses are invaluable. Here rambler roses and wistaria are combined to form a shady retreat.

2. An elaboration of the usual single rope and pillar is here shown. Wichuraiana, or rambler roses, can be trained to form a living " chain."

3. Section and elevation of pillar used in **2.** Four upright posts are set in a concrete block 1 ft. 3 in. square. The posts, which are 7 ft. 6 in. high, are topped with a carved block and connected by small cross-bars at intervals.

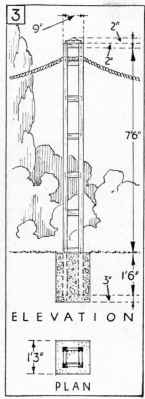

RAMBLERS TO BORDER STEPS

Yet another position for the indispensable rambler rose is the balustrade on either side of a flight of steps. On the bank itself plants can be set 5 ft. apart and the shoots pegged dow to cover surface. Main shoots 18 in. apart se out side shoots from which flower trusses gro

ALONG A LOW WALL

Roses scrambling along a low partition between different sections of the garden make a charming informal break and do not obstruct the view beyond the wall. If no other plants are grow in the bed by the wall the roses may be allowe to grow rampantly with little prunin

COTTAGE RAMBLER

No cottage is complete without a rose rambling it will round the windows. Crimson Rambler will repay good cultivation by a wealth of bloom. Fasten the branches firmly by wrapping with felt or sacking and nailing to the wall, and tie in all new shoots. Prune after flowering.

CLIMBER FOR THE ROOF

Paul's Scarlet Climber is one of the brightest roses for growing on a house or wall. The growth is very vigorous and the flowers, which are large and vivid, are borne in profusion.

A FORMAL ROSE GARDEN

A small formal rose garden in one corner of the lawn is always an attractive and neat feature. Small beds of separate varieties set in York stone paving can here and there be given height and interest by the addition of standard rose trees of similar or contrasting colour

A FINE BED OF BUSH ROSES

It is well worth while to plant a whole bed with the same variety of rose. Here a large bed has been devoted to the variety Princess Margaret Rose, a salmon pink flower on bush with healthy green leaves and even habit growth. Keep well hoed all the summer

STANDARDS AND WEEPING STANDARDS

and **2.** Many bush roses can be grown as standards, which, if used in moderation, lend eight and dignity to the rose garden. Suitable arieties for this purpose are: Betty Uprichard, almon; Dame Edith Helen, pink; Etoile de Hollande, red; Lady Forteviot, yellow; Mrs. Van Rossen, orange; Frau Karl Druschki, white, Mrs. Sam McGredy, coppery orange, splashed red. **3.** Rambler roses grown as weeping standards form attractive specimens in the lawn. The variety Dorothy Perkins makes a solid head of pink blossom. Excelsa, crimson, is good.

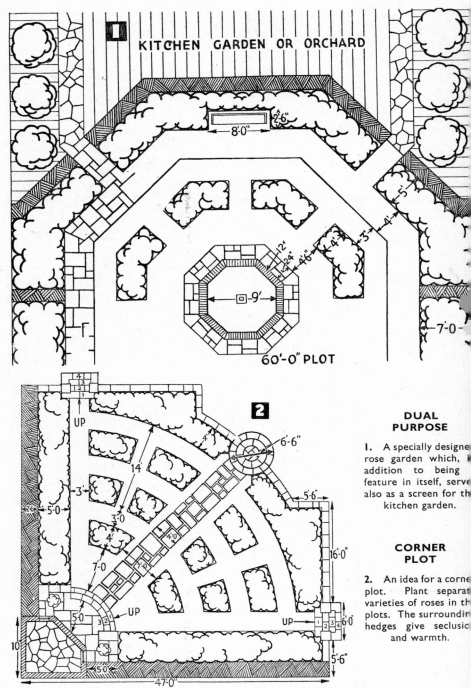

1 KITCHEN GARDEN OR ORCHARD

60'-0" PLOT

2

DUAL PURPOSE

1. A specially designe rose garden which, i addition to being feature in itself, serve also as a screen for th kitchen garden.

CORNER PLOT

2. An idea for a corne plot. Plant separat varieties of roses in th plots. The surroundin hedges give seclusio and warmth.

ROSES IN FRONT GARDENS

e row of gardens above gives an impression
unity with their many roses grown as bushes,
andards, weeping ramblers and ramblers on
ence. In the lower garden standard roses are
well placed in beds bordering the way to
the door, with bedding plants used as a carpet.
Post and chain partitions are very pleasing in
a built up area; they give uninterrupted views.

Purity, a perfect white Wichuraiana rose. A strong grower and very thorny.

MODERN BUSH ROSES

Variety	Type	Colour
McGredy's Ivory	H.T.*	Creamy white
Julien Potin	Pern.	Golden yellow
Etoile de Hollande	H.T.	Bright dark red
Betty Uprichard	,,	Salmon pink carmine
Mrs. H. Bowles	,,	Rose
Christine	Pern.	Golden yellow
Picture	H.T.	Clear rose pink
Phyllis Gold	,,	Golden yellow
Shot Silk	,,	Orange rose, shaded yellow
Mrs. S. McGredy	,,	Coppery orange red
McGredy's Yellow	,,	Pale yellow
Southport	,,	Vivid scarlet
Golden Dawn	T.	Pale lemon yellow
Emma Wright	H.T.	Pure orange
Barbara Richards	,,	Maize yellow, flushed rose
Comtesse Vandal	,,	Reddish copper, edged pink
Crimson Glory	,,	Deep crimson
Charles P. Kilham	,,	Brilliant nasturtium red
Pres. Hoover	,,	Orange and gold
Mme. Butterfly	,,	Flesh pink

DWARF POLYANTHA ROSES

Variety	Type	Colour
Paul Crampel	Dwarf	Deep orange re
Cameo	,,	Flesh pink
Golden Salmon	,,	Vivid golde salmon
Ellen Poulsen	,,	Bright cherr rose
Coral Cluster	,,	Pale coral pink
Little Dorrit	,,	Coral salmon

HYBRID POLYANTHA ROSES

Variety	Type	Colour
Else Poulsen	Hybrid	Pink
Karen Poulsen	,,	Bright red
Anne Poulsen	,,	Bright crimson
Salmon Spray	,,	Salmon pink
Donald Prior	,,	Bright scarl shaded crin son
Alice Amos	,,	Rose cerise

CLIMBERS

Caroline Testout	H.T.	Warm pink
Mme. Butterfly	,,	Pink
Etoile de Hollande	,,	Dark red
Mme. Edouard Herriot	,,	Terra-cotta
Hadley	,,	Red

* T.—Tea Rose   H.T.—Hybrid Tea   Pern.—Pernetie

The name "Poulsen" is the hall-mark of t hybrid polyantha roses. The member of t family illustrated is Karen, a brilliant scarle

MERMAID AND JULIEN POTIN

An unusual but very beautiful climber is e sulphur yellow single-flowered Mermaid. he beauty of the flower is further enhanced y the cluster of deep yellow stamens. It requires the slight shelter of a south wall. 2. The richest yellow bush rose is Julien Potin; it is a sweet-scented and free-flowering Austrian briar hybrid with finely cut leaves.

AN AUSTRIAN BRIAR HYBRID

A newer yellow of a paler shade is Christine, Austrian briar hybrid. The Austrian briars ve been largely used by rose breeders because of their good colours of yellows and bronzes. Persian Yellow and Soleil d'Or are other well-known members of this attractive group.

INNOCENCE

1. There are only a few single roses, but all are worthy of cultivation. The flowers of this variety, Innocence, are 5 in. in diameter, the petals being pure white, the centre mahogany.

CHARLES H. RIGG

2. This lovely rose has much to commend it—flower of vermilion scarlet shaded to rose pink, a beautifully shaped flower held on a stiff stem, and a good scent.

ETOILE DE HOLLANDE

3. A good red rose is difficult to find; the two best are Christopher Stone and Etoile de Hollande, both seen here. When choosing a new red rose, be sure to see a full blown bloom. Many reds have lovely buds, but fade to an ugly purple when opening in strong sunlight.

MINIATURE ROSES

4. A delightful miniature rose for the rock garden or cool greenhouse is Rosa Peon, a new red-flowered dwarf. The pink-flowered Rosa Rouletti also deserves a place in the rock garden. Rosa Pumila is another delightful little rose, slightly larger than the other two.

DAME EDITH HELEN
This rose has large full flowers of pure glowing pink growing on a very vigorous bush.

LADY SYLVIA
2. Has flowers of rich prawn pink, shaded with apricot and fine dark glossy leaves.

PRUNING OF ROSES

Most beginners in gardening are afraid of rose pruning. They fear that irreparable damage will be done by cutting away the stems. The effect of not pruning roses can sometimes be seen in old gardens where bushes have been neglected for many years, with the result that the blooms are small, flimsy and semi-double.

We prune to admit sunshine and fresh air, to promote larger blooms characteristic of the variety, and shapely bushes. Rose species are usually left unpruned; kinds like R. Hugonis make beautiful specimen bushes if grown singly in small beds in the lawn, but the bulk of bush roses must be pruned annually to get the best results.

Newly planted roses should not be pruned until the end of March. The sap in the stems for a few months after planting helps the roots to make growth and establish themselves.

The pruning of hybrid tea roses deferred until the end of March so that the young growths which spring from the base of the stems after pruning are not destroyed by late frosts. Late (March) planted roses are pruned at the time of planting.

For pruning use leather gloves and a sharp pair of secateurs. First cut away weak growths and suckers which spring from the stock. Next cut away dead and old wood that has lost its vigour; finally prune all the growths made last year to about half their length. Some varieties are pegged down, such as Zephirin Drouhin, Hugh Dickson and Mermaid; the weak growths in this case are cut out and the long growths are merely tipped. In this way a larger quantity of flowers, especially for cutting, is obtained.

Tea roses are best pruned the first week in April; they are more tender than hybrid tea roses, which can be pruned the last week in March. All prunings should be burnt to prevent the spreading of disease. Old wood is

1.   Starting to prune the bush rose.

2.   Shows weaker growth cleared out.

3. Completed work: stronger shoots have been headed back.

etained on some varieties of roses where the young growth springing from them s fairly thick and likely to carry blossoms. This should be shortened back to three or four eyes where it springs from the old wood.

CLIMBING AND RAMBLER ROSES

The pruning of rambler roses and climbing roses is a puzzle to many beginners in gardening, who find it hard to recognize the essential difference between the two types.

The true ramblers, like American Pillar, bloom on the young wood made the previous season, which usually springs from the base of the plant. Therefore, the best time to prune all this class of roses is when they have done flowering. This usually occurs about August, and the easiest method is to undo all the ties, cut away the old wood and to tie up the new shoots. These new shoots are sometimes produced in excess of the number required, in which case they are thinned out, leaving the strongest to be tied up.

The chief mistake often made with newly planted climbers and ramblers is in the keeping of long trailing growth. Severe cutting back is essential. Different varieties will, however, need different treatment. The strong shoots of crimson ramblers and other climbing polyanthas (e.g., American Pillar, Waltham Bride) should be cut back to 12 in. and the weak shoots to 6 in.; whereas the Wichuraianas (Hiawatha, Dorothy Perkins, etc.) should have strong stems left to a length of 4 ft., and 3 ft. of weaker shoots can be left.

The necessary thinning out of dead wood and of shoots liable to overcrowd the plant, and the removal of the worn-out wood, will keep the plant in full vigour.

The true climbing roses of the hybrid tea or tea class, such as Gloire de Dijon, climbing Caroline Testout, etc., are pruned quite differently. They bloom on young wood, but it is young wood which is made from growths on the previous year's shoots. In other words the climbing tea roses do not throw up abundant growths from the base each year and for this reason newly planted climbing hybrid tea roses should not be pruned, otherwise the climbing habit is lost. The method of pruning is to shorten the young growths to about two-thirds their full length, to cut out weak growths and old worn-out shoots and to encourage one or two fresh leaders to spring from as low down the tree as possible each

PRUNING RAMBLERS

1. Unpruned condition. Note weak straggl[
side shoots, remove or spur these back[

2. Remove complete branches of oldest woo[
just above a new branch, leave no snag[

3. Tie up shoots securely with tarred string[

year. There is, as it were, a supply o[
young wood coming on to take th[
place of the old over a period of tw[
or three years.

As a general rule, hybrid perpetuals[
hybrid teas, teas and noisettes requir[
moderate pruning only. It is usuall[
best to cut out dead, unripe an[
weak shoots, and others which ar[
likely to cross when full grown. Th[
remaining strong well-ripened las[
year's shoots should be cut back t[
from six to eight buds. Certain varie[
ties (e.g., Frau Karl Druschki, Hugl[
Dickson, etc.) require even lighte[
pruning ; shoots from the base shoul[
be left about 8 in. long, and the lateral[
on the older wood can be cut back t[
four or five buds.

VALUE OF SUMMER PRUNING

The flowering season of a border of hybrid tea roses can be prolonged by cutting the blooms with long stems to a healthy outward-facing bud. This constitutes light summer pruning and keeps the bushes growing vigorously, producing large-sized blooms. The stronger growing varieties of roses need not be cut so hard as the weaker ones, as they have more vigour to develop the extra blooms springing from the several buds which are left to grow.

A BORDER LEFT UNPRUNED

An experiment was made in that this border was left completely unpruned. The result was a quantity of rather loose, medium blooms. The method is advocated by some who prefer tall natural bushes, for roses in a mixed border, or alongside low-growing flowering shrubs.

G—G*

1. ROSA CANINA

2. ROSA SETIPODA

3. ROSA MACROPHYLLA

4. ROSA DAVIDII

5. ROSA RUBIGINOSA

6. ROSA SWEGINZOWII

7. ROSA MOYESII

WILD ROSES OF EUROPE

The wild roses of Europe are among the most useful of our autumn shrubs. In addition to their colourful and distinctive fruits the single yellow, red, pink, white and orange flowe give a good display in early summer. Most these roses demand the minimum of prunin

PROOF AGAINST TOWN ATMOSPHERE

No flower thrives better in or near towns than the iris. The grey bloom on the leaves serves as a protection against the evil effects of a smoky atmosphere and gives a fresh appearance. A raised border with a dry supporting wall provides an ideal setting for the flowers, and they can then be viewed at eye level. The crevices of the wall can be planted with aubrietia in mixed colours, for the cushion foliage contrasts well with the blades of the iris, while along the top mixed dianthus and rock roses would grow well and offer more contrast.

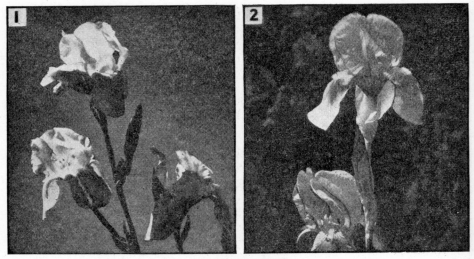

BEARDED IRISES

This group is most largely grown in gardens and nurserymen list a very large number of named varieties. They have stout root stocks called rhizomes, which lie flat on the ground, and from these the roots go down into the soil. Roots are formed annually immediately after flowering and last for a whole year, therefore irises are best moved as soon as the flowers fade so that the new year's roots are not broken. Clumps should be divided when they become too thick and the strongest new growths replanted. They will produce healthy leaves in a shady border, but to get a good mass of flower spikes these irises need plenty of sun.

NAMED VARIETIES

1. Helios has large flowers with yellow standards and the falls lightly veined with violet.
2. Lord of June, a lovely bloom; the standard is a silvery-blue and the long falls are a light violet. Goes excellently with pink lupins.

3. Ambassadeur, coppery bronze and maroon purple. Gives depth of colour to the border.
4. Mrs. Valerie West is noted for the perfect shape of its flowers; the standard is a light bronze and the falls are a rich crimson purple.

BULBOUS IRIS

Iris species add interest to the garden and make pleasing groups in the rock or flower garden. The four shown here are all bulbous. Plant in well-drained soil in September.

2. *Iris tuberosa* is a most unusual flower, but quite easy to grow in shady positions. The flowers are bright green and purple black on stems I ft. high. Known as the Snake's Head iris.

1. *Iris histrioides* has fine flowers of a deep shade of blue in February. Only 5 in. high.

3. *Iris orchioides* has flowers of a clear yellow with distinct markings, and sappy foliage growing sometimes as high as 2 ft.

4. The well-known white, yellow and blue flowers of the Dutch iris are excellent for use as cut blooms. They appear at the end of May a little earlier than the Spanish irises, from which they were bred with *Iris tingitana* as the other parent. They are favoured by growers for their clear colours and stiff stems.

IRIS RETICULATA

1. *Iris reticulata* is an excellent subject for a sheltered corner of the garden or for forcing in bowls in the house. The purple scented flowers appear in March. Two good named varieties are Cantab, pale blue, and Krelagii, rich plum, the falls veined with gold.

IRIS DANFORDIAE

2. *Iris Danfordiae* has a similar habit to *Iris reticulata*, but the flowers are golden yellow and they appear in February. In some districts it is wiser to grow this plant in the cool greenhouse. Planted in small pots and a layer of small pebbles or limestone chippings used to cover the soil, they look charming on the greenhouse shelf with early flowering alpines.

IRIS INNOMINATA

3. A less common but very attractive little iris is *Iris innominata*. The flowers are golden yellow with distinct markings and the foliage is narrow and grass-like. Another iris with grass-like leaves is *I. graminea*, the plum iris, with fragrant purple flowers.

IRIS PUMILA

4. *Iris pumila* is a miniature form of bearded iris. It grows in a sunny well-drained position in the rock garden and can be divided after flowering in the same way as other rhizomatous kinds. Many named varieties of *Iris pumila* can be obtained in white, cream, yellow and shades of blue and mauve; some are slightly larger than the type, but all deserve a place in the garden.

1. *Iris tingitana* is one of the parents of the well-known Dutch irises. The variety Supreme is shown here.

2. *Iris sibirica* is lovely planted in groups near water. There are white and blue flowered forms.

3. *Iris stylosa*, or more correctly *Iris unguicularis*, produces lovely pale lavender flowers from November until March. It requires the shelter of a sunny south wall, and the plants should remain undisturbed from year to year. Pull buds to flower indoors.

4. *Iris Kaempferi* is a lovely plant which needs a moist, peaty situation, preferably near a stream or pond.

INDIVIDUAL EFFECT

As irises are neat in appearance at all seasons they can be planted in the more prominent parts of the garden, as in this border against the house. They do well in full or half sun.

BEDS FOR MASS EFFECT

Irises form the main planting in this sunk garden. The garden is at its best during May and June, but in order to prolong the display lilies should be introduced wherever possible.

A CLUSTER OF " HARVESTER " CHRYSANTHEMUMS
Early flowering double decorative, yellow shaded bronze, very free growing up to 2 ft. in height. This variety can be grown in sprays or disbudded.

CHRYSANTHEMUMS

Why is the chrysanthemum so popular? Probably because it lasts so long when cut. Cottagers like it because it keeps the garden gay almost to the year's end.

The real chrysanthemum fan likes it because it is under his control right from babyhood to maturity. A complete cycle of little attentions needed month by month through the whole year makes chrysanthemum culture a satisfying hobby.

Early flowering chrysanthemums make a brilliant display from August to November, and deserve a prominent position in the garden. The range of colours gives a variety of interest. Nearby borders against a wall can be devoted entirely to outdoor chrysanthemums, and they will also be most effective if grown against a background of climbing shrubs. All varieties are suitable for cutting and decorative purposes, but the grower should aim for flowers of perfect form and good colour, with long straight stems, and good lasting qualities when cut.

An "all purposes" collection of varieties which are easy to grow and give flowers of useful size before the frosts are likely to cause damage is as follows. These will bloom outside, unprotected.

EARLY FLOWERING VARIETIES
Double. Bronze Early Buttercup, chestnut bronze ; Conqueror, rich crimson ; Dawn, salmon pink ; Dictator, bronze scarlet ; Framfield White, white ; Freda, rich pink ; Gertrude, salmon pink ; Goldfinder, orange yellow ; Harvest Moon, golden yellow ; Harvester, shaded bronze ; Herbert Sutcliffe, golden yellow ; Leda, mid-shade pink ; Mayford Red, bronze red ; Mrs. Phil Page, red bronze ; Peveril, rich golden yellow ; Rose Precoce, bright rose ; Salmon Precoce, salmon ; September Glory, orange bronze ; Sanctity, pure white ; Sunbeam, deep yellow ; Wendy, bright orange bronze ; Yellow Gown, deep yellow.

Single. Doreen Woolman, golden flame ; Peerless, golden yellow ; Shirley Terra-Cotta, fine spray variety, terracotta.

Koreans. New race of hardy chrysanthemums useful in borders. Apollo, Mars.

1. A bold group in the herbaceous border.
2. Border decoratives Kitty and White Boy.
3. Mass grouping of Fleur d'Argent.
4. Effective group of the mauve variety, Kitty.

OUTDOOR CULTURE

Make sure that the ground is dug at least two spits deep and see that it is well drained. If farmyard manure is not available, good results are obtained by digging in either fish manure or bone-meal during the winter and feeding the plants during growing season with some specially prepared chrysanthemum manure. Do not apply nitrogen in the form of soot, farmyard manure, nitrate of soda, or sulphate of ammonia without balancing with a potash or phosphate or it will make the flowers very liable to damping.

In well-drained soils, plants can be

1. Butterscotch, a yellow single decorative.

left in the ground quite safely ; but heavy wet soils will, however, cause them to rot, and old stools should be lifted, shaken free from soil, and placed in frames in a frost-proof place. The main stem should first be cut down about 4 in. from the ground.

If slugs are likely to be troublesome, wash the stools before putting into the frames. In the spring young growth will appear, and these shoots, which should be short jointed, can be taken as cuttings when 2 in. to 4 in. long. The cut should be made just below a joint, and make sure that the central growing point has not been pinched out by birds. Cuttings

3. Bronze Marcus, a dwarf decorative.

should be inserted round the edges of boxes or pots, and it is an advantage to use a compost containing granulated peat (one part) to two parts sifted loam and one part silver sand. The peat holds moisture and the cuttings will therefore not get dry. A close atmosphere is important to encourage rooting. The frame must be kept closed until after rooting. Later the air can be admitted more freely and towards the end of April lights can be left off altogether.

In early May they may be safely planted out, either in groups of five or six together, leaving 15 in. between, or where flowers are required for cutting, it is usual to plant in one or two rows, with 15 in. between plants and 18 in. between rows.

Stopping and disbudding is dealt with on pages 213 and 214. During the early part of the growing season, the soil must on no account be allowed to become hard, and much hoeing will be necessary.

There has been a certain amount of vagueness as regards classification of types of chrysanthemums. The term

2. Dareth Jewel, a fine single decorative.

"Japs" has referred to large exhibition varieties, and the term " decorative " had a confused sense. The following standard classification is more specific :—

Indoor cultivation. (1) Incurved, flowering in most cases in November and excellent for decorative purposes, e.g., Dorothy Wilson. (2) Exhibition Japanese, e.g., H. E. Trueman and Majestic. (3) Singles, flowering October to December, e.g., Butterscotch. (4) Anemone-centred, e.g., Aphrodite, Caleb Cox, etc. (5) Cascade, e.g., Swallow and Fugino.

Outdoor cultivation. (1) Hardy border varieties. (2) Hardy singles.

4. Dorothy Wilson, rich canary yellow.

INDOOR CHRYSANTHEMUMS

After the plants have finished flowering they are cut down to within a few inches of the ground, and the pots are left in the cold greenhouse to encourage the production of new basal shoots. A small mulch of fine loam and leaf-mould will encourage the formation of strong shoots for cuttings. The compost for rooting cuttings is similar to that used for outdoor propagation and the methods followed are also similar.

Cuttings of Japanese types must be taken in December or January. There

7. Majestic, Exhibition Japanese variety.

5. Henry E. Trueman, pure white Japanese

are various opinions as to time for striking the Decorative types, but February or March can be taken as a fair compromise. December-struck cuttings will be ready for potting on into 3 in. pots in February, using a compost of loam, leaf-mould, a little sand, mortar rubble and chrysanthemum fertilizer. Before the pots become full of roots, shift into 5 in. pots, disturbing the roots as little as possible. Add a little more manure, but the application should be more frequent as summer advances.

The final shift will be about the middle of June into 8 in. or 9 in. pots, and the

6. Bernea, Exhibition Japanese Incurved.

plants should then be stood outside in a sheltered position and given a proper support (*see* Staking, page 214).

Methods of stopping and disbudding are dealt with on pages 213 and 214.

From early in August the plants require feeding with weak liquid manure and soot water two or three times a week, or with liquid manure and sulphate of potash alternatively, but feeding must cease as soon as the flowers are three parts open. At the end of September the plants should be housed, allowing at

8. Canada, Exhibition Japanese variety.

least 4 in. space between the pots, which can stand either on the staging or on the ground. Overcrowding encourages mildew. It is important to syringe several times a day over a few weeks. Heat will not be required until early November, and then the temperature should not exceed 50 degrees Fahrenheit.

Outdoor varieties can be transferred from border to greenhouse in October, but only those flowering late in the season should be selected. Transplant only when soil is moist, and keep the house closed for a few days. Water in well and they will soon recover from the shift, and the buds will open freely.

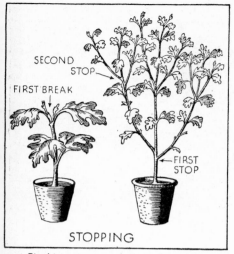

STOPPING

Pinching out central tip, and results.

STOPPING

This term signifies the removal of the central shoot tip with a view to securing fine blooms in perfect condition, or at a desired date, or in the case of singles and decoratives in ensuring an increase in the number of shoots.

If bushy plants are wanted it will be necessary to pinch out the tip when the plant is about 6 in. high. Side shoots will appear in the leaf axils of the main stem and will continue to grow with the production of the first crown bud (i.e., the first bud that forms after the natural break). The actual number of " breaks," or side growths, will depend on how many pairs of leaves are left on the main stem after " stopping " has been done.

A second stopping, in early summer, will mean the removal of the first crown bud on each lateral growth, or by pinching out the tip of each side growth before the production of the first crown bud. This should postpone the flowering period and secure the second crown bud.

It is important to get the right first crown bud forming after the natural break. The second crown bud will form about six weeks after the natural break.

For sprays it is best to stop twice and then let the buds develop freely.

Some varieties of Japanese and incurved chrysanthemums will break naturally without stopping. In this case the number of side shoots should be retained, according to projected number of flowers wanted. If there is no natural break, the growing point must be pinched.

There is no strict ruling as regards whether or not plants should be stopped or allowed to break naturally. It will depend largely on experience and on growers' ambitions. Some may want only exhibition blooms, others only singles and decoratives, and others may be growing for market purposes. Time of flowering will vary with district or locality, and this must be considered just as much as quality, colour, etc.

Flowering time may be early in August or not until late September, and it should also be borne in mind that the first crown bud gives the largest flower, and the second crown bud the deeper colour. Some growers of early flowering chrysanthemums make a rule of stopping twice, and aim to secure about six second crown flowers to each plant. The first stop is made before planting out, and the second in May soon after planting.

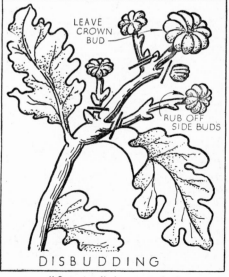

DISBUDDING

" Securing " the crown bud.

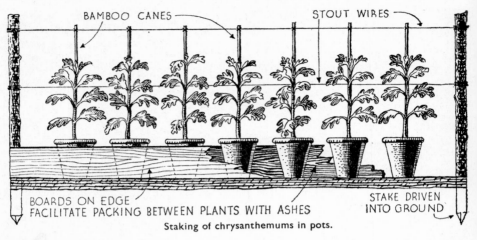

BAMBOO CANES ———   STOUT WIRES ———

BOARDS ON EDGE
FACILITATE PACKING BETWEEN PLANTS WITH ASHES   STAKE DRIVEN INTO GROUND

Staking of chrysanthemums in pots.

DISBUDDING

Disbudding and the " taking " or " securing " of the central bud is an important operation from the end of July until the second week of August. Only one bloom is wanted on each shoot, but it will be noted that at the apex of the shoot there is often a central bud and buds clustered around.

As soon as the plant is established, it is therefore important to secure the crown bud by removing the side leaf axil shoots early, either with a penknife or with the thumbnail, when they are not more than $\frac{1}{8}$ in. in size. Great care should be taken not to damage the peduncle or stalk bearing the central first crown bud, as this is the foundation of the perfect bloom. If the central bud has been blighted, disbud and encourage the development of one of the side buds instead.

After the break induced by stopping the plants some four to six or even up to ten lateral growths may be produced. If exhibition blooms are wanted, not more than three breaks should be retained and the rest removed ; but in cutting these away, remember that the laterals which break highest up on the plant and nearest the natural break will be liable to flower first, but the breaks from the leaf axils lower down will have longer stems.

For ordinary cut blooms, an average of nine blooms can be taken ; if numbers are limited, better quality will be the reward.

How much time should be estimated between the securing of the bud and the actual flowering? As a general rule, six weeks can be taken as an average, although certain very large flowering varieties, such as Peveril and Purple King, will take up to eight weeks.

STAKING

Chrysanthemums require to be staked when they are about 1 ft. high ; small canes should be fixed to be replaced later with one or three canes according to the height of the variety. Where chrysanthemums are grown in pots one of the stakes could be tied to a wire stretched between two posts ; this prevents the chrysanthemum from being blown over during gales.

Ordinary raffia is the best tying material, and with each tie it should be passed once round the stake. Where chrysanthemums are allowed to make many shoots a strand of raffia can be tied to the canes, which are pushed in the form of a triangle into the sides of the pots, and can be passed round the plant to secure all the loose branches. Take care that the stake, when the large blooms are developing, does not damage the swelling buds. It should be cut off just underneath the bloom.

1. A typical flower of the perpetual flowering carnation, a well-shaped head of evenly arranged petals on a stiff, slender stem.

2. The flower of the Malmaison carnation is fuller than that of the perpetual flowering carnation and is a delicate pink.

GROWING CARNATIONS

The carnation is a flower that should find a place in every garden. Owing to the thin grey film of wax which coats its leaves the carnation can tolerate the smoky atmosphere of towns and is equally at home at the seaside, its native haunt. It is said that the carnation came over with William the Conqueror ; it grows wild on the cliffs of Normandy. There are many types of carnations. The most popular is the perpetual flowering, most suitable for the cold greenhouse. The border carnation is a distinctive family and gives a wide range of choice colours. It is easily cultivated. Beginning with young plants of named varieties, these are set out in the border 1 ft. apart each way. Provided the soil is deeply dug and enriched with leaf-mould and bonemeal, excellent results can be expected the first year. Lime is an important compound to be mixed with the soil and can be applied in the form of builders' lime, mortar rubble or powdered chalk. Half a pound to a square yard will do.

The method of propagation is to place a little prepared soil round the base of the plant and to layer about half a dozen of the healthiest shoots, which are formed about the time the plant is in full bloom, into this prepared soil. In cold wet soils the layers are best lifted and potted in 3 in. pots to be kept in the cold frame until they are ready for planting out in March.

Carnations from Seed. It is now possible to raise border carnations from seed. If these are sown in February in the cold frame they will bloom the first season. With carnations, as with all slow-growing flowers, no check should be given to the plants at any stage during their growth.

If large blooms are desired, some disbudding should be done. This consists

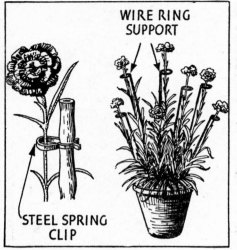

FOR SUPPORTING BLOOMS
The steel clips and rings shown here are handy devices for fastening blooms to a wooden stake.

of removing the little side buds which appear in a cluster round the large centre bud.

For Cutting. For cut blooms there is nothing to beat the French Chaubaud. This is a family of carnations easily raised from seed, and in a bed of one hundred plants from a good strain of seed, scarcely one plant with single blooms can be found. They are all doubles. It is best grown as an annual, seeds being sown early in the year to

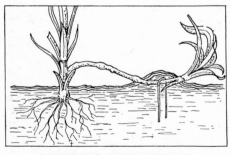

LAYERING CARNATIONS
When propagating carnations by layering, select a shoot near the ground, make a sloping cut on the underside of the shoot, peg down firmly and cover with soil. When roots are formed, sever the layer from the main plant.

be transplanted where they are to bloom. A bed of this about 4 ft. wide and 6 ft. long would keep the average household with cut blooms for many months during the summer and autumn.

The Malmaison carnation requires similar treatment to border carnations, but need only be stopped once. It should not be placed outside in the summer, and the approximate winter temperature should be 45 degrees Fahr.

Clove carnations are a hardy border type, which should be planted in March or April. The picotees and pinks are also closely allied to carnations and are propagated in the same way. Spring planted pinks resent frequent disturbance and are best left in position for several years, the soil being limed periodically.

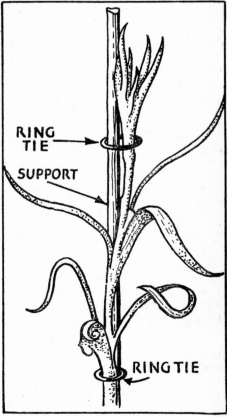

Ring tie and support.

1. Shows a typical flower of a border carnation with smooth-edged petals. Variety Sussex Maid.

2. A fine bunch of modern border carnations which are obtainable in a variety of colours, including the fancies as illustrated. Good varieties are Sussex Beauty, Sussex Maroon, Sussex Pink and Sussex Maid. The last-named, illustrated in 1, is white, flaked rose pink.

BORDER CARNATIONS

Border carnations were one of the first carnations to be introduced into our gardens and have remained popular for a hundred years. They are hardy and easily grown, have a good habit and well-shaped scented blooms. They are classified according to the flower colour into bizarres, flakes, clove, picotee, white ground and yellow ground.

4. The class of border carnation known as picotee all have flowers margined in a contrasting shade. This variety, Firefly, is yellow with crimson markings. Disbudding is not necessary.

3. *Dianthus Allwoodii* is the result of a cross between the perpetual flowering carnation and the hardy border pink. Various colours of whites, pinks and maroons, both plain colours or with deep or white eyes, can be obtained. They are exceedingly hardy dwarf-growing little plants and flower from May to October. They are excellent for the rock garden.

DIANTHUS FAMILY

I. There are annual and biennial members of the dianthus family which should find a place in every garden. Sweet-williams are easily raised from seed sown in a nursery bed from May to July. The young plants may be put in their flowering quarters the following autumn. On some soils they give a good show of flower the second year.

2. With the introduction of the blue dianthus, a new colour has been introduced into this family. It grows 9 in. high and flowers in nine months.

3. *Dianthus Heddewigii* is an annual dianthus. and the plants may be easily raised from seed. Seed may be sown outside in March or April and the plants transferred to their flowering positions when large enough to handle. The flowers are multi-coloured in shades of crimson, pink and white.

4. A cross between Sweet Wivelsfield and a rock pink has resulted in dianthus Rainbow Loveliness. The spidery flowers are deep mauve.

5. Rooted carnation cuttings potted up singly.

As the dahlia is showy and free flowering, mass it for display. It is invaluable for the border. The plants need to be stoutly staked, and it will be found that 1-in. stakes about 4 ft. to 4 ft. 6 in. high, and painted green, will serve the purpose admirably. Use green string for tying.

DAHLIAS FOR DISPLAY

No flower gives more satisfaction for so little trouble than the dahlia. It is showy, free flowering and easily cultivated. The only drawback is that it has no scent. It is obtainable in the following types : Cactus, decorative, dwarf decorative, pompon, charm, dwarf bedders, peony-flowered, and single-flowered.

The dahlia thrives best in a fairly rich soil with plenty of moisture during the growing season. It is a tender plant and cannot be subjected to the slightest touch of frost. For this reason the tubers should not be started into growth too early. About April is early enough in the cold frame and if the tubers are placed close together in shallow boxes of sandy soil, they sprout and the roots are easily divided up into cuttings with roots and some pieces of tuber attached. Each of these can be potted into a 3-in.

pot in a soil containing one part loam, one part leaves and one part coarse sand, with a little rotted manure worked in. The cuttings are set close together and the frame kept moist for a few weeks until they are hardened off in readiness for planting out the first week in June.

The distance apart depends upon the variety. Dwarf bedders like Coltness Gem can be planted 18 in. apart, while the taller varieties, such as Jersey Beauty, need 3 ft. or 4 ft. between the plants.

Staking is best done at the time of planting, because the dahlia is a rapid grower and the succulent stems need tying almost once a week during growth. All the attention required after planting is to thin out the growth and to keep the main stems tied up to prevent breakage in heavy winds.

Some varieties of dahlias begin to

bloom in July and most come into full bloom in August, but they all go on blooming until the frosts come. It is important to keep dead flowers removed to prevent seed formation and, during dry seasons, to give the plants a good soaking with water and a little general fertilizer to improve the quality of the blooms.

1. Fine full blooms with petals of even texture, typical of the decorative class.

FOR CUT FLOWERS

For getting good cut blooms the small decoratives and singles are the best types to use. These are obtainable in a variety of colours and any good dahlia catalogue should be consulted for varieties.

The dahlias may be planted either in a bed by themselves with early blooming annuals in between, or they may follow spring flowers, such as wallflowers and bulbs. Another way is to plant them in small groups of three or five in the mixed flower border. Here they can be so arranged as to take the place of earlier flowers like the doronicum, oriental poppies and lupins.

Not many garden pests attack the dahlia. Earwigs are the most troublesome. These are best caught by making traps of wisps of hay pushed into flower pots and placed on the top of the stakes ; the traps must be examined daily and all the earwigs killed. They go into the hay to hide during the night, so the morning is the best time to examine the traps ; failure to do so merely provides the earwigs with a good hiding place even

nearer the dahlia bloom than their usual home in some crevice. Slugs can be troublesome when the tender young plants are first put out in the open ground, but a ring of soot or lime, or plenty of poisoned slug bait, should protect the plants which quickly become woody.

WINTER CARE

Lift the roots when the tops have been blackened by frost. Cut down the tops to within 6 in. of the soil. Tie the label with the name of the variety to each root and store in a dry cool frost-proof shed or cellar.

Dahlias may also be raised from seeds. These should be sown early in a warm frame. When they are about 2 in. high the seedlings are potted on and planted

2. A good decorative dahlia is Lady Lawrence.

out in June in the ordinary way. Mixed dahlia seedlings are a bit of a gamble, but occasionally an interesting colour will develop which can be kept through the winter by means of tubers in the ordinary way.

SHOW BLOOMS

When extra large blooms are required, the plant should be kept to a single main stem and a certain amount of disbudding should be done, leaving only one flower bud on each of the side branches ; either the central bud may be left or one of the side buds if the flowers are required later. Plants from new cuttings which have grown steadily without any check produce the best and largest blooms for showing.

DAHLIA CLASSES

Single. One row of overlapping ray florets (or petals) round the open central disk.

Star. Two to five rows of ray florets slightly turned back at the margins round an open disk.

Peony. Semi-double flowers having up to five rows of ray florets, sometimes having additional dwarf florets round the

5. Brentwood Yellow has a beautiful symmetrical flower with slightly pointed petals.

3. Lovely blooms of Fabian, a variety with red and yellow flowers.

Cactus. Double flowers with most of the petals having the margins turned back to form a tube for more than half of their length.

Semi-cactus. Similar to the cactus dahlia, but the tubular formation is less than half of the floret, the portion near the centre being flat.

Collarette. One row of ray florets with the addition of a ring of small petals generally of a different colour round the central open disk.

Pompon. Full double flowers, ray florets blunt-tipped and arranged spirally and turned inward ; the whole flower is ball-shaped or slightly flattened.

Mignon. Flowers similar to the single dahlia, though slightly smaller. The whole plant is of a dwarf habit and should not exceed 18 in. in height ; largely used for bedding purposes.

4. Gold Rush produces a large quantity of rich amber flowers.

central disk. This class is divided into two sections : large, with flowers more than 7 in. across ; medium, with flowers 3½ in. to 7 in. across.

Decorative. Full double flowers with slightly pointed florets arranged irregularly. The outer petals turn back slightly and the inner petals turn inwards, forming a cup. The class is divided into three sections for show purposes, according to width of average bloom of the variety.

6. Mrs. D. Ingamells is another charming variety of the decorative class.

DAHLIA TYPES

1. Adel is one of the pompon class, terra-cotta shaded buff. The large flowers of a decorative dahlia show the striking difference in size and form between the two classes.

2. Sheila is an orange-flowered dahlia of the collarette class; notice the ring of short " collar " petals round the open centre. In this variety they are the same colour as the ray petals, though many varieties have the two kinds of petals of different colours or shades of the same colour.

3. Wild dahlias vary considerably in height. This variety, *Dahlia imperialis rosea*, grows to 10 ft. high. It needs the protection of a cool greenhouse.

4. A typical flower of a semi-cactus dahlia, showing the tips of the petals fully curved back.

5. Mrs. E. Staines is an example of the cactus class, having the petals curved back for the whole of their length.

MIGNON DAHLIAS

All these dahlias are very free flowering and of a dwarf habit, generally growing to a height of about 18 in., and are very suitable for bedding or as groups in the front of borders. They form bushy plants which fill the bed quickly and, once a fair stock has been raised and a frost-proof shed is available for winter storage, they provide an inexpensive form of summer bedding. They continue flowering until late autumn.

1. L'Innocence is a charming little white flower of free growth and compact habit.

2. Albatross is another good white-flowered variety of this class. Has strong yellow eye.

3. The variety Pembroke has pale yellow flowers shaded to deeper yellow at centre.

4. Winsome, a free-flowering dahlia of this class.

POMPON DAHLIAS

Pompon dahlias vary in the amount the petals turn in to form a ball.

I. Shows a rather loosely formed flower. Only the base of the petals is curled into a tube.

ELECTRA

2. The variety Electra is deep orange and has a very solid compact flower. Though perhaps less showy than the other classes, there is a quaint charm in the stiff arrangement of the petals of these flowers.

NERO

3. Stiff little balls of deep red petals standing erect on short stems are characteristic of the variety Nero. Flowers opening late in the season have not the same depth of colour.

FANNY LANG

4. Fanny Lang is another pompon dahlia of intermediate habit. All these dahlias have the advantage of being less battered by rough weather than the looser flowering kinds.

ALL PART OF ONE GARDEN

The rock garden is an informal part of a garden, a reproduction of the natural setting of alpine plants, and must not be too near formal arrangements of flower beds. Here, solitary rocks are placed as outcrops in the lawn which gradually merges into the rock garden proper, and blends the whole garden into one scheme. Choice of plants will add the finishing touch. They should be selected with a view to long period bloom and harmony.

BUILDING A ROCK GARDEN

1a and **1b.** Here is shown how a steep and rather badly shaped bank was made to look effective with bold groups of alpine plants. Full advantage has been taken of the possibility of reflection by raising the level of the water. The planting of a broad stretch of light-coloured flowers up the full height of the bank adds interest to the reflection in the still water of the pool.

A SMALL CASCADE

2a. The most suitable pieces of stone were chosen for the cascade and a natural effect obtained by the small outcrop of rock in the turf. The bottom of the pool was covered with shale to hide the concrete. **2b.** On closer inspection it will be seen that suitable alpines planted in between the rocks on either side make a charming foreground to the falling water.

AN ARTIFICIAL POOL

3a. The completed pool before planting is done presents a very bare appearance. The positions for flowering shrubs and dwarf conifers are chosen and the trees planted to give a framework upon which to plan the places for the other plants. **3b.** Carefully chosen plants are used to disguise the concrete sides of the pool. In less prominent positions the turf is brought right to the edge to soften the effect.

A GLIMPSE ACROSS WATER

4a. The rocks established in position and the grass growing will show promise of the future charms of this rock garden.
4b. In a single year the rock garden takes on a very different look. Irises introduced near the water's edge provide a contrast with the horizontal lines of the rocks beyond. The group of older shrubs on the height behind the top of the cascade provide a fine setting for the whole rock garden.

CHOOSING YOUR STONE

1. Wherever possible, local stone should be used, both from the point of view of economy and more natural effect. Here Delabole slate has been most ingeniously used. Plants do not, however, take too kindly to this stone.

2. At this early stage of construction the stratification of weather-worn Westmorland stone is clearly seen. Compare the horizontal lines of the strata in this construction with the vertical ones in 1. Both give attractive effects.

STONE FOR CASCADES

3. Westmorland water-worn stone provides the perfect setting for cascades and pools. It is one of the easiest kinds to lay in a natural formation. The dwarf conifer is well placed.

4. Sussex sandstone is used in this pleasing little arrangement of rocks and cascades. Plants with upright leaves contrast well with it, and dwarf junipers planted above add height.

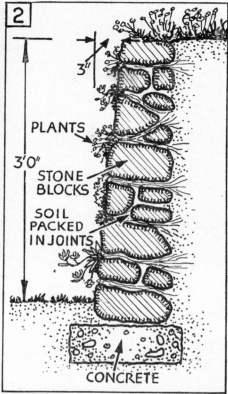

3"

PLANTS

3'0"

STONE
BLOCKS

SOIL
PACKED
IN JOINTS

CONCRETE

DRY WALLS

The term dry wall is applied to a wall built with soil between the stone instead of mortar.

1. A dry wall flanking steps. The corner is cemented to give a firm support for the wall.

2. The wall should lean backwards slightly.

3. A dry wall at the turn of a pathway.

FLAGSTONE PATHS

1. Flagstone paths can be made a little less austere by the judicious choice of neat-growing alpines. Restraint in planting is important; most crevices should be planted with thyme, sedum and acaena. Stones can be set with an irregular margin, and if placed flush with the lawn will not impede the lawn mower. Allow the grass to encroach between some flagstones.

PAVING PLANTS

2. *Dianthus caesius* is an ideal subject for paving. The grey-green hummocks are attractive at all seasons, and in June are smothered with bright pink blossoms. Effective also on old walls.

3. A few of the other low-growing types of dianthus hybrids may also be included such as the one grown here. The small-leaved sedum at the bottom of the picture is ideal.

ROCK GARDEN SHRUBS

1. Dwarf and prostrate shrubs should be included in the rock garden to give variety of texture and height. Here, *Cotoneaster horizontalis* is used to give autumn colour. The spreading branches lie flat on the ground and grow down to the water's edge.

2. *Daphne Cneorum* has a wealth of pink, fragrant blossom in early May and makes a neat little evergreen bush.

3. For a spectacular display, choose *Cytisus praecox*; the pale yellow flowers appear in May, most freely on a light soil. *Cytisus kewensis* has deeper yellow flowers and should be planted above a rock, where its trailing branches will show to best advantage. *Cytisus purpureus*, as the name suggests, has purple flowers and flowers also in May; it grows to about 1½ ft. high and can be planted in a similar position to *Cytisus praecox*.

4. In leafy soils rhododendrons give of their best. The pink flowers of *Rhododendron oleifolium* appear on quite young plants. As with most of the rhododendrons, this plant does not tolerate lime. Where pockets of peat soil are being made, care must be taken that water draining through limy soil cannot get into the peat pocket, or it will need renewing very frequently.

CONIFERS IN THE ROCK GARDEN

1. The Spanish savin, *Juniperus Sabina tamaris-cifolia*, is an attractive prostrate conifer for the rock garden. The flat branches are a lovely blue-grey colour, and once established it grows fairly quickly, covering several yards, and makes a beautiful evergreen patch among the rocks.

TREES IN MINIATURE

2. The most perfect feathery pyramid for the rock garden is the glaucous blue *Cupressus Lawsoniana Fletcheri*. Full height about 4 ft.

3. Of the dwarf spruce firs, *Picea abies* variety *pygmaea* makes a neat bush. Thrives on many soils. Dark mature foliage, shoots pale green.

THE FOUR MOST POPULAR ROCK PLANTS

1. *Alyssum saxatile*, Gold Dust, is easily raised from seed. It is a bright mustard yellow; the variety *A. saxatile citrinum* is a pale yellow.

2. *Arabis albida flore pleno* is a fine double white trailing plant, increased by cuttings. A single-flowered form has variegated leaves.

3. The dark green tussocks of armeria show the deep pink flowers to advantage. Note the trailing white *Gypsophila repens* on the wall.

4. There are now many different colours and varieties of aubrietia, in shades of red, pink, mauve and purple. Cut back after flowering.

PLANTS FOR SUN AND SHADE

1. *Anemone Pulsatilla* is but one of the many delightful windflowers suitable for the rock garden. The silky mauve flowers appear in March on beautiful hairy stems. It flourishes in semi-shade and much prefers chalky soils.
2. Rocky steps in shady corners will soon become covered with the moss-like foliage of *Arenaria balearica*, called Spilt Milk because it is covered with white, starry flowers in June.
3. The double form of *Alyssum saxatile* is even more showy than the single. This form has to be increased by cuttings as seed is not formed.

DWARF CAMPANULAS

1. *Campanula carpatica* is a useful plant in the rock garden. The bell-shaped flowers on 6 in. to 9 in. stems open from June till August. Small plants increase rapidly and form fine clumps in a few years. It will flower in sun or semi-shade. The common form is blue, but there is also a white-flowered variety.

2. For a deeper blue include *Campanula muralis*. This has a creeping habit and the upturned bells are carried on 4 in. to 6 in. stems which lie along the rocks. The foliage makes tufts of bright green, and the plant with its purplish blue flowers, looks well planted near paving stones or on brick or stone walls.

BLUE STARS

3. *Campanula garganica* and its varieties will give colour in the rock garden from June to September. The pale blue starry flowers with white eyes smother the grey hairy foliage. The variety Profusion has deeper blue flowers and the leaves are a clear green without hairs on them. After flowering, remove the dead heads to keep the plant neat. Increase by division.

DIANTHUS

1. One of the easiest rock plants to raise from seed is *Dianthus caesius*. Seedlings will often be found growing round the parent plant.

2. The Allwoodii hybrids between carnation and pink can be had in varying carnation shades.

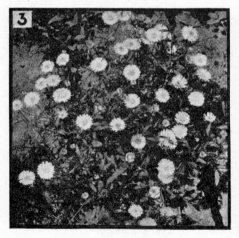

FOR CREVICES

3. *Erigeron mucronatus* has little pink and white daisy flowers. It forms a large quantity of seed and many self-sown plants will be found.

4. In warm sheltered pockets, gazanias make a bright splash of colour; brilliant orange with a black centre. Winter in a cold frame.

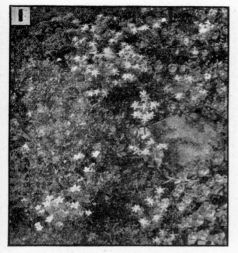

A PRETTY STONECROP

1. Stonecrops will root anywhere without difficulty and require very little water once they are established. *Sedum spathulifolium* has glaucous rosettes that produce 6 in. stems of yellow flowers. Flowers from June to August.

A DWARF GERANIUM

3. The cranesbills, or geraniums to give them their proper name, are vigorous little plants, with attractive foliage and gay blue, purple, pink or crimson flowers. The one shown is *Geranium napuligerum*, a dwarf-growing type.

A YELLOW GENTIAN

2. An unusual gentian both for colour and size is *Gentiana lutea*. It has deeply ribbed foliage and tall spikes of citron yellow flowers in late July. Plant in an out of the way corner.

ROCK VIOLAS

4. Violas make delicate splashes of colour through the early summer; some prefer a shady nook and others thrive in the sun. *Viola lutea* is one of the easiest to grow, producing attractive masses of delicate yellow flowers. The variety Lady Crisp has pale mauve flowers of the same shape.

SAXIFRAGES AND SHORTIA UNIFLORA

The family Saxifraga present a great variety of suitable subjects for the rock garden, some liking very well-drained limy soil in full sun, and other sections requiring some leaf-mould in the soil and a position in semi-shade.

1. Perhaps the most frequently grown of the family is *Saxifraga decipiens* and its varieties with red, pink or white flowers.

2. The pink flowers of *Saxifraga umbrosa primuloides* bloom in May and June and grow 6 in. high. Likes semi-shade and moist soil.

3. *Shortia uniflora* is an alpine treasure for leafy, lime-free soils in almost complete shade.

4. From large individual rosettes of silvery foliage, long arching sprays of white flowers appear in May and June on *Saxifraga longifolia*.

MASSED PRIMULAS IN A MOIST CORNER

The primula family is particularly useful in the garden and especially in the rock garden. They vary in height from a few inches to 4 ft. and nearly every colour is found. Most thrive in leafy pockets in sun or semi-shade. This delightful corner has several species of primula nestling among the rocks—rich magenta *Primula Wanda* in the foreground, behind which are the pale yellow wild and blue cultivated primroses. A small group of *Primula denticulata* is seen on a higher ledge. The semi-shade of an overhanging ledge is an ideal spot for *Primula Allionii*

FORMAL POOLS

1. Water gives character to the garden and can be introduced in a variety of ways. A variation of the circular pool is shown here. Note the restraint in planting and the all-green setting to provide a restful atmosphere.

2. Here two pools are united by a narrow canal forming the central feature of a small garden. The lead ornament of unusual design is not hidden by excessive planting.

3. A more intricate design is accentuated by placing tubs of bronze Japanese maples at the corners. The grey and pink dianthus grows freely on the paved edge surrounding the pool.

POSITIONS FOR FERNS

1. Here is a simple idea which could be carried out in many gardens. The cool, moist root-run beneath the cobbles is ideal for ferns and trollius, and the water remains crystal clear. 2. Cascades need a rocky setting. For these ledges, choose stone with a rounded edge to give a water-worn appearance. Vary the heights of the cascades in a series to give variety. Small native ferns can be planted by the falling water; the damp atmosphere will encourage their growth, and ferns thrive much better by running water than by still.

WATER LILIES

3. This formal pool is filled with flourishing water lilies. Gardeners are sometimes deterred from planting water lilies because of the idea that all these lilies need a large pool for successful growth; this is not so. There are many dwarf-growing varieties which will thrive in only 1 ft. of water and can even be grown in a half barrel buried in the ground. Be sure to notice the depth of water required before deciding which variety to buy. When planting in a concrete pool, water lilies are generally placed in a wicker basket or sack of suitable soil and the whole dropped into the water; the container will rot away after a couple of years, by which time the lily is well established in the mud at the bottom of the pool.

A GRASSLESS GARDEN

In town gardens it is most difficult to cultivate grass. The solution to the problem here has been to concrete the spaces between the flower beds and mark them to look like crazy paving. Such a method has the advantage of saving labour. The beds are closely planted with vigorous plants and tubs of flowers are added to give as much colour and variety as possible.

THE MINIMUM OF PLANTS

Plants are difficult to cultivate in smoky atmospheres and the minimum furnish this garden. Megasea and laurel stand out well against the wall, and a touch of colour is provided by the thickly planted scarlet geraniums at one end of the pool. Evergreens in tubs can be replaced by others of the same size when one of the line dies, much more easily than in borders.

1. Still the best of bedding plants for culture n boxes or troughs is the ivy-leaved geranium.

2. Plants for town gardens are limited, but tomatoes appear to grow quite successfully.

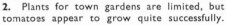

3. A cheap plant to furnish boxes with a bright display in the summer is the petunia.

4. Daffodils brighten the vases by these steps before geraniums are ready to be planted.

HINTS FOR WINDOW BOX GARDENS

Raise box to allow air to circulate; make drainage holes; line bottom with crocks; use good fibrous loam, leaf-mould, some sharps, a little charcoal, and a handful of bonemeal.

A disused sink of the old-fashioned type will provide a home for alpines.

A kitchen garden should be as carefully laid out as any flower border.

THE KITCHEN GARDEN
PREPARING THE SOIL

SINGLE DIGGING

Soil that has been used for growing crops will be in a more or less fertile condition, according to the treatment it has received. It should be deeply dug in the autumn, and there are two ways in which this may be done. If the ground has recently been double dug, all that is necessary is to turn over the surface 10 in. of soil, i.e., one spade blade deep, or one spit deep. This is what we call single digging. The really important points to observe in dealing with soil in this way are first that each spadeful should be completely reversed, so that all weeds are buried—not just tipped on one side. Secondly, that the finished plot should be roughly level. Some people dig evenly and their plots remain level, while others tend to throw up soil into heaps in one place, and finish elsewhere with a shallow depression. Even digging should be aimed at, and if this is found

difficult when single digging is done, a trench should be opened as for double digging, and the soil always turned into the previous trench.

DOUBLE DIGGING

If the cultivated soil has not been well dug for some time, or has been only dug over as above described, it will benefit from double digging in autumn or winter. Double digging really means that the soil is broken to double the depth of the spade blade, but it also means that though the top spit is turned over it remains at the top, while the underneath soil is broken up well with a large digging fork, so that the roots can penetrate deeply, and so that moisture can pass freely through the lower soil.

It is quite easy to double dig a plot of ground if it is tackled in the right way. This is how to proceed. Begin by marking off a strip of soil 18 in. wide. If

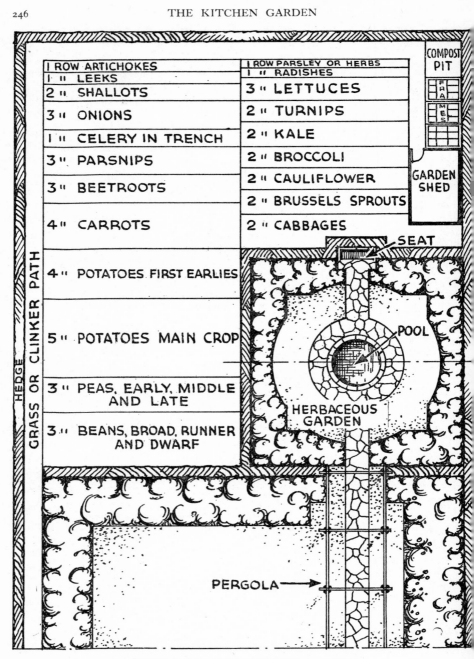

I ROW ARTICHOKES	I ROW PARSLEY OR HERBS
I " LEEKS	I " RADISHES
2 " SHALLOTS	3 " LETTUCES
3 " ONIONS	2 " TURNIPS
I " CELERY IN TRENCH	2 " KALE
3 " PARSNIPS	2 " BROCCOLI
3 " BEETROOTS	2 " CAULIFLOWER
	2 " BRUSSELS SPROUTS
4 " CARROTS	2 " CABBAGES
4 " POTATOES FIRST EARLIES	
5 " POTATOES MAIN CROP	
3 " PEAS, EARLY, MIDDLE AND LATE	
3 " BEANS, BROAD, RUNNER AND DWARF	

COMPOST PIT

FRAMES

GARDEN SHED

SEAT

POOL

HERBACEOUS GARDEN

HEDGE

GRASS OR CLINKER PATH

PERGOLA →

SCREENING THE KITCHEN GARDEN

The kitchen garden in this plan is well hidden from the pleasure grounds by a carefully placed belt of flowering trees and borders of tall herbaceous plants. The layout for vegetable cropping is a suitable one for a first year planting, showing grouping for easy rotation

PLOT	1ST YEAR	2ND YEAR	3RD YEAR
A	**BRASSICAS** *CABBAGES* *CAULIFLOWER* *SPROUTS. BROCCOLI* *KALE. TURNIPS*	**ROOTS**	**PEAS AND BEANS**
B	*POTATOES. PEAS* *BEANS, RUNNER* *„ FRENCH* *„ DUTCH BROWN* *ONIONS. LEEKS* *CELERY*	**BRASSICAS**	**ROOTS**
C	**ROOTS** *CARROTS* *BEETROOT* *PARSNIPS*	**PEAS AND BEANS**	**BRASSICAS**

Reference plan for a three-year rotation in the vegetable plot.

grass has grown over the plot, or if surface weeds are very rampant, strip them off to a depth of 2 in., and pile this mass of weeds on one side to be buried at the bottom of the last trench.

Then dig out the top spit of soil, and stack this also in a heap. If you can conveniently move these heaps at once to the part of the plot where digging will end, so much the better, but a tip to allotment cultivators is to divide the plot in two, dig the trenches across one half of the plot only, proceeding down one half and up the other, so that the digging ends near to where it began. You do not have to move the excavated soil from the first trench quite so far!

When you have opened your trench, which should go well down at the side, so that the bottom is square-angled, get into it, and clear out any loose soil. Then take the largest digging fork, and with it break up the soil all along the trench. Over this loosened soil throw the surface turf and weeds from the next strip of soil, and any available organic manure (i.e., grass clippings, leaves, household refuse etc.), and finally fill in the trench by turning over into it the soil from the next 18-in. strip across the plot.

This of course will leave you with a second trench, alongside the first, which you will treat in exactly the same fashion, and so continue all down the plot, until at the end, you can fill into the last trench the weeds, and then the top soil taken from the first.

While you are digging you may come across large brickbats and stones : unless these are really very large indeed you need not remove them. Just drop them into the trenches below the organic refuse : they will help soil drainage, and will not harm crops. On no account try to remove all small stones from heavy stony soils or you will do more harm than good.

TRENCHING

Trenching is a different matter from ordinary digging. It implies that the general position of the soil layers is altered. It is necessary sometimes on new land to get rid of surface rubbish left by builders, or deposits of unfertile clay, chalk, or gravel dug out during excavations for foundations or for drainage works.

It is generally pretty obvious if the infertile subsoil has been distributed over the top of the old soil, as the top fertile soil of any land is darker in colour, and different in texture from the subsoil,

PLOT	1ST YEAR	2ND YEAR	3RD YEAR	4TH YEAR
A	BRASSICAS CABBAGES CAULIFLOWER SPROUTS. BROCCOLI KALE. TURNIPS	LEGUMES	ROOTS	POTATOES
B	LEGUMES PEAS FRENCH BEANS RUNNER BEANS DUTCH BROWN BEANS WAXPOD BEANS	ROOTS	POTATOES	BRASSICAS
C	ROOTS CARROTS BEETROOT PARSNIPS	POTATOES	BRASSICAS	LEGUMES
D	POTATOES ONIONS LEEKS CELERY	BRASSICAS	LEGUMES	ROOTS

Reference plan for a four-year rotation in the vegetable plot.

on account of the decaying vegetation, fibrous roots, etc., that it contains.

If you should find that some or all of the ground you have to dig is in this condition, i.e., with the fertile soil buried under rubbish or subsoil, trench the land at once, for to leave the infertile soil on the surface will ruin the chance of good crops for several years.

The procedure is not unlike that of double digging, with the exception that the trench must be opened to two spits deep, and the top infertile layer of the next strip thrown into the open trench first, and followed by the darker fertile layer. This will leave you, as before, with a well broken layer of infertile subsoil, and a top layer of darker fertile soil.

VIRGIN SOIL

If you are breaking up what we call virgin soil, where turf forms the top layer, work exactly as described above for double digging, but as you mark out each 18-in. width for digging, strip off the turf to a depth of 2 in., and throw this *upside down* in the open trench. The turf will decay and form excellent manure.

INTERCROPPING

The owner of a small garden can often get as much produce from his plot as the man with twice the area of ground. This is done by a carefully thought out method of intercropping.

Intercropping is based on the fact that different crops vary in the time they take to reach maturity (*see* maturity chart). Main crop peas for example take a long time to mature, but the ground between can be used in the meantime for another crop which matures before the taller crop requires the light.

A few suggestions of what is meant by intercropping will illustrate this method of cultivation.

In February early peas are sown $3\frac{1}{2}$ ft. apart. These are sown in shallow trenches with a little soil left on each side of the row to be drawn to the plants when they are a few inches high. Early in April a row of early potatoes is planted

Lettuces grown as a catch crop on the mound of soil between two trenches.

etween the peas. The peas would be cleared before the potatoes and the land where they are grown is forked over to make way for brussels sprouts. When these are planted and are growing away nicely, the potatoes would be lifted and again the land would be forked over to make way for a row of winter spinach and onions. In this way there are actually three crops obtained from the same piece of land in a single season.

Take another scheme. Shallots are planted 1 ft. apart each way in January. In March two broad beans are sown between each shallot in every third row. The rows of broad beans would therefore stand 3 ft. apart. The shallots would be pulled at the end of June and the beans a month later. Then fork over the ground and plant with broccoli 2 ft. 6 in. apart and sow early shorthorn carrots between the rows of broccoli. The carrots will follow on for use in late autumn when earlier maturing carrots will have become tough and the broccoli would then follow on for winter use. Broccoli have spreading leaves and will need the full space after the carrots have been pulled.

A point to bear in mind is that nearly all vegetable crops have early maturing varieties. These are the varieties to select for intercropping. They enable the land to be cleared sooner so that the maximum use can be made of the space available during the warmer months of the year.

Another suggestion would be to open up the celery trenches early in the spring and to plant on the ridges french beans and cos lettuce. On wet heavy soils in a normal season this is the most effective method. In June the celery is planted out and by the time the french beans and lettuce are cleared, the soil of the ridges can be used for earthing up the celery.

Summer spinach is a valuable catch crop for growing between tall rows of peas. To get a rich crop of tender leaves sprinkle a little decayed manure along the line where the seeds are to be sown, and lightly turn this in so that it is buried 2 in. or 3 in. below the soil. On this sow the spinach. Lettuce can be grown in the same way.

Another factor which should be remembered when intercropping intensively is

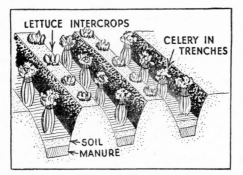

LETTUCE INTERCROPS

CELERY IN TRENCHES

←SOIL
←MANURE

Celery intercropped with lettuce.

the need for plenty of manure in the soil. It is folly to suppose that three or more crops can be obtained from the same area of land within a year without a liberal dressing of organic manure and the use of artificials during growth. But

the succession of one crop with another does, in part, contribute to the nourishment of each crop, and it is this which taken together with the manure and fertilizer, enables intercropping to be carried out successfully. Success also depends on using all the space all the time.

Easily soluble fertilizers are quickly washed down by rain below the depth of plant roots, by keeping the ground filled with successive crops full value is obtained from all manures.

It has been discovered that some crops help each other. For example, peas grown near potatoes pass on some of their nitrogen to the potato crop through the soil moisture. The beginner in gardening will find many interesting opportunities for intercropping, so that truly "Two blades of grass are made to grow where one grew before."

THE USE OF CLOCHES FOR INTERCROPPING

The space between rows of peas allows for the introduction of a line of cloches, enabling tender plants to be put out much earlier than would be possible without such protection

QUICK REFERENCE SOWING TABLE

Vegetable	Time to Sow	Distance between plants	Distance between rows
Bean, broad ..	Nov. to April	6–9 in.	2–3 ft.
,, dwarf french	May to July	8–12 in.	1½–2 ft.
,, runner ..	May and June	9–12 in.	5–8 ft.
Beet	March to July	9 in.	12–15 in.
Broccoli	March to May	2–2½ ft.	2–2½ ft.
Brussels sprouts ..	March and April	2–2½ ft.	2–3 ft.
Cabbage			
,, (spring sown)	March to May	1–2 ft.	1½–2 ft.
,, (autumn sown)	Early August	1–2 ft.	1½–2 ft.
Carrot	March to July	6–9 in.	½–1 ft.
Cauliflower ..	March to May	1½–2 ft.	2–2½ ft.
Celery	April	6–9 in.	4 ft.
Cucumber, frame	Feb. to Oct.	—	—
Kale	March to May	2–3 ft.	2–3 ft.
Leek	Feb. and March	½–1 ft.	1½ ft.
Lettuce	March to Sept.	9–12 in.	1 ft.
Onion	March to August	6 in.	9–12 in.
Parsley	March to July	½–1 ft.	1 ft.
Parsnip	Feb. and March	1–1½ ft.	1½ ft.
Pea	March to July	2–3 in.	2–6 ft. according to height
Potato	Plant Jan. to April and July	1–1½ ft.	1½–3 ft.
Radish	March to Sept.	6 in.	9 in.
Savoy Cabbage	March to May	1–2 ft.	1–2 ft.
Shallot ..	March	9 in.	9–12 in.
Spinach			
,, (summer)	Feb. to August	9–12 in.	12–15 in.
,, (winter) ..	July to Sept.	6 in.	12–15 in.
,, (perpetual)	April to July	6–8 in.	12 in.
Swede(garden)	April to July	6–9 in.	15 in.
Tomato, frame	April	15–18 in.	1½–2 ft.
Turnip ..	April to August	6–9 in.	12–15 in.
Vegetable Marrow	May	2 ft.	4–5 ft.

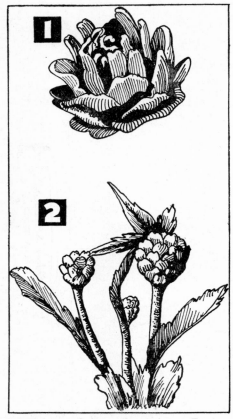

1. Globe artichoke cut for cooking. Tenderness is essential; do not allow the heads to get old and tough. 2. Typical branched head.

ARTICHOKE, JERUSALEM

General. Easily grown. Useful for soups. Stems cast heavy shade, therefore choose a position accordingly.

Plant. February-April. 1 ft. apart in rows 2 ft. 6 in. apart.

Cultivation. Dry soil is best. Manure well. Dig in vegetable matter. Apply 2 oz. sulphate of potash and 3 oz. superphosphate of lime per square yard before planting.

Variety. New white.

Quantity. Seven lb. for 50 ft. of row.

Season of use. Lift after the tops die down as required. Be sure to lift

every one, as any portion left behind wil grow next season.

ARTICHOKE, CHINESE

An oriental plant grown for its tuber Plant March-April in sunny spot. Us during winter.

ARTICHOKE, GLOBE

General. A large decorative perenni plant, needing plenty of space. Onc established, it needs little care.

Plant. Raise from seed in March, o plant young plants in April. Plant 18 i apart and 3 ft. between the rows.

Cultivation. Deeply dug rich soil needed to obtain good crops. Hoe durin the summer months. Fork the groun round the plants each autumn and give dressing of decayed farmyard manur In cold districts the crowns should b covered lightly with dry leaves.

Varieties. Purple Globe, Gree Globe.

Quantity. A small packet of seed wi produce more than enough plants fo the average garden. Buy the number o grown plants required for the space.

Season of use. The young flower bud are cut for eating during the summer.

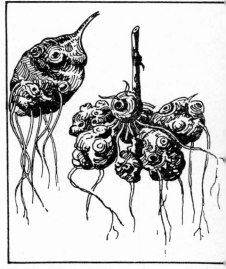

Single tuber and whole root of Jerusale artichoke.

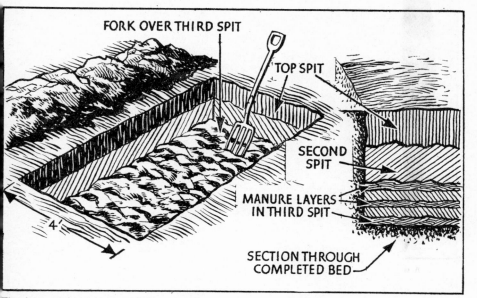

FORK OVER THIRD SPIT

TOP SPIT

SECOND SPIT

MANURE LAYERS IN THIRD SPIT

4'

SECTION THROUGH COMPLETED BED

The diagram shows how manure is mixed with the third or bottom layer of trenched soil, and its ultimate position in the ground.

ASPARAGUS

General. When once prepared, the bed is little trouble to maintain and one or two rows are sufficient for a small family.

Plant. Two-year-old crowns in March for quickest results ; 1½ ft. apart in two or three rows 1½ ft. apart.

Cultivation. Good drainage and generous manuring are essential. Bastard trench 3 ft. deep and bury plenty of vegetable refuse 2 ft. deep. Rotted seaweed is a valuable top-dressing ; apply 4 in. thick. Replace the soil to form raised bed. Apply 1 oz. nitrate of soda per square yard in spring.

Varieties. Connover's Colossal.

Quantity. Seventy plants for 50 ft. of double row.

Season of use. March to early June. No cutting should be continued after the beginning of June and in the case of young plants only one or two shoots should be cut the first year ; more may be cut the second year and as required later.

Asparagus shoots are gathered by cutting with a sharp knife just below the surface of the soil.

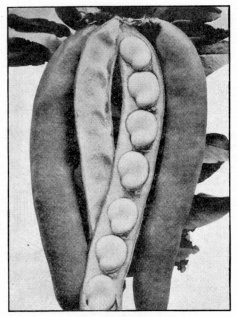

A well filled pod of broad beans.

BEANS, BROAD

General. This is an easily grown and very accommodating crop. Rich in protein, the vegetable substitute for meat.

Sow. November, Longpod types ; March, Broad Windsor types. Drills 6 in. wide and 2 ft. 6 in. apart each to take a double row of seeds 4 in. apart.

Cultivation. On good ground organic manure need not be dug into the soil. On light soils a mulch given in the spring is beneficial. Apply 2 oz. of basic slag per square yard in the autumn prior to sowing. If an attack of black aphis is discovered the simplest remedy is to pinch out the tops of the plants.

Varieties. Seville Longpod, Exhibition Longpod, Early Giant Windsor.

Quantity. One pt. for 30 ft. of row.

Season of use. July and August.

BEANS, FRENCH OR KIDNEY

General. These are easily grown and are useful in order to have beans a fortnight before runners are ready. Rich in protein.

Sow. Mid-May onwards. Make three sowings at intervals of a fortnight. Drill 6 in. wide and 2 ft. apart each to take three staggered rows of seed 6 in. apart.

Cultivation. Good on sandy soil, as they withstand drought. No heavy manuring is necessary before sowing. Apply basic slag in the autumn after digging. Apply ½ oz. sulphate of potash and 1½ oz. superphosphate per square yard when sowing.

Varieties. Masterpiece, Canadian Wonder.

Quantity. Half a pt. for 60 ft. of row.

Season of use. Late July.

BEANS, RUNNER

General. They give a good return for the small space occupied. In addition to the usual method of supporting them on rods they may be trained up trellis or against a fence or wall.

Sow. End May. Drills 6 in. wide each to take two staggered rows of seed 6 in. apart. Two drills 18 in. apart to each set of poles.

Cultivation. Any soil is suitable. No heavy manuring is required before sowing. Bonfire ash is very good if applied freely to the surface when sowing. Alternatively, apply 1½ oz. superphosphate and ½ oz. sulphate of potash per square

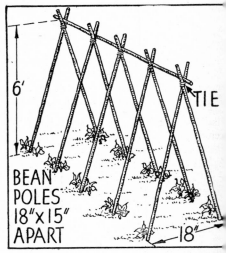

Poles arranged for scarlet runner beans.

French, or kidney, beans.

/ard at this time. Stake with poles set
one to each plant on either side of the
double row. Cross them at the top and in
the V's thus formed lay another pole and
tie securely into position.

Varieties. Scarlet Emperor, Prize-
winner.

Quantity. Half a pt. for 30 ft. of row.

Season of use. August until the first
frost comes. Fresh beans may also be
preserved in salt for use in winter.

BEANS, WAXPOD

General. This type is grown for
cooking whole, the pods being stringless.

Sow. Mid-May onwards. As with
French beans, three sowings may be
made. Drills 6 in. wide and 2 ft. apart,
each to take three staggered rows of seed
5 in. apart.

Cultivation. Sandy soil suits them
best. No heavy manuring is required
before sowing. Wood ashes are useful.

Varieties. Golden Waxpod, Giant
Waxpod.

Quantity. One pt. for 60 ft. of row.

Season of use. July-August.

BEANS, DUTCH BROWN

General. These are grown for use
like grocer's butter beans, the seeds being
removed from the pods after drying.
Rich in protein.

Sow. End May. Drills 6 in. wide and
2 ft. apart, each to take three staggered
rows of seed 6 in. apart.

Cultivation. They grow best on a
light soil, but with deep digging and
attention to drainage they may be sown
on any soil with success. Wood ashes
are good.

Variety. Dutch Brown.

Quantity. One pt. for 60 ft. of row.

Season of use. When the pods are
fully grown, pull up the entire plant and
hang in a dry airy place. After a few
weeks the beans may be easily taken from
their pods and stored in jars.

BEET

General. This root crop has a great
dietetic value. In addition to the usual
use in salads and with cold meat, it is
excellent when boiled or steamed.

(*Upper*) Round, and (*lower*) long, beetroot.

Sow. April-May, and again in July.
Drills 1 ft. apart. Sow three seeds
together at intervals of 6 in. Thin the
seedlings so that the strongest remain.

Cultivation. They can be grown
successfully in any soil. Hoe the rows
continuously, taking great care not to
damage the roots. Freshly manured
ground must be avoided. During October
the roots will be ready for lifting. Do this
during a dry spell and avoid damaging
them or they will be spoilt through
bleeding. The leaves must be twisted off.

Varieties. Long : Blood Red, Perfection. Globe : Crimson Ball.

Quantity. One oz. of seed will sow
150 ft. of row.

Season of use. August onwards.
Store in a clamp as for potatoes or cover
them with dry sand.

Two fine heads of broccoli.   These vegetables can be obtained in succession from early autumn t
late spring.   Protection from frost is obtained by breaking some of the leaves over the head

BROCCOLI

General. By careful selection from the four divisions, heads of broccoli can be produced for use practically all the year round.

Sow. For autumn, mid-March in a frame ; for winter, late April in a seed bed outside ; for early spring, April in a seed bed outside ; for late spring, May in a seed bed outside.

Plant. The young plants may be planted out when they are large enough to handle, 2 ft. apart in rows 2 ft. 6 in. apart.

Cultivation. A firm, somewhat heavy soil produces the closest curds (heads), and if broccoli follows a crop that received deep digging, single digging will be sufficient. Newly turned soil, especially of a light nature, should be trodden down to make a firm bed. Apply a slow-acting fertilizer, such as bonemeal, when planting, at the rate of 2 oz. per square yard, followed by nitro-chalk at the same rate. Alternatively, apply 1½ oz. of super-phosphate and ½ oz. of sulphate of potash prior to planting. To protect the heads

in a hard winter the plants may be heeled over to the north by removing a little soil on one side, pushing them over at an angle and replacing the soil on the other side.

Varieties. Autumn : Veitch's Self Protecting, Michaelmas White, Extra Early Roscoff. Winter : Roscoff No. 1, Roscoff No. 2, Early Feltham. Early spring : Roscoff No. 3, Roscoff No. 4, Snow's Winter White. Late spring Roscoff No. 5, Late Feltham, Whitsuntide.

Quantity. ¼ oz. seed for 50 ft. of row

Season of use. September-May.

BROCCOLI, STAR

General. This type produces several heads on one plant and is therefore particularly useful for the small household.

Sow. April-May in a seed bed outside

Plant. When large enough to handle 2 ft. 6 in. apart in rows 3 ft. apart.

Cultivation. As for ordinary broccoli

Varieties. Nine Star, Bouquet.

Quantity. Quarter of an oz. of seed for 50 ft. of row.

Season of use. Throughout the spring if successional sowings are made.

BROCCOLI, SPROUTING
General. This is hardier than the hearting broccoli, needing no winter protection.
Sow. March-April in a seed bed outside.
Plant. When large enough to handle.
Cultivation. As for ordinary broccoli, 2 ft. apart in rows 3 ft. apart.
Varieties. Early Purple, Late Purple.
Quantity. Quarter of an oz. for producing five hundred plants.
Season of use. September-April. It is the loose flower heads that are used.

BRUSSELS SPROUTS
General. A very popular late autumn vegetable to follow celery.
Sow. Early March in a cold frame. Early April outside in a seed bed. Drills 9 in. apart. Transplant the seedlings to another part of the nursery plot, 6 in. apart.
Plant. April-June, 2½ ft. apart in rows 2½ ft. apart.
Cultivation. A particularly long

he Nine Star broccoli produces a cluster of small cauliflower heads in early spring.

G—I

growing season and plenty of space in which to develop is required. The soil should be bastard trenched, and if manure is obtainable this should be dug in. Failing this, add plenty of decayed vegetable matter; this should not be

Pure white, well-shaped cauliflower.

near the surface. Apply fertilizers—1½ oz. superphosphate and ¾ oz. sulphate of potash per square yard.
Varieties. Evesham Special, Clucas Favourite, Matchless.
Quantity. Quarter of an oz. of seed for 50 ft. of row.
Season of use. October-February. Pick the lowest sprouts first.

CAULIFLOWER
General. Cauliflowers fill the gap between the early summer and autumn crops of broccoli. They are less hardy The flavour is more delicate.
Sow. January-February in boxes in gentle heat; prick out into frames April-May in a seed bed outside.
Plant. April-June, 1½ ft. apart in rows 2 ft. apart.
Cultivation. As for broccoli.
Varieties. Snowball, Early Giant.
Quantity. Quarter of an oz. of seed produces five hundred plants.
Season of use. August-October from successional sowings.

Brussels sprouts ready for picking.

CABBAGE

General. Greenstuff is an important item in the food supply, and where salads are short, raw young tender cabbage hearts may be finely shredded and will prove acceptable.

Sow. For spring, early August in a seed bed outside ; for autumn, March and April in a seed bed outside.

Plant. For spring : September, 1 ft. apart in rows 1½ ft. apart. For autumn : May and June, 1½ ft. apart in rows 2 ft. apart.

Cultivation. For good hearts cabbages need a firm soil, therefore avoid planting them on newly dug ground. It needs, however, to be well drained with organic manure previously dug in at the rate of one barrow load to 10 sq. yd. Light dressings of a nitrogenous fertilizer, 1 oz. per square yard at intervals are beneficial to avoid any check to the plants. In this way they are more tender.

Varieties. Spring : Harbinger, Offenham, Ellam's Early. Autumn : Christmas Drumhead, Winningstadt. Savoy : Ormskirk Early, Ormskirk Medium, Ormskirk Late.

Quantity. Three-quarters of an oz. of seed for producing five hundred plants.

Season of use. All the year round. Although called spring and autumn cabbage, successional sowings will give a supply throughout the year.

Spring cabbage, smooth leaves, pointed heart.

Savoy cabbage, rough leaves, round heart.

Mammoth Red capsicum.

Quantity. Quarter of an oz. of seed for producing seventy-five plants.
Season of use. Autumn.

CHIVES
General. Chives belong to the onion family and are used as flavouring in soups and salads. Only the green leaves are used. Mild flavour.
Sow. Spring.
Plant. As an alternative to seed, offsets

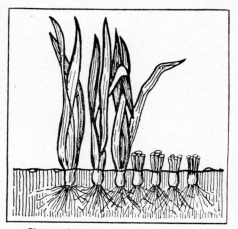

Chives, showing where to cut for use.

CAPSICUM
General. In wartime it is as well to aim at producing everything that will be required in the kitchen. This includes plants grown for seasoning.
Sow. March in heat.
Plant. June, 1½ ft. apart.
Cultivation. Sun heat is the chief factor for success and therefore capsicum should be grown on a very sunny border. A leafy soil is best.
Variety. Mammoth Red.
Quantity. Quarter of an oz. for 50 ft. row.
Season of use. Gather in August.

CARDOON
General. This is similar to celery but grows to a greater length and is of a distinct flavour.
Sow. April in boxes in cold frame. Prick out on to a hotbed.
Plant. June, 15 in. apart. One row is usually sufficient.
Cultivation. Deep digging and the addition of organic manure or vegetable refuse are essential. During the growing season, liquid manure should be given and in dry weather water also.

Cardoon, blanched and tied.

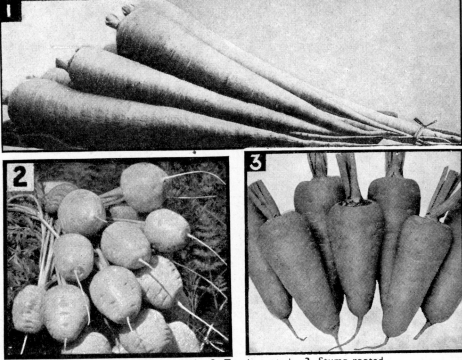

Carrots: **I.** Long rooted.   **2.** Turnip rooted.   **3.** Stump rooted.

(that is small bulbs) may be planted in spring.

Cultivation. They will grow in any ordinary soil, but like dry conditions.

Season of use. Spring and summer.

COLEWORT

General. This is the equivalent of a little winter cabbage.

Sow. May-June in a seed bed outside.

Plant. July, 1 ft. apart in rows 15 in. apart. Alternatively, sow in rows 15 in. apart and thin to 1 ft. apart.

Cultivation. As for cabbage.

Variety. Rosette.

Quantity. Half an oz. of seed for 50 ft. of row.

Season of use. Winter. Cut as required.

CARROT

General. From successional sowings young carrots can be obtained in season throughout the spring and summer and the main crop will give a supply for the winter.

Sow. January-February on a hotbed. March-April outside, also July. Drills 9 in. apart. Thin the seedlings gradually to 6 in. apart.

Cultivation. As for all root crops, a soil that does not contain stones is most suitable ; otherwise only stumpy varieties can be successfully grown. Stones cause the roots to fork. Do not dig in manure prior to sowing. During the growing season a general fertilizer can be applied along the rows in showery weather.

Varieties. For forcing : Early Shorthorn. For main crop : James Scarlet Intermediate, Long Surrey.

Quantity. One oz. of seed will sow 150 ft. of row.

Season of use. All the year round. For storing, lift the roots in autumn store in a clamp or dry sand.

CELERIAC
(TURNIP-ROOTED CELERY)

General. Celeriac has many advantages for the small garden or allotment owner. Whereas the flavour of celery and celeriac are similar, the latter does not need earthing. Also, a point very much in its favour is its keeping quality. It may be used for salads and cooked in the same way as celery.

Sow. March on a hotbed.

Plant. June, 1 ft. apart.

Cultivation. It is a gross feeder and therefore must have plenty of vegetable matter dug in. Apply bonemeal at the rate of 4 oz. per square yard before planting. Liquid manure should be given occasionally. To blanch the stem root which grows near the surface, hoe soil up to it.

Quantity. Quarter of an oz. of seed for producing seven hundred and fifty plants.

Season of use. November-January. Store the roots in dry sand.

Only the swollen root of celeriac is eaten.

CELERY

General. As soon as beans are withered by the frost, celery will be ready for the table.

Sow. February-March in boxes in heat or on a hotbed. Prick out the seedlings on to a hot bed.

Plant. June, in trenches specially prepared in early spring so that they may become weathered. Make the trenches 1½ ft. wide and 1½ ft. deep. Stack the soil neatly between the rows to form flat-topped ridges on which a catch crop may be grown. In the bottom place a 4 in. layer of rotted manure, tread it well down and cover with 5 in. or 6 in. of soil. Celery is a gross feeder and this preparation is important. Set two rows per trench, 9 in. apart, staggered with 1 ft. between the plants.

Cultivation. After thorough preparation of the trench, keep both the trenches and ridges weed free so that earthing up is not made difficult. Water is essential to good celery cultivation, and in dry weather water really thoroughly twice a week. Liquid manure occasionally is

In dry weather, water the trench thoroughly before planting out young celery plants.

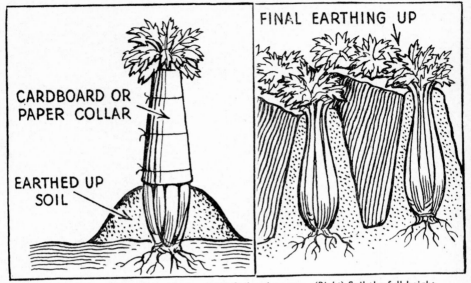

CARDBOARD OR PAPER COLLAR

EARTHED UP SOIL

FINAL EARTHING UP

Two methods of blanching celery.   (*Left*) Soil and paper.   (*Right*) Soil the full height.

good. Any suckers that may appear must be removed. Begin earthing up in August. Turn the soil from the ridges against the plants, allowing the leaves to project. Smooth the surface, so that rain drains off. Another two earthings-up will be required later. On a wet soil the paper collar illustrated is more satisfactory.

Varieties. Solid White, Giant White.

Quantity. Quarter of an oz. of seed for 50 ft. of row.

Season of use. After frost the flavour is improved. Lift then as required.

CELERY, SELF BLEACHING

General. This can be grown on a flat bed and needs no earthing up.

Sow. February-March in boxes in heat or on a hotbed.

Plant. June, 9 in. apart in rows 1 ft. apart.

Cultivation. This type needs plenty of manure and when digging plenty of organic matter should be added. Liquid manure during the growing season is good.

Variety. Golden Self Bleaching.

Season of use. Lift as required in the autumn after frosts.

CELERY CLEANED AND TRIMMED

When trimming the roots off celery, leave as much as possible of the root stock; this part has an excellent flavour and is particularly good eaten raw. A soft scrubbing brush is best for removing the soil from celery, which needs very careful washing, especially when soil-blanched.

Forcing chicory under the staging.

CHICORY

General. This is a useful winter salad. The blanched leaves are eaten as lettuce.

Sow. May-June outside. Rows 1 ft. apart. Thin to 9 in. apart.

Cultivation. Grow it on good but not freshly manured soil. Keep the ground hoed regularly. In the autumn, lift the roots for forcing. Pack them tightly, upright, in boxes with fine soil between and place them in a warm dark place. Beneath the staging of a greenhouse is a suitable place or a coal cellar or shed. The warmer the place the quicker they will be ready. The time varies from three to five weeks.

Variety. Large Brussels.

Quantity. Quarter of an oz. of seed will produce three hundred and fifty plants.

Season of use. Cut when 5 to 6 in. long. Ready during the winter.

COUVE TRONCHUDA
(SEA-KALE CABBAGE)

General. This crop serves a double use, for in addition to the cabbage-like heart that can be cut the lower leaves have thick fleshy ribs that may be used as sea-kale.

Sow. April in seed bed outside. Prick out 9 in. apart in a nursery bed when the seedlings are 3 in. high.

Plant. June, 2½ ft. apart.

Cultivation. As for cabbage.

Quantity. One-eighth of an oz. of seed will produce two hundred and fifty plants.

Season of use. Winter.

CUCUMBER, FRAME

General. Although usually grown in glasshouses, this type of cucumber can be successfully cultivated in a frame on a hotbed.

Sow. February-March, one seed in a 3 in. pot and stand on a hotbed to promote rapid germination.

Ridge cucumber for outdoor culture.

A fine frame cucumber, Carter's Gourmet.

Plant. End of April and early May on a hotbed. One plant to a 4 ft. by 4 ft. light, placing it in the centre of the bed.

Cultivation. After planting, keep the frame closed for four days and then increase air gradually each day. Perfect drainage is essential as the plants have to be given so much water. All water given should be tepid if possible. To train, pinch out the growing point soon after planting. This will encourage side growths, four of which should be kept and trained towards the corners of the frame. As flowers appear, all male blossoms must be pinched out to avoid seedy cucumbers. Throughout the life of the plant, water must be freely given In hot weather syringe twice daily, at

midday and again at about 4 p.m. Liquid manure is also helpful to keep the plant growing strongly. Side shoots as they appear must be cut out, but in this process young ones can be left to replace old ones that have finished fruiting.

Variety. Telegraph.

Season of use. Summer.

CUCUMBER, RIDGE

General. Where there is no frame, this type of cucumber may be grown.

Sow. Mid-April in pots in a box covered with a piece of glass.

Plant. End of May.

Cultivation. Hillocks of old bonfire rubbish or fermenting organic waste are excellent. When six leaves have developed the plants should have their growing point pinched out to encourage several shoots to develop. Watering with plain water and manure water at intervals is the only attention needed.

Variety. Long Green.

Season of use. Summer.

EGG PLANT (AUBERGINE)

General. The egg plant is a delicious vegetable that is seldom grown. It takes up little space and is a welcome change

Fruiting plant of aubergine.

to have occasionally. It is grown like tomatoes.

Sow. February in heat.

Plant. June, about 1 ft. apart.

Cultivation. The base of a south wall is the best position, because here the plants can be kept warm. The soil should contain plenty of leaf-mould.

Varieties. Purple, White.

Season of use. August.

Oval-leaved endive, showing blanched centre after the tie has been removed.

ENDIVE

General. The leaves are blanched and used as an addition to winter and summer salads.

Sow. April-August at intervals of about a fortnight. This will give a regular supply through the autumn and winter. Drills 1½ ft. apart. Thin the seedlings to 15 in. apart.

Cultivation. No special treatment is required. To blanch, gather the leaves together and tie round with raffia or

Moss Curled endive blanched under a pot.

PG—I*

Moss Curled endive tied for blanching.

cover with flower pot or tile as illustrated. The plants must be quite dry for this operation. Blanching takes approximately a fortnight.

Varieties. Moss Curled, Round-leaved Batavian.

Quantity. Quarter of an oz. of seed for 50 ft. of drill.

Season of use. Summer and winter.

Tile in position for blanching endive.

GARLIC

General. Leaves of garlic are often appreciated as an addition to the salad bowl, and as it takes up very little room it can be included where desired.

Plant. February, 2 in. deep and 6 in. apart.

Cultivation. Deeply dug, well-drained soil is all it needs.

Season of use. Throughout the summer.

HORSE-RADISH

General. A large quantity of horse-radish is not as a rule required in the ordinary small garden. It is a very accommodating kind of herb and will grow in any out-of-the-way corner.

Plant. Plant in February in rows 15 in. apart, the roots being 8 in. or 9 in. distance from each other; cover with 3 in. or 4 in. of soil.

Cultivation. It grows well in any soil, but gives the best results in well-cultivated land and does not mind being in the shade or in the sun. The roots should be lifted every other year during February, but if the roots are left undisturbed for several years they will not harm. For replanting, select straight roots about 10 in. in length, each root should have a crown or bud and be planted crown end uppermost.

Varieties. Only the native *Cochlearia armoracia* is grown.

Season of use. Lift roots as required.

KALE

General. This is a grand green vegetable for winter, which is improved by the frost. It can be cut again and again.

Sow. March-April in a seed bed outside.

Plant. June-July, 2 ft. to 2½ ft. apart.

Cultivation. A heavy soil is best. Those of a light nature need vegetable matter added, but it is preferable to let kale follow a crop that has been well manured and not to add it just before this is planted. It will quite satisfactorily follow early potatoes. Apply 2 oz. of superphosphate and ¾ oz. of sulphate of potash to the soil before planting.

Varieties. Hardy Sprouting, Asparagus (this may be sown as late as June for spring use).

Quantity. Quarter of an oz. of seed will produce 750 plants.

Season of use. Late winter and early spring.

KOHLRABI

General. This is a fine crop for dry soils and seasons and under such conditions can be grown as a substitute for turnips.

Sow. April-June where they are to grow, 9 in. apart in rows 15 in. apart.

Cultivation. They need nothing special beyond regular hoeing.

Varieties. Early Purple, Early White.

Quantity. Quarter of an oz. of seed will produce 750 plants.

Season of use. Use roots when they are half-grown for the best and mildest flavour. Older roots, although larger in size, are so tough that they cannot be eaten.

LEEK

General. This is a useful crop that can be used any time during the winter when other vegetables are scarce. Very hardy.

Sow. February, in heat. Prick out into boxes when 1 in. high. Mid-March in a cold frame. Transplant when large enough to handle into a further frame 8 in. apart.

Plant. 1, Drills on manured ground

Well-blanched leeks are pure white.

6 in. deep and 1 ft. apart ; set the plants 8 in. apart. 2, Holes 6 in. deep in rows 1 ft. apart and 8 in. from hole to hole ; drop the plant into the hole and do not fill in. 3, Trenches 9 in. wide, 6 in. deep, 1½ ft. apart ; this method is for the production of extra large leeks and so they should be set 1 ft. apart in the trench. For any of the above methods the soil must be deeply dug and well manured.

Cultivation. Fertilizers are important during the growing season. Soon after planting, apply 1 oz. of superphosphate and ½ oz. of sulphate of potash. A fortnight later give a dressing of nitrate of soda at the rate of ¾ oz. per square yard.

Varieties. Giant Musselburgh, Prizetaker.

Quantity. Quarter of an oz. of seed for 50 ft. of row.

Season of use. October onwards.

A row of young cos lettuce.

Cabbage lettuce should have a firm heart.

LETTUCE

General. Lettuces can be had all the year round with the use of a greenhouse, cold frame, cloches and hotbed.

Sow. For succession : 1, October in boxes in a cool greenhouse ; prick out into boxes ; transplant to a hotbed in December. 2, October in boxes in a cool greenhouse ; transplant to a cold frame. 3, February in a cold frame ; prick out into boxes ; plant out into a warm border in March. 4, March onwards outside. 5, July outside. 6, August and September on a warm border or in a cold frame.

Cultivation. A well-cultivated soil with rotted vegetable refuse dug in, but near the surface. Hoeing is essential. Plenty of overhead watering during dry weather. A mulch of leaf-mould or grass clippings is useful.

Varieties. *Cabbage* : 1 and 2, Early French Frame ; 3, May Queen ; 4, Market Favourite ; 5 and 6, Imperial, Hammersmith. *Cos* : 1, 2, 3 and 4, Nonsuch Superb White ; 5 and 6, Hick's Winter White.

Quantity. Half an oz. of seed will sow 100 ft. of row.

Season of use. 1, February-March ; 2, April-May ; 3, May-June ; 4, July-October ; 5, November ; 6, winter.

MARROWS, VEGETABLE

General. This is a very easily grown vegetable that is particularly useful for preserves. It is quite accommodating and can be grown in any odd corner of the garden or allotment. Both bush and trailing forms are available.

Sow. March, in pots.

Plant. May, when frosts are over.

Cultivation. An old bonfire or other heap makes a suitable home for the

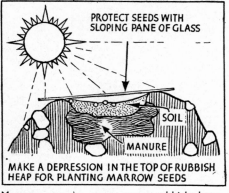

MAKE A DEPRESSION IN THE TOP OF RUBBISH
HEAP FOR PLANTING MARROW SEEDS

Marrows can be sown on a rubbish heap.

marrow plant. Its chief requirement is vegetable matter in a state of decay. A mulching of grass clippings given periodically during the summer helps to conserve moisture.

Varieties. *Trailing* : Long Green, Long White. *Bush* : Green, White.

Quantity. One trailing or three bush plants are sufficient for the average household.

Season of use. August until frost comes. Cut when young. Marrows can be preserved to make pickles and jam.

MINT

General. When once established it will always be in the garden. As it spreads very freely, mint should be given a corner to itself.

Plant. Spring or autumn, 1 ft. apart.

Cultivation. No special treatment is required. To force, lift a few roots during the winter and plant them in boxes which should be placed in the greenhouse. Even without heat the shoots are ready by March.

Season of use. May-August (naturally); December onwards (forced).

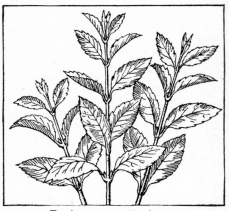

Tender young mint shoots.

MUSTARD AND CRESS

General. Popular salad crops that can be produced at any time.

Sow. Thickly over sifted soil pressed firm in boxes. Sow cress three or four days before mustard.

Cultivation. Keep moist and in a dark place to lengthen the stems. Bring into the light three or four days before cutting. Both need warm greenhouse in cold months.

Varieties. Cress : Plain or Curled. Mustard : White.

Season of use. All the year round.

Mustard and cress should be sown in separate punnets.

SPAWNING A MUSHROOM BED

I. Break the spawn into small pieces and distribute it evenly over the surface of the bed.

Insert the pieces of spawn and mark the position of a few to examine before casing over the bed.

2. Unbroken mushroom spawn.

MUSHROOMS

General. Where a cellar is available, it can be utilized for mushroom growing, or a dark, dry shed is suitable.

Cultivation. Beds are made any time from July to February. Stable manure is essential for mushroom cultivation and no substitute will do. A fresh supply should be obtained, and before using, the heap must be turned three times. After this, form a flat bed by packing solidly, treading it as necessary to a depth of

READY FOR PICKING

3. Fill the holes left after picking mushrooms with a little fine soil and leave it level.

8 in. When the temperature falls to 75 deg. F., spawning may be done. Insert pieces of spawn the size of a walnut at intervals of 1 ft. at the surface of the bed. After a few days, during which time the mycelium (fine white fibres) will penetrate, the bed can be cased with moist soil. The bed should be kept in the dark at all times. If there are any windows in the shed they must be covered, or if the beds are made beneath the staging in a greenhouse sacking

An outdoor mushroom bed (*left*) is generally ridge-shaped and covered with a thick layer of straw to conserve heat and moisture.

should be hung down in front to shut out the light. After about a month, watering may be necessary if the soil appears to be getting dry. Avoid excessive moisture as this is fatal to mushrooms.

Season of use. Gathering will commence 7 or 8 weeks after spawning.

6" STRAW COVERING

2'6" MANURE   1½" SOIL CASING

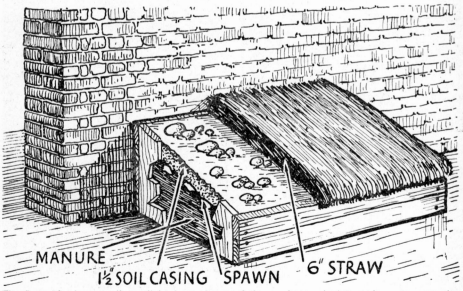

MANURE   1½" SOIL CASING   SPAWN   6" STRAW

The floor of a house cellar will be kept cleaner if the mushroom bed is made up in a wooden frame made to fit the available space. The sides should be just higher than the soil casing.

Mushrooms can be grown in small boxes stacked as shown in the diagram. Such small boxes cannot hold much heat, so are only suitable for warm sheds or cellars, and to save floor space.

PARSLEY

General. New plants must be grown from seed at regular intervals of a few months as the young leaves are best and it is a biennial.

Sow. March for summer use. June for winter use. August for spring use.

Cultivation. It will grow on any soil and can be used as an edging to the vegetable plot. It germinates very slowly so that if the soil is full of weed seeds radishes may be sown with it so that the rows may be determined early. In severe weather, protection may be given to the winter crop by using cloches.

Quantity. $\frac{1}{4}$ oz. seed for 100 ft. of row.

Season of use. All the year round.

Moss Curled parsley.

PARSNIPS

General. The easiest root crop to grow ; will succeed in any but stony soils.

Sow. End February and March in drills $1\frac{1}{2}$ ft. apart. Thin to 8 in. apart. Sow thickly as germination is poor. Alternatively, make holes 3 ft. deep and 3 in. in diameter with a crowbar. Fill these with sifted soil and sow two or three seeds on top. Thin these to one, leaving the strongest. The holes should be 12 in. apart in rows $1\frac{1}{2}$ ft. apart.

Cultivation. No special treatment is required, but fresh manure must not be given.

Varieties. Tender and True, Hollow Crown.

Quantity. $\frac{1}{4}$ oz. seed for 50 ft. of row.

Season of use. As required, November onwards. The flavour is improved after frost.

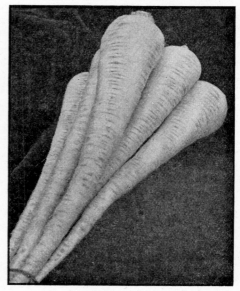

Well-grown parsnips.

THINNING ONIONS
Leave the plants 6 in. apart at the final thinning. The thinnings can be used for salads or flavouring soups. In dry weather loosen the soil with a small fork before attempting to pull the onions.

ONIONS

General. Every garden should contain a few onions, as they are particularly useful for flavouring many dishes. During spring the thinnings find favour for the salad bowl. Autumn sown onions ripen earlier than spring sowings and are seldom attacked by onion fly.

Sow. 1, February in boxes in heat; prick out into further boxes; plant outside in rows 9 in. apart, with 6 in. between the plants, in May. 2, March and April, where they are to grow in rows 9 in. apart; thin the seedlings to 6 in. apart. 3, August and September, where they are to grow in rows 9 in. apart; thin to 6 in. apart in spring.

Cultivation. A very firm bed is essential, especially where seed is sown direct. Onions prefer a light sandy soil with a deep root run, but with no organic manure in the top 9 in. of soil. Wood ash spread on the surface before sowing is beneficial, together with 1 oz. of sulphate of potash and 2 oz. of superphosphate ten days before planting. In August the tops may be bent over to assist the ripening of the bulbs, the autumn sowings being done early in the month and the spring sowings towards the end.

Varieties. For spring salads, White Lisbon; for summer use, Giant Rocca; for storing, Bedfordshire Champion, Ailsa Craig (for sowing under glass).

Quantity. Quarter of an oz. of seed for 50 ft. of row.

Season of use. Thinnings from the autumn sowing will be of use for salads in the spring, and the mature bulbs will

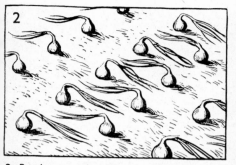

2. Bend over onion tops, as shown above, to get full sun on the bulbs and promote ripening.

be ready at the beginning of August for lifting and storing. Towards the end of August the spring-sown crop will be ready for lifting and storing for winter use. Remove the tops, clean off soil, and store in a dry place.

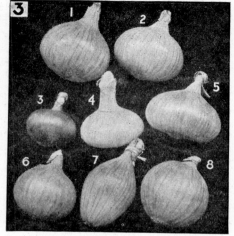

3. I, Carter's Record; 2, Carter's Holborn; 3, Carter's Blood Red; 4, Carter's White Emperor; 5, Carter's Autumn Queen; 6, James's Keeping, Carter's Re-selected; 7, Carter's Long Keeper; 8, Carter's Selected Ailsa Craig.

PEAS

General. Peas are the most popular vegetable and very easily grown. *Best substitute for meat, full of protein.*

Sow. February in a warm border—earlies ; March and June—earlies ; April —second earlies ; May—late. Drills 6 in. wide, 2 ft. to 6 ft. apart according to the varieties, two or three rows in each drill.

Cultivation. Peas are able to use atmospheric nitrogen and therefore need supplying only with potash and phosphate. Fork organic manure in bottom of drills. Flood drills with water in dry

Stake peas early—it gives some protection and prevents the plants falling over.

Well-filled pods of main crop peas.

the potatoes on end in shallow boxes, setting the end with the most eyes uppermost. Stand the boxes in a light airy frostproof place to sprout. Allow only one or two shoots to grow ; all others should be rubbed off.

Plant. Mid-March to mid-April on the ridge system (*see* illustration). Rows 2 ft. to 3 ft. apart, according to whether they are first or second earlies or main crop. The tubers should be 12 to 18 in. apart. The later the variety the farther apart they should be planted. To prepare the soil, dig deeply and leave ridged. Place manure in the bottom of the furrows and set the tubers in position on this. Cover them with soil to a depth of 4 in. to 6 in. so that the ridges now run over the tubers and the furrows between the rows. When the shoots appear through

weather. Light soils are best. Apply 3 oz. superphosphate and 1 oz. of sulphate of potash before sowing. Hoeing is very important and mulching with lawn mowings alongside the rows is beneficial. Support peas with sticks of hazel placed either side of the rows or special nettings sold for this purpose.

Varieties. *First earlies* : Early Bird (2 ft.), Little Marvel (1½ ft.). *Second earlies* : Thomas Laxton (3½ ft.), Gradus (3 ft.). *Lates* : Autocrat (3½ ft.), Alderman (5 ft.).

Quantity. Two pt. will sow 100 ft. of row.

Season of use. Earlies, eleven to twelve weeks after sowing ; second earlies, twelve to thirteen weeks after sowing ; lates, thirteen to fourteen weeks after sowing.

POTATOES

General. The importance of this crop cannot be over estimated. By sprouting potatoes (*see* illustration) prior to planting the crop will be ready for lifting a few weeks earlier. Seed should be the size of an egg and about 2 oz. in weight. It should be obtained from a locality farther north than your garden or allotment. By planting immune varieties you will not be troubled with wart disease.

Cultivation. During the winter, place

As soon as the potato sprouts are growing well, select the two strongest on each potato and rub off all the other unnecessary ones

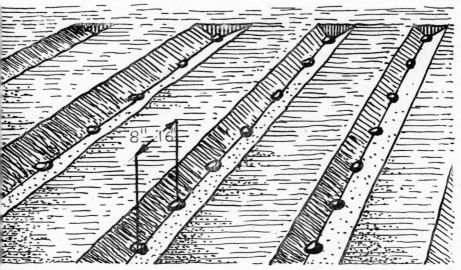

POTATO DRILLS

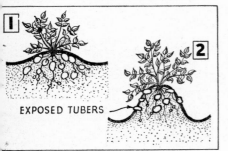

EXPOSED TUBERS

Above is shown potato drills drawn over the whole plot. The potatoes are placed in the drills 8 in. to 16 in. apart, the wider planting for main crop varieties. Below is shown the position of manure with each line of potatoes. In this plan the first drill is filled with the soil dug out for the second and so on across the plot.

1. A mature potato planted to the correct depth (6 in.) and properly earthed up; all the tubers are well covered with soil.

2. A shallowly planted potato; many tubers are rendered useless by exposure to the light.

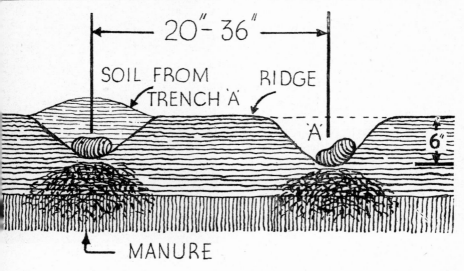

The crop you ought to get.

the soil and are 8 in. high they may be
earthed up. Continue earthing at fortnightly intervals, adding 1 in. of soil.
Spray with Bordeaux mixture in July and
again in August if necessary against blight
disease.

Varieties. *First early*: Arran Pilot
(immune). *Second early*: Arran Banner
(immune), Doon Star (immune). *Main
crop*: Gladstone (immune), King Edward
VII.

Quantity. 7 lb. seed for 100 ft. row.

Season of use. First early, June;
second early, July; main crop, August
onwards. The main crop should be
stored in a clamp or in sacks in a dry shed
away from frost and light.

RADISHES

General. This is a quick maturing
crop that can be sown as a catch crop
between the main rows of vegetables or
taken off ground before cabbage and
broccoli is planted.

Sow. December-February on a hotbed; March-September outside. The
seed can be broadcast or sown in rows
6 in. apart.

Cultivation. Hoeing is the onl
important operation, and in dry weathe
give a regular supply of water.

Varieties. French Breakfast an
Wood's Frame (for hotbeds), Turnip
shaped red, Sparkler.

Quantity. One oz. of seed will so
100 ft. of row.

Season of use. All the year round.

SAGE

General. This is a useful herb, a fev
bushes of which may be grown in th
flower border or any other part of th
garden.

Plant. Spring or autumn, 1½ ft. apa
if more than one bush is required.

Cultivation. No special treatment i
required. To renew, take cuttings i
May.

Season of use. Shoots may be cu
throughout the year, but if required fo
drying this should be done in August.

SALSIFY (VEGETABLE OYSTER

General. The variety of winter vege
tables is somewhat restricted and thi
crop makes a welcome change.

Collected types of radish.

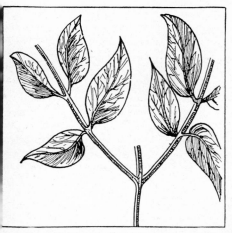

Cut shoots of sage during the summer and dry them for winter use. Store in jars or tins.

Sow. April. Drills 1 ft. apart. Thin the seedlings gradually to 8 in. apart.

Cultivation. A general fertilizer should be applied about fourteen days before sowing. A suitable mixture is made of one part sulphate of ammonia, two parts sulphate of potash and four parts superphosphate, applied at the rate of 4 oz. per square yard.

Variety. Mammoth.

Quantity. Three-quarters of an oz. of seed will sow 100 ft. of row.

Season of use. Dig as required throughout the winter.

Whole stools of rhubarb lifted and brought into the greenhouse or put in a cold frame will give a crop of tender shoots early in the season.

RHUBARB

General. A few plants will provide sufficient sticks for the average family for several years.

Plant. March, 2½ ft. apart.

Cultivation. Ground that is to receive rhubarb roots should be very deeply dug and well manured, as after this preparatory work the roots will not be disturbed for several years. During each winter a top dressing of rotted vegetable matter may be given. Any flower heads that appear must be removed.

Variety. Champagne.

Season of use. Pull sparingly the second season, and unless the crowns are very large none the first season after planting. In future years, rhubarb can be pulled until August. Do not on any account eat the foliage.

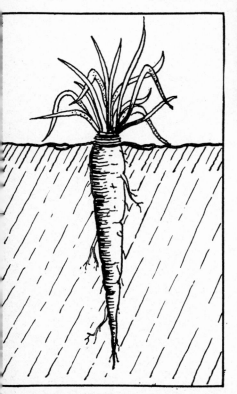

Salsify grown in deeply dug soil has a good straight root with no branches, which makes it easier to prepare for cooking.

(Left) A sea-kale root ready for planting. *(Right)* A blanched shoot of sea-kale fit for use.

SEA-KALE

General. This vegetable is grown solely for the blanched stems.

Sow. March in a nursery bed. Drills 1 ft. apart. Thin the seedlings to 6 in. apart.

Plant. Following March. Alternatively pieces of root 4 in. to 6 in. long can be planted, thick end uppermost, 15 in. apart in rows 2 ft. apart.

Cultivation. This crop requires plenty of manure in order to obtain large crowns for forcing. Dig the soil deeply, adding farmyard manure if available or any other organic material. Rotted seaweed is a valuable top dressing; apply 4 in. thick. In autumn the plants are lifted and trimmed, leaving about 6 in. of the thick main root with the crown on the top. Those not required for immediate forcing can be packed in moist sandy soil in a shed. The remainder should be placed close together in a box with fine leafy soil between them and placed in a

warm dark position, such as beneath the greenhouse staging. Here sacks will be necessary to exclude the light. The heads are cut when about 6 ins. long, a small portion of root being left attached.

Variety. Ivory White.

Season of use. Winter.

SHALLOTS

General. These are especially useful where attacks of onion fly are prevalent as they are not affected by this pest. To economize in space they can be grown on the ridges between celery trenches, a they will be off the ground before the celery requires earthing up.

Plant. February-March. Push the bulbs into the soil to half their depth 9 in. apart in rows 1 ft. apart.

Cultivation. The soil must be well drained, and for this reason too the celery ridges are particularly suitable. Before planting, spread wood ash over the surface of the soil together with 1 oz. of sulphate of potash and 2 oz. of super phosphate per square yard. At the end of July when the leaves turn brown the bulbs should be pulled up and left on the

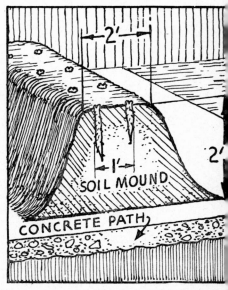

Beds can be made up in a dark shed for forcing sea-kale. For very early crops heat is required

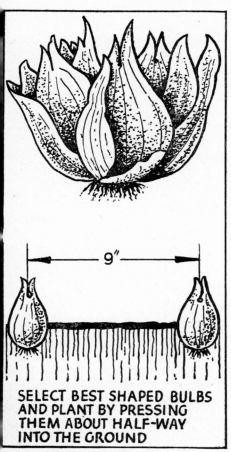

SELECT BEST SHAPED BULBS AND PLANT BY PRESSING THEM ABOUT HALF-WAY INTO THE GROUND

It has been said of shallots: "Sow on the shortest day of the year and pull on the longest."

soil to dry. Turn them over once or twice during this period.

Variety. Yellow Shallot.

Quantity. One hundred and thirty bulbs will plant 100 ft. row.

Season of use. July-March. The bulbs should be stored in a dry place.

SCORZONERA

General. Another winter root crop that gives variety when little else is available.

Sow. April. Drills 1 ft. apart. Thin the seedlings gradually to 8 in. apart.

Cultivation. Apply a general fertilizer a fortnight before sowing. A suitable mixture is made of one part sulphate of ammonia, two parts sulphate of potash and four parts superphosphate applied at the rate of 4 oz. per square yard.

Quantity. Three-quarters of an oz. of seed will sow 100 ft. of row.

Season of use. Dig as required throughout the winter.

SPINACH, SUMMER

General. This type is not hardy and quickly runs to seed. Sowings should be made little and often.

Sow. March-July. Drills 1 ft. apart. Thin the seedlings to 6 in. apart.

Cultivation. Plenty of organic matter should be dug into the soil to hold the moisture. Fish and bonemeal mixed in equal quantities and applied at the rate of 4 oz. per square yard is beneficial.

Variety. Long Standing Round.

Quantity. Half an oz. of seed will sow 50 ft. of row.

Season of use. Pick regularly. It does not matter how much is taken from the plant at one time.

SPINACH, WINTER

General. This is the hardy type, but in very severe weather the use of cloches may be advisable.

Sow. July-September. Drills 9 in. apart. Thin the seedlings to 4 in. apart.

Cultivation. Dig in organic matter

Spinach must be well thinned to produce good leaves. Thick, heavy leaves are best for cooking.

Young plants of sweet corn in their permanent positions. Plant out in rows 3 ft. apart.

prior to sowing. Apply fish and bone-meal mixed in equal quantities at the rate of 4 oz. per sq. yd. before sowing.

Variety. Prickly.

Season of use. Pick the largest leaves only as required during the winter.

SPINACH, PERPETUAL (SPINACH BEET)

General. This type can be had all the year round, but is particularly useful for winter picking.

Sow. April and August to obtain a succession. Drills 15 in. apart. Thin the seedlings to 1½ ft. apart.

Cultivation. No special treatment is required, but water in dry weather.

Variety. Perpetual.

Quantity. Half an oz. of seed will sow 50 ft. of row.

Season of use. Pick the leaves as required. Do this regularly in order to keep up the supply.

SWEET CORN

General. Sweet corn is a popular American dish. The plant should be better known in this country: it can be raised without heat in the southern counties.

Sow. End of May.

Plant. One and a half ft. apart in rows 3 ft. apart when large enough to handle.

Cultivation. A well-worked and well

Well-filled cobs of sweet corn make an appetizing dish which is rapidly becoming more popular in this country. Served on the cob with butter, or off it in flavoured sauce.

Round white turnip.

drained soil is the chief requirement with an ample supply of water. Occasional applications of a general fertilizer will speed up growth and so reduce the time required to cook the cobs.

Variety. Improved Sweet Corn.

Season of use. August.

SWEDE

General. A very useful vegetable in times of emergency.

Sow. March and April. Drills 1 ft. apart. Thin the seedlings 9 in. apart.

Cultivation. If possible, swedes should be sown on land that has been manured for a previous crop. The soil should be friable and the application of a general fertilizer before sowing is beneficial.

Varieties. Purple Top, Bronze Top.

Quantity. Half an oz. of seed will sow 50 ft. of row.

Season of use. August, pulled from the ground as required; autumn onwards, stored roots. Roots are stored like potatoes in a clamp.

TOMATO

General. Although tomatoes are generally grown under glass, they may be planted in a frame or on a warm border against a south wall of the house. Any tubs in the garden may also be utilized where space is limited. For outdoor culture, choose an earlier ripening variety.

Sow. February-March in heat in pots. If you have no means of raising your own plants they can be bought during May. Choose sturdy, dark green plants; refuse leggy thin specimens. Avoid any with side shoots.

Plant. If you have a glasshouse in which they are raised, leave them inside until the first flower truss has formed. In this way ripe fruit will be ready a week or two earlier. Under ordinary conditions, plant them outside at the end of May, when all fear of frost has passed. Set them 15 in. apart.

Cultivation. The soil should contain plenty of organic matter. Good drainage is important. Before planting, apply 2 oz. of sulphate of potash and 4 oz. of bone flour per square yard. Apply liquid manure every week unless the weather is dull, when it should be given less frequently. Train the plants up canes, removing all side shoots as they grow. After four trusses have set, remove the growing point of the plant, as no further fruit would mature under outdoor conditions. During August the lower leaves may be removed. To grow tomatoes in a cold frame the same soil treatment should

Outdoor tomatoes should be stopped after setting three trusses to ensure early ripening.

be given. Set the plants in position in a row along the front of the frame 15 in. apart and as they grow tie them to bamboo canes set in position one to each plant from front to back and 6 in. from the glass.

Variety. Sunrise.

Season of use. August and September. Ripe fruit may be bottled whole or as pulp and green fruit used for chutney.

Hang up bunches of thyme to dry for winter use.

THYME

General. This is a useful herb for seasoning and can be grown as an edging plant in any part of the garden, or even in the rock garden.

Sow. April.

Cultivation. No special treatment required.

Season of use. When the flowers appear, cut the shoots and hang them up to dry in a light shed.

TURNIP

General. This vegetable belongs to the cabbage family and in a rotation of crops should be on the same plot, as both are subject to club root.

Sow. February on a hotbed, drills 6 in. apart, thin to 4 in. March-April outside, drills 1 ft. apart, thin the seedlings to 6 in. apart. June and July outside for winter supplies.

Cultivation. After digging, apply lime at the rate of 4 oz. per square yard. A fortnight before seed sowing, apply a general fertilizer at the rate of 4 oz. per square yard. A suitable mixture is made of one part sulphate of ammonia, two parts sulphate of potash and four parts superphosphate.

Varieties. Early Snowball (for growing on hotbeds), Golden Ball, Red Globe, Chirk Castle (for winter storage).

Quantity. Half an oz. of seed will sow 100 ft. of row.

Season of use. Pull as required from early sowings. The main crop roots may be stored in a clamp.

CONCLUSION

The foregoing cultural directions will give the beginner a useful guide for the time at which the various operations should be performed. Naturally, all dates are subject to variation according to locality and altitude.

Never put off autumn digging until " next week " ; a thorough tidying up of all empty space in the kitchen garden will save weeks if the following spring is unusually wet, as the first spell of good weather can be used for sowing instead of catching up arrears of preparation of the ground.

Lift turnips before they become woody.

Daffodils in the orchard beneath the trees give colour before the apple blossom opens.

THE FRUIT GARDEN
HOW TO STOCK AND MAINTAIN IT

All soils will grow some kind of fruit and every garden, however small, can produce something. The individual requirements of each fruit need to be understood, but once the principles of cultivation are grasped subsequent maintenance is quite simple.

The main operations are pruning in winter, spraying in winter and spring, feeding in spring and autumn, thinning in summer, gathering and storing.

In making a new garden, give careful consideration to planning the fruit section; this is a permanent crop which, once established, cannot be disturbed and planting should not therefore be undertaken too hastily.

The chief factors to be considered are :—

Soil. A good loam with careful cultivation will grow practically all fruit ; but even a clay, gravel or chalky soil will produce certain fruits. It is important to choose, therefore, the most suitable type, and it is a mistake to try to grow every type and few of them well.

Aspect. Although in most gardens it is difficult to select the ideal aspect, the most can be made of any situation by careful choice of fruit to be grown. Frost and the consequent thaw cause damage to the blossom, but this can be avoided to a certain extent by planting so that the trees are not exposed to the early morning sun. Protection from cold north winds can be afforded by shelter belts.

Variety. In a small garden where space is limited the few fruits grown should give crops in succession, bearing in mind those that will keep in store.

Plant mostly dessert varieties rather than cooking, in order to get the full value of really fresh picked fruit from your garden.

The following are fruits in order of ripening :—

Strawberries, cherries, gooseberries, black currants, red currants and raspberries.

Plums, apples, pears, according to variety.

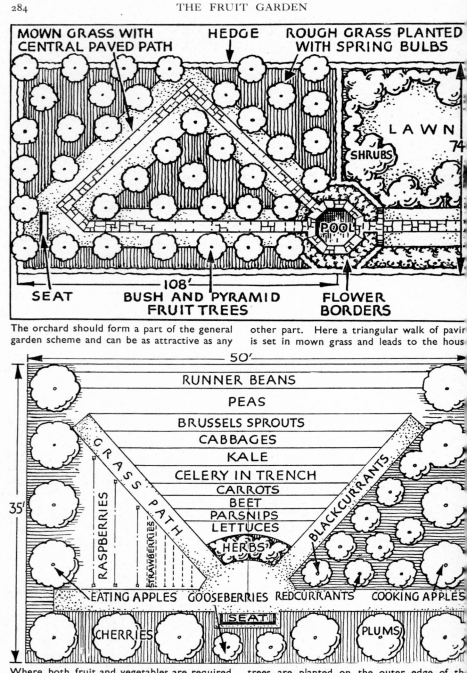

MOWN GRASS WITH CENTRAL PAVED PATH — **HEDGE** — **ROUGH GRASS PLANTED WITH SPRING BULBS**

LAWN
74

SHRUBS

POOL

108′

SEAT — **BUSH AND PYRAMID FRUIT TREES** — **FLOWER BORDERS**

The orchard should form a part of the general garden scheme and can be as attractive as any other part. Here a triangular walk of pavin is set in mown grass and leads to the hous

50′

RUNNER BEANS

PEAS

BRUSSELS SPROUTS

CABBAGES

KALE

CELERY IN TRENCH

CARROTS

BEET

PARSNIPS

LETTUCES

HERBS

GRASS PATH

RASPBERRIES

STRAWBERRIES

BLACKCURRANTS

35′

EATING APPLES   GOOSEBERRIES   REDCURRANTS   COOKING APPLES

SEAT

CHERRIES   PLUMS

Where both fruit and vegetables are required careful planning enables the owner to make the most use of the space available. Here bush trees are planted on the outer edge of th plot with soft fruits towards the centre an the vegetable section is not overshadowed

FRUIT TREES IN GROUPS

. Where it is possible to group the fruit trees together in an orchard the labour of cultivation is reduced to a minimum. It should be borne in mind, however, that fruit can be introduced into the garden scheme with excellent effect. For instance, small trained trees can be used as a background to flower borders; as a screen between one part of the garden and another; or if very low growing to outline the beds in the kitchen garden.

TREES ON THE LAWN

. Fruit trees can fulfil a decorative as well as useful purpose: nothing is more charming than a specimen standard apple tree grown on the lawn, or pear trees trained to form a pergola. The trees are beautiful when covered with blossom in spring, and the ripening fruit supplies colour in autumn. A large cherry is beautiful and does not shade the lawn too much.

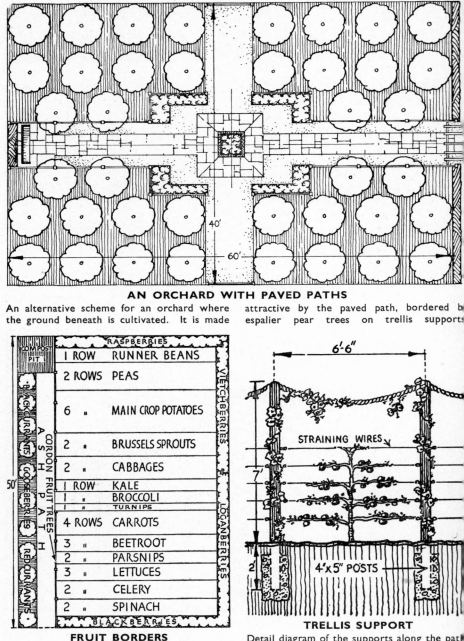

AN ORCHARD WITH PAVED PATHS

An alternative scheme for an orchard where the ground beneath is cultivated. It is made attractive by the paved path, bordered by espalier pear trees on trellis supports

FRUIT BORDERS

In this plan, berried fruits are trained against the surrounding fence with cordon apples alongside the path, not shading the vegetables.

TRELLIS SUPPORT

Detail diagram of the supports along the path in both the plans on this page. The upright supports are set in concrete 6 ft. 6 in. apart and wires run at even distances between them

STANDARD AND HALF-STANDARD

Modern fruit production is based on the correct use of stocks, that is to say, the ultimate size of the tree, the quality of the fruit and the age at which the tree comes into bearing can be determined by the different root-stocks used for grafting. It is therefore essential to purchase trees from a reliable nurseryman telling him the space you have at your disposal as well as particulars of soil, locality and the type required. Research stations have done years of work on this subject and produced a range of suitable stocks.

1. A half-standard requires slightly less space and can be pruned and sprayed more easily. The trunk is 4½ ft. high and permits cultivation beneath the branches.

2. The largest type of tree is the standard; the trunk of the tree is clear of branches for 6 ft.

Double horizontal cordon.

TRAINED CORDONS

Cordon trees can be trained to suit various positions, and produce fruit in places which would otherwise be unproductive.

The double horizontal cordon shown above is used as an edging. The branches may be tied along wires stretched at the correct height, or fastened to a peg by tying the tips to a stake. Protect the shoot with felt before fixing the string.

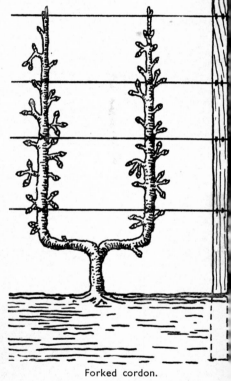

Forked cordon.

Single cordon.

The forked cordon shown above is used on fences or walls. Forked cordons are generally planted in rows where a screen is needed to cut off some part of the kitchen garden, or as a wind break. The single cordon is used in the same way, and a fine row of them is seen in the left-hand photo. Apples from cordons are well coloured, being exposed to the sun more than those from large orchard trees.

BUSH TREES

1. Bush trees are suitable for the small garden; pruning, spraying with a hand syringe, and fruit gathering are easy. They have a clear trunk of 2 ft. only, the branches radiating evenly at that height to form an open centre.

PYRAMID TREES

2. The pyramid, on the other hand, has a central stem clear for 1½ ft. from which tiers of branches grow on all sides. This type is also suitable for small gardens; the branches do not cast so much shade as a standard tree.

UTILIZE ALL YOUR SPACE

3. In a small garden, fruit trees are apt to take up too much room unless small-growing varieties are selected. Although cordon-trained trees are more expensive to buy than bush or standard forms, they take up very little space and give a good return of high quality well-coloured fruit. They are usually planted at an angle of 45 degrees and tied to bamboos held in position on straining wires set 1 ft. to 2 ft. apart. Mature stems do not need the bamboo.

PG—K

ESPALIER AND FAN TREES

Trees trained as espaliers have an upright trunk, with horizontal branches at regular intervals.

Trees trained as fans have a very short trunk from which the branches grow out fanwise.

Square planting.

Quincunx planting.

LAYING OUT AN ORCHARD

When laying out an orchard the positions of the permanent trees must first be considered. Full grown standard trees need to stand 30 ft. apart; as they take some years to come into bearing, the usual practice is to interplant with bush trees of apples and pears, which produce crops more quickly, or with bush fruits such as gooseberries and currants. These will give crops for the early years after laying out the orchard, while the permanent trees are growing a framework of strong branches and producing no fruit.

The square planting system seen above is usually adopted as the final scheme.

When trees are planted on the quincunx system alternate rows should be bush trees; these are left to grow as long as space permits, and on their removal it is seen that the standard trees are left at the required spacing of 30 ft. each way. An alternative method is to plant five currant or gooseberry bushes between each standard tree in the line, and use the space between the lines for vegetables.

In all cases where interplanting is practised avoid the temptation of allowing the catch crop to stand too long; remember that the standard trees are to be the main source of income, and must have light and air for full development.

PLANTING DISTANCES

APPLES

Cordon	. .	2 ft. in rows 7 ft. apart.
Espalier	. .	15 ft.
Bush & pyramid		12 ft. to 20 ft. (according to habit).
Half-standard	.	20 ft. to 30 ft. (according to habit).
Standard	. .	20 ft. to 30 ft. (according to habit).

PEARS

Cordon	. .	2 ft. in row 7 ft. apart.
Espalier	. .	15 ft.
Bush & pyramid		12 ft. to 15 ft.

Half-standard	.	18 ft. to 24 ft. (according to habit).
Standard	. .	20 ft. to 30 ft. (according to habit).

PLUMS

Fan	. . .	15 ft.
Bush	. . .	15 ft. to 18 ft.
Half-standard	.	20 ft. to 24 ft.
Standard	. .	24 ft. to 30 ft.

CHERRIES (Sweet and Morello).

Fan	. . .	15 ft.
Bush	. . .	9 ft. to 12 ft.
Standard	. .	24 ft. to 30 ft.

STAKING WHILE PLANTING
At least 2 ft. of the stake must be underground.
Make sure that both tree and stake are firm.

STAKING

Where standard trees are planted in an open position exposed to winds, a double stake as illustrated will give better support. Two stakes are driven in, one on either side of the tree and when in position their tops should not reach into the branches. To the top of each stake a crossbar is nailed and the trunk of the tree is tied securely to this. Before tying wrap a piece of felt or rubber round the bark to prevent injury.

While the trunk of the tree is smaller than the upright stakes a crossbar may be nailed on each side of the stakes; this will help to ease the strain of the tie against the young trunk. In districts where rabbits are troublesome fine mesh wire netting should be wrapped round the stakes, so as to enclose the trunk, to a height of 2 ft. 6 in. This will save the trees from having the bark eaten.

Planting and staking should be done together. Both are important operations; the life of the tree depends on them. After a hole sufficiently large to take the

roots well spread out has been made and the tree set in position, a stake should be driven in without injury to the fibrous roots. It is impossible for the roots to become established unless they are well anchored in the soil, and the stake should therefore be at least 2 ft. below ground. The soil is replaced gradually, worked among the roots and trodden down layer by layer. Never plant on a wet soil or during frost; if trees arrive from the nursery during bad weather heel the roots in, or, if this is not possible, cover them with sacking or straw to keep them damp to plant in time.

FOUR METHODS

There are many ways of staking fruit trees, but only four will be dealt with here. In fairly sheltered districts one upright stake, such as the one shown on the left, is sufficient. Where there is a prevailing wind a stake should be put in slantwise against the wind. In more exposed districts it is necessary

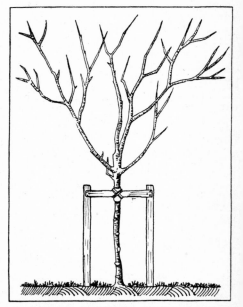

CROSSBAR STAKING OF STANDARDS
Note the tie which should be of soft cord over a wrap of old felt, or rubber, so that the cord does not cut into the bark of the tree.

SINGLE STAKE METHOD

The stake should be placed slantwise in districts where there is a prevailing wind, but where really boisterous weather is not normal. For exposed districts use tripod staking.

to provide more elaborate forms of staking.

A tripod can be formed of three posts or two upright posts can be joined by a crossbar. Whichever form is adopted the stakes must not reach higher than the top of the trunk and the bark must be protected in some way or other. Wire or twine will cut into the bark and cause irreparable damage, so it is necessary to encase the stem in a wrapping of sacking or rubber. These ties must be examined periodically, because the stem will expand, and the ties must then be loosened.

It is in fact advisable to renew the tie every year, so that there is no danger of hurting the bark as the tree swells in size. Always use a soft cord and make sure that there is an adequate underwrap.

Before being driven into the ground, the stake should first be pointed off, to facilitate driving. It will wear better if it is dipped into creosote or tar up to 2 ft. from the tip. It is possible that the mallet may roughen the top of the stake when this is knocked into the ground ; if this happens smooth off any roughness, so as to avoid possible damage to the bark.

After frosts both stakes and trees may be found to be rather loose. It is a wise precaution to go round and test for this, and where necessary to stamp the soil firm again. Always remember that fruit trees are properties that will last a lifetime, and that they are therefore worth much trouble.

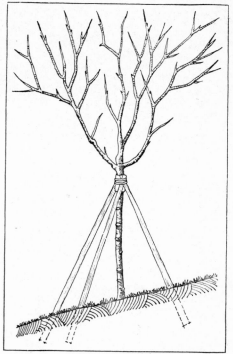

TRIPOD STAKING

The three post method is best for trees in districts exposed to high winds. The stakes should reach to just below the lowest branch, but not above. The bark must be carefully protected by wrap before tying.

LORD DERBY

1. Apple Lord Derby is an exceptionally upright grower. When pruning in the young stages, shoots should be cut in every case to an outside bud. This will promote an open centred tree.

REV. WILKS

2. Apple Rev. Wilks is of a spreading habit, and in order to keep the tree a good shape the pruning of young trees should be to inside buds. This will produce more upright branches.

VARIETIES OF APPLES

Apples are the easiest of all fruits to grow. The ideal soil is a deep, well-drained loam with plenty of vegetable matter worked into it. A heavy soil should be dug deeply to render it suitable for planting young trees. The vigour of apple trees varies considerably, and a heavy soil requires a stronger growing variety.

Young unpruned trees called maidens can be bought quite cheaply. For those who do not fully understand the early stages of pruning it is much better to pay an extra shilling or so and purchase a tree with the first branches already formed.

Strong-growing varieties are: Bramley's Seedling, spreading ; Lord Derby, upright ; Newton Wonder, spreading ; Warner's King, spreading ; Beauty of Bath, tends to spread to one side ; Blenheim Orange, spreading ; Wealthy, spreading ; Ribston Pippin, spreading.

Weak and dwarf varieties are: Lane's Prince Albert, spreading ; Stirling Castle, compact ; Rev. Wilks, spreading ; Cox's Orange Pippin, slightly spreading ; D'Arcy Spice, slightly spreading.

Most varieties of apples produce fruit on short shoots called spurs. Hard pruning is practised on these varieties to encourage the production of more fruit buds at the base of the shoots.

Others carry fruits at the extremities of long thin shoots and are known as tip-bearers. When pruning, do not remove the fruit bud that will be found at the end of these growths. Typical tip-bearers include Barnack Beauty, Beauty of Bath, Mr. Gladstone and Grenadier.

JAMES GRIEVE

An apple that ripens in September is James Grieve. It can be relied upon to crop regularly.

COX'S ORANGE PIPPIN

Cox's Orange Pippin is the best dessert apple for flavour. It is ready for picking early in October.

DESSERT APPLES

The following varieties of dessert apples are listed in order of ripening :—

Variety	Pick	Season of use
Irish Peach	Last week July	Eat from tree
Beauty of Bath	1st week August	Eat from tree
Devonshire Quarrenden	2nd week August	Eat from tree
St. Everard	4th week August	Eat from tree
Worcester Pearmain	2nd week September	September to October
King of the Pippins	2nd week September	September to October
Allington Pippin	3rd week September	October to December
James Grieve	3rd week September	September to October
Ellison's Orange	4th week September	September to October
Charles Ross	1st week October	October to December
Blenheim Orange	2nd week October	November to January
Cox's Orange Pippin	2nd week October	November to March
Barnack Beauty	2nd week October	December to March
Ribston Pippin	3rd week October	December
Fearn's Pippin	3rd week October	December to March
Annie Elizabeth	3rd week October	December to May
D'Arcy Spice	3rd week October	March to May
Reinette de Canada	3rd week October	March to May

RELIABLE COOKING APPLES

Where space is limited and only one tree of cooking apples can be grown this should be a Bramley's Seedling. This variety can be picked for use before it is fully ripe, and when the fruit is ready for gathering it can be kept in store until March for use as required. The following half-dozen are the best cooking apples : Bramley's Seedling, Early Victoria, Golden Noble, Lane's Prince Albert, Lord Derby, Newton Wonder.

TWO GOOD CROPPERS

The fruiting branch shown in the picture on the right is of Lane's Prince Albert, a good quality cooking apple which keeps well. It is a regular and heavy cropper.

The tray of apples seen below is the dessert variety Ellison's Orange, a medium-sized well-coloured apple of good flavour ready for use in October. It is the result of a cross taken from the well-known Cox's Orange Pippin and is becoming increasingly popular.

A group of bush pears in a mixed garden.

GROWING PEARS

Pears, like apples, require a deep well-drained soil with plenty of humus, especially in the young stages. Newly planted pear trees are apt to stand still for a year or two, due partly to faulty planting, but chiefly to insufficient food of a nitrogenous character. Manure and decaying leaves added to the soil at planting time will prevent this.

Pears will succeed on heavy soils if attention is paid to drainage. As with most plants, waterlogging is fatal, so dig the ground really deeply before planting. Aspect is another factor to which pears are very accommodating. By careful choice of varieties, they can be grown on north as well as on south walls.

As pears bloom fairly early in the year, they are likely to be damaged by late spring frosts, so that where a sheltered position is available this should be selected, although it is not essential.

Like apples, suitable stocks have now been selected from the numerous ones originally used and these are now made available to nurserymen under the names of Malling A, B and C. All are quinces, but they make the best root system for all varieties of pears. Malling A produces the most vigorous tree; B, a tree of medium vigour; and C is suitable for trained types, such as cordons and espaliers.

Some varieties of pear give even better results if they are double grafted. By this it is meant that the root system is a Malling type (as above) on to which a variety of pear is grafted. A year later on to this variety is grafted a second variety which will produce the ultimate fruiting branches. This method has been found to give more certain control over age of bearing, quality and strength of tree. Choose a reliable nurseryman and you will be sure that the trees you buy are properly worked.

Upright types are trained as open centred bushes.

Doyenne du Comice grown against a wall.

VARIETIES OF PEARS

COOKING	Type of Growth		Sterility	Ready for Use	
Catillac	Strong	Spreading	Self-sterile	Dec.	The best cooker
Fertility	,,	Upright	,,	Sept.	Regular cropper
Pitmaston Duchess ...	,,	Spreading	Partially self-fertile	Oct.–Nov.	Very large fruit
DESSERT					
Beurré d'Amanlis ...	,,	,,	Self-sterile	Sept.	A good cropper
,, Hardy ...	,,	,,	,,	Oct.	Excellent flavour
,, Superfine ...	,,	,,	Rarely self-fertile	Sept.–Oct.	Very juicy
Clapp's Favourite ...	,,	Upright	Self-fertile	Mid. Aug.	Use immediately
Conference	Weak	Spreading	,,	Nov.–Dec.	Very juicy
Dr. Jules Guyot ...	,,	,,	,,	Early Sept.	Good flavour
Doyenne du Comice	,,	,,	,,	Oct.–Nov.	Exquisite flavour
Durondeau	,,	,,	Sometimes self-fertile	Oct.–Nov.	Tender and highly flavoured
Emile d'Heyst ...	,,	,,	Rarely self-fertile	Oct.	Juicy, use immediately
Jargonelle	Strong	,,	,,	Aug.	Rich and juicy
Josephine de Malines	Weak	,,	Self-sterile	Jan.–March	Juicy flavour
Laxton's Superb ...	,,	,,	Partially self-fertile	Aug.	Heavy cropper
Louise Bonne of Jersey	,,	Upright	Partially self-fertile	Oct.	Excellent flavour
Marie Louise	,,	Spreading	Self-fertile	Oct.–Nov.	Superb flavour
Pitmaston Duchess ...	Strong	,,	Partially self-fertile	Oct.–Nov.	Good flavour. Also for cooking
Williams's Bon Chrètien	Weak	Upright	Self-fertile	Aug.–Sept.	Good flavour. Use immediately
Winter Nelis ...	,,	Spreading	Rarely self-fertile	Nov.–Feb.	Small deliciously flavoured fruits

STANDARD PLUMS

Plums grown as standard trees will yield a larger crop than bushes. They should be grafted on Myrobalan B stock.

PLUM GROWING

Plums require a light soil such as sand, gravel or chalk. The latter is the most suitable, as a certain amount of lime is necessary. Sandy and gravelly soils need to have lime added at the time of planting. Mortar rubble is a convenient form, and each autumn in the following years hydrated lime can be applied to the surface soil.

This should be applied at the rate of $\frac{1}{2}$ lb. per square yard. Scatter it on the soil surface under the trees to the extent of the branches.

Lime or any of the fertilizers should not be heaped round the bole of a tree as it is the tips of the roots that are the feeding organs. As the branches extend, so do the roots. Thus, the spread of the branches indicates approximately the position of these root tips under the soil.

Liming promotes " stoning " in plums, and although the fruit may set it will not mature if there is lack of lime. Fertilizers must be given in addition to keep a healthy balanced tree increasing in size gradually each year, and at the same time

bearing regularly. Suitable fertilizers are nitrate of soda and sulphate of ammonia. Care must be taken using these manures, and no dressing given if the trees become sappy and produce too much leaf growth.

Like apples and pears, plums are grafted, and in this case a wild plum is used. The two types selected and now used by all good nurserymen are Myrobalan B, for vigorous trees, and the Common Mussel, for dwarf trees.

Plums are most frequently grown as standards, although for limited space bush trees can be had. For walls they may be trained as fan-shaped trees, and in this case a south or west wall must be selected as plums bloom very early in the year. In other aspects they would be liable to damage by cold winds and frosts.

Where birds are troublesome, small trees can be cottoned or large areas sprayed with a bud protective spray. Trees on walls can be covered with fish netting, which will, in addition, keep off frosts.

BUSH PLUMS

Plums grown as bushes are convenient where space is very limited or where the shadow cast by a large standard would be a nuisance. For bush trees choose varieties grafted on to the Common Mussel stock.

PLUMS

Varieties for standards or bushes. *Dessert :* Oullin's Golden Gage, Denniston's Superb, Early Transparent Gage, Jefferson, Reine Claude de Bavay, Coe's Golden Drop, Comte d'Althan's Gage, Pershore, Late Transparent. *Cooking :* Czar, Purple Pershore, Victoria.

Varieties for growing on a wall or fence. *South aspect :* Early Transparent Gage, Denniston's Superb, Jefferson, Coe's Golden Drop, Reine Claude de Bavay, Golden Transparent. *North aspect :* Czar, Victoria, Oullin's Golden Gage. *West aspect :* Early Transparent Gage, Oullin's Golden Gage, Denniston's Superb, Jefferson, Victoria, Czar. *East aspect :* Comte d'Althan's Gage, Victoria, Coe's Golden Drop.

Varieties of spreading growth. *Red plums :* Comte d'Althan's Gage, Victoria. *Yellow plums :* Coe's Golden Drop, Pershore. *Purple plums :* Czar, Purple Pershore.

Varieties of upright growth. *Yellow plums :* Denniston's Superb, Jefferson, Late Transparent, Oullin's Golden Gage, Reine Claude de Bavay.

Pollination. " No fruit following excessive flowering " is the complaint of numerous amateur plum-growers. The importance of pollination must be remembered. Only three of the best varieties are self-fertile. These are Czar, Purple Pershore and Victoria. All others must be cross pollinated with another plum nearby. Unless bees and other insects can carry pollen from one to the other, no fruit will set, however freely blossom is produced.

Order of ripening:—

Early Transparent Gage	Early Aug.
Czar	Early Aug.
Oullin's Golden Gage	Mid-Aug.
Denniston's Superb	Mid-Aug.
Pershore	Aug.
Purple Pershore	Late Aug.
Reine Claude de Bavay	Early Sept.-Oct.
Jefferson	Early Sept.
Late Transparent	Sept.
Victoria	Sept.
Coe's Golden Drop	End Sept.
Golden Transparent	Oct.

Damson. The Merryweather.

DAMSONS

Damsons require a similar soil to plums and general treatment is also the same. In windswept gardens they are frequently used as shelter trees. They will withstand gales, and if planted along the boundary of the garden will provide a certain amount of protection for other plants and trees.

The trees require little attention and no pruning is necessary beyond the occasional removal of dead or badly placed branches. Paint over any large wound made with tar or specially prepared paint to keep out the spores of fungus diseases which can enter the healthy wood through newly-made cuts.

Varieties of damsons. Aylesbury Prune, ready October to November ; large fruit, reliable cropper. Bradley's King of the Damsons, ready September ; medium size, good flavour. Farleigh Prolific, ready September ; small, poor flavour, very heavy cropper. Merryweather Damson, ready September ; very large fruit, used for cooking. Shropshire Damson, ready September ; large fruit, best for jam.

A cherry orchard in bloom.

CHERRY GROWING

For the successful culture of all cherries the soil must be light and well drained. Gardens on sand or chalk will give the best results, but a heavy loam can be made quite suitable if it is very deeply dug prior to planting and some system of drainage adopted. A heavy clay soil cannot, however, be brought into a suitable condition for cherries though a medium clay over a light sub-soil such as gravel often produces heavy crops of good quality fruit.

The sweet cherries require as much sun as possible, but sour cherries, particularly the Morello, can be grown successfully on a north wall.

The remarks on liming made under the heading of plums also applies to cherry growing. Lime is required for successful stoning, and other fertilizers needed are basic slag in autumn or superphosphate and muriate of potash in the spring, unless the trees are not growing freely. Then a balanced fertilizer, such as the 1:3:1 mixture described elsewhere, would be more suitable, applied at the rate of 4 oz. per square yard.

Cherries, too, have a special root stock on to which good varieties are grafted. This is the Gean, *Prunus avium*. Others formerly used are no longer considered worth while, so intending planters are advised to make sure that they obtain cherries grafted on the Gean.

Cherries are most frequently grown as standards, although bushes can be had. They are very beautiful trees when laden with their white blossom and could very effectively be made part of the ornamental flower garden. They will grow well as specimens in the lawn, for cherries are one of the best fruit trees for planting in grass. A small grass orchard of cherries is another idea that can be added to the garden as a feature. The diagram illustrates how a vacant corner of the plot can be turned into an attractive part of the garden scheme.

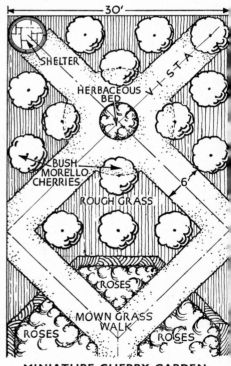

MINIATURE CHERRY GARDEN

The beauty of a cherry orchard can be reproduced in miniature using bush Morello trees planted in rough grass that has mown pathways.

A wall or fence can be covered with a trained cherry tree. On north walls Morello cherries will grow well, but on a south or west wall sweet cherries can be grown.

Varieties. *Sweet cherries :* Black Heart, early July. Frogmore Early, early July ; large, pale yellow, mottled with red. Early Rivers, end June ; large, glossy black. Bigarreau Schrecken, June ; a very early black. Governor Wood, early July ; large, yellow and red variety. Napoleon, white. Waterloo, large, deep black, red flesh of good flavour. *Sour cherries :* Morello, large, round, dark red, deepening to purple when ripe. Kentish Red, end of July ; acid, red. *Duke cherries :* May Duke, June ; agreeable acid flavour.

Pollination. Cherry growing, as far as the setting of fruit is concerned, is even more complex than plum, as in addition to many varieties being self-sterile (not setting fruit with their own pollen) there are many that will not

YOUNG FAN CHERRY
Cherry trees grown against a wall should be trained as a fan. This work must be started when the tree is only a year or two old, and when purchasing you should tell your nursery-man that it is to be grown in this way.

cross pollinate either with certain varieties.

Much experimental work has been carried out and results enable the experts to advise on suitable varieties to grow in the gardens. The results are too extensive to give here, but the following are a few of the successful combinations :—

Black Heart   + Early Rivers or Big-
                   arreau Frogmore.
Early Rivers   + Governor Wood, or
                   Waterloo.
Governor Wood + Emperor Francis, or
                   Big. Frogmore.

Big. Frogmore, Big. Napoleon and Big. Schrecken appear to pollinate numerous varieties.

Three self-fertile varieties are Morello, Late Duke and Flemish Red.

Order of ripening. Early Rivers, mid-June ; Governor Wood, end of June ; Knight's Early Black, early June ; Black Heart, mid-July ; Kent Bigarreau, end of July ; Big. Napoleon, early August.

CHERRY WOOD
To keep the trunk clean spray the whole tree each winter with a tar oil wash.

GOOSEBERRIES

Soil. Gooseberries will grow on almost any soil. The extremes of heavy and light only should be avoided.

This fruit is generally grown as a bush, although cordons can be trained. In an orchard these plants can be set 4 ft. to 6 ft. apart between the apple and pear trees, but where kitchen garden and fruit garden are combined a row can be planted in any convenient part provided the position is sunny. Lack of a free circulation of air is the greatest deterrent to growth. This encourages mildew, which affects both the shoot and the fruit.

Planting. Bushes or cordons can be put in any time from autumn to spring. Plant 6 ft. apart.

Manures. Gooseberries respond to both organic and artificial manures. If farmyard manure is obtainable, dig that in before planting and during the lifetime of the bush apply fish or meat meal in the spring, 4 oz. per square yard. An alternative is to use basic slag, 4 oz. per square yard, if you have a heavy soil, or kainit if it is light, applied at the same rate.

Gooseberry grown as a standard.

Lime is essential for good gooseberries, and should be given each autumn, 8 oz. per square yard.

Cultivation. Frequent hoeing during the summer months to keep the soil open and control weeds. Give a light forking between the bushes in late autumn and leave the surface rough.

Pruning. Gooseberry bushes will gradually increase in diameter, so that a further number of branches can be allowed to grow. Most young bushes start life with five or six branches. Prune to avoid overcrowding by removing dead and weak shoots. Sun and air should be able to enter the bushes on all sides to ripen both fruit and wood.

If branches tend to droop, cut them back to a suitable upward pointing bud and those tending towards the centre to an outward facing bud.

Varieties. Careless, for cooking, green; Lancashire Lad, for dessert, red ; White Lion, for dessert, white.

Note the open framework of branches on this young gooseberry bush just breaking into leaf. There is no danger of mildew where air can circulate freely. Cut back branches that droop.

BLACK CURRANTS

Soil. Of all soft fruits black currants need the most moisture. They will grow well in a heavy soil, provided there is some form of drainage to prevent the roots being waterlogged.

Shelter, too, is an advantage as it assists in the pollination of the blossoms.

Manures. Organic matter gives the best crops. If you can obtain any spent hops this is excellent for mulching the bushes in autumn.

Planting and pruning. Autumn is the best season and the bushes should be 4 ft. to 6 ft. apart. Bushes are the only form of black currants. After planting young bushes all the shoots should be cut down to two buds to encourage strong healthy shoots to spring from the base. Good black currant bushes should produce such new basal shoots every year enabling old worn out shoots to be

BLACK CURRANT FRUITING

The fruit clusters of black currants are produced on the young shoots of the previous season's growth.

removed. In the following year if three shoots are more than 2 ft. long they can be left uncut and all others again cut back to two buds.

After the initial pruning, to form the foundation of a bush that will be productive for many years, pruning consists of cutting out the oldest wood and weak shoots : weak growth is a burden on any tree and will never be fruitful.

Cultivation. Beyond keeping down weeds, little attention is required. The only likely trouble is an appearance of big bud. Picking off any swollen buds may remedy the trouble, but a surer means is by spraying. When the leaves are the size of a shilling spray with lime sulphur.

Varieties. Baldwin, a very prolific short-bunched variety ; Goliath, large sweet fruit with tender skin ; Boskoop Giant, vigorous grower with large berries, rich and sweet ; Davison's Eight, heavy cropper, large juicy berries ; Laxton's Raven, strong grower producing very heavy crops.

BLACK CURRANT IN WINTER

Black currant bushes should be kept as open as possible to admit plenty of air. During the annual pruning in winter cut out old wood, leaving young wood to carry the next season's crop. Remove dead, broken and weak shoots. The bush shown still needs thinning and the broken branch should be cut at the nearest outward pointing bud.

RED CURRENTS

Soil. Red currants are lovers of light soil—sand, gravel or chalk, and are most unhappy in any that is at all cold and damp. They will, however, grow under apples, pears and plums quite successfully and so in the small garden can occupy that space in which few fruits or vegetables can be grown productively.

Types. Red currants have a different habit from the black currant, the clusters of fruit hanging from the same spurs on old wood year after year. In this way it is possible to grow bushes with or without a small " leg " and train single, double and triple cordons.

Bushes should be planted 5 ft. apart, but of course, cordons can be as close as 1 ft., if only one stem is taken up.

Manures. This currant requires less organic manure and more artificial, particularly potash and phosphates, than the black form. Apply in the spring a little farmyard manure to each bush, about a forkful, as a mulch, and a dusting during the growing season of 2 oz. sulphate of potash, 2 oz. superphosphate and 1 oz. sulphate of ammonia.

Pruning. Training in the early stages of the red currant consists of obtaining

RED CURRANT FRUITING
The fruit of red currants is produced on spurs of old wood which remain fruitful for many years. Be careful to protect against birds.

six or seven main branches placed at equal distances to form an open-centred basin-shaped bush. These main branches are then each treated as a cordon and closely spur pruned each winter. It is an advantage to cut the laterals to 4 in. in length before picking the fruits. This helps to swell the fruit buds at the base of the shoot for next year's fruit. The leading shoots are cut annually to within 6 in. of the base of the current year's growth.

Varieties. Raby Castle, late bearer ; Fay's Prolific, very large berry, easily broken.

WHITE CURRANTS

White currants are similar to red currants in flavour and are used chiefly for dessert.

Their method of growth and fruit production is the same, and they are cultivated in the same way as red currants in every respect.

Varieties. White Dutch, prolific cropper, very good flavour ; White La Versaillaise, large and sweet.

RED CURRANT IN WINTER
Red currant bush after pruning. Note the open framework of seven main branches each treated as a cordon; the side shoots have been spurred back and only the leaders left long, to produce new shoots to form additional spurs.

Strawberries starting to ripen. The bed well strawed and netted.

GROWING STRAWBERRIES

Soil. Any soil that is warm, firm, and will work into a fine tilth is suitable. The position selected needs to be sheltered so that late spring frosts do no harm to the flowers. Varieties can be selected to suit the particular soil and so make a good crop more certain. For heavy soils choose Sir Joseph Paxton, while on a light soil grow Royal Sovereign. Where the soil is peaty, Jucunda will do best.

Planting. August to October is the season for making new strawberry beds, the earlier the better. Choose a showery period so the plants have a good chance of taking root. The depth to plant is important. You will find each plant has a crown, and this should be level with the soil surface. If it is too deep or too shallow poor results will follow, if the plant does not fail entirely. Too shallow planting is even worse than too deep.

If you are unable to plant until spring, give the plants a chance to establish themselves before they are called upon to bear a crop.

Strawberry beds are planted with year-old plants set in rows 1 ft. apart.

The life of a strawberry bed is from three to four years, and the best crop is from plants in their second year. In order, therefore, to have plants in the garden that are always at their peak, part of the bed should be replanted annually, a third or a quarter according to whether plants are to remain three or four years.

Cultivation. Strawberries are surface rooting so the soil cannot be deeply cultivated. Keep the hoe going on the surface until it is time to put straw in position. Top dress with guano in spring.

As soon as the weight of the fruit bears down the trusses, it is time to straw the plants. Clean dry straw should be used, and not only does it help to keep the fruits clean but it acts as a mulch and conserves the moisture supply. If mildew should make an appearance, dust the plants with flowers of sulphur when the dew is still on them.

When all the fruit has been gathered, the straw should be removed and attention may then be paid to the runners.

Varieties. Royal Sovereign, Sir Joseph Paxton, Jucunda, Tardive de Leopold.

Strawberries in the greenhouse. The fruit has been thinned to produce large berries.

Propagation. The best method of propagation is by layering runners early in July. Vigorous runners with compact centres should be selected, but do not allow a plant to retain more than four runners at the most. It is best to peg down runners in small 3-in. pots rather than direct into the ground, using wire pins or wooden layering pegs. Place a small piece of turf over the drainage hole in the pot and fill up with a mixture of loam and leaf soil. The pot is then plunged into the soil, to avoid drying out of soil or upsetting. It is important to keep the soil moist.

Cultivation under glass. Propagation similar to outdoor cultivation, but young plants should be potted up about the middle of August into 6-in. pots, filled with a compost mixture of coarse turfy loam (three parts), well-rotted manure (one part), and broken up brick rubble and lime (one part). This is improved by dusting over with bonemeal and soot. Make sure the pots are well drained. Stand the pots on well rammed ashes.

Wintering in a frame. In late autumn if frosts become severe, pots should be sunk up to the rim in ashes in a cold frame, but with care not to let leaves come close to the glass. The pots must not be allowed to become dry, and ventilation should be given whenever possible.

Forcing. It is possible to have strawberries early in April if pots are moved about the middle of January and placed on shelves near the glass in a vinery or peach house ; if these are not available a heated frame will serve just as well. The heat should be gradual at first (50 degrees Fahrenheit by night and rising 5 degrees Fahrenheit by day, but taking due note of heat of sun).

Keep atmosphere dry while plants are in flower and each day, about midday, gently shake the flowers or dust the centre of each with a rabbit's tail to make sure of cross pollination.

Damp floors in hot weather and keep plants syringed to prevent attacks of green fly and red spider.

Raspberry Pyne's Royal.

RASPBERRY

Soil. This fruit does best in soil that will hold moisture—new ground should be trenched and manured 2 ft. deep. Stable manure should be worked in well *near the surface.* If this is not available, any decaying vegetable rubbish will help to conserve moisture.

Partial shade is an advantage, and raspberries can be grown successfully either out in the open, or in the shelter of fences or walls.

Planting. Plant young canes in November or spring, singly 2 ft. apart in rows 5 ft. from each other. When planting, dig a trench about 4 in. deep and wide enough to allow roots to be spread out horizontally. Top roots should not be more than 1 in. below the surface : do not plant too deeply. Work the soil well in among the roots, and take care not to break off the buds at the base of the cane when planting, as these will in due course produce fruiting canes.

The most practical way of supporting the canes consists of three wires strained horizontally at heights of 2 ft., 3½ ft. and 5 ft. from the ground.

Early in March cut the newly-planted canes down to within 9 in. to 12 in. from the ground, to encourage production of strong fruiting canes for the next year.

Pruning. In June cut out suckers and weak shoots. The strongest must be tied up and water given to the roots. Fruit is borne only on one-year-old shoots ; hence the importance of cutting down to the ground in the autumn all old canes that have borne fruit that season. The only other pruning which will be required consists of cutting off the sappy tops of the young canes in March to encourage formation of laterals on which the fruit is borne.

An autumn crop. It is quite possible to obtain fruit in September and October if the old canes are cut away entirely in June, thus preventing summer fruiting. Mulching with well-rotted manure in June will encourage production of flower buds which will bear fruit in the autumn. Water liberally in dry weather.

Varieties. *Summer fruiting.* Lloyd George, Laxton's Bountiful, Devon. *Autumn fruiting.* October Red, Hailsham Berry, Belle de Fontenay, Surprise d'Automne, November Abundance.

Raspberry Red Cross.

LOGANBERRY

A cross between the American raspberry and the blackberry. It is self-fertile. This fruit will grow well on heavy soils, but will thrive best on a moist, but well-drained deep rich loam. Treatment is similar to that of raspberries but the loganberry will often flourish where the former gives unsatisfactory results.

Propagation. By layering in August. The new plant should be ready for planting in permanent position in October to November. Propagation by division of roots in October is also practised.

1. Loganberry.

Planting. Should be done in October, 5 ft. to 6 ft. apart ; the shoots should be trained fan-wise, or as an espalier on a trellis or wire fence. Growth is much more rampant than with raspberries and the plants require more careful training.

Pruning. After fruiting time, all old growths should be cut right down to the base, and only the most vigorous growing of the new shoots should be kept and carefully tied to the wires.

Plants will continue to bear fruit from 10 to 15 years.

2. Veitchberry.

BLACKBERRIES

Although common hedgerow plants will do well under cultivation, only good fruiting kinds of nursery grown stock should be used.

VEITCHBERRIES

A cross between the November Abundance raspberry and the common blackberry. The fruits are a mulberry colour and ripen after raspberries and before blackberries. Cultivation as loganberries.

LOWBERRIES

Black fruits similar in shape to the loganberry, but with the flavour of the blackberry which it also resembles in habit of growth.

3. Lowberry.

MULBERRIES

The fruit of mulberries is produced all over the tree from the axils of the leaves on the small twigs. When ripe it drops to the ground.

MULBERRY

A fine mulberry tree is often seen as a feature in old gardens, but of recent years fewer have been planted.

Almost any garden soil suits the mulberry, but on heavy clay the fruit may not ripen properly. It can tolerate the smoky conditions of town gardens, but appreciates a position on a wall or in a sheltered corner in cold localities.

Mulberry leaves are much in demand by children who keep silkworms, as the worms thrive on them.

The fruits resemble large red blackberries and have a pleasant acid flavour ; they ripen in August and September and fall from the tree when ripe. For this reason mulberries are best planted in lawns, where the falling fruit can be gathered easily. When the tree is on dug ground, much of the fruit is spoilt by getting covered with soil. Mulberry jelly can be made and the berries are delicious in tarts.

QUINCE

Quinces are seldom grown for their fruit these days, the chief use being as a stock for grafting pear trees ; for this purpose they are raised in vast quantities by nurserymen.

A light soil with an ample supply of moisture is best for quinces, and a full-grown tree 15 ft. to 20 ft. high is a lovely sight in flower.

The fruit should be left to ripen late on the trees : they do not keep very long and are easily bruised. November is the usual time for gathering the fruit.

Quinces are used for making jams and jellies, which are great favourites with many people. The addition of a small proportion of quinces to an apple pie gives a distinctive flavour.

Some varieties of quince are called apple-shaped : these have large golden yellow fruits rather like an apple. Champion is an American variety of this type and is a vigorous grower.

The pear-shaped quince is another type which is usually grown as an ornamental tree ; it produces a large crop, but the flavour is inferior to the apple-shaped variety.

Portugal quince produces a smaller crop than the others, but the fruits are larger and have a better flavour ; it is particularly suitable for culinary purposes and turns red when cooked.

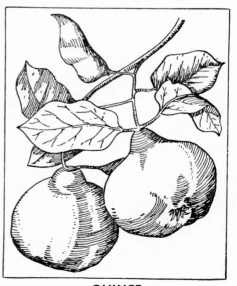

QUINCE

The fruit is a rich golden-yellow and has a powerful yet pleasant smell.

VARIETIES OF NUTS

Hazel, or Cobnut and Filbert. In this country, Kent is the home of the nut; but where the wild hazel grows is a sure guide to the suitability of the local soil. If hazels grow near your home you can plant nuts with a good chance of success. Good drainage is necessary and loam overlying chalk or sand is best.

Nuts do well under dense shade, so here is a useful subject for that awkward spot in your garden. If you are planting more than one bush, put them at least 15 ft. apart—or more if possible.

They do not require staking when planted. The trees are trained to a basin shape and pruned in late February or early March. By this time the female flowers will have been pollinated by the catkins and there will be no fear of severing shoots that bear the catkins before their work is completed. The leaders are shortened and the laterals thinned and shortened. Wood that fruited the previous year must be spurred back, as for apples, to two or three buds.

Suckers springing from the base are a very great source of trouble and must be broken away. Do not cut; this only increases the trouble. These suckers are called "wands" and are very useful as garden sticks, growing often 4 ft. to 6 ft. high and very straight.

Nuts should be in cultivated ground and not grass. Avoid quick-acting nitrogenous fertilizers. Fur or hair waste or shoddy material is the most satisfactory.

Nuts are ready for gathering about mid-September when the bushes are turning yellow. They can be kept dried and stored in a heap, but this should be turned constantly.

The **sweet** or **Spanish chestnut** thrives in a light gravelly loam in full sun. Though produced in large quantities, the nuts in this country are generally rather small. Plantations of chestnuts are chiefly used for the production of poles; the shoots from the base develop into fine straight stakes, the wood is hard and does not rot quickly.

The **walnut** is a good tree for a large garden. It has some properties repellent to flies, and any one sitting under a walnut will not be bothered by midges or gnats—a great consideration on summer evenings.

Research is being done to discover a really satisfactory strain of walnuts which is hardy in this country and produces good quality, large-sized nuts.

1. Cannon Ball.　2. Cosford Cob.　3. White-skinned Filbert.　4. Kentish Cob.

1. A well-trained fig tree in a sunny position.

CULTURE OF FIGS

Figs are sometimes called the lazy man's fruit. In the southern counties they thrive well, especially if given the protection of a wall.

Soil should be poor and well drained, with an ample quantity of lime and plenty of water given when the fruit swells. Very little pruning is needed, but trees growing too rampantly may be root pruned. The tree forms two crops of fruit each year, but only the autumn crop ripens in this climate ; the fruit is ready for picking when it turns brownish purple and parts easily from the branch. Birds are very fond of the fruit and sometimes ruin most of the fruit by pecking at each one.

Figs grown on walls are usually fan trained and need a certain amount of pruning ; restricted root growth will counteract the tendency to form too much leaf.

The variety Brown Turkey is most frequently grown, though Negro Largo and White Marseilles are also often seen in gardens.

2. Fruiting branch of fig.

A FAN TRAINED PLUM

When plums are chosen for wall culture only the very best dessert varieties should be planted. Coe's Golden Drop has fruits of amber colour with red spots and is a good cropper.

FRUIT TREES ON WALLS

A well-built brick wall provides the perfect background for trained fruit trees. They retain the heat of the sun and generally have a smooth surface. Stone walls can also be used, but all cracks and fissures should be filled with cement, as these harbour pests which attack the trees and ripening fruits. Plant the choicer dessert varieties of fruits against walls and get the full benefit of well-ripened fruits.

Every aspect will grow something, and the following are a few suggestions :

North walls. *Pears :* Marie Louise d'Uccle, Roosevelt. *Cherries :* Morello.

South walls. *Apricots :* Frogmore Early, Moorpark. *Nectarines :* John Rivers. *Peaches :* Duchess of Cornwall, Golden Eagle. *Figs :* Brown Turkey. *Vines :* Royal Muscadine, Black Hamburgh.

West walls. *Plums :* Coe's Golden Drop, Giant Prune, Victoria. *Pears .* Jargonelle. *Red currants :* Comet, Laxton's Perfection. *Gooseberries :* Howard's Lancer, Leveller, May Duke.

East walls. *Pears :* Late flowering varieties. *Apples :* Late flowering varieties. *Gooseberries :* Lord Derby. *Cherries.* Morello.

Trees grown against walls need to be trained and the fan-shaped style is the most usual. Various forms of cordons and espalier trees are also popular. The best method of securing the branches is to tie them to straining wires. These are placed at intervals of 12 in. to 18 in. up the wall, and 4 in. to 6 in. from it. The wires may be secured to posts at either end or attached to special wall nails. Trees grown in this way do not receive much rain and should, therefore, be thoroughly watered periodically during spells of dry weather in summer.

permanent wooden framework covered with netting to protect soft fruits from birds.

PROTECTING FRUIT FROM BIRDS

Do you find birds troublesome? Most soft fruits, such as strawberries, raspberries and currants, are frequently damaged by birds. To avoid this a fruit cage may be erected. If you have any spare timber, a permanent one can be constructed for a small cost—well worthwhile when you think of the labour and the value of the fruit saved. Erect the framework of timber and cover the whole with wire netting. Leave a door at one end, and make sure that this fastens securely so that birds cannot get in through it blowing open.

A cage of a less permanent nature may be made from fish netting. A portable timber framework should be set up and hemp netting thrown over this. Care must be taken to see that the strips are joined thoroughly and lap over sufficiently at the entrance to prevent birds getting through at this point.

When planting your soft fruits, remember this need for protection from birds, and plant them near one another in a neat formation so that one cage will serve the entire quantity of soft fruit bushes.

Against a wall it is a simple matter to throw netting from the top and an even better idea is to erect a small canopy framework at the top of a fence or wall so that the netting hangs in front of but not touching the branches.

In large orchards where birds are troublesome and netting impossible owing to the size of the trees and cost of the netting, various methods such as the scarecrow and hanging tins to frighten birds are tried. These are seldom much use. The occasional firing of a gun will help to keep birds away, or a small boy walking through the orchard beating a tin protects the fruit to a certain extent.

We should always remember that we welcome birds to help us keep down insect pests and eat weed seeds. Provided they are not too rapacious, should we grudge them a small share of the fruits?

BEEHIVES IN AN ORCHARD

Pollination is a very important factor in fruit production. Some varieties of apples, pears, plums and cherries are self-fertile, but there are others that need the pollen of some other variety in order that the blossom may set. Insects, particularly bees, are natural carriers of such pollen, and where possible a hive may be introduced into the orchard during blossom time, as has been done in this case. Note the fruit trees trained on the walls of this barn

CROSS POLLINATION

Certain varieties of apples, pears, plums and cherries must be pollinated with another variety of the same fruit to obtain a crop.

Apples. The varieties Bramley's Seedling, Rev. W. Wilks, Stirling Castle and St. Everard are the only self-fertile ones. All other varieties need pollen from another tree, Beauty of Bath, Blenheim Orange and Cox's Orange Pippin being completely self-sterile.

Pears. The varieties Conference, Dr. Jules Guyot, Durondeau, Marie Louise and Williams's Bon Chrètien are self-fertile. All other varieties need pollen from another tree, Catillac, Doyenne du Comice, Fertility and Winter Nelis being self-sterile. As the flowering period of many varieties does not coincide, for pollination those that blossom at the same time must be grown. This information can be obtained from the nurseryman.

Plums. Self-fertile plums are Czar, Denniston's Superb, Early Transparent Gage, Farleigh Damson, Golden Transparent, Pershore, Purple Pershore, Reine Claude de Bavay (greengage) and Victoria. All other varieties require cross pollination and again it is important to grow varieties blooming at the same time.

Cherries. All sour cherries are self-fertile and sweet cherries are self-sterile. Any variety, however, will not necessarily pollinate another and when making a choice consult your fruitgrower.

Peaches. All are self-fertile, but it is advisable to pollinate the flowers by hand using a rabbit's tail on a stick, especially under glass where they bloom before many bees are flying.

Cherry tree in full bloom.

FLOWERING SEASON OF FRUIT

APPLES	PEARS	CHERRIES	PLUMS
Irish Peach	**1.** Jargonelle	**1.** Noir de Guben	**1.** Monarch
Beauty of Bath	Louise Bonne of	Early Rivers	Jefferson
Ribston Pippin	Jersey	Black Tartarian	Early Transparent
Stirling Castle	Conference	Old Black Heart	Diamond
Allington Pippin	Emile d'Heyst	Bedford Prolific	Reine Claude de
Cox's Orange Pippin		Emperor Francis	Bavay
Allison's Orange	**2.** Beurre Superfin	Black Eagle	Denniston's Superb
James Grieve	Beurre Hardy		Coe's Golden Drop
King of the Pippins	Winter Nelis	**2.** Bigarreau de	
Worcester Pearmain	Josephine de Malines	Schrecken	**2.** Golden Trans-
		Governor Wood	parent
Barnack Beauty	**3.** Catillac	Roundell	Victoria
Bramley's Seedling	Fertility	Waterloo	Barleigh Damson
Charles Ross	Laxton's Superb	May Duke	Compte d'Althan's
St. Everard	Williams's Bon	Napoleon	Gage
Blenheim Orange	Chèrtien	Amber	
Laxton's Superb	Dr. Jules Guyot		**3.** Pershore
Lord Derby	Doyenne du Comice	**3.** Morello	Purple Pershore
Rev. W. Wilks	Marie Louise	Kentish Red	Czar
Early Victoria		Tradescant's Heart	Pond's Seedling
Lane's Prince Albert			Late Transparent
			Oullin's Golden Gage
Annie Elizabeth			
Gascoyne's Scarlet			
Royal Jubilee			
Crawley Beauty			

Varieties given in the lists above bloom approximately at the same time and will pollinate each other.

FERTILIZERS FOR FRUITS

Apples. In early years trees require nitrogenous manure to build up the head of the tree, then a balanced fertilizer should be given each spring. If the leaves show marginal browning, potash is needed; if growth is excessively vigorous and fruit greasy and of poor keeping quality, the trees are getting too much nitrogen; but if the leaves are small and yellow, nitrogen is needed.

Pears. The general requirements are the same as for apples. Apply farmyard manure in autumn; this is specially necessary for young trees. In autumn give 4 oz. basic slag and 1 oz. kainit to a square yard, and in spring 2 oz. superphosphate and 1 oz. sulphate of ammonia to a square yard.

Plums. The most important requirement is lime. Where this is not present in sufficient quantities in the soil, dressings should be given annually. The trees grow vigorously by nature and only on exceptionally poor soils need nitrogenous manures. When the new wood shoots are very short and weak fertilizers are needed. Light dressings of an all-round fertilizer for a couple of seasons will bring the tree back into full vigour.

Cherries. An essential factor in the successful culture of cherries is lime, and if they are not being grown on a chalky soil a dressing of $\frac{1}{2}$ lb. per square yard should be given in the spring. During their early years, nitrogenous fertilizers will be needed to encourage the growth of the main branches. After this the land may be grassed down when no further manure will be necessary.

Gooseberries. Gooseberries, like black currants, need plenty of manure. If manure of an organic nature is not available, give a heavy dressing of basic slag if the soil is heavy or kainit in the case of light soils. From 2 oz. to 4 oz. per square yard is an average amount.

Black Currants. This fruit has to produce a certain amount of new wood each year to keep the bushes strong and healthy and therefore give best results if they are mulched each summer with farmyard manure, spent hops, or some similar organic material. They do not respond always to artificial fertilizers. Fish, meat and bonemeal can, however be given.

Red and White Currants. Crops on these bushes are carried on old wood and do not need so much organic matter. They will respond to artificial fertilizers, particularly potash. A little nitrate of soda and superphosphate should, however, be included in the general feedings, especially if the new wood is short and weak.

Strawberries. Ground freshly prepared for this fruit requires deep digging with free supply of organic matter dug in. Animal is best if obtainable. Artificial manures given after planting and in subsequent seasons should be of an organic nature, such as bone and meat meal or guano applied at the rate of 4 oz. per square yard. During the early spring mineral fertilizers consisting of sulphate of ammonia, sulphate of potash and superphosphate can be applied.

Raspberries. This fruit has to produce entirely new wood each season and therefore a plentiful supply of food should be available. This is most easily given by applying a dressing of farmyard manure each spring. A suitable substitute is a hop manure or other organic material. Artificial fertilizers are not required, but a plentiful supply of water is important if the season is dry.

Loganberries. These and other berried fruits are not so exacting in their requirements, but an annual top dressing in autumn and spring is certainly beneficial. Grown against walls this top dressing helps to conserve the moisture in the border.

Figs. Too rich a soil is not recommended for this fruit, only if the tree fails to make a fair amount of growth each season should organic manure be given. Against a sunny wall grass cuttings laid on the soil helps to retain moisture.

1. Cluster of apples before thinning, young fruits very overcrowded.

THINNING FRUIT

Branches of fruit trees, especially standard or half-standard trees should not be allowed to carry an excessive quantity. During June a certain amount falls naturally, but after this " June drop " hand thinning will probably be necessary. No diseased, misplaced or touching fruit should remain on the tree. In the case of apples and pears, they should be thinned to approximately 6 in. apart : this varies with the size of the variety. By doing this each fruit will grow to a better size and shape and will colour evenly and be of good flavour. Remove leaves that shadow the fruit.

2. The same cluster thinned, each fruit with room to develop.

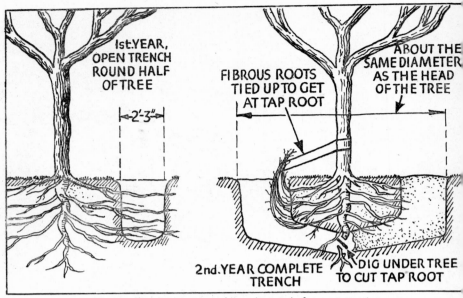

Diagram showing position of trenches made for root pruning.

INCREASING FRUITFULNESS

Beginners often think that the more manure they can give their fruit trees the heavier will be the crop. This is not so. A tree which is growing very rapidly and producing long shoots does not make fruit buds in such quantities as one making less leaf growth.

Various methods can be adopted to counteract this production of too much wood and several of them will be decribed in detail. Before starting any of these laborious methods be certain that the trouble is not due solely to the application of too much fertilizers. Reduce the dressings given for a season and if the tree continues to grow too fast start more drastic treatment.

ROOT PRUNING

Root pruning is a method of trenching around the tree to cut away the tap roots. This has the same effect as "ringing" in helping a tree to become more fruitful. It needs to be done carefully. I once carried out the operation on a pear tree grown against a wall which, owing to an exceptionally dry summer, caused th loss of the tree.

We root prune the tree, of course, whe it is transplanted, because no matter ho carefully this operation is done consider able quantities of roots are removed whe a tree or shrub is lifted. In nurseries, tree are lifted every year so that they are in fit condition to be moved when ordere by clients without undue loss of roc system.

When root pruning to induce a tre to become more fruitful, I would recom mend that it be done in halves. Tr cutting a semicircular trench, say 3 f away from the tree. Work under th tree root and cut away any tap roots m below say 18 in. or 2 ft. of soil. This shown in the diagram. This will hav some effect in restricting the growth the tree, and if you notice that it increas the fruitfulness but does not quite retar the growth sufficiently, you can the after two years, root prune the other hal The operation is best carried out durin the winter, when the tree is dormant.

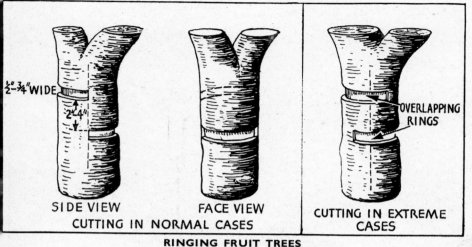

SIDE VIEW   FACE VIEW

CUTTING IN NORMAL CASES

CUTTING IN EXTREME CASES

RINGING FRUIT TREES

Left: Half-rings removed.   *Right:* Overlapping rings.

Trees, such as cherries, plums, pears and apples, may be treated in this way.

The only roots that need to be cut away during root pruning are the thick anchorage roots and not the fibrous roots. An important precaution after root pruning is to stake the tree securely to prevent it being blown down during a gale.

Sometimes a fruit tree—pear or apple—will produce an abundance of wood and leaves without bearing fruit. One method of promoting fruitfulness is to ring the stems as shown in the illustration.

The theory of ringing is that by cutting the bark the flow of sap from the leaves down to the roots is partly prevented. This restricts root development, thus preventing excessive growth of branches and foliage.

METHOD OF RINGING

The method is as follows : With a sharp knife remove the two half-rings of bark ½ in. wide and about 2 in. to 4 in. apart and on opposite sides of the stem. The cuts end so that a line drawn vertically up the trunk would touch the ends of the two half-rings. The best time is when the trees are in bloom. After making the cuts, pull out the bark down to the white wood and paint over the cut portion with white lead paint.

Ringing prevents the dropping of unripened apples, and cases are known where pears which have flowered without fruiting have been brought into bearing.

SUMMER PRUNING

Summer pruning is seldom performed on large standard trees, but for apples and pears grown as cordons or espaliers it is most efficacious in controlling leaf growth.

On young and vigorous trees the tips of the side shoots can be nipped out while still soft in May or June ; leaders should never be shortened. Older trees growing more slowly should be left till August, when the shoots are cut back with secateurs to five or six fully-developed leaves.

Shoots must never be cut back very severely as this would cause the dormant buds to grow and form additional shoots. Very vigorous shoots can be broken through half way and left to hang on the tree. This is unsightly, but by continuing to grow they still use sap and prevent the lower buds from developing.

All these methods conserve the strength and encourage the production of fruit buds. In addition, the removal of some leaves allows more sunlight to reach the fruit and give it colour and flavour.

SUMMER PRUNING

The photo above shows summer pruning in progress, with secateurs being used. On the right is a diagram of the branch seen above. The relative positions of two seasons' winter pruning and the intermediate summer pruning are clearly marked. Notice that the leader is left uncut in the summer and is only shortened to about eight buds during the winter pruning. Apples and pears may both be cut during the summer without damage. Plums and cherries must never be cut, as they are both liable to "gum." Any necessary summer pruning must be done by pinching out the soft tips of the shoots while still young.

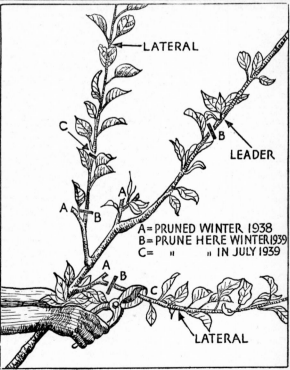

LATERAL

LEADER

A = PRUNED WINTER 1938
B = PRUNE HERE WINTER 1939
C =   "   "   IN JULY 1939

LATERAL

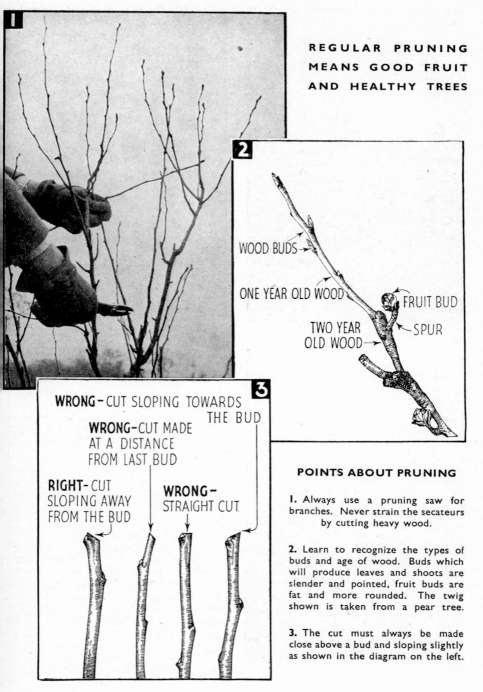

REGULAR PRUNING
MEANS GOOD FRUIT
AND HEALTHY TREES

WOOD BUDS →

ONE YEAR OLD WOOD

TWO YEAR
OLD WOOD →

FRUIT BUD

SPUR

WRONG – CUT SLOPING TOWARDS
THE BUD

WRONG – CUT MADE
AT A DISTANCE
FROM LAST BUD

RIGHT – CUT
SLOPING AWAY
FROM THE BUD

WRONG –
STRAIGHT CUT

WRONG –
STRAIGHT CUT

POINTS ABOUT PRUNING

1. Always use a pruning saw for branches. Never strain the secateurs by cutting heavy wood.

2. Learn to recognize the types of buds and age of wood. Buds which will produce leaves and shoots are slender and pointed, fruit buds are fat and more rounded. The twig shown is taken from a pear tree.

3. The cut must always be made close above a bud and sloping slightly as shown in the diagram on the left.

1. The unpruned tree.

2. Cutting a leader.

3. The completed work.

PRUNING FRUIT TREES

First decide which are the leaders, that is, the shoots that are to form the main branches, then prune all other shoots for spurs. These should be cut back from five to seven buds according to strength—the weaker the shoot the harder it should be cut—and the leaders can then be attended to.

The most important stage in the pruning of fruit trees is during the first three or four years. It is then that the framework of the tree is formed. Bush, half-standard and standard trees should all have branches radiating from the trunk more or less at the same point to form an open bowl-shaped head.

For the first three or four years after the tree is planted the leaders are cut back by a half and afterwards annually by a third of their total length. The pruning in earlier years is to encourage the production of a few really strong main shoots on each branch. Later work consists of shortening spur shoots, with leaders treated as before.

Medium sized modern greenhouse with sun-blinds.

IN THE GREENHOUSE

Only the owner of a small heated greenhouse knows the joys of gardening in the dull days of winter. As early as December the first spring bulbs give a bright and welcome contrast from the cold and dismal weather outside.

Although there are now many newer types of greenhouse on the market the one of wooden construction has not been ousted. It requires painting every two or three years, but wood has the definite advantage over other materials in that it is a slow conductor of heat. This means that it absorbs the heat of the sun slowly and is capable of holding it for a long time.

It is important to give the house a thorough cleaning every year. Choose a time between crops and wash over all the glass and woodwork with soft soap and water to which is added a little disinfectant such as carbolic or lysol. This makes certain of getting rid of any pests. The brickwork of the walls should be whitewashed, and the paths, if they are also of brick, thoroughly swilled down.

Watering is as important a part of greenhouse cultivation as ventilation and shading. Some plants like a moist atmosphere as well as water at their roots, whilst others prefer to be kept on the dry side. As a general rule very little water should be given in the winter, and more should be added as the growing season advances until the resting period is again reached. Water should not be given in driblets, but a plentiful supply applied when necessary, filling the pot to the rim. Rapping the pots with a rammer or the knuckles shows whether or not water is required : a high-pitched tone denotes dryness.

Do not give water when it is not needed as this makes the soil waterlogged. On hot days spray the paths and walls of the greenhouse with water. Not all plants like water on their leaves, and care should be taken not to cause mildew and damping off by this method.

SITING YOUR GREENHOUSE

1. Sudden bursts of sunshine in spring and early summer can do untold damage to plants under glass. It is necessary to guard against this, but not, as here, by using trees for shade.

SHADING FROM SUN

2. The most convenient form of shading is slatted blinds which can be pulled up or down according to the weather. Another method is to give the glass a light coating of "Summer Cloud," a pale green wash; ordinary whitewash can be used, but this is too dense to be effective.

SECTIONAL GREENHOUSE

The metal greenhouse can be readily assembled by the amateur. Moreover, it is sectional and can be extended at any time. The wooden staging is movable and can be taken away if the house is needed for tomatoes, or any crop which can be planted direct in the ground.

METAL AND CONCRETE

The value of this new type of greenhouse is the wide expanse of glass admitting all the available light and sunshine. All the rest of the construction is of concrete which eliminates the possibility of rotting and has no crevices to harbour pests. Suitable for town gardens.

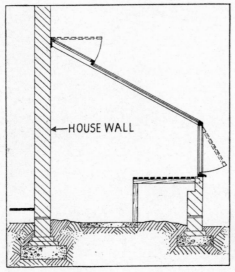

Section of lean-to greenhouse.

LEAN-TO GREENHOUSE

A lean-to greenhouse enables the gardener to take full advantage of a bare wall. A southern aspect allows for a wide choice of plants, but any aspect other than due north can be satisfactorily employed.

THREE-QUARTER SPAN

A three-quarter span is a more elaborate method of constructing a greenhouse against a wall. It affords light and ventilation on both sides, the ridge being

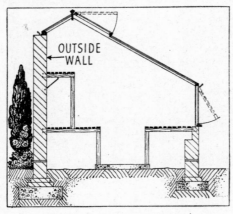

Section of three-quarter-span greenhouse.

slightly higher than the top of the wall.

In the three-quarter-span type of house staging can be had on both sides of the path. Against the wall it should be raised on two levels to enable the plants to gain the maximum light. In a lean-to house a border for a vine, peach or ornamental climber is left against the wall.

VENTILATION

Top ventilation is the most essential of all types. Wherever possible the ventilators should be on both sides so that opening can be adjusted according to the wind. Always ventilate with a rising

Span-roof greenhouse.

temperature and never allow the thermometer to stand too high before air is given, thus causing a sudden drop. Side ventilation is only used in summer weather when it cannot cause a draught. Always close the house early, particularly in the duller months, so as to shut some of the sunshine into the house to maintain a genial atmosphere during the night. This applies to both types of ventilators.

STAGING

Having decided upon the type of heating apparatus and ventilators the interior plan of the greenhouse should be considered. Shelves should be arranged so that water does not drip on to plants below. The path should be no more than

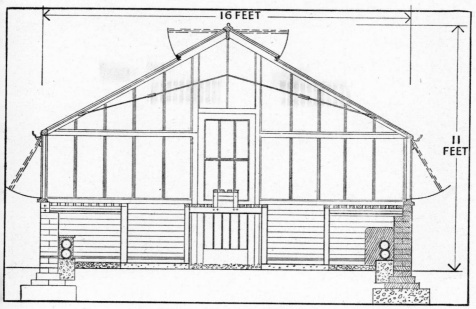

Section of span-roof greenhouse.

the width of the door, usually 2 ft. 6 in. Staging of slatted wood to allow free circulation of air around the plants is most often used. Solid stagings of sheet zinc, or other metals which do not rust, supported on solid wooden framework, are often used in conservatories. These must be covered with coarse sand, washed pebbles, or clean small clinkers. This has the advantage of conserving moisture and during the annual cleaning can be washed,

in a sieve. When adopting this method the edge of the staging can be clothed with tradescantia or helxine rooted in a narrow ribbon of soil.

During the early spring the house is always very crowded with annuals and vegetables for first crops being raised. An extra temporary shelf makes room for many more boxes. Wooden planks about 1 ft. wide slipped into metal supports fixed to the roof are easily moved.

Wooden staging should be painted regularly.

FIRE HEATING

The old method of heating the greenhouse by hot water pipes and a coke stove is quite satisfactory. Stoking is necessary two or three times a day to maintain an even temperature.

ELECTRIC HEATING

Where electricity is easily available and reasonably cheap it is the most labour-saving method of heating the greenhouse. The temperature can be automatically controlled by a thermostat.

GREENHOUSE PIPING

When installing heating pipes in a greenhouse do not try to economize by reducing the length of piping to be fitted. The most satisfactory results are obtained from large areas of low temperature pipes. Very hot pipes tend to dry the atmosphere too much, and encourage attacks of red spider. Stoking is easier with plenty of piping, as a large quantity of water will retain its heat all night in cold weather; an extra stoking late in the evening is essential when the house has insufficient piping. As well as the extra labour involved the fuel bill will be higher. Avoid the temptation of throwing rubbish under the staging. The ground round the pipes must be kept scrupulously clean.

OIL AND GAS HEATING

1. For the small greenhouse a paraffin oil heater is very convenient. The blue-flame lamps will burn for forty-eight hours without attention. Most are fitted with a trough in which water can be placed to keep the atmosphere humid.

2. By gas heating a winter night temperature of 45 degrees Fahr. can be maintained. The inside boiler surface supplements pipe heat.

THE SERVICE CORNER

The key to the successful and economic garden is the service corner. Here the tender plants can be protected during the winter, and half-hardy annuals and vegetables raised from seed prior to planting out in their permanent quarters. For ease in working the potting-shed with its supply of soils, the greenhouse and frames should all be in close proximity.

FOR SUN AND AIR

1. Where possible set the greenhouse running north and south and the frames facing south to obtain the maximum amount of sunshine. Ventilating should be away from the wind.

2. A span frame gives more scope than the ordinary one- or two-light frame because it allows for taller plants, and it also gives opportunity for ventilating more freely even in windy weather.

1. Seedlings in boxes in the frame.

2. Early vegetables grown on a bed of soil.

FRAMES FOR PROPAGATING

Frames used for propagating will house pots and boxes of seedlings and cuttings until they are ready to be stood outside. Successive batches can be handled throughout the spring and early autumn, thus using the frame to its fullest capacity. During the summer, indoor plants and bulbs can occupy the space while ripening off, and frame will also be useful for forcing tulips, narcissi, lilies of the valley, etc. Alternatively, a bed of good soil can be made up in the frame to grow early lettuces, carrots, brussels sprouts, cauliflowers and radishes.

Perpetual flowering carnations.

CARNATIONS IN COLD GREENHOUSE

Although in a small greenhouse a variety of flowering plants have to be grown together, if carnations are to be grown they should be kept separate. They require careful heating, watering, ventilation, and a dry atmosphere. The types grown in the greenhouse are the perpetual flowering, for which a little heat may be introduced during the winter, and in a cold house the perpetual border carnation.

For success carnations must have good light and plenty of air. Young plants may be obtained and these should be potted up in 3-in. pots and stood in the greenhouse close to the glass. Before the pots are full of roots the plants should be potted into 5-in. pots. This size is usually large enough for general use. If exhibition blooms are to be grown a further potting on is advisable into 8-in. pots.

The compost for the first potting should consist of five-sixths loam, one-twelfth sand, one-twelfth manure and wood ash. For all further pottings the compost should consist of one-sixth manure, one-twelfth wood ash, one-twelfth mortar rubble, a little sand and the rest loam. The manure used should, if possible, be well decayed cow manure, but if this is not obtainable, a recognized carnation fertilizer may be used. The mortar rubble in the compost is important, as all members of the dianthus family require lime in the soil.

After the final potting, completed by the end of June, the plants should be stood in a frame ; they require plenty of sun to ripen the wood. During this period watering should not be neglected and overhead watering is permissible if done moderately. To check insect pests syringe once or twice a week with tepid water. It is also possible to feed plants occasionally with light dressings of an approved carnation fertilizer.

Staking should be attended to before the plants flop ; the various methods that may be adopted are shown in another chapter. During August the plants should be housed with all ventilators fully open so that plenty of air is admitted at all times. Continue to syringe twice a day if the weather is hot and bright. This is done as a control for red spider, which can be very troublesome on carnations, as it flourishes in the dry atmosphere needed for the plants. Use the syringe vigorously to apply the spray with as much force as possible.

A flowering shoot produces one central bud and several small side buds. Allow only the central one to develop. Disbudding should be done early.

When gathering the flowers, cut them with long stems. New shoots spring from the base of the old ones and the lowest on the stem are the strongest. Leave two or three pairs of leaves and each will send up a healthy shoot for subsequent flowering.

There are many fine named varieties, of which a selection can be made from a nurseryman's catalogue according to the colours required.

GODETIA

1. Godetia makes a good pot plant and gives colour in the house in spring. Put one only in each pot to allow it to develop in its natural pleasing form. Named varieties include both double and single-flowered forms in many lovely shades of pink, salmon, cerise, clove and white.

ANNUALS

3. Clarkia and schizanthus are easily grown under glass, but for good display attention must be paid to staking. Plants that are stopped require a stake to each shoot, unstopped plants need only one central cane.

STOCKING FROM SEED

Raising plants from seed for greenhouse flowering is an inexpensive and fascinating hobby. It provides occupation during the winter when so often outdoor work is at a standstill. The golden rules are: constant attention, plenty of space and air for the plants, and the avoidance of coddling.

BALSAM

2. A plant for certain success is balsam or *Impatiens*. It is easily raised from seeds or cuttings and bears white, pink, scarlet and crimson flowers on fleshy stems.

CALCEOLARIA

4. Calceolaria can be sown in the early spring. The many colours available range from yellow through bright orange to scarlet.

FOR THE HOUSE WITH HEAT

I. A deep cornflower blue perennial for the winter months is *Coleus Frederici*. The plants grow 2 ft. to 3 ft. high and require an 8-in. pot at the final potting.

2. Cyclamen are worth a little trouble. They may be raised from seed but the young plants like a cool moist atmosphere created by syringing without allowing water to remain round the tubers.

3. Many shrubs can be readily forced into bloom in the early months of the year; among the easiest is forsythia. Young plants should be kept in small pots and encouraged to produce flower buds by constant syringing.

BULBS AND TUBERS

Bulbs and tubers play an important part in furnishing the greenhouse with flowers throughout the year. All have a resting period; some, like daffodils, hyacinths, lachenalias and cyclamen during the summer; others, like gloxinias, arum lilies, begonias, hippeastrum during the winter. During this time they require little or no water, but supplies can be gradually increased from the time they commence growth up to the flowering period.

1. Lachenalias must have excellent drainage and a fibrous compost with a little manure in it. From the time the flower buds form until they open, weak stimulants can be given.

2. The arum lily likes a warm moist atmosphere, and appreciates plenty of water until the flowers open. Syringe daily during growth.

3. Gloxinias like a compost of fibrous loam and leaf-mould, and plenty of warmth until they flower. Increase by seed or leaf cuttings.

SPRING FLOWERS IN THE GREENHOUSE

1. Narcissi will give colour in the cool greenhouse from Christmas till April. The bulbs should be planted in August and September.

2. All early flowering bulbs can be used for greenhouse decoration, particularly the dwarf red, yellow, and orange double tulips and hyacinths in blue, pink, white and yellow.

3. Where no heat is available alpines could be grown. They need plenty of light and air and can be selected to give bloom at most seasons, particularly during the spring months.

FOLIAGE PLANTS

1. Foliage plants in the greenhouse hold almost as important a position as flowering plants. Plants such as eucalyptus, grevillea, ferns and kentia (palm) are effective when used as a background to primulas, as seen here, or other small, bright flowered subjects. When furnishing a central staging a permanent group of foliage plants generally occupies an area in the middle, and during seasons when flowering plants are scarce ferns are placed in groups between the pots of flowers.

TERRACED BORDERS UNDER GLASS

Tender plants are usually grown under glass in pots, but here, in place of the usual staging, terraced borders have been constructed either side of a central pathway faced with rock.

PRIMULAS

This is a useful family for the greenhouse because they are easily raised from seed, simple in their requirements and suitable for houses of various temperatures. Guard against dampness; remove dying leaves without injury to the plant; apply water at the side of the pot.

1. *Primula malacoides* in shades of white, pink and lavender blooms during the winter from an August sowing in a cold house.

2. *Primula obconica* can be in bloom from autumn until early spring by sowing seed at regular intervals from February to July. Second year plants give quite good results.

BEGONIAS

To increase your floral display include begonias Besides those illustrated here, there ar pendulous varieties suitable for planting i hanging baskets in the conservatory.

3. Tuberous-rooted begonias are started int growth in boxes of leaf-mould in a warm hous in March. The young plants are later potted u in leafy soil. There are many named varieties both double and single, in rich and delicat shades of a large range of lovely colours

4. *Begonia manicata* bears delicate sprays c pale pink flowers over large leaves in winter

1. Tomatoes can be planted in boxes standing on the staging in a light and airy greenhouse.

2. Tomatoes can be grown in cold frames and trained up canes placed 6 in. from the glass.

TOMATO GROWING

Tomatoes are fairly accommodating and will grow in any receptacle provided it is filled with a good compost and has proper drainage. Here both pots and boxes are used ; large pots are needed to take the plants, a 9 in. or 10 in. being the best size. Margarine boxes will make very good containers and should have holes bored in the bottom to allow surplus water to drain away.

The floors of span-roofed houses can also be used, provided they are well drained. The plants should be started on a small mound of soil, as near to the light as possible, and the earth added as the roots develop. The soil is an all-important factor in successful tomato growing. The best results are obtained with a mixture of fibrous loam, to which is added a little sharp sand, some leaf-mould and some well-decayed manure in adequate proportions. Good results are also obtained by adding some fine bone meal, a 5-in. potful to a barrowload of loam with well-crushed mortar rubble and a shovelful of wood ash. It is always advisable to follow the principle of building up the soil with additional compost as the plants develop.

Overmanuring is liable to cause un-fruitfulness, and only well-rotted manure should be used at any time, or some specially prepared tomato manure. As soon as the fruits are setting well, a top dressing with some such manure will assist cropping, but if this is not available, a pinch or two of kainit, superphosphate, or nitrate of potash at intervals during the growing period will suffice.

Seeds should be sown in early spring in pans filled with light rich soil. Sow thinly and not more than $\frac{1}{4}$ in. deep, cover with glass and paper and place on a shelf near the glass. When the first central leaf is visible the seedlings should be potted off, still placed near the glass, to keep them short jointed.

1. A useful cluster of young tomatoes.

as well as giving a humid atmosphere, which is necessary for a good set. This should only be done during the morning. To shut the house at night in a damp condition makes for disease attacks, especially leaf-mould. Moisture in the soil may be readily conserved by mulching. Although not frequently done, it is useful to remember when going away for a holiday that by placing straw on the soil after thoroughly soaking them the tomatoes will remain moist for at least a week if in pots or boxes and much longer when grown in borders.

Ventilation also plays an important part in atmospheric conditions. Every day the ventilators should be opened and the amount of air admitted can be regulated according to the wind and temperature. On very warm days the door may be left open, but it and the ventilators should be closed before the temperature drops. There should not be more than 10 to 15 degrees Fahrenheit

2. Hand pollination is advisable. Brush across flowers gently with a rabbit's tail. Choose a warm sunny day and do at midday.

When ready for planting into the final quarters they should be placed 1½ ft. to 2 ft. apart, with occasional wider spaces for reaching the fruit and easier working.

The training of tomatoes is as important as the preparation of the soil in which they grow. By nature the plants produce many shoots, but when cultivated they must be restricted to one main stem. As the side shoots appear in the axils of the leaves they should be pinched out. Each plant should be tied to a bamboo cane, and where they are grown in boxes on the staging these canes must be held in position 6 in. from the glass. Plants growing in the border can be tied to canes pushed in alongside the plant.

After planting tomatoes need thorough watering in and can then be left until they show a very slight bluish tinge. Thereafter, water by giving a thorough soaking, and then leaving unwatered for several days. Overhead damping will help to keep the plants in sturdy growth

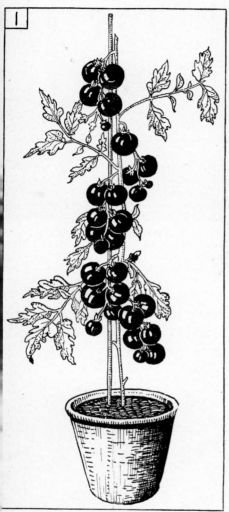

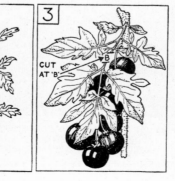

difference between the day and night temperature in the house.

To encourage early ripening of the lower trusses of fruit the plant is generally stopped, and the top side shoot can be grown on for later fruits if desired. Earliest crops may be stopped after the third truss, while later crops can be left to develop five trusses.

When the fruit begins to ripen additional light should be admitted by removing some of the foliage. Leaves which shade the fruit should be shortened as shown in the diagram, and when the lower leaves begin to change colour they may be pulled off. Do not remove all the leaves, as foliage is required to keep the plant growing.

1. After the fifth truss of blossom has set fruit the growing point should be removed to concentrate energy.

2. The young plants produce side-shoots A which when large enough to handle should be pulled out as shown at B.

3. As the clusters of fruit begin to colour, the leaves can be shortened by half to admit more sunshine.

4. The fruit can be picked when it parts easily from the stalk.

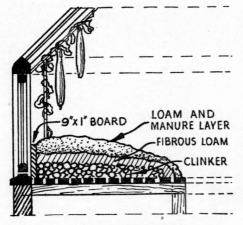

CUCUMBER BED

First cover the staging with a thick layer of clinkers or coarse ashes for drainage. On this put a thin layer of fibrous loam and finish off with a mixture of loam and rotted manure. The whole soil depth should be about 1 ft.

PLANTING CUCUMBERS

The young plants are generally raised in pots and are planted out 2 ft. apart when they have three or four leaves. Plant on a small mound and no deeper than it was in the pot. The stem at soil level must be kept as dry as possible.

BED OF YOUNG CUCUMBERS

Cucumbers are surface rooting, and therefore they must be continually supplied with fresh nourishment. This may be done by covering the bed at intervals with a few inches of strawy manure and loam in equal quantities. Dried blood may also be given once a week.

CARE OF CUCUMBERS

Cucumbers are gross feeders and require very liberal quantities of well-rotted manure. Seed is sown any time from February to April, one seed being placed in a 3 in. pot. The pot should be stood on a shelf near the glass in a heated greenhouse. When the seedlings have grown their first pair of proper leaves they are ready for planting in the border. The bed is made on or near the hot-water pipes. First plenty of draining material, such as large clinkers, is necessary, and over this a 3 in. layer of fibrous loam. A further layer from 6 in. to 9 in. deep of fibrous loam mixed with half its quantity of decayed manure is placed over this.

The temperature required is 65 degrees Fahrenheit, and in very sunny weather it will be necessary to shade the plants to prevent scorch. This is most easily done by lime washing the glass on the outside.

Should the fruits hang low enough to touch the bed, place glass beneath them.

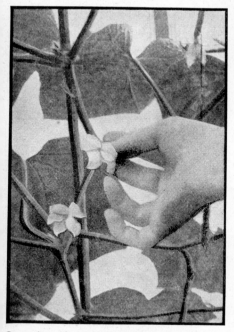

Cucumber plants bear both male and female flowers and the moment the male ones appear they must be picked off, or the female flowers will become pollinated and the cucumbers full of seeds, and have a bitter flavour.

Daily syringing, morning and afternoon, is very necessary. If possible, keep an open tank in the house full of water, as this is warmer than water from a tap.

The shoots on the cucumber plant grow very rapidly in the hot moist atmosphere and they require weekly attention in the matter of training. The main shoot should be tied in position to the bamboo cane set alongside each plant and all side shoots as they grow should be stopped after the second leaf. From these further shoots will grow, which should be stopped after the first leaf and all should be tied to the wires so that they do not break off with the weight of the fruit.

Cucumber plants continue to bear fruit for the greater part of the summer, but if they show signs of ceasing to crop they should be left unwatered for ten days, but the syringing continued. After ten days renew the water supply, and this should give the plants a new lease of life.

YOUNG VINE ROD

When pruning cut the shoot to an outward pointing bud. The upper spur has only one bud. The lower shoot if left with only one bud would be wrong ; the position indicated by the second line is the correct one in this case.

GROWING GRAPES

The treatment of vine rods during the winter is important for the production of good quality clean bunches of fruit. They should first be untied from the wires and all aerial roots trimmed off. The rods should then be pruned as illustrated. Grape vines are usually trained to one or two rods—that is, main stems—along the full length of which there are fruiting spurs. In their first season all side shoots should be cut back to within two buds of their base. In subsequent seasons, shoots which arise from these buds should be cut back each winter to one or two buds. The position of the cut depends on the direction in which the bud is pointing. The cut should be made immediately above a bud that points away from the rod. Having pruned the rods in this way, all loose bark should be scraped off and

the rods painted with Gishurst compound as a disease preventative.

Early in the year the vine rod may be started into growth by giving heat, but if no heat is available it will break into growth naturally towards the end of March. In the early part of the season the ventilator should be opened slightly in the morning and should be closed by about three-thirty. This will preserve the sun heat. The amount of air given each day can be increased as the weather improves, but care should be taken to avoid draughts especially in windy weather. If the current of air is not thus regulated, the leaves and fruit will become mildewed. Control the temperature in this way so that the house is at all times about 55 degrees Fahrenheit.

Even when pruned to only one visible bud each spur generally produces several shoots. When these are a few inches long all but the strongest should be removed from the base.

Vines require syringing once a day with water, preferably rain water from a tank. In a heated house the pipes, too, should be damped. As soon as the flowers appear, syringing should cease, but may be continued for a few days when they have set. Syringing should not be

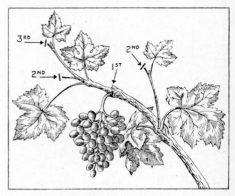

STOPPING VINES

Vines are rampant growers and the house would soon be filled with leaves unless the shoots are " stopped." The diagram shows the position of the first three stoppings on a young shoot. Subsequent stopping is done in the same manner throughout the growing season.

RIPENING BUNCHES

The vines shown are carrying a well-spaced crop of bunches. Stopping has been thoroughly carried out and there is an adequate network of leaves without over-shading the bunches.

continued for long after this period or a deposit will be left on the fruit.

To assist the fruit to set, the wires supporting the vine rod may be tapped gently and this will release a certain amount of pollen. Midday on a warm sunny day is the best time. The rods require constant attention in the matter of training. As soon as the flower clusters appear, all the shoots should have their growing points pinched out two leaves beyond the flower cluster.

As a result, further shoots will grow and these should be stopped after the first leaf. Eventually, only one bunch of fruit should hang from each shoot, the best being selected and others cut out.

A mature vine rod can carry eight bunches. The fruit in each bunch will require thinning in order to obtain good-sized berries, and for this purpose a pair of pointed scissors is used.

Avoid touching the berries with the hands or head while working, as this can cause the skins to become brown. A thin stick or split label will help to hold the berries while thinning, and with a little practice is easier to use than the fingers. At the first thinning the smallest berries are removed; seedless berries will never swell and can be cut away at once. Later remove misplaced berries; by this time it will be seen that some berries are being squeezed; all these must be cut and space left for all the remaining berries to develop. The shoulders must be left full to give the bunch the correct shape; on larger clusters the top two or three sprays which will form the shoulders may be lifted and tied loosely to the wires.

Varieties. Early and mid-season: Black Hamburgh, Madresfield Court; black.

Late: Black Alicante, Muscat of Alexandria; the choicest green.

INDOOR PEACHES IN FLOWER

At this stage the atmosphere must be kept as and a good set assured. Artificial pollination is
dry as possible, so that pollination is thorough essential to set fruit on the earliest varieties.

GROWING PEACHES

Although in milder districts peaches can be grown outside, a good crop of fruit is more certain in a glasshouse. Unless the soil is a good, well-drained loam, obtain a special load of fibrous loam at the time of planting. The border in the greenhouse should be filled with this. The trees are planted about 12 ft. apart and fan-trained trees used. When planting, dig a semicircular hole 8 in. deep, with a radius 6 in. longer than the roots. Into the bottom of the hole, fork in 3 oz. per square yard each of bone meal and sulphate of potash. The roots will then be spread out in the hole. Into the soil used to cover the roots add artificial manure as before. Tread the soil very firm and give a thorough soaking with water. Take great care not to injure the roots as this will lead to gumming.

In the young stages the object of pruning is to obtain a fan of branches covering the space allotted to the tree, in the same way as trees are trained on a wall. Having obtained the framework, the shoots are pruned twice annually. The aim of summer pruning is to train new growth to replace the shoots that have fruited. As the shoots grow all are rubbed out except the uppermost on each branch, the one nearest the base and one half-way between these two. The lowest shoots will be tied in during the winter in place of the one carrying the fruit, but the other two shoots are left merely as sap drawers.

After leaf fall, winter pruning may be done. Cut out the shoots that have fruited, just above the lowest new shoot. Tie this in place of the old one. The

SYRINGING

A daily syringing with clear water should be done early, before the sun would burn the leaves. Apply the water with force and the trees will be clear of aphis and red spider.

house may now be cleaned and all the branches untied from the framework of wires ; for convenience the branches are tied in bunches so that the buds are not injured. After cleaning the house they may be placed in position and at the same time washed with Gishurst as a preventative against red spider. Tie back the main branches first, then the semi-main branches, and so on.

Peaches grown in a heated house should begin to break naturally before the heat is turned on or the buds will drop off. Bud drop is also caused if they ever become dry at the roots. Throughout the year, except when the trees are in flower and the fruit is colouring, they should be syringed with water daily.

A free circulation of air is important, also regular feeding. A general fertilizer of two parts sulphate of potash, one part sulphate of ammonia and two parts

superphosphate may be given every ten or fourteen days, or liquid manure may be used.

The fruits must be gradually thinned, and this commences when they are the size of a pea. First remove those that are badly placed and likely to touch the wood or glass when they are larger and those that will be bruised by branches. Where several fruits grow from one point on the stem, all but one should be removed. Ultimately, the fruit should be about 9 in. apart.

Peaches ripen at different seasons and the following will give a succession : Hale's Early (July), Peregrine (August), Belle de Barde (September), Sea Eagle (late September).

Nectarines require the same treatment as peaches, and the following three varieties are good : Early Rivers (July), Humboldt (August), River's Orange (September), Victoria (October).

SWELLING FRUITS

Water the borders thoroughly when the surface shows signs of drought. The swelling fruit needs plenty of moisture to develop to its full size. Drought causes the skin to split.

The cold frame is covered by lights, which are the framework holding the sheets of glass. These lights are made in two sizes, 4 ft. by 4 ft. and 4 ft. by 6 ft. They can also be obtained unglazed and unpainted and if purchased in this way they are of course less expensive. To economize even further the framework to support the lights can be constructed at home.

Frames are made on a slight slope so that water runs off, but the back wall should not be more than 6 in. higher than the front wall. Wood is the usual material used, although bricks are more permanent and in any case a row of bricks should be used as the foundation for the wooden frame, as otherwise if the wood is placed directly on the wet soil it will quickly rot. Regular painting helps to preserve the wood : white paint should be used, as this reflects most light. During the season the glass is apt to become dirty and should be washed occasionally so that the maximum amount of light can penetrate to the plants.

HOTBEDS

Very much more use can be made of the cold frame if the ground is prepared as a hotbed. To do this, soil should be taken out to a depth of 18 in. and the space filled with 9 in. of strawy manure, if it is available, or material from the rot heap or leaves that are decaying and therefore giving off heat. This should be trodden down very firmly so that the heat is conserved, and then covered with a 6 in. layer of sandy soil. The heat generated will encourage growth so that early salad crops can be raised and seeds that are normally sown in heat, such as leeks and celery, can be raised on the hotbed instead.

COLD GREENHOUSE

A cold greenhouse serves much the same purpose as a cold frame, but of course it enables a much larger quantity of plants to be raised. If there are borders on either side, salads may be brought to maturity in the house, and where there is a staging boxes of young

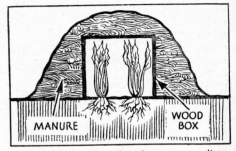

A wooden box covered with manure or litter can be used for forcing sea-kale or rhubarb.

plants may be brought on earlier for planting outside. By May the borders will be empty and ready to take tomatoes and cucumbers. Even if the house is to have staging, construct a central concrete path only and leave borders on either side. Should the whole floor be concreted over, there will be nothing to absorb the water draining from the pots and boxes.

HEATED GREENHOUSE

A heated greenhouse has a great advantage over the cold greenhouse for the early raising both of plants for setting outside and of crops to mature under the glass. The installation of a coke, gas or electric heating apparatus may prove too

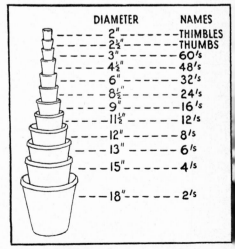

DIAMETER	NAMES
2"	THIMBLES
2½"	THUMBS
3"	60's
4½"	48's
6"	32's
8½"	24's
9"	16's
11½"	12's
12"	8's
13"	6's
15"	4's
18"	2's

The standard sizes of flowerpots.

expensive, but much can be done with a small oil stove which will only require attention every forty-eight hours.

Young plants, such as leeks, celery and onions, may be raised ; and early crops of tomatoes, cucumbers and lettuces can be grown. These sowings can be made early in February, whereas in a cold frame it could not be done until the end of March or, if the seeds are sown outside, until the end of April. Tomato seed can be put in pots in October and at intervals throughout the winter, and the plants will fruit a month or two earlier than those which, under cold conditions, cannot be planted out until the end of May. Successional sowings of lettuce can be made throughout the autumn, winter and early spring at intervals of a fortnight or three weeks. Sow little and often so that there is a constant supply of fresh, solid-hearted lettuce.

During the winter the greenhouse may be used for the forcing of chicory, mustard and cress, rhubarb and sea-kale. This last can be placed underneath the staging with sacks hung from the staging to exclude light.

SCREENS

If no glass is available, much can be done to protect growing crops during the winter by various forms of screens. Wattle hurdles are particularly useful as barriers against strong winds, but where these are not available much valuable protection is afforded by the aid of brushwood, particularly pieces of fir tree or other evergreen. Place these along the windward side of the vegetable plot or nursery seed bed, sticking them into the ground to form a little hedge. Even a few twigs inserted on either side of the rows will shield the young plants slightly. Seedlings which are just showing through the soil can be protected a little from the cold wind by hoeing up ridges of soil either side of the rows. Another form of protection is hessian fastened to stakes and set as a screen all round the vegetable plot, or on the windward side only.

PROTECTIVE COVERINGS

During very cold spells additional protection from the cold is necessary, and although brown paper or newspaper is quite protective, something of a more permanent character may be found more convenient, such as hessian held taut on wooden laths, sacks, old mats, straw, heather, etc. The last two can be easily put on and taken off the frames if they are tied in a number of small bundles. Home made matting of broad bean haulms is also very useful. When the last pods have been picked off the broad beans, the plants are pulled up, tied in bundles and hung in a shed to dry. The dry haulms can then be tied together to form mats—tie them together in small handfuls, joining a dozen or more alongside each other.

1 COMPOST

PIECES OF BROKEN POT CONCAVE SIDE DOWN   LAYER OF ROTTING LEAVES

2

3

WATERING SEED PANS

Seed pans, and pans of newly pricked out small seedlings, should not be watered with a can ; this washes away too much soil. The best method is to let the water seep up through the soil by placing the pan in a shallow vessel. Use wooden labels when handling small seedlings.

CLOCHES

Gardeners aim at getting crops off the ground a week or two earlier than the normal time. To do this, they must be sown earlier and protected from cold in their young stages. This applies more especially to peas, beans and salad crops that cannot be raised in a frame and transplanted when the weather is more favourable. A cloche consists of two or four pieces of glass, held together by metal or wooden clips, which can be placed end to end over the rows of seedlings. There are several types on the market and the type required will vary with the crop that is to be protected. The tent shape, made of two pieces of glass, is sufficiently large to place over lettuces, whilst that made of four pieces, known as the barn shape, provides more height and is therefore more suitable for peas and dwarf beans. Other types with metal sides are obtainable and serve an equally useful purpose. As soon as the crops grow too large, the cloches may be transferred to other seedlings of a subsequent crop.

Barn type of garden cloche suitable for peas and beans. Handles are of galvanized wire.

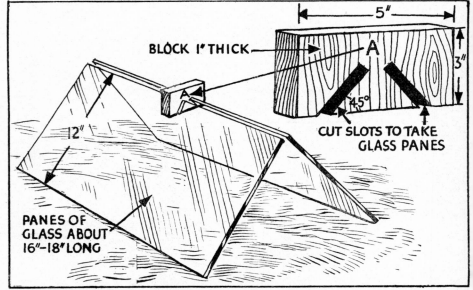

BLOCK 1" THICK

5"

3"

45°

CUT SLOTS TO TAKE GLASS PANES

12"

PANES OF GLASS ABOUT 16"–18" LONG

It is a simple matter to construct a tent cloche. Two panes of glass are secured by a wooden block in which slits have been cut. The angle of the slits will vary according to the width of cloche required. They can also be obtained with wire framework similar to that seen above.

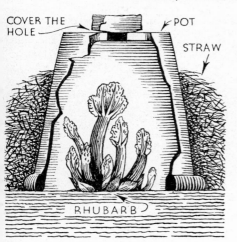

Utilizing a flowerpot for forcing.

FORCING

A simple aid to outdoor forcing or blanching is a flowerpot inverted over each plant. If the plant is to be forced strongly, the flowerpot should be surrounded by strawy litter to keep the plant warm.

Butter boxes or large packing cases are useful for covering big clumps.

STAKES

In the vegetable garden only two crops require staking : peas and beans. When the peas first show through the ground they should be given a few short twigs, and when they have reached the extent of these they will require tall hazel boughs. Place these either side of the row, close to the plant, so that they slope very slightly inwards.

Runner beans can be supported in two ways, either on tall wooden rods or on strings. Set the rods either side of the row and cross them at the top so as to form a V. In this V lay another rod lengthwise and tie securely at the point where all three rods meet. If you find it difficult to obtain bean rods, the plants can be trained up strings. Set a stout post at either end of the row, connect them at the top and bottom by two horizontal wires and tie the strings to these wires.

WATERING APPLIANCES

For long gardens with no taps a hose-pipe saves much water carrying. When not needed as a sprinkler it can flow into a barrel from which cans are filled and the walk to the scullery tap saved. When buying a hose be sure the connexion is the right size for the tap from which it will be used.

Watering cans are made in various sizes : for kitchen garden work a strong $2\frac{1}{2}$ gallon can is as large as is convenient for most people ; while in the greenhouse a light 1 gallon can with one fine and one coarse rose is the handiest.

A hand syringe is needed in the greenhouse for damping leaves and applying insecticides. The bucket syringe is a useful adaptation, having a length of hose which remains in the water and saves filling the syringe for each stroke.

All watering appliances last longer if kept clean ; they must be thoroughly washed after using spraying fluids.

LIQUID MANURES

Suspend a sack of manure in a barrel of water as shown. Dilute with water to the colour of light beer before use or it may burn the roots.

Cucumbers	Summer spinach	chokes	Kale
Peas		Beet	Leeks
		Broccoli	Parsnips
JULY		Brussels sprouts	Salsify
Broad beans	Endive	Cabbages	Savoys
French beans	Kohlrabi	Cardoons	Scorzonera
Waxpod beans	Peas	Celeriac	Sea-kale
Cabbages	Shallots	Celery	Shallots
Cucumbers	Summer spinach	Chicory	Winter spinach
		Colewort	Swedes
AUGUST		*All the year round:—*	
Broad beans	Cabbages	Cabbages	Parsley
Runner beans	Capsicum	Mustard and cress	Potatoes
Waxpod beans	Cauliflowers	Lettuce	Radishes
Beet	Cucumbers	Onions	Turnips

FOOD VALUE OF VEGETABLES

It is well known that the human body contains certain minerals, and constantly suffers the loss of these to a greater or less degree. Such losses must be repaired, and the inclusion of fresh vegetables in the diet is one of the best ways. Here are a few examples of the substances which are replaced by vegetables.

Calcium found in asparagus, beans, cauliflower, dandelion, endive, kale, peas.

Phosphorus in beans, sprouts, peas, nuts, mustard.

Iron in dried beans, cauliflower, dande-

Vitamin D. The sunshine vitamin, essential to bone and tooth development. Prevents bacterial infection on skin.

Sources : General vegetables.

Vitamin E. The vitamin that affects reproduction.

Sources : Lettuce, and to a less extent any green leaves and whole grain cereals.

Vitamin F. Lengthens life and assists general health.

Sources : Beet leaves, spinach (raw), apples, cress, dandelion and other

Weather

Snow and ice, with outdoor jobs at a standstill ; all hands busy in the potting shed, preparing seed boxes and composts, oiling and sharpening tools. Or, if a mild spell occurs, work on paths, fences, pergolas, and screens. Beware of the temptation to move plants : roots dislike disturbance when frosts are about, and January weather is treacherous.

January Work

Turn over vacant soil.

Bastard trench vegetable plots if weather permits, and if this has not been done already.

Ridge heavy soil : it will break up easily after frost.

Use lime, i.e., chalk (on light soils) or builder's lime (on heavy soils).

Use soil fumigants and winter washes.

Spread manure during frosts.

Order seeds.

Apart from the usual seeds, make a note to try out one or two new or unusual varieties—Golden Wonder potato for flavour, alpine strawberries, or the Paramount sugar pea. A practical novelty or two will give additional interest to your garden.

Food Plots

Thoroughly prepare food plots by single or double digging, ridging, and liming. Annual dressings of lime are better than very heavy dressings once in three years.

Set seed potatoes to sprout, rose end up in shallow trays, in a light, frost-proof place.

Plan the plot for sowing ; order seeds.

Order sufficient seeds for the season, but sow only a part at a time, so that crops are raised in succession.

Plan for a rotation of crops ; no ground

should lie idle for any great length of time, particularly in spring and summer.

If a warm sheltered plot is available, the first sowing of the year—a row of broad beans—can be made.

Fruit Garden

Prune hardy orchard trees : apples, pears, plums, damsons, but not peaches, cherries or apricots.

Cut back trees that are to be grafted. Heel grafting scions into the ground where they will lie dormant.

Use winter washes.

Avoid planting this month.

Flower Patch

Loosen the soil surface on vacant flower beds, so that plenty of air penetrates the top spit.

Inspect the stock of tools and accessories.

When mild spells occur, loosen the soil between bulbs that are showing.

Protect autumn sown annuals with mats, newspapers, etc.

Wheel manure to beds that are intended for spring sowing of annuals.

Dust powdered lime between herbaceous plants, if no renovation of the borders has taken place recently.

General Maintenance

Make and repair paths.

Keep evergreens free from snow as far as possible.

Use creosote or white lead paint on all garden woodwork except oak, teak and red cedar : these woods need no preservative.

If cement is used in repair work, keep it well covered during frosty weather, until it is quite dry, otherwise it will crack badly.

Repair all non-living edges ; use stone or tiles to separate grass from gravel, but not wood, or insect pests will be encouraged.

Take stock of tools, fertilizers and insecticides. These can usefully be

Movable wattles make a good windbreak.

ordered for the season now, to save time when the rush of outdoor work begins.

Sort over stakes and plant labels. Order stocks of these and also of tying material.

Wash all pots, and also the pieces of crock to be used for drainage. A disinfectant bath for these will prevent many losses among seedlings.

Prepare and paint, if necessary, tubs, flower-boxes and plant vases.

In mild spells climbers, from pots, can be planted : prepare good soil beds for these, remembering that they have to make a great deal of growth if they are to be really effective.

Press back the soil round all growing plants if it has been loosened by frost ; this will prevent losses in all parts of the garden.

Under Glass

Make up the first hotbed of the year with leaves and manure ; this will create enough heat to raise many half-hardy vegetables and flowers.

Shorthorn carrots and early cauliflowers are useful first crops for the hotbed.

Cold frames and cold greenhouses should be ventilated on mild days, the lights and windows being closed again an hour before sundown. This conserves solar heat.

Set cloches in position over rhubarb and sea-kale in the open.

Use rows of continuous cloches over early lettuces and early peas sown in the open garden. Such sowings should only be made now on warm borders.

Sow onions in boxes in the frame—preferably in boxes raised a little over a hotbed.

Leeks and parsley can also be sown in a frame if plenty of room is available.

Radishes and mustard and cress can be forced when opportunity permits ; a hotbed will produce good radishes in a few weeks.

Sweet peas can be sown now in deep boxes, covered with a sheet of glass, and stood under a south wall if no frame is vacant. Raise the glass $\frac{1}{2}$ in. when the first sign of the seedlings is shown.

MARCH

Weather

Erratic! An ounce of March dust is worth a king's ransom. In other words, March is sowing time and a dry dusty March makes the ground surface in good condition for sowing. But beginners should note that the experienced gardener does not sow by the calendar, but by the weather. Wait for favourable conditions, and meanwhile continue with the indoor work of sowing and pricking out.

March Work

Sow seeds outdoors, beginning with the hardiest kinds. Sow both on the plot and on nursery beds.

Plant almost anything — herbaceous plants, hardy bedding plants, roses (during the first half of the month), shrubs (except tender evergreens), and hardy annual seedlings.

Renovate and alter the arrangement of small gardens.

Prune roses (during the last week of the month) and other shrubs as necessary.

Use slug killers ; these pests are very troublesome among tender seedlings, but any of the modern slug killers will solve the problem.

Make and repair lawns. Begin to mow regularly.

Food Plots

Plant potatoes, beginning with first earlies.

Sow most of the small seeds, i.e., a part of each packet of quick maturing crops like lettuce; and the whole packet in the case of such crops as parsnips, which are to stand.

Hoe and rake the top soil thoroughly and use fertilizer according to the intended crop before you sow the seeds. Two or three inches of fine crumbly soil should form the surface.

Draw drills in this fine crumbly soil, alongside a line stretched taut, so that the lines are straight and parallel. Move the line before covering the seed.

Prepare a nursery bed for sowing such crops as cabbages, sprouts, and broccoli that are to be set out permanently later. Sow on a favourable day, broadcast or in rows, and thin out the seedlings as necessary to prevent crowding.

Outdoor sowings on the plot include broad beans, carrots, onions, radishes, parsley, parsnips, peas, spinach, garden swedes and turnips.

Plant out lettuces raised in the hotbed in February. Cloches are sufficient protection for these on the plot.

Dig deeply and manure well the trenches where celery is to be grown. (Sow celery seed under glass.)

Seed beds need a finely-raked surface.

If birds are troublesome on the food plot, set a board studded with nails at each side, and criss-cross black cotton over the rows of young plants.

Fruit Garden

Protect the opening blossom of wall fruits from frost and birds.

Hoe and use fertilizers as needed round orchard and bush fruits.

Finish planting; when buds have burst it is dangerous to move trees.

Begin grafting, if trees were headed back in January for the purpose.

Spray pears in the green bud stage with lime sulphur or bordeaux mixture against pear scab.

Flower Patch

Plant out chrysanthemums, carnations and similar hardy bedding plants.

Plant gladioli and hardy lilies.

Sow all hardy annuals, dwarfs for edging in both ornamental and in food gardens, and taller varieties for border display and to cut for the vases.

Divide rock plants of suitable kinds such as mossy saxifrage.

Sprinkle the paths with weed killer.

General Maintenance

Break down the surface of ridged soil, ready for seed sowing and planting.

Repair all grass walks : use fertilizer as for lawns.

Order new plants for water gardens (April and May are times to put them out).

Order fruit netting, straw for strawberries, pea sticks for the food plot, bean sticks and flower stakes if the present stock is not sufficient.

Make or re-lay crazy paving paths ; cement work can usefully be done in springtime.

Apply weed killer to paths.

Hedge bottoms should be cleaned out before growth begins. They harbour weeds and pests. Fork over the soil and hand pick the roots of perennial weeds, devil's twine, nettles and the like. Then, if the roots invade the garden plot, cut these off with a sharp spade close to the side of the hedge. Any gaps can be filled in with little plants like the hedge.

Keep the hoe going amongst crops every two weeks. Work with sharp tools.

Under Glass

Cloches are of supreme importance this month. Seedlings of lettuce, etc., raised in hotbeds can be transferred to the open garden if a row of cloches can be set over them immediately.

Seeds sown under cloches will produce early crops of spinach, carrots, mustard and cress. All these are crops rich in vitamins.

Prick out or plant out under cloches all January sown seedlings.

Sow all half-hardy annuals, tender annuals that are to be grown on indoors, and seeds of perennials likely to flower in the first season, such as Japanese chrysanthemums, bedding dahlias and carnations.

Sow broccoli, leeks, lettuce, onions, peas, celery, tomatoes and vegetable marrows under glass for outdoor cultivation.

Ventilate freely but avoid draughts.

Maintain a frost-free temperature in hotbeds by the application of fresh stable manure round the sides

black currants. Spraying with lime sulphur wash when the foliage is about the size of a shilling, and again a fortnight later is a certain cure.

Use bordeaux mixture on pears to prevent scab (if this was not done last month).

Loosen the surface of autumn dug ground.

their season of growth can be dried and stored.

Sow half-hardy annuals where they are to flower. The South African annuals—venidium, heliophila, ursinia, and dimorphotheca, etc., can be sown this month in the open.

Dress beds with bonemeal where annuals are lifted to make way for summer bedding plants.

Sow biennials and perennials in a nursery bed. Such plants as wallflowers and forget-me-nots should be raised in quantity for use in spring borders and to edge food plots. Aquilegias, hollyhocks, and Russell lupins are examples of the flowers that can be raised from present sowings, for planting in the herbaceous borders next season.

Under Glass

Prick out asters, stocks and other half-hardy annuals sown in February.

Sow runner beans, cardoons, marrows, and ridge cucumbers for the food plot.

Plant out frame cucumbers on a hotbed.

Prick out tomato and celery seedlings.

Harden off and plant out brussels sprouts, celery, and all other seedlings as soon as possible.

Keep litter handy for protection of cold frames.

APRIL

Weather

Showers, with a good prospect of sunshine and mild open spells. In a favourable April all the work of seed sowing for the summer crops and summer flowers can be completed. Beware of too much haste in setting out plants that are not quite hardy.

April Work

Sowing — almost every flower and vegetable grown for summer use can be sown now in the open—and planting out occupy the main part of the gardener's time this month.

Delicate evergreens can be moved where their sites are needed for the food crops. If showers do not occur frequently afterwards, an overhead spray with the hose morning and evening will help them to recover the shock of removal.

Grafting and spraying, the taking of cuttings from started dahlia and other plants, and the first steps against active

the rows, and at the same time, pull out by hand weeds actually in the rows.

If seedlings are disturbed by hoeing or weeding, press them immediately back ; unless the roots are in close contact with moist soil, the plants cannot grow.

Sowings delayed through bad weather in March must be carried out now. Seeds that must be in the ground before the month ends are onions, main crop carrots, radishes, summer spinach, swedes. Other seed sowings for the month include beet, salsify, scorzonera, endive, kohlrabi, lettuce (for succession), peas (tall varieties), and perpetual spinach.

Plant out hardened seedlings only ; remember that frosts are still probable. Keep light litter, mats, and other material handy for the protection of open-air plants should severe frosts come.

Thin crops sown on the plot as soon as convenient : two thinnings are best,

MAY

Weather

Probably some hot sunny weather, but still the possibility of frost at night. The most critical month of the whole year for raisers of bedding and vegetable garden seedlings.

May Work

Plant out hardy plants from frames.

Sow quick maturing annuals for succession.

Sow tender vegetables in the open.

Watch the progress of the weather, and be prepared with protection for all seedlings.

Prepare beds and sow seeds of biennials.

Keep the plot and borders clean.

Hoe regularly.

Mow regularly.

Fight pests : many of the worst are now busy laying eggs.

Prepare to plant out tender summer bedding plants, and plan how to fill gaps in the summer colour scheme.

Food Plots

Crops should be well advanced, and will now be liable to attacks of pests.

Onion and carrot flies in particular come this month to lay their eggs. Soot and lime, or whizzed naphthalene dusted along the rows will keep the flies away. Whizzed naphthalene is obtainable from all horticultural chemists.

Black fly on beans is likely to come too. Spray to prevent its appearance, using derris powder in liquid form.

Derris insecticide is also useful to keep green flies away from peas and other crops ; it is harmless to animals and can be used freely in the food garden.

Use quick-acting fertilizers. Nitrate of soda will effect a quick change when used on crops that ought to make more

growth—lettuces, greens and onions in particular benefit. A teaspoonful to a yard of row, dissolved in water or watered well in after distribution is sufficient for a fortnightly dressing.

Rotted waste matter is useful as manure, but not if weed seeds are present. Burn weed plants that already carry seed pods.

Earth up potatoes : this helps to keep the tubers a good colour and also protects the growing shoots in case of late frosts.

Set small twigs amongst pea seedlings as a first support.

Sow now french, runner, waxpod and dutch brown beans in the open garden. Cloches over the rows will be of great help, specially in late frosts.

Sow more peas, beet, endive, radishes, sweet corn, chicory and summer spinach on the plot.

Hoe frequently, especially in dry weather.

368

Sow cauliflower and broccoli in the nursery bed.

Plant out brussels sprouts, savoy, broccoli, colewort and cauliflower from the nursery beds.

Plant out March-sown frame cucumbers on the hotbed.

Plant marrows and tomatoes in sheltered positions at the end of the month.

Fruit Garden

Mulch with manure all fruits on light dry soils.

Prune apricots, Morello cherries, nectarines and peaches as required.

Reduce the number of runners on the strawberry plants, leaving only those that will be required for fresh autumn plantings. Dust fertilizer along the rows, and hoe it in before placing straw or other litter round the plants.

Flower Patch

Plant out bedding plants, beginning with the hardier kinds ; leave tender subjects such as dahlias, cannas, eucalyptus, standard fuchsias, heliotropes, etc., until the end of the month.

Sow peas for succession.

Sow biennials and perennials as desired.

Divide such rock plants as arabis, aubrietia, cushion saxifrage, primulas, and double daisies when the flowers have faded.

Thin out, stake, and peg down annuals as they need this attention.

Trim away faded flowers from rock plants and early summer bedding plants unless seed is required.

Watch for green fly and other pests on roses. Derris dust is a good general insecticide, and green sulphur powder a good cure for fungoid diseases such as mildew. Apply with powder bellows.

General Maintenance

Syringe newly planted trees both early and late in the day.

Water newly pricked out seedlings ; hoeing is usually sufficient among established large plants, but the roots of seedlings only penetrate a shallow surface layer of soil.

Lift bulbs, and if they are fully ripened store them for autumn planting. If the foliage is still green replant the bulbs in some odd corner until they are ready for storing.

Daffodils, snowdrops, and bluebells are better left undisturbed. Hyacinths, tulips and such edging bulbs as scillas and grape hyacinths can be lifted annually.

Under Glass

Be ready with night protection : frosts may occur as late as the last week in May.

Turnips and carrots on hotbeds under glass should be ready to pull as required, from about the last week of this month.

Plants raised for outdoor culture can be moved from the hotbed to the cold frame and gradually hardened off. These include both food crop plants and flowers.

Keep the cloches in use ; nights are cold and all newly planted seedlings will benefit from slight protection. Remove the cloches early if the weather is fine.

JUNE

Weather

Flaming June, if we are lucky : in any case a fair amount of sunshine and warmth. Showers may well turn out to be heavy thunder-showers, which will test the rigidity of rose pillars and other plant supports.

Avoid root damage this month, and if plants must be disturbed, as in the case of bedding-out material, keep up the water supply artificially for a time.

June Work

First crops are ready to harvest—salads, summer spinach, a few peas and early potatoes.

Hoe, and keep on hoeing! This keeps down weeds and aerates the soil.

Finish all summer bedding.

Plant out seedlings from nursery beds on to the food plots as opportunities occur.

Use one-three-one or a good general fertilizer. It can be used anywhere.

Put scrap of annual weeds unseeded, grass clippings, vegetable parings from the house on the compost heap. A dusting of sulphate of ammonia over organic matter will accelerate decay.

Food Plots

Dig the first early potatoes as they are ready. Potatoes to be stored, even for a short time, should lie on the ground to dry for an hour after digging.

Hotbed cleared of carrots and turnips can be used without further additions for the cultivation of marrows and ridge cucumbers.

Fresh manure, if available, can be used to make up mushroom beds.

Transplant from the nursery bed to the plot : kale, savoys, cabbages, cauliflowers, brussels sprouts, and broccoli.

Move from frames to the open : outdoor tomatoes, leeks, couve tronchuda, aubergines, celery, celeriac.

Sow, for succession : french, runner, waxpod and brown dutch beans, also quick-maturing peas.

Sow, also for succession, such crops as endive, chicory, kohl-rabi, lettuce, parsley, radishes, and summer spinach.

Stake peas and runner beans.

Keep up the water supply : hoeing is best, but in long dry spells it may be necessary to use the hose or the can.

Feed regularly when plants are well established ; never feed newly planted seedlings or sickly plants.

Grass cuttings are a good mulch for dry soil. Between turnips they are specially good. This mulch is turned in when the crop is cleared, so that it eventually decays and enriches the soil.

Water new lawns in the evenings.

Fruit Garden

Thin out superfluous shoots on fruit trees, and pinch or stop as required.

Provide support for trees that are cropping very heavily.

Use derris powder freely against caterpillars and green flies.

Raspberry and loganberry beetles can be controlled by dusting derris powder into the open flowers. As they open in succession, treatment should be carried out daily for a few weeks.

Net cherries and other fruits where birds are troublesome.

Summer prune red and white currants.

Layer loganberries if more stock is wanted.

Remove weak, unwanted canes from raspberries. Keep sufficient to ensure a good crop next summer. Six young canes to a root are generally sufficient.

Water strawberries during a dry spell.

Summer prune grape vines as soon as convenient.

Flower Patch

Cut away dead flowers to encourage further blooms.

Dust raspberries with derris powder.

Disbud roses, carnations, chrysanthemums as necessary.

Spray with insecticides and fungicides: prevention is better than cure.

Cut rose blooms with long stems : this ensures better blooms for the second crop.

Finish all bedding out.

Prepare a cutting plot : double wallflowers, sweet rocket, etc., can be propagated there.

Sow more perennials, such as delphiniums, lupins, and hollyhocks.

Provide a sufficient number of stakes and ties in the mixed borders.

Save all bulbs by storing in a dry cool place. Tulips should be cleaned and stored in a shallow box. Daffodil bulbs can be left in the soil to come up another year. Lilies if given ample drainage when planting can be left permanently in the soil. Bulbs naturalized in grass should now be cut down and the grass mown in the ordinary way.

General Maintenance

Take a daily walk with the lawn mower and roller.

Use fertilizer still on lawns and among all growing plants.

Clean out the frames as plants are removed to summer quarters. White lead paint is useful on the window frames, particularly inside, as it reflects all available sunlight in winter.

Dig over and lime all vacant seed beds and prepare them for use again.

Prepare a propagating frame : many plants root best in summer.

Hoe! Hoe regularly! Hoe everywhere!

Under Glass

Give plenty of air to all seedlings and plants left under glass.

Shade very young seedlings from brilliant noonday sun.

Keep cucumbers sprayed and trained in the frames.

Fumigate cold greenhouses and frames if pests are troublesome. If mildew occurs, use green sulphur powder and allow more ventilation.

JULY

Weather

Hot and close, with drought and heavy rains in the balance. Staking becomes necessary, and neglect often means a ruined herbaceous border just when it should be at its best.

July Work

The fruit harvest occupies some time this month. Currants, gooseberries, strawberries, and raspberries are ready to use.

Gather soft fruits as they can be dealt with; they preserve best when freshly gathered.

Preserve surplus harvests of vegetables when possible. Cut and dry mint and other herbs. Make potpourri.

Hoe, weed, water, and top dress with mulches of old manure or with prepared rich soil, as possible.

Food Plots

The harvest this month includes salads, peas, spinach, french and waxpod beans, carrots, turnips and beetroots, summer cabbages and cauliflowers (these last two from the hotbeds).

Look after the tomatoes on the plot. Pinch out all side stems, leaving a single cordon growth.

Feed tomato plants with fertilizer, or with liquid manure made from animal droppings and soot.

Remove male flowers from cucumbers; this will prevent seed formation, and the flavour of the fruits will be improved.

Take up and store shallots as the foliage begins to wither.

Well-formed seed from a few plants that have no more flowers to set can be saved to provide seeds of peas and french beans.

Lift the second early potatoes; dry and store them carefully.

Earth up the main crop potatoes.

Keep the hoe going between the late crops; intercrop with lettuce and radish.

Watch for "blight" disease on potatoes; spray whether it appears or not, using bordeaux mixture. Spray on both sides of the foliage. (Affected potatoes will not store.)

Wash all utensils used for copper sprays immediately after use.

Sow turnips, beet, and carrot for winter in beds previously planted with peas, etc.

Winter spinach can now be sown.

Plant out celery, if not already done. Also plant out late sowings of cabbage, sprouts, and broccoli.

Fruit Garden

Thin out fruits and overcrowded growths on fruits of all kinds.

Keep a sharp look out for pests, and cut out diseased wood.

Woolly aphis on young apple shoot.

Water loganberries and any other fruits that require this attention.

Train cordon and espalier trees.

Watch for mildew and spray or dust with sulphur.

Summer prune as needed.

Bud fruit trees if stocks and buds are available.

Silver leaf will be easily detected amongst plums and cherries now that they are in full leaf. The branches attacked show a distinct silvery colouring and begin to die back from the tips. The affected branches should be cut clean away and burnt. Cut back to healthy wood; the diseased wood has a brown stain in the centre. Paint over the cut portion with white lead paint, sterilize the secateurs or pruning knife with strong carbolic solution frequently during pruning operations.

Flower Patch

Layer border carnations that have flowered.

Take cuttings of hardy plants under cloches or in a propagating frame.

Sow pansies and violas.

Try saving your own dianthus seed.

Mulch, stake and tie up dahlias and other tall herbaceous plants to bloom in late summer.

Prick out and plant out seedlings of hardy flowers raised in frames and nursery plot.

Train flowering climbers.

Bud roses.

Remove dead flowers; stake, and water regularly.

General Maintenance

Hoeing, weeding, and watering are the tasks of the month in most parts of the garden.

Keep down weeds on paths, and cut and roll lawns regularly.

Attend to the shrub borders; some need pruning at this season after the spring flowers have passed.

Many shrubs can be increased by layering, and this simple method of increase does not encroach on the space of frames and pits.

Collect tops of early perennials, unwanted stumps from the cabbage patch, etc., and put all material that will rot into the compost pit. Burn other waste matter and use the ash immediately on the flower beds, or on vacant food plots.

Make plans for winter storage of surplus crops. Some crops can be stored in sacks in shed or cellar, but large harvests of roots are better stored in the open. Straw is needed for this.

Under Glass

Sow Brompton stocks and border carnations in frames for next season.

Give plenty of ventilation to tomatoes, aubergines, etc., in cold frame and greenhouse.

Propagate carnations by layers or cuttings, stake and tie those that are coming into bloom.

Stake, tie, and pinch or disbud chrysanthemums as desirable.

Propagate perennial herbs by cutting or division.

Wash, repaint, and put into good order all frames and greenhouses not at present occupied; they will be needed for food crops later if not for flowers.

SEPTEMBER

Weather

First frosts probable. With luck, and perhaps a little extra care, summer flowers may be kept unharmed through the first night frosts, and if so, there is a probability that they will continue to produce blooms for several extra weeks. Keep your weather eye open!

The gardener's year begins this month. Plan autumn alterations to the garden. Fresh from your holidays you will be full of ideas. By planning to carry these out while your ideas are fresh you will get better results.

September Work

Move tender plants under glass, and plant out those that are to stand the winter in the open.

Clean up the garden as vegetables, flowers and fruit complete their season.

Order autumn and winter fertilizers.

Plan autumn planting and make out orders for plants, trees and shrubs.

Move immediately any evergreens that have to be transplanted ; it is not safe to move them when the soil has become cold.

Food Plots

Clear away finished crops. Dig over the ground. If it is not to be immediately replanted, trench it and bury below the top spit material taken from the compost pit.

Lift any potatoes that remain. If you are to keep your own seed potatoes, select tubers about the size of eggs, i.e., weighing approximately two ounces each. Only perfectly healthy tubers must be chosen, and only from potatoes that were grown from fresh seed, i.e., seed from a distance, this year.

Lift onions that have ripened.

Preserve surplus runner beans and other summer vegetables for winter use.

Lift and store roots. Jerusalem artichokes are ready for use when the tops turn yellow, but these need not be stored in clamps ; like parsnips, they can be left in the ground and dug as required. Any roots can, however, be lifted and stored in clamps if this is more convenient.

First sowings of endive may now be ready to be blanched. This can be done by inverting a clean flowerpot over each plant, laying a piece of tile over the hole, to exclude light.

Some of the celery and leeks will be ready for earthing up.

Watch for caterpillars on cabbages, and for their eggs, which are laid on the underside of the leaves. Pick these colonies of eggs off and burn them.

Lift main crop potatoes

Dust derris powder over the remaining foliage.

Winter spinach and onions can still be sown in the open.

Spring cabbages can be planted out as soon as the plants and vacant ground are ready.

Gather tomatoes, green or ripe, before the frosts come, and bring them indoors to ripen. Green tomatoes are useful for pickling.

Fruit Garden

Harvest and store such fruits as apples and pears, but only as they become ripe, or ready for gathering.

Apply grease bands to trees. This prevents the winter moth from reaching the top of the tree.

Cuttings of small fruits—gooseberries, red, white and black currants—can be taken now.

Prune raspberries and black currants if this has not already been done.

Plant out rooted strawberry runners to make a new plantation.

Thin out fruits on apples and pears if they are overcrowded.

Plant out spring bedding.

Plan new fruit gardens and order the trees and bushes required.

Flower Patch

Take cuttings of such bedding plants as antirrhinums, hollyhocks, petunias, pentstemons, if specially good varieties are present and an increased stock is desired.

Plant spring bulbs of all kinds, except tulips. October plantings are satisfactory, but the sooner the bulbs are in the better.

Sow hardy annuals for early flowering.

Plant peonies, delphiniums, oriental poppies and iris, and other border plants that flower early in the year.

Examine the ties on roses that were budded in June. Loosen them if the buds have taken.

Plant hardy lilies among border shrubs.

Plant out biennials, perennials, seedlings, and rooted cuttings from frames and nursery plots as convenient, leaving all the space possible in the sheltered corners for those plants that dislike our hard winters.

General Maintenance

Watering is not generally needed this month in the open, as nights tend to be dewy even if the weather is not showery.

Hoeing must be continued. Beds made quite weed free during this month will not suffer if they are left untouched for several months in the winter.

Sweep and roll lawns and where necessary, make new lawns from seed.

Prepare all glass structures for the winter.

Under Glass

Pot up bulbs for indoor flowering.

Bring under cover all tender plants from beds and borders.

Take plenty of cuttings ; young plants are often stronger than old ones and so survive winter better.

Reduce the water supply under glass, and if summer shading has been used, wash it off the glass.

Fumigate the greenhouse before stocking it for the winter.

Weather

Night frosts become almost inevitable, and plant growth slows down. Leaves begin to fall.

Tops die back in the herbaceous borders.

Fully grown plants mature, fruits ripen, but the development of seedlings is very slow. Nature is settling down to a long rest.

October Work

Prepare ground. Main winter digging can begin.

Prepare glass and other forms of protection—mats, screens, hurdles, straw.

This is the gardener's new year, and stocks of plants, fertilizers and soils should be overhauled.

Perennial plants, trees and shrubs should be ordered and a garden planting plan made so that they can be prepared for in advance.

Food Plots

Continue to hoe and weed.

As ground becomes vacant, clear away rubbish to the compost pit and the bonfire, and begin to trench.

Lime can be used immediately after digging.

Trim away yellow leaves from cabbages and sprouts. Throw them into the compost pit to decay.

Gather any remaining fruits on tomatoes ; burn the old haulms.

Clear asparagus beds and cut down stems. Cover the beds with manure to a depth of two inches.

Lift and store celeriac, carrots and beet.

Blanch celery and leeks by earthing and the use of paper collars.

Finish planting out cabbage seedlings ; any plants not set out this month should be left in the nursery all winter.

Watch for frost ; protective covering will often save a late crop.

Cauliflowers can be protected in the open with portable cloches.

Corn salad and dwarf early peas can be sown on a warm south border in the sheltered parts of the country.

Plant rhubarb. This is a permanent crop, and should be planted where the ground will not be required for any other crops.

Onions sown in beds last month can be thinned, but care should be taken not to disturb the remaining seedlings.

Fruit Garden

Prepare holes for new orchard fruits, and dig over plots intended for new plantations of raspberry, currant or gooseberry.

Bring late chrysanthemums under cover.

Towards the end of the month planting can begin.

Apples and pears can still be gathered and stored.

Some pruning can be done this month, if convenient.

Old fruit and old wood that is not wanted can be cut out from fig trees now. This allows room for full development of the remaining new growths.

Grease bands, if not yet in position, should be put round orchard tree trunks immediately.

Flower Patch

Clear away summer flowers from the beds and after forking the soil and manuring as needed, replant them with bulbs and spring herbaceous flowers.

Lift and store gladiolus corms, dahlia tubers, and bedding (tuberous rooted) begonias.

Renovate herbaceous borders; lift and divide perennials, and treat the soil with bonemeal before replanting.

Fork lightly over the soil surface of borders that do not need to be completely renovated. A dusting of lime between the plants is useful.

Plant or renovate herbaceous borders.

Plant hyacinths, narcissi, and other bulbs in groups in the mixed border.

Plant beds or border edgings of anemones.

Sever carnation layers, and plant the new plants in permanent or winter quarters.

General Maintenance

Make new lawns from turf.

Dress old lawns for worm trouble.

Prick over and use fertilizer or sifted soil and manure on lawns in poor condition. A sandy, leafy top dressing works wonders at this season.

Clean up lawns and paths; keep the fallen leaves in a heap to decay. They are best just damp, but should not be left in a very wet heap, or they do not decay satisfactorily.

Bring under cover sifted soil, sand, leaf-mould, and other materials likely to be wanted for pots and boxes during the frosty weather; you cannot easily obtain soil from a frostbound garden.

Under Glass

Watch temperatures carefully. Keep frost out by the use of mats, straw, strawy manure piled round the sides of the frames, hurdles used to keep off winds or any other means that suggest themselves.

Pot up more bulbs for indoor flowering.

Bring chrysanthemums indoors — the border varieties to winter packed closely together in a cold frame, and the late flowering types in their pots, to provide colour in the cold greenhouse.

Sow sweet peas in a frame.

Prick out cauliflower seedlings into frames.

Begin to force rhubarb if desired.

Lift parsley, mint, etc., and pack into soil in a frame if fresh winter supplies are wanted.

Clear away old hotbeds. The bulk of the old manure can be used in mixing potting soil.

Sow lettuces in good rich soil in the greenhouse. Radishes and mustard and cress are other good winter salads to grow under glass.

Weather

Cold and misty, perhaps frosts, but usually not so severe that they last through the day. Just right for pruning, tree and shrub planting, and winter digging unless an exceptionally wet or cold spell occurs.

November Work

Sweep the leaves; these will have all fallen and the garden, including lawns and paths, can this month be cleaned up thoroughly for the winter.

Dig and ridge all vacant land.

Plant protection becomes an urgent matter. Newspapers, mats, straw, mats made of the old broad bean stems, hessian, cloches, evergreen twigs, bracken —all these are useful protective material.

Keep the bonfire going; woody waste matter and any seeding weeds or diseased plant waste that might be the cause of future trouble should be burned.

Tree prunings should be burned and any large wounds made by cutting out branches of forest trees should be painted over to keep out rains.

Food Plots

Dig and trench vacant ground. If no manure is available, and the compost pit does not provide sufficient humus, use hop manure as a substitute.

Spread lime over dug soil, particularly over heavy soil; it helps to break down the lumps so that a fine tilth can be secured.

Soil infested with pests such as wireworms should be treated now with soil fumigant, which must be dug in below the top spit.

Lift and store all root crops. Parsnips are best after a light frost has touched them, but if left in the ground too long, there may be a difficulty in digging.

Indiscriminate manuring is wasteful, and some fertilizers are quite expensive. Ground to take peas and beans should need little nitrogenous food, and therefore will be sufficiently manured with the contents of the compost pit. Ground to take cabbages would benefit from a dressing of rich stable or poultry manure.

Cover the manure on asparagus beds with a layer of soil now.

Remove bean poles, pea sticks, etc., and sort and clean them before storing.

Watch growing crops of spinach, turnips and onions for signs of slugs. Any modern slug killer will prevent trouble.

Lift sea-kale roots and store them for forcing as required. They can be put into sand or ashes in the open.

Lift rhubarb for forcing under glass.

Start to prune apple trees.

Sow broad beans if you have a position ready on a warm, sheltered border.

Plant horseradish.

Fruit Garden

Plant fruit trees and bushes of all kinds.

Prune fruits of all kinds.

After pruning, fruit trees benefit by a dusting of fertilizer; a tree never really goes to sleep; you will notice the fruit buds swell between November and February. A good tonic for clay soils is basic slag, this supplies phosphates, 1 oz. to 2 oz. per square yard' is sufficient. Kainit is also slow acting and can be applied now at the rate of 2 oz. per square yard.

Take cuttings of gooseberries and currants if further plantations are desired.

Lift cuttings that were rooted last year and plant them in permanent homes.

Spread manure between strawberry rows if available.

Flower Patch

Complete remodelling of the flower garden can take place now if desired.

Spread lime on newly-dug soil.

Plants lifted should have their roots protected from frost while they are out of the soil.

Do not divide roots except of very hardy plants such as Michaelmas daisies; leave others to be divided in March.

Plant roses. These are labour-saving flowers, and excellent for the wartime gardener.

Clear away fallen leaves, specially from the rock garden.

Arrange for the protection of such plants as Christmas roses that are to flower in the open in winter.

Arrange for woolly-leaved rock plants to have protection from the worst rains.

Plant tulips in shrubbery, borders and formal beds.

General Maintenance

Attend to constructional details : gate hinges and latches, greenhouse doors and frame hinges. A touch of oil or a coat of paint may make years of difference in wear.

Clean all glass ; sunshine is scarce enough, and none should be lost through films of dirt on windows. Limewash inside walls of lean-to greenhouses.

Repair pergolas, paths, screens and fences.

Plant protective screens ; wattle hurdles as temporary shelters help the young hedge plants to establish themselves quickly.

Under Glass

Ventilate and fumigate as needed.

Bring indoor bulbs into the greenhouse or living-rooms from the cold frames. Do not bring in every bowl or pot at once, but allow for a succession of bloom.

Watch for yellowing leaves on geraniums and similar plants ; remove these and burn them. Ventilate as much as possible, avoiding frosts, but water sparingly.

In mild weather, take the frame lights off cauliflowers and similar vegetables that are being grown in the frame ; they will stand mild winter days well enough, and are best kept hardy.

DECEMBER

Weather

Unfit for any serious disturbance of plant roots. Probably cold if not actually frosty, and usually either rainy or snowy. Garden work indoors is probably more useful than outdoors unless the days are dry enough for digging.

December Work

Make plans for next season. Planting pans are needed both for flower and vegetable garden.

Work out in detail systems of plant rotation, what fertilizers are to be used, and where, what insecticides are needed, what seeds will be required.

Clean, sort, tie in bundles and store all idle plant stakes, labels, etc.

Clean up tool sheds. Wash pots. Reorganize the non-living details of the garden such as pegs for tools, bins for fertilizers, storage places for soils, new compost pits and so on.

Tour the garden and see that wind breakages and damage through snowfalls are quickly repaired.

In many ways December is the best month to bring pests that trouble the garden under control. American blight and other pests that attack fruit trees can be destroyed with a tar oil wash. Soil pests like wireworm and leather-jackets can be reduced by applying naphthalene during digging. It should be well below the soil to get the maximum results. All weeds whether in paths or under hedges should be removed and dumped in the compost pit.

The foliage from rose bushes attacked by black spots should be raked or picked off the beds and burnt.

Lawns can receive a dressing of lawn sand which will help to control weeds and prevent these spreading during the winter months.

Food Plots

Dig, dig, and dig again! You need to trench or bastard trench vacant ground annually for the best results.

In addition, fork the top spit of soil over as many times as possible during the winter; it aerates the soil, and also brings pests to the surface to be preyed on by birds.

Do not dig when the ground is very frosty; on such days do the work of wheeling manure from place to place, setting it out in heaps for easy distribution as digging is done.

Watch stored roots—remove any that become rotten or they will infect the whole store.

Protect broccoli from frost by bending a leaf over the flower that is forming.

Garden soil is most easily sterilized

Spray fruit trees on windless days.

with chemicals, and this can best be carried out during winter, when the soil is vacant.

Very little sowing can be done between November and February on the plot, but in a mild spell a few broad beans could be sown in a sheltered border.

Where peas are growing in the open, draw a little earth up against them as a protective measure. Treat broad beans in the same way.

Fruit Garden

Prune outdoor grape vines.

Prune other fruits as required, but pruning must be avoided during very heavy frosts.

Spray fruit trees and bushes with tar oil winter wash. If green crops are growing below the fruits, cover them with sacking or hessian before you spray.

Burn dead wood and prunings.

Remove and burn big buds from black currants if present. Make a note to spray these with lime sulphur in spring.

Continue planting only if the weather is mild and open.

Mix potting soil for use in frosty weather.

Flower Patch

Protect Christmas roses with pieces of glass. Otherwise the blooms get ruined by rain splashes.

Finish bulb planting if any bulbs are still out of the ground.

Protect autumn sown anemones with light litter.

Protect autumn sown annuals with evergreen twigs pushed in close to them.

Protect tender roses by strewing light litter among the stems.

Distribute rotted manure over the herbaceous borders, forking it lightly in when opportunity occurs.

General Maintenance

Distribute winter fertilizers—lime or kainit or both—as required.

Potash is specially needed by orchard fruits, and kainit applied now is a good way to supply the required potash.

Lime for heavy soils and chalk for light soils must be applied in winter. Order supplies immediately.

Repair work of all kinds is urgent—order gravel, surfacing chips, paving stone, and any new posts and trellis that may be needed.

Give a coat of paint or creosote where needed.

Under Glass

Rhubarb, sea-kale and chicory are ready for forcing. Light is best excluded from all, as the flavour is thereby improved.

Seed potatoes, if already in hand, can be set to sprout. These do better if allowed some light.

Clean and limewash the greenhouse if this has not already been done.

Prepare potting and seed composts.

Pay great attention to ventilation ; all the air possible without endangering the plants should be admitted daily.

Reduce water supplies for resting plants to a minimum. Fuchsias and similar plants in pots can lie over on their sides for the present.

Keep up the supply of small saladings. Mustard and cress can be grown still from fortnightly sowings under glass.

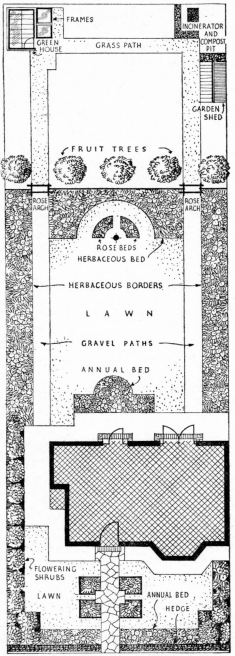

A TYPICAL SUBURBAN GARDEN IN PEACE TIME

HOW TO ADAPT YOUR GARDEN IN WARTIME

I have seen many thousands of gardens on housing estates in various parts of the country, and on the whole I think the wisest course to adopt in the present emergency would be to devote, say, half to two-thirds of the back garden to vegetable culture. This would leave an area of lawn and flower beds near the rear of the house for recreational purposes. It will mean sacrificing some of the lawn area and possibly a few beds and flower borders in the front garden. I suggest the borders might be widened to make way for more flowers for cutting purposes and also to provide a home for treasures amongst the perennial flowers, shrubs and roses which would have to be moved to make way for the vegetables in the back garden.

To present this problem of adapting the garden to wartime needs, I have prepared two sketches, one showing the garden as it is now, and the other how it can be converted to wartime needs most economically. This should be taken merely as a guide. Every garden will have its own problems, and since no two gardens are alike it is impossible to lay down hard and fast rules. But the main idea is to work to a preconceived plan so that your garden can be adapted easily, and when necessary reconverted to its former use.

The illustrations show an ordinary suburban plot about 35 ft. wide, with a rear garden length of 100 ft. (The actual proportions have had to be modified to fit the page.) The house is a typical semi-detached type. As will be seen the scheme is laid out at present in three sections—the front formal garden, ornamental garden at the rear and at the farther end of the plot a small kitchen garden containing some fruit trees, garden shed, small greenhouse and compost pit. The paths in the kitchen garden are all grass and those in the formal garden are gravel.

To convert this plot to provide suffi-cient space for keeping a family of four or five people for at least part of the year, it will be necessary to double the size of the present kitchen garden. Where a large family is to be fed an allotment should be considered. On this would be grown main crop potatoes, cabbage, dutch brown beans and similar food crops.

DON'T DESTROY PLANTS

I have not advised more than doubling the vegetable area in order to leave a small section, adjacent to the house, which can be used for recreational purposes, and for the replanting of portions of the herbaceous border. It will not be necessary in this instance to destroy any of the plants, as sufficient accommodation can be found in the formal front garden and the recreational portion to take all existing plants. In the late autumn, when the roses are dormant they can be shifted into the fore beds of annuals in the front garden, and a certain amount of the herbaceous plants can be disposed of among the shrub borders. The fruit trees and rose trellis are left; these are permanent fixtures and will entail considerable trouble and expense if shifted.

The greenhouse may now be used either as a store or kept for raising seedlings, forcing rhubarb and growing early vegetables and salads. A greenhouse, even if unheated, is an asset, and can be used for tomatoes in summer.

HAVE SOME CHICKENS

The Anderson pattern air raid shelter is situated in an inconspicuous spot near the greenhouse and the area between the compost pit and greenhouse can be converted into a small chicken house and run on the intensive system. Sufficient fowls may be kept in this area to provide the family with nearly all the eggs necessary for a household of this kind. Half a dozen chickens let loose in a small orchard will keep the ground clear of pests. I have always noticed that where poultry are kept fruit trees are healthy and free from pests. Poultry are not advised among bush fruits they peck off the foliage and fruit.

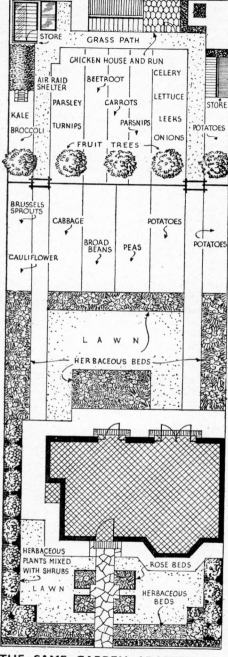

THE SAME GARDEN ADAPTED TO WARTIME NEEDS

PG—N

The area of the kitchen garden, including the new section, is divided into three portions. In the first portion a large amount of greens, such as cabbages, sprouts, cauliflowers, etc., may be grown. The second central section is given over entirely to legumes and root crops, such as peas, beans, carrots, etc.; the third section is taken up with the first and second crop early potatoes, and possibly the main crop. An area is also left for salads, such as lettuce, celery, onions, small herbs, etc.

INTERMEDIATE CROPS

The idea of dividing the garden into three main plots is to provide for ease in crop rotation. This is of prime importance in the cultivation of vegetables.

There are, of course, several intermediate crops which are not indicated on the drawing, such as spinach, chives, parsley, etc., which can be introduced in spare areas as the original plants drop out of cultivation. It is amazing how much can be grown in a small area by careful planning.

On the rose screen it may be possible to train certain of the soft fruits, such as loganberries and cultivated blackberries. These give an excellent return the second year after planting. The site where these are planted will need careful preparation. First take out a hole 2 ft. by 2 ft. and break up the subsoil. If the soil is poor replace this with fresh rich soil, mixed with rotten manure before planting.

ROWS NORTH AND SOUTH

Some plots face practically due south. This is an advantage in the cultivation of vegetables, for if the rows run lengthwise with the plot as shown, they will obtain the maximum amount of sun and air. It is important, however, to remember not to screen any of the lower growing plants, such as cabbage, by placing in the line of light taller plants such as bean rows, otherwise the crops will become drawn out and straggly. Rows should run north and south. You can adjust your rows without altering the layout.

FEATURES TO RETAIN

The compost pit and incinerator should certainly be retained as these two items will prove invaluable in the long run. Only use the incinerator for really woody material that will not decompose in the pit. Details of making a compost pit are given elsewhere in this book, and the incinerator will be found very useful for producing the potash so necessary on sandy soils.

In many gardens there are features which it is not economical to move. Rockeries, for example, are costly and they usually occupy quite a small area and can be left alone. Pools and ponds are also costly details in gardens and should be retained. A shallow pool can be converted into a watercress bed by placing a layer of loamy soil in the bottom and planting this with cuttings of watercress. All that is required is to supply fresh water from time to time.

DIG UP LAWNS

Lawns are so easily raised from seed that the sacrifice of a lawn area is not great. The turf can either be dug in, using the double digging method, as described elsewhere in this book, or it can be skimmed off to a thickness of about 2 in., and used for patching or making potting soil or supplying compost for filling cold frames.

Trees up to an age of ten or fifteen years may be moved successfully if sufficient care is taken and due preparations made. Standard laburnums, for example, that have been in their present position for three or four years, could be moved in the following way :—

First make a hole about 2 ft. or 3 ft. in diameter and about 18 in. deep. Break up the subsoil. Next dig a trench around the tree to be moved, and work underneath the ball of soil around the roots, cut off any tap roots ; try and remove a ball of soil about 2 ft. in diameter, and 1 ft. to 1½ ft. in depth.

A statutory allotment will provide the family with vegetables for eight months in the year.

ALLOTMENT GARDENING

In the war of 1914-18 allotments came into prominence ; over two million were taken up by amateur gardeners all over the country. Many of these were retained as permanent allotments managed by local allotment societies or committees of the local council, and these have a national organization.

Readers anxious to get into touch with the local allotment society should inquire, in the first instance, to the National Allotment Society, Drayton House, Gordon Street, W.C.1, for the address of the local secretary. Local plots may be immediately available ; if not, application should then be made in writing to the Town Clerk or Clerk to the Parish Council.

For food production during wartime a million new allotments are to be provided and land is to be acquired compulsorily under the War Emergency Legislation.

A statutory allotment is 10 rods, or 10 yd. by 30 yd., i.e., 300 sq. yd. This is regarded as sufficient land to provide a small family with fresh vegetables for two-thirds of the year. Rents are approximately 1s. a rod. More than this area of land may be obtained in many localities, and an extra 5 rods would be useful for main crop potatoes. But do not take on more than you can manage. Better cultivate 5 or 10 rods well than a larger area badly.

In renting an allotment try and secure as long a tenure as possible. The agreement is usually terminated by six months notice either way, expiring with the year of tenancy. I think it takes three years' crops to repay the initial labour in getting virgin land into good condition. A form of agreement is provided by the allotment society, and the rules are framed to help the members of the society to make a success of their allotment.

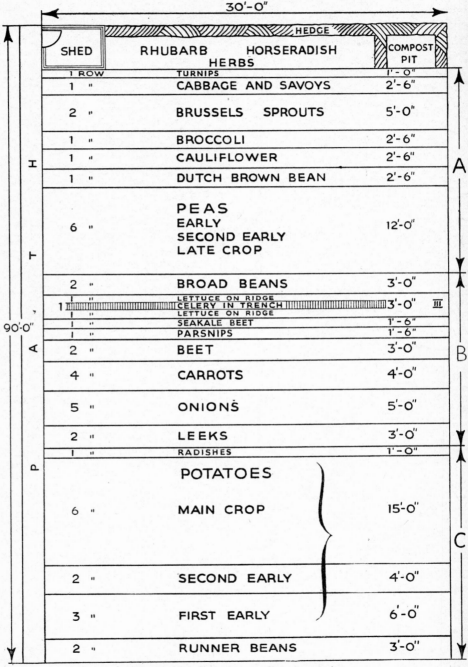

Cropping plan for statutory allotment garden.

PREPARATORY WORK
GETTING SOIL IN GOOD CONDITION

Before signing the agreement for an allotment certain factors should be taken into account. The plot should be unshaded by trees ; preferably it should have a southern aspect and be protected from the north by a hedge, tree or wall. It should be easy of access and as near as possible to the cultivator's own home.

The easiest way to test soil is to dig two or three holes at different parts of the plot. Cut the hole about 1 ft. square and 2 ft. deep. Good soil should show a surface depth of turf about 2 or 3 in. then rich brown soil to a depth of 1 ft., and under this subsoil, which will vary according to the locality. Usually it will be of clay, gravel or sand. Clay, although more difficult to work, is really the most fertile.

Water on the plot is an immense asset. I would like to see on all groups of allotments a proper system of irrigation installed so that water can be turned on from a tap at will. A little agitation in this direction by a group of plot holders might prove effective. Expense might be the chief objection. Should water be nearby, a small electric pump could be fixed to lift it to a dipping well or tank.

DIGGING AND RIDGING

Having selected your plot, and decided whether the soil is of good depth and texture, check up your pegs before doing any digging.

The usual allotment is best treated by the double digging method, described elsewhere in this book. This enables the surface grass to be buried so that it will rot and form plant food in the soil. Very heavy soil can be ridged. There is a special spade known as a "trenching tool" which I have found most suitable for ridging heavy clay soil. There is a knack in ridging, but a little practice will soon initiate the beginner.

Allotment societies are often able to buy quantities of road sweepings or similar material from the local authority, which, by arrangement, can be tipped at the end of the plots in readiness for wheeling on to the ground. It will save a lot of labour if each load can be carted as near as possible to each plot to avoid unnecessary wheeling.

APPLYING LIME

Newly-broken ground always requires a surface dressing of lime after digging. Remember to dust it over the surface after digging, because if it is thrown haphazardly at the bottom of the trench it will be lost through rains washing it away. *A fortune is lost every year in this country through fertilizers being buried too deeply, soon to dissolve and drain away.*

The easiest method of liming a plot is to obtain 75 lb. of burnt quicklime. Give the ground a dressing of approximately 4 oz. to the square yard. If this is obtained in unslaked lumps and placed in several heaps over the plot it will absorb atmospheric moisture and break down into a powdery condition in a day or so, and can then be scattered with a spade evenly over the soil. This is the most economical method because lime absorbs 40 per cent of its weight in moisture, and if it is bought all ready slaked you are really buying water. Failing this, powdered chalk, really calcium carbonate, can be applied at the rate of $\frac{1}{2}$ lb. to a square yard. Acetylene waste is another substitute. It needs to be left on the surface for a few weeks before being forked into the soil.

Gas lime is available in some districts. It should be used with care and applied to barren land in the autumn. If it is left on the surface for seven or eight weeks before forking it into the soil it will have lost its harmful properties.

The same applies to waste tannery lime. The value of lime is known to every allotment holder, although perhaps he is not always aware of the action it has on the soil and how exactly it is of such value to plant life. Many gardeners, I find, do not realize the comparative values of the several forms of lime available, and this I will try to explain. The action of lime on the soil is explained elsewhere in this book.

The three types are : Burnt lime (i.e., caustic or quicklime) ; hydrated lime (i.e., slaked lime) ; carbonate of lime (i.e., chalk and ground chalk and ground limestone).

It is the percentage of calcium oxide contained by each that determines the value.

Burnt lime. Is the result of burning limestone or chalk in kilns. It contains 65 per cent to 90 per cent of calcium oxide. When water is added to it great heat is given off until a powder results. It is therefore important to use it only on vacant land.

Hydrated lime. The resulting powder is hydrated lime. This form contains less calcium oxide but has the advantage of being a dry powder which may be more easily spread.

Carbonate of lime. Is the natural form as is found in chalk and limestone. This contains 50 per cent to 55 per cent of calcium oxide and is rather slower in action than either of the previous two forms.

WINTER MANURING

Some crops should not have rotted manure dug into the soil prior to sowing. This does not mean a poor soil is needed : they should be sown or planted in ground that has been vacated by a crop that received heavy manuring.

Broad beans	Dutch brown beans
French beans	Beet
Runner beans	Carrots
Waxpod beans	Peas
Parsnips	Swedes
Turnips	Chicory
Kohlrabi	Salsify
Scorzonera	

These crops require moderate manuring, one full barrow being sufficient for 20 sq. yd.

Jerusalem artichokes	Lettuce
	Vegetable marrow
Broccoli	Onions
Brussels sprouts	Parsley
Cabbages	Shallots
Cauliflowers	Spinach (summer,
Colewort	winter and per-
Couve tronchuda	petual)
Endive	Sweet corn
Kale	Tomatoes
Leeks	

These crops require heavy manuring one full barrow being sufficient for 10 sq. yd.

Asparagus	Mushrooms
Cardoon	Potatoes
Celeriac	Rhubarb
Celery	Sea-kale
Cucumber	

SOIL IMPROVERS

Wood ash. Some crops require plentiful supplies of potash during the growing season, and this is most easily given before sowing in the form of wood ash or ashes taken from the bonfire. The crops that benefit most are :—

Broad beans	Onions
French beans	Peas
Runner beans	Potatoes
Waxpod beans	Shallots
Dutch brown beans	

Soot. Light-coloured soil tends to be colder than dark soil. The addition of soot when digging will help to darken and so to warm a cold soil. Fresh soot contains a small quantity of nitrogen and is often used for making a liquid manure.

FERTILIZER QUANTITIES

Directions for application of fertilizer generally tell you how much is needed for a square yard ; then comes the problem of how much to buy for the allotment. Below is given a table of quantities needed for a rod at different rates per square yard.

$\frac{3}{8}$ oz. per sq. yd.	$=$	$\frac{3}{4}$ lb. per rod
$\frac{3}{4}$ oz. per sq. yd.	$=$	$1\frac{1}{2}$ lb. per rod
1 oz. per sq. yd.	$=$	2 lb. per rod
$1\frac{1}{2}$ oz. per sq. yd.	$=$	3 lb. per rod
2 oz. per sq. yd.	$=$	4 lb. per rod

$Rod = 5\frac{1}{2} \times 5\frac{1}{2}$ yd. $(30\frac{1}{4}$ sq. yd.$)$.

An attractively designed hut is an ornament to the allotment.

TOOL SHEDS AND BOXES

Tool sheds are sometimes provided by the societies, but if, owing to the emergency, this is not possible, a wooden chest with a padlock could easily be constructed at one end of the plot. This enables tools to be left, thus avoiding the bother of carrying them backwards and forwards. A chest 4 ft. by 2 ft. by 2 ft. would be ample and would serve as a seat at one end of the plot.

The diagram shows the kind I have in mind. You may find it advisable to have it fixed to the ground so that there may be no chance of its disappearing! If you are living only a few minutes away from your allotment you will be able to take the wheelbarrow to and fro and at the same time cart bags of fertilizers. Failing this, then a shed may be necessary.

Here you can help the council to keep your town tidy. In the past the sheds on allotments have been the source of much criticism. The owners have been guilty of constructing the shoddiest eyesores possible. If you cannot afford a neat little shed, and they will be difficult to obtain now owing to the timber control, perhaps you can arrange to share one with one or two other allotment holders. Or, better still, a keen allotment society will provide suitable lock-ups for a small rental. I know of some that cost only 2s. 6d. per annum.

I am very much in favour of this communal idea. No space is wasted on individual plots, overshadowing is avoided and the area is not rendered unsightly. A field of allotments planned with main and side pathways and a service centre of huts convenient to all is neat and economical of space. A field covered with huts differing in size, shape and material is ugly and uneconomical.

The plan seen on page 393 is of a communal allotment. You will see that the huts are quite simply arranged on the paths which are branching from the central road.

Many allotment fields are quite newly formed with no allotment association in

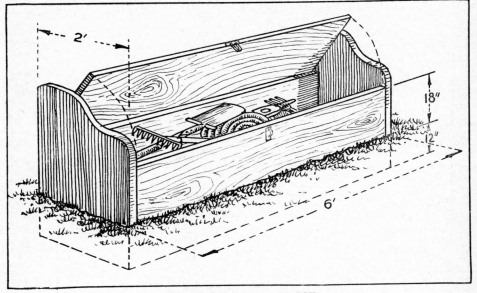

A HANDY TOOL CHEST

When sufficient money is not available for building a tool hut a good idea is to obtain a few lengths of seasoned deal, give them three coats of creosote and arrange them in trunk form, which can be sunk into the ground to render it inconspicuous. If the two ends of the trunk are carried up and shaped as shown in the sketch the closed trunk can be used as a seat.

the district. If you are renting such a one, get some of the holders together and see what can be done to form a new society. Then bear in mind the communal centre idea and work for its organization.

ROTATION OF CROPS

On allotments it is important to adopt some system of crop rotation. The effect of rotation is to obtain a better yield and to avoid diseases which will attack certain crops if they are grown continuously on the same plot of land. Onions are the only crop which can be grown on the same land year after year, provided suitable manures and fertilizers are applied.

In practice I have found that many allotment holders follow the two year rotation, half the plot being taken up by potatoes and the remainder with other crops. In such a case the operation is simply to rotate the crops alternate years, but the best method is to adopt the three year rotation.

Although attention is directed to the rotation of crops in other sections of the book it is such an important point that there is no harm in repeating it.

By a rotation of crops the same land does not carry the same vegetables in successive years. For convenience we divide our crops into three groups : 1, peas and beans ; 2, cabbage, broccoli and other greenstuff, turnips and swedes ; 3, root crops. Lettuce, spinach and other saladings are treated as intercrops, whilst leeks, onions and celery are placed on spare land in any one of the sections, preferably the cabbage sections, but as these are usually the most numerous this is not always possible. Each section is treated differently, the requisite digging being done and fertilizers applied. In this way only one section need be double-dug each winter. This obviates much heavy work.

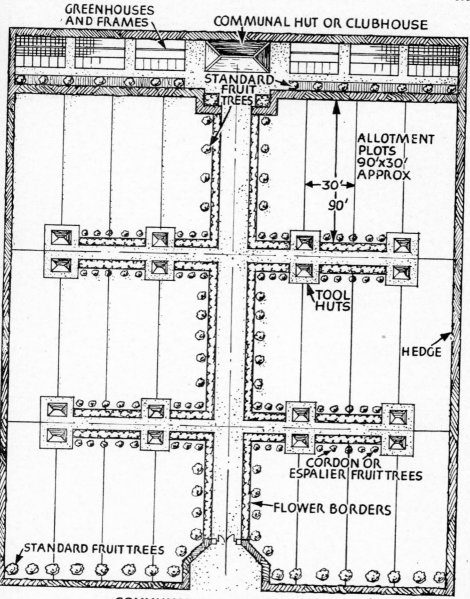

GREENHOUSES AND FRAMES

COMMUNAL HUT OR CLUBHOUSE

STANDARD FRUIT TREES

ALLOTMENT PLOTS 90'x30' APPROX

←30'→

90'

TOOL HUTS

HEDGE

CORDON OR ESPALIER FRUIT TREES

FLOWER BORDERS

STANDARD FRUIT TREES

COMMUNAL ALLOTMENT SCHEME

layout for a small communal allotment scheme nowing the disposition of individual tool sheds, ames and greenhouses, fruit trees, flower orders and the central communal hut. The entral hut can be used either as a clubhouse, lay centre for children, or a resting place for the older members. The roadways should be well constructed to allow the passage of carts or lorries bringing manure and fertilizers. Members may find it advantageous to combine for the purchase of seeds and manures, as the cost of carriage is lower for larger quantities.

full grown and before they become tough and the average size of well developed fruits.

WHITE SPROUTING BROCCOLI
An exceptionally useful vegetable, the shoots
of which can be picked as required.

Before leaving this subject perhaps I should say a little more about *intercrops*. Between rows of early potatoes autumn cabbage can be planted out ; between peas and beans rows of spinach may be sown and on celery and leek ridges lettuce can be planted. This is intercropping—the growing of a quick maturing crop between rows of slower growing main crops. Before the latter can overshadow the intercrop it is off the ground.

The growing of a quick maturing crop on land that is awaiting the main crop sowing or planting is *catch cropping*.

NUMBERS OF ROWS

The approximate number of rows for an allotment is given in the following table :

TABLE

Crop	No. of Plants	Yield
Pea (early)	1 row	52 lb.
,, (mid)	,,	47 lb.
,, (late)	,,	41 lb.
Bean, broad	,,	68 lb.
,, runner	,,	131 lb.
,, dwarf	,,	38 lb.
Celery	double row	72 lb.
Leek	,, ,,	72 lb.

Crop	No. of Plants	Yield
Potatoes (early)	4 rows	2½ cwt.
,, (main)	7 ,,	6¾ cwt.
Shallot	2 ,,	61 lb.
Onion	5 ,,	137 lb.
Carrot	4 ,,	98 lb.
Parsnip	3 ,,	82 lb.
Beet	4 ,,	67 lb.
Marrow	5 plants	27 lb.
Lettuce	—	10 doz.
Radish	—	40 bunches
Cabbage	2 rows	50
Cauliflower	1 row	24
Brussels sprouts	2 rows	38 lb.
Cucumber	4 plants	18
Rhubarb	—	18 bundles
Parsley	1 row	25 bunches
Herbs	—	—

The estimated cost of these vegetables if purchased in a shop is £13 9s. 9d. (pre-war) and the cost of seeds, potatoes, farmyard manure, fertilizers and rent is £2 7s. 0d. This is, of course, for an allotment given special attention in all cultural details, but it can be achieved by any one following the simple instructions given in this book.

A good rule to follow in cropping an allotment is to grow crops that are dear to buy and quickly perishable. Fresh cauliflowers, beans, peas, lettuce and early potatoes always taste sweeter from one's own garden.

For reasons of health also this advice is valuable. There is a world of difference between a crisp lettuce freshly picked and one that has travelled from grower to market, from market to retailer and from retailer to purchaser.

Kohlrabi, a useful allotment vegetable.

HANDY REFERENCE PAGE

FOR THE TEN-ROD PLOT

Approximate Cost of Tools, Equipment and Seed

	£	s.	d.
Spade		7	9
Fork (four prong)		7	6
Dutch hoe		3	0
Draw hoe		2	6
Rake (fourteen teeth)		3	0
Garden line		1	3
Canterbury hoe		3	3
Trowel		2	9
Water can		8	6
Syringe	1	0	0
Barrow	1	1	0
Labels (9-in.)		1	8
Indelible pencil			4
Pea sticks		2	6
Bean sticks		2	0
Lime (4 cwt.)		12	0
Farmyard manure ..		15	0
Sulphate of ammonia (7 lb.) ..		1	0
Sulphate of potash (7 lb.) ..		1	6
Superphosphate of lime (14 lb.)		1	3
Naphthalene (14 lb.)		4	6
Burgundy mixture		1	3
Caterpillar insecticide		2	0
Slug killer		1	0
Quassia extract		3	0
Mildew fungicide..		3	6
	£6	**13**	**0**
Seeds		12	6
Potatoes		9	9
	£7	**15**	**3**

N.B. The above prices are based on pre-war costs, with an allowance made for a wartime increase in prices.

Many new allotment holders will find it possible to reduce the capital outlay considerably below the above figure; they will already possess tools, pea and bean sticks can be cut from hedges, and wheelbarrows can be made at home if a small wheel is purchased separately.

MATURITY TABLE

Vegetable	Time for Germination	Ready for use in:
Jerusalem artichoke	—	7–8 months
Broad beans	2 weeks	4 months
French beans	8–10 days	2½ months
Runner beans	8–10 days	2½ months
Dutch beans	8–10 days	3½ months
Beet	10–15 days	4 months
Broccoli	5–10 days	10–12 months
Brussels sprouts	5–10 days	6 months
Cabbages	5–10 days	4½ months
Capsicum	12 days	5 months
Cardoon	30 days	6 months
Carrots	10–14 days	5 months
Cauliflowers	5–10 days	5 months
Celeriac	10–20 days	5–6 months
Celery	10–20 days	6 months
Chicory	6–8 days	6 months
Chives	10 days	4 months
Colewort	5–10 days	6 months
Couve tronchuda	5–10 days	6 months
Cress	3 days	15 days
Ridge cucumbers	6–12 days	2½ months
Egg plant	10–14 days	5 months
Endive	10–12 days	4 months
Kale	5–8 days	7 months
Kohlrabi	5–8 days	3 months
Leeks	8–10 days	7 months
Lettuces	5–8 days	2–3 months
Marrows	6–12 days	4 months
Mushrooms	—	7–8 weeks
Mustard	5 days	12 days
Onions	8–10 days	6–7 months
Parsley	13–16 days	4 months
Parsnips	15–21 days	8 months
Peas	8–14 days	2½–3 months
Potatoes	—	4 months
Radishes	4–7 days	3–6 weeks
Salsify	8–14 days	7 months
Scorzonera	8–14 days	7 months
Shallots	—	6 months
Spinach	12–18 days	3 months
Sweet corn	8–10 days	3–4 months
Swede	5–9 days	5 months
Tomatoes	6–12 days	6 months
Turnips	5–9 days	3 months

This maturity table assumes reasonably good weather conditions. In extremes of heat or cold germination may be quicker or slower according to the crop; carrot seed, for example, can remain in the ground for weeks or even months without germinating if there is a dry spell after sowing.

WALLFLOWERS

Although chiefly used for bedding or in flower borders these beautiful plants are well suited to allotment culture. Grown in lines between vegetables, some of the young plants can be sold in autumn and the remainder left for use as cut flowers in spring.

cut flowers, and find their way into the markets in bunches.

Other common annuals grown for cutting include cornflowers (often best if sown in autumn to stand the winter in the open), calliopsis, gaillardia, annual chrysanthemums, godetias, sweet sultan, Shirley poppies, candytuft, clarkia and larkspurs. In a warm garden or where the winters are not too severe these can all be sown in autumn, but spring sowing is safer in some districts.

BIENNIALS FROM SEED

Biennials are often sown in lines across the plot, say between rows of some vegetable crop. The seedlings are not thinned out, but carefully transplanted, so that every seedling is grown on to maturity. Wallflowers, Canterbury bells, sweet-williams, sweet scabious, and forget-me-nots are plants grown from seed one season to flower the next spring and early summer.

Finally there are the innumerable seedlings of so-called half-hardy plants that are always on sale in April and May, for immediate planting out where they are to mature, such as stocks, asters, double daisies, tobacco flowers, salvias, antirrhinums and so on. These plants are sown early under glass, and by the time they are on sale are nearly at their flowering stage.

A VALUABLE ASSET

Such seedlings are a worth-while investment for busy food gardeners. They can be set out immediately they are bought, and if the water supply is kept up at first, and the hoe used later to keep the soil surface aerated, they need very little other attention, and will repay the gardener with quantities of good cut flowers, and with a greatly improved appearance in the kitchen garden.

To sum up, the allotment gardener need not turn a blind eye to flowers, for they take up very little space, can be managed with the vegetables, and will prove one of the garden's most valuable assets.

ESCHSCHOLTZIA

Seed sown where the plants are to flower gives a patch of colour for many months.

STORING AND PRESERVING

NATURAL STORAGE OF ROOT CROPS

It is not necessary for all crops to reach maturity before they can be used. Very young carrots are delicious, and it is well known that the thinnings from autumn-sown onions may be used in spring salads. Many of the root crops, such as beet, turnips and parsnips, are more tender before they are fully grown, and kohlrabi should never be left until fully grown. Peas and beans are often sweeter in flavour when gathered just before they reach their full size ; they are liable to become stringy and lose their delicate flavour if left till later. In addition to this, regular picking is important, so that the strength of the plant is concentrated on developing pods and plants will not cease to be productive before their time. For this reason, when seed has to be saved, it is not until the last pods are forming that they are left ungathered.

Vegetable and fruit storing may be divided into two types : (1) Storing in their natural condition, for use as required, and (2) domestic preservation.

Artichoke (Jerusalem). Through the winter tubers can be left in the ground and dug as required.

Artichoke (Globe). Heads are best cut early in the morning.

Beet. The main crop should be lifted when the leaves are showing a lack of freshness, and a flabbiness of the outer leaves. After lifting, remove the leaves by a sharp twist (not by cutting). Beet can be stored in heaps in a shed. Cover with about 4 in. of straw, and then in the following week with a 2-in. layer of moist, sifted soil. Alternatively they can be dried and packed away in dry sand in a frost-proof place. Beet stored thus should remain in good condition until the following April. Long or winter beet of the Cheltenham green-top type is best for storage.

Carrot. As already noted, very young carrots are delicious, but the main crop should not be lifted until late autumn. A natural curling of the leaves, and a dulling of colour is an indication that it is time to lift. Cut off the leaves close to the carrot root, but take care not to damage the root, or shrivelling may result. Roots should be stored in a frost-proof place, in boxes or on the floor of a shed, and covered with dry sand or fine coal ash. Layers can be built up in this way. The carrots should be placed crown outwards. Covering with sacking or straw is advisable as a precaution against severe frosts. Large crops will require clamping like potatoes.

Celeriac. In late autumn roots should be lifted and stored like potatoes.

Onion. When bulbs are properly matured (indicated by drying off of leaves), they should be dug up and spread either in the open air in a sunny place or in an airy shed until the tops are dead, and then tied up in rope form and hung up in a cool, dry place.

Three pieces of strong string are required, which are tied together in a knot at one end and hung from a hook at a convenient height for working. The onions are placed in position one by one and the strings wound round the necks in a similar way to plaiting.

Parsnip. Roots can be left in the ground until they are required, but they can also be lifted and stored in sand in the dark early in March after first trimming off tops. If the frosts are severe, protect with straw, bracken or ashes.

Potato. Early potatoes should be dug for immediate use, but as a general rule second earlies and main crop can be left in the ground until the tops are dead. They should be lifted with a fork placed well under the tubers to avoid damage. Clinging earth must be cleaned off and the potatoes left to dry in the sun for a few hours, after which they can be stored either in a cellar or in a frost-proof

HARVESTING OF GREEN CROPS

Brussels sprouts. If the sprouts are allowed to remain on the plants very long they are inclined to become slimy and yellowed.

Spinach. Only the leaves of *winter* spinach should be picked. They should be pulled outwards and then to the side. If they are pulled upwards they are liable to damage. *Summer* spinach can be used whole when young.

FRUIT GATHERING AND STORAGE

Apples. Different varieties require different treatment. Certain early dessert kinds, such as Beauty of Bath, Lady Sudeley, James Grieve and Grenadier (cooking) are best left to ripen on the tree, and are more suitable for immediate use, whereas other varieties have late-keeping qualities and if gathered too soon they will be liable to shrivel and lose their flavour, e.g., *dessert:* Cox's Orange Pippin, Blenheim Orange, Ribston Pippin ; *cooking:* Newton Wonder, Lane's Prince Albert, Bramley's Seedling.

These are, however, gathered before they are absolutely ripe in order to store before the frosts set in. This applies especially to the larger proportion of cooking apples. Fruit that is damaged by maggots, etc., will drop early, and this must not be taken as an indication that the good fruit is ripe.

Always gather fruit in dry weather, preferably in the late morning or after-noon. Ripe fruit will separate easily from the twig to which it is attached.

Pears. Fruit of early kinds, such as Clapp's Favourite, Doyenne du Comice, etc., should be gathered before it will separate easily from the twig, when care-fully raised on a level with the stalk. It is best laid out and allowed to ripen for a few days prior to eating. The crop can be brought a few at a time into a warm room. Very few early varieties can be stored. It may be necessary to protect fruit still on the tree from attacks of wasps and birds. Thin muslin bags will be sufficient.

Late dessert kinds should be left on the tree till mid-November, e.g.,

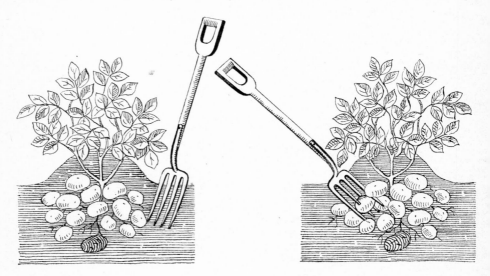

RIGHT METHOD   WRONG METHOD

LIFTING POTATOES

When lifting potatoes care must be taken not to cut or spear the tubers. A special fork with long prongs is the best implement to use and should be inserted as shown on the left.

Pitmaston Duchess, Easter Beurré, etc. The same applies to certain stewing varieties such as Catillac, Bellissimo d'Hiver.

The large proportion of pears should be gathered towards the end of October.

Storing of apples and pears. Fruit should first be sweated by being laid in heaps and left to heat for about fourteen days, and then be stored away on trays or boxes in single layers, keeping the varieties separate, preferably in a cool, dry, dark cellar. There will be no need to cover except during frost. An average temperature of 45 degrees Fahrenheit is sufficient. Fruit must be looked over periodically and any decaying fruit removed.

If a cellar is not available, a dry, well-ventilated shed, preferably with a brick or concrete floor, may be utilized. For very choice keeping varieties of apples, e.g., Cox's Orange Pippin, Lane's Prince Albert, etc., a good method is to wrap each fruit in clean white tissue paper or in specially prepared sulphate wraps.

Clamping of apples. If storage space is limited, apples can be clamped in the same way as potatoes and will keep well. Heap the apples on a layer of clean straw, making sure that the ground is well drained and level. They can be left to sweat for some ten days. After sorting out the uncertain apples, the rest should be covered with clean

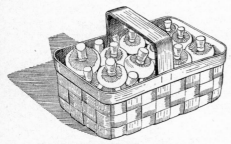

MARKETING MUSHROOMS
For marketing purposes mushrooms are packed in chip baskets and small punnets. The stalks are cut and the tops of the mushrooms brushed with a soft brush to remove any specks of dirt. The cleaned mushrooms are then placed in layers as shown in the diagram.

straw, and over this a 6-in. layer of fine, dry soil. Put in the straw a small drain-pipe for ventilation. The bottom of straw wisp or pipe should actually touch the apples, as this will ensure proper liberation of moisture and heat. By digging a small trench all round, surplus water will be drained off.

BUSH FRUITS

Currant. *Black:* Should be picked just before they are quite ripe, but when the larger proportion of berries have turned black.

Red: For dessert use should not be picked until all the berries in the bunch are red, but for cooking they can be picked whilst yet only a pinkish red colour. Red currants are less suitable than black for bottling as they are inclined to be seedy.

Gooseberries. To get the best results the largest berries should be picked first round about Whitsuntide ; this will give the others a chance to swell. Picking about every fourteen days is a good ruling. The best varieties for bottling are Lancashire Lad (red) Cousin's Seedling (yellow), and Careless (green).

Loganberries should be picked when quite red, before the deep reddish purple colour is evident. Picking with the stalk is not necessary.

Raspberries can be left until quite ripe if intended for jam making and picked without stalks. If they are for dessert purposes the berries should be picked when fairly firm and just turning red in colour, but do not leave until quite ripe, and leave the short stalks attached. Raspberries are very easily bruised, and great care is necessary if they are intended for bottling. It is an advantage to pick straight into the bottles. The fruit must be firm and in quite sound condition, as it is liable to deteriorate quickly, and it is unwise to leave time between picking and preserving.

Strawberries should be picked before fully ripe. Pinch off from the stem with the finger and thumb a short distance

Plums. Only certain varieties are suitable for drying. The Victoria plum and Pond's Seedling are the most satisfactory. The fruit must be washed and then laid on the drying tray and placed in the oven, but taking care not to raise the temperature above 120 degrees Fahrenheit until the skin shows signs of shrivelling. The temperature can then be raised to 150 degrees Fahrenheit and kept thus until the process is complete. This can be tested by squeezing the plums and noting if the skin remains intact and without exudation of juice. At this stage the fruit can be taken out of the oven, laid aside for about twelve hours and then packed away.

Small fruits are not worth drying as they shrink and lose colour.

Cooking of dried fruit. Always soak dried fruits in water for some two days prior to cooking. The water in which they have been soaked should then be boiled, and boiling gently continued until the fruit is tender. Do not add the sugar at the beginning but only a short time before boiling is completed.

Dried herbs. It is useful to have a store of dried herbs during the winter months. The procedure is quite simple. Always gather the young plants just at the flowering stage, and when quite dry. Leaves should be picked from the stalks of the large-leaved herbs, but this will not be necessary with the small-leaved kinds. With the former, the leaves should be tied in muslin and dipped into boiling water for a minute, and then after shaking, placed in a cool oven, keeping the temperature to between 110 degrees and 130 degrees Fahrenheit.

The small-leaved kinds such as thyme, etc., must first be washed, then tied into bundles, covered with muslin and hung up to dry near the kitchen range.

In both cases, when dried and crisp, the herbs should be crushed with a rolling pin, powdered, and then stored in bottles and kept in the dark.

If parsley is being dried, it is better to place in a hot oven for a minute rather than use the slow method. Scorching must be guarded against.

PRESERVING FRUIT AND VEGETABLES

Garden owners will find that the home preservation of fruit and vegetables is a major economy, as it not only reduces the household expenses, but also adds to the excellence of the table. Even if you cannot grow your own vegetables, but watch the markets carefully, and buy at the moment when fruit is cheap but in first-rate condition, and then follow the instructions in the art of bottling, making of jams and jellies, etc., you also can enjoy the benefits of reduced household expenses. There are, as you will see, ways of bottling fruits without sugar. More stress is laid on the bottling of fruit than vegetables, as the bottling of vegetables is more difficult than fruit, and requires a rather more elaborate sterilization process and equipment.

This economy can, however, only be effectively made by following directions in detail, and in noting the reasons why faults in bottling are entailed and how they can be avoided. The same applies to jams, jellies, pickles and chutneys, and to the more luxurious forms of preservation such as the making of candied fruits which, since they are luxuries, have been omitted from these pages.

BOTTLING OF FRUITS

General rules. Although rules will vary for different fruits, there are certain rules which are applicable in every case, and if these rules are not observed, bottling is liable to be a failure.

1. Always choose sound fruit, and slightly under ripe. The fruit should be "firm ripe." Over ripe fruit will lose shape and flavour and become very soft or break during sterilizing. It is most unsatisfactory to pack fruit at different stages of ripeness in the same bottle.

2. Bottles and jars should be absolutely clean and free from flaws and cracks. They should be steamed and the insides left moist as the fruit will then pack more easily.

3. Fruit must be picked *dry*. If there is an unexpected shower of rain, stop picking until the fruit is quite dry again.

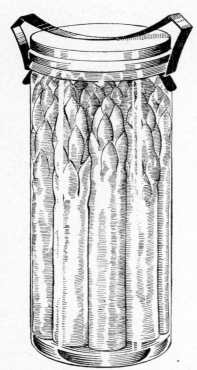

Correctly packed asparagus in clip-top bottle. The bottle is filled with brine and is ready for sterilization in a pressure cooker.

4. Wash the fruit if necessary. Soft fruit will retain its firmness and good flavour if left unwashed, but if it is unavoidable, it should be done *after* the fruit has been packed into the bottles. The bottles can then be filled with water and emptied out two or three times. Hard fruits, such as gooseberries, plums, may be washed before packing; the best way is to place the fruit in a colander and rinse under the tap.

5. Grading of the fruit according to size and ripeness will ensure even heating with much more attractive results.

6. All utensils, rings and covers should be sterilized by dipping into boiling water.

7. Rubber rings must not have any flaws and their edges should be smooth.

8. Hot bottles straight from the sterilizer should never be placed on a cold surface or they may crack. Stand the bottles on a piece of wood or on asbestos.

Raspberries and currants will make a useful mixed fruit salad. This clip-top bottle is packed correctly and the fruit is covered with syrup and ready to be placed into the sterilizer.

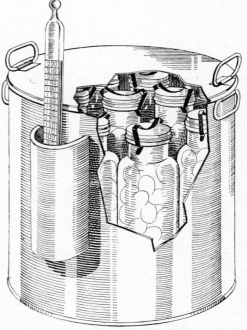

Practical type of sterilizer with copper bottom, showing bottles packed and sealed ready for water sterilization. Sterilizers of this type are made to hold from eight to twenty-four bottles.

9. Test the thermometer in boiling water before using it, and see that it registers 212 degrees Fahrenheit.

10. Before putting the sterilized bottles into store, test all the seals by removing the clip or screw and lifting the bottles by the lid. There will be no need to replace the clips, and if screw bands are replaced, they should first be greased with vaseline and then only lightly screwed down.

SPECIAL PREPARATION FOR DIFFERENT FRUITS

Apples. To prevent browning when peeled, each fruit should first be halved and one half should be laid flat with the cut side down, whilst the other is cut into rings, quarters, or whatever is desired. These sections must be placed without delay into a weak brine (2 teaspoonfuls salt to 1 quart water), and a plate placed over the pieces to keep them from rising. When ready to pack, they should be quickly rinsed, in cold water, and packed into the bottles, and covered immediately with syrup (8 oz. sugar to each pint of water). The remainder of the fruit can be left in the brine until required.

If economy in bottles and storage space has to be considered, a slightly different method can be used. The pieces of apples should be removed from the salted water, and dipped in boiling water for three minutes, or steamed in a colander over a pan of boiling water until tender. The fruit will shrink ; much more can be packed into one bottle than by the other method. The packing must be very close, and very little water or syrup will be added. Apples packed in this way will be very useful in tarts, pies and puddings.

The best varieties of cooking apples suitable for bottling are : Bramley's Seedling, Lane's Prince Albert, Lord Derby, and Annie Elizabeth.

Pears. The same treatment of weak brine is applicable to pears. Peeled pears will discolour if exposed to air. A quick and neat way of coring pears is to use a strong teaspoon to hollow out the core after the fruit has been halved. The choice of variety in the case of pears is more difficult than for apples as the best bottled pears are obtained only when a well-ripened dessert is used. Good results have been obtained with such varieties as Pitmaston Duchess, Beurré Hardy, Catillac, and the familiar Williams's Bon Chrétien pear. The same method is followed as with apples, but if you are dealing with cooking varieties or dessert varieties that do not ripen well, the pieces should be stewed gently until quite tender in a syrup (4 oz. sugar to 1 pint water), and after draining off the water they should be packed into the bottles and covered with the syrup in which they have been cooked.

Stone fruits. Large plums and apricots are difficult to pack into bottles without wasting bottle space, but a good pack for home use can be made by halving the fruit and removing the stones, though it is advisable to include a few stones in each bottle to maintain the true flavour. They can be packed in the centre of the jar, out of sight. Fleshy varieties of plum such as Victoria, Pond's Seedling and Magnum Bonum will bottle well, but make sure the fruit is firm ripe. After packing, cover with syrup (8-12 oz. per pint water for whole plums, and 12 oz. for halves) and sterilize according to directions. Greengage, Mirabelle and Early Rivers will bottle well whole.

Apricots should be ripe and well coloured. They will pack well in halves with stones removed and cut surface facing the bottom of the bottles. Varieties Moorpark and Shipley will pack well.

Soft fruits. When dealing with soft fruits such as raspberries, it is better to pick them straight into the bottles. Only firm, sound fruit should be used, the stalk being removed carefully. If the fruit has to be left overnight, and cannot be picked straight into bottles, it must not be left in the baskets, but should be spread out on trays or sheets of paper to prevent heating, and left in a cool, dry place. It should then be packed as for soft fruit and covered with syrup (12 oz. per pint water) and sterilized according to directions. Varieties: Lloyd George, Duke of Cornwall, Pyne's Royal, and Superlative give the best results.

Blackberries must be picked early in the season as they are liable to lose their flavour later. Cultivated varieties such as Himalayan Giant will bottle well, but it is very important to select berries which are firm ripe, and after removing the stalks these should be washed well in cold water. Use syrup (8 oz. per pint water) for covering after packing. Blackberries and a good cooking variety of apple make a very nice mixture if bottled together.

Currants of all kinds can be used for bottling, but the black give the best results, although it is necessary to select only the firm ripe good-sized, thin-skinned currants. Stalks should be removed, and the currants gently washed in cold water. After packing according to directions for soft fruits, cover with an 8-12 oz. per pint strength syrup.

Gooseberries. Green varieties of medium size are preferable, and the fruit should be picked before quite ripe. The stalks and blossom ends should be removed (referred to as " topping " and " snibbing "). Pack as for hard fruit and use the 8 oz. per pint syrup.

Cover jar with two sheets of paper dipped in hot milk and tie down firmly with string.

Loganberries. This is the best of the soft fruits for bottling and will keep its colour, flavour and shape well. Use before quite ripe and do not wash unless absolutely necessary. Use a 12 oz. per pint syrup. If there is a sign of maggots in the fruit, berries should be soaked in salted water ($\frac{1}{2}$ oz. to 2 pints water) for one hour. The berries can be rinsed in cold water and packed without risk.

Strawberries. These are not very satisfactory to bottle as they so quickly lose colour and shrink during sterilization.

Tomatoes. Young and firm fruit should be chosen, and stalks removed. Fruit should then be washed and blanched. This is most conveniently done by tying in a piece of cheese cloth or muslin, or placing in a blanching basket and dipping in boiling water for a minute or less, according to ripeness of fruit. This will loosen the skin and facilitate peeling. Plunge at once into cold water to make the fruit firm and easily handled. The skin should be peeled off, and it may be necessary to remove existing hard core. Small tomatoes can be packed whole, but there is an advantage in halving medium size and large fruits, as every part of the bottle is more easily utilized, and ripe tomatoes with broken skins can be used. For whole tomatoes fill to the brim with a solution of 1 teaspoonful of salt to 1 pint of water, taking care to pack firmly, and for cut tomatoes, pack tightly layer upon layer, and improve the flavour by adding $\frac{1}{4}$ oz. salt and 1 teaspoonful sugar to each 2 lb. tomatoes. No liquid should be added as the juice of the tomatoes is sufficient to cover them. Rubber rings, lids and clips or screw bands should be fixed on the bottles which should be placed on a false bottom in the sterilizer and covered with cold water. The temperature is brought up to 190 degrees Fahrenheit in one hour and should be maintained thus for about thirty minutes. After the bottles are removed, and screwbands have been used, these should be tightened immediately. It is very important that the bottles or jars are completely airtight.

vary with type of fruit. An average proportion of sugar for a syrup is 8-12 oz. per pint of water. The syrup should be allowed to become quite cold before pouring over the fruit. If a sugar solution of sufficient strength is used in vacuum bottles, the fruit can be served immediately without re-cooking.

Only a very weak syrup need be used with home-made seals. A syrup of 2 oz. per pint of water is a safe strength.

METHODS OF STERILIZATION

Oven sterilization. This method is especially practicable when small quantities of fruit ripen daily. Only a moderate oven (about 240 degrees Fahrenheit) is needed. Cook after the fruit has been packed into the bottle, but before the syrup is poured on. The fruit should be packed right to the top of the jars and covered with patty pans or saucers and then placed in the oven. Leave for three-quarters to one hour, turning the bottles occasionally to ensure even heating. It is safest to place the bottles on a shelf at least 6 in. above the bottom plate of the oven. Slow cooking is better than too much haste, as the latter will cause bursts and pulping of the fruit. In about forty-five to sixty minutes the fruit begins to look cooked and sinks in the bottles with the juice running freely. Take the bottles out of the oven one at a time, and have ready a kettle of boiling water or a pan of boiling syrup. The patent cap and home-made seal must be affixed immediately while steam is still rising freely from the bottle; put on the lid, clip or screwband if the patent stopper bottles are used. In this case do not insert the rubber rings until after removing from the oven, as the rubber is liable to perish.

Fruits such as raspberries or damsons will bottle better in dry sugar than in water. The sugar and fruit are packed alternately in the bottles (average proportion 1 lb. fruit to 8–12 oz. sugar), and the bottles are then oven sterilized as above. There is, however, often considerable shrinkage by this method, and it may be necessary to fill up one bottle from another and replace in the oven for about ten minutes to ensure sterilization. The somewhat sad appearance of the fruit after sterilization is compensated for by the delicious flavour.

Water sterilization. Cover the fruit with cold syrup or water before heating, and when patent bottles are used, fit the rubber ring, top and clip screwband. When packing the fruit the use of a thin stick will be helpful. Packing particularly well under the shoulder of the bottles is important. Make sure there is no particle of fruit left on the rim of the bottle where the band fits as this may cause an unsealed bottle. If you are using the screw type of bottle, screwbands should first be screwed tightly and then unscrewed a quarter to half turn to allow for the glass to expand during heating. After removing from the sterilizer the bands should be screwed down again tightly. In the clip top type the spring of the clip gives enough to allow for any expansion during

Well bottled plums.

heating or contraction during cooling.

The sterilizer pan or boiler must be filled with *cold* water up to the shoulder of the bottles and the sterilizer must be covered to keep in the steam and placed on the stove. The water should be brought slowly up to simmering point, taking about one hour in the process. Maximum temperature will vary for different fruits, but a guiding rule can be taken as 100 degrees Fahrenheit in the first half-hour, 170 degrees Fahrenheit in one and a half hours and maintaining at this temperature for ten minutes, i.e., a total of one hour and forty minutes heating. If a thermometer is not used, the water should be brought up to simmering point in one hour and maintained thus for ten minutes, but take great care to raise the heat very gradually, especially during the first half-hour. After removing from the hot water, place the bottles on a wood or asbestos surface to cool, and then test the seal.

STORAGE OF BOTTLED FRUITS

Bottles should be kept in a cool place and away from a strong light. Brown paper can be fastened with drawing pins over the fronts of shelves; these can be turned back easily to examine the contents from time to time, as there is always a possibility of occasional fermenting or moulding. If this is the case, the bottle must be removed immediately and the contents destroyed, care being taken to keep them away from domestic animals. Open fermenting bottles with caution as a certain amount of pressure may have been produced inside.

FAULTS IN BOTTLED FRUITS

There are often disappointments in bottling; either the fruit does not keep well, the seals do not hold, there is poor flavour, the covering liquid is cloudy, fruit rises in the bottles or sinks, air bubbles are evident, fruit turns brown at the top or has a poor colour generally. It is, however, possible to avoid all these faults by careful handling.

Fruits do not keep well unless a sufficiently high temperature has been

The result of faulty bottling.

maintained. Insufficient heating and faulty sealing also spoil fruit.

Faulty sealing is nearly always due to some defect in the bottle or top, or in the rubber rings.

Poor flavour is due to using under- or over-ripe fruit or fruit in a stale or bruised condition, or unsuitable varieties. As already noted the use of water only as a covering liquid tends to acidity.

Cloudy covering liquid noticeable just after removing from sterilizer indicates over-cooking or the use of over-ripe fruit, but if the cloudiness is apparent some time after the fruit has been in store, it may be due to some bacterial action, in which case the contents of the bottle must be discarded as unfit for use.

Fruit rising in the bottles is usually caused by loose packing or the use of too heavy a syrup. If the fruit sinks in the bottles it is usually due to over-heating, heating too quickly or using over-ripe fruit.

USEFUL AND ECONOMICAL RECIPES

Obviously there is not room in this chapter to review all the culinary possibilities of all garden crops. However, there are certain facts which ought to be known both to the cultivator and to the cook, and it is rather to make these clear that this chapter is included.

First, the general principles of **vegetable** cooking and of balanced diet with all sorts of foods. Generally speaking, the number of calories of energy required is less when *uncooked* food is eaten than when the diet consists mainly of cooked food. This suggests that wherever possible, appetizing dishes should be made with foods in their *raw* state. There is a tendency to include only the well-known salad crops in this category, but besides lettuce and radish and beet, the turnip, carrot, onion, leek, heart of cabbage, spinach, etc., if eaten young and uncooked are very nourishing. If we are likely to become short of certain of the more usual items of diet, we must try to get the best possible value out of our vegetable supplies.

There are two suggestions which serve to emphasize this means of economy :—

First, that wherever possible, *appetizing* dishes should be made with foods in their raw state.

This applies also to the second suggestion in regard to the family appetites and taste of cooked food. It is a principle which is rarely mentioned in cookery books. It is useless to force any one, child or adult, to eat unpalatable food. Every one knows by experience that such food does very little good. On the other hand, it is very important that diet should be well balanced, and naturally it is important, too, that there should be no waste. It is therefore the cook's business to prepare foods that might, in ordinary guise, be rejected, in a palatable form. For example, five or six people out of ten will refuse to eat Jerusalem artichokes if they are plain boiled. Some will eat them if they are plain boiled but with an onion added to the boiling water to disguise the "smoky" flavour, and some will eat them if they are thinly sliced, rubbed over with an onion, and fried in batter. Some will take them best in the form of white cream soup. There is hardly any one who could not be given these artichokes in some form and eat them with enjoyment, yet there are families that will refuse to grow them, or waste them after they are grown, because they "don't like artichokes." Such cases could be multiplied indefinitely with all kinds of vegetables.

It is proposed, therefore, in these pages to suggest general ways and means, rather than to go into great detail concerning cooking methods. Any experienced home cook will be able to follow out the suggestions for herself. The various garden crops are treated alphabetically for easy reference.

A third suggestion concerns old-fashioned cooking methods which are definitely wasteful if not harmful. For instance, the practice of cooking vegetables in large quantities of water which is afterwards thrown away is particularly wasteful, as the valuable mineral salts the vegetables contain are thrown away with the water. It is also wasteful to boil green vegetables with soda. Carbonate of soda keeps the fresh green colour, but robs the vegetable of some of its value. Washing soda, which was used by old-fashioned cooks, is even worse.

Conservative cooking methods, steaming, or cooking in a minimum of water so that nothing need be thrown away, are best from every point of view, except possibly appearance, and this, after all, is merely a matter of habit and personal prejudice.

Artichokes. The green globe artichoke cannot be regarded as a profitable garden crop, but those who have it in quantities in the garden should make the best use of it. Gather the flower-heads while still firm, and not fully opened. Trim away the stem, and some of the roughest of the base leaves. Wash the heads, put them into salted water and boil for about half an hour. The heads can be served as they are, one to each person, together with a little melted butter. For economy this should be served separately, as the artichoke leaves are picked off and dipped into butter as they are eaten. If a small quantity of melted butter is supplied to each person, the remainder, after the artichokes are eaten, could be used by each individual on the potatoes of the next course, so that there is no waste. Prepared mayonnaise dressing could be used in place of the butter.

Jerusalem artichokes are a much neglected dish. They are second in food value only to potatoes among the allotment crops, and every effort should be

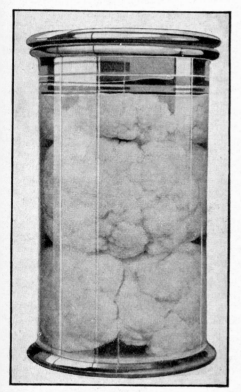

Cauliflowers.

made to serve them palatably. The tubers are lifted, washed and peeled. Boiling takes generally about half an hour, but small young tubers will cook more quickly. An onion added to the water when the tubers are cooked will improve their flavour. A good supper dish is made by parboiling the tubers in salt water with an onion, then slicing them to the thickness of about $\frac{3}{8}$ in., flouring each, dipping it in batter, and frying to a nice golden brown. The remaining onion and water makes the base of a good gravy to serve with them.

For a cream soup, boil the artichokes well, with half the weight of onions. Press these through a sieve, and reheat, together with sufficient ground rice to thicken the soup nicely. Some milk should be used as an addition at the last moment ; the proportion of milk to water in the soup is a matter of judgment. A sprinkling of chopped chives, chopped parsley or other soup flavouring can be added at will.

Asparagus is a luxury crop, dependent on good soil and years of cultivation. If supplies are available, the most economical way to cook them is by steaming the heads. Tie them in bunches, after cleaning, and stand these bunches upright in boiling water that comes nearly to the green part. Let them cook for forty minutes in this, and the stems will be soft while the tips will not be overcooked, so that there is not a great deal of waste.

Broad beans should be young enough for there to be no black " eye " to the bean. If they are older, the skins of the beans will be tough and the bean itself less palatable. Old beans can, however, be used for soup making, the skins being left behind when the beans are sieved. Twenty to twenty-five minutes is all that the young beans should require for boiling. They are nice served with parsley sauce. Shell just before cooking ; part of the flavour is lost if beans are left long after shelling.

Broad bean stew can be made by boiling shelled beans for about ten minutes in salted boiling water until and of course the salt and pepper finish. On an average use about three times as much liquid as vegetables.

Artichoke, broad beans, cabbage, carrots, celery, celeriac, marrow, onions, parsnips, peas (dried or green), spinach, sprouts, tomatoes and turnips can all be used as ingredients.

White soups. In this category will come the soups made with cabbage and sprouts, but all the other vegetables named can be used alone or mixed either as white soup or brown soup. The green vegetables are chopped small and stewed in fat in a covered saucepan slowly for about five minutes, and care taken not to burn. Add boiling water and simmer till tender (about forty minutes) and then add milk and seasoning and watch the thickening. A tablespoonful of cornflour can, if required, be added to the milk. Simmer again for about ten minutes. The addition of a chopped onion will add taste.

Brown soup entails the browning of the chopped vegetables when frying prior to adding the liquid. Blended soups such as carrot (three parts) to onion (one part), flavoured with parsley or a mixed vegetable soup can all be made to advantage.

If fresh vegetables are not available, dried split peas or haricots may be used, but all dried pulse should be washed before cooking. This is easily done by stirring in hot water a few times.

As a soup thickener the use of breadcrumbs or oatmeal will be a useful economy, but stir in early so that it is well cooked along with the vegetables.

Meat stock consisting of bones or meat scraps should be made in a closed saucepan, and the outer leaves of cabbage, lettuce, leeks and onions can be added. Vegetable stock alone is, however, equally useful, as for example the water in which roots, beans and peas have been boiled. Cabbage water has a high food value, but the flavour will be too strong unless the cabbage has been scalded prior to boiling.

Sieving stock is only necessary in the case of meat stock, to get rid of the small pieces of bone, in vegetable stock to remove fibrous matter.

Seasoning should not be limited only to salt and pepper. The addition of chopped parsley and other herbs, a few gratings of nutmeg, a few cloves, or a little essence of celery, or some ketchup will make all the difference.

Old green peas will also make good soup. Do not throw away pea pods. Wash them carefully in salt water and boil till tender in a saucepan with onion, carrot and herbs if they are available. Then pass through a sieve and thicken with some cornflour and margarine. This will make a really good green soup.

Most of these recommendations seem to refer to vegetables available in every season except the spring, but here is a recipe which is truly springlike. Shred a lettuce and slice some spring onions thinly. Fry in a saucepan with dripping for a few minutes. Add stock and a little milk and simmer for about ten minutes. Add a tablespoonful of cornflour with some more milk and pour into the soup, stirring well until it boils. Allow to simmer and add seasoning and a nutmeg flavouring. Pour over dry crisped bread which has been cut into strips and garnish with parsley.

Vegetable Hot-pot. Chop up some carrot, turnip, potato, leek, onion or whatever is available, mix with butter beans and herbs and seasoning in a casserole filled with water or stock, and cook slowly. Strain off the liquid, except for what is needed for sauce. The sauce is easily made by stirring in flour with melted margarine in the pan and boiling. Add the pepper and salt and some grated cheese. This poured over the vegetables will make a very nourishing and economical meal. Another good way of using up vegetables is the so-called colcannon method. Mash potatoes and other vegetables through a sieve, allowing more potatoes in proportion to the rest, and add a tablespoonful of butter. Put into a fire-proof dish and sprinkle with breadcrumbs and some dabs of margarine. Bake until it has a golden brown appearance.

Salads in variety.

SALADS AND FRUIT DISHES

"A salad a day keeps the doctor away." Lettuce, endive, mustard and cress, cucumber and other green salad crops are too well known to need any special comment here, except that growers might remember that surplus quantities of such crops that cannot be used in salad bowls might more often be cooked. Lettuce cooked with garden peas, for instance, is quite good, and almost any saladings might go into the soup pot at times.

There is no reason why we should despise cooked salads, although the importance of raw vegetables has already been emphasized. Jerusalem artichokes, beet, beans, carrots, celeriac, onions, parsnips, peas, kohlrabi can be boiled and sieved, and if served with grated nutmeg, lemon, tomato juice, etc., on toast will make an excellent relish. On the cold vegetables it can be cut into small pieces and mixed with salad dressing and served in a salad bowl.

Apart from the green salad crop already mentioned, corn salad (or lamb lettuce) is an interesting addition to the winter salad bowl. It needs no special preparation beyond washing.

A very tasty mixed raw salad can be made by chopping up endive, spinach, carrot, radish, onion, leek, turnip and beet and dressing with lemon juice and a little sprinkling of sugar.

Beetroot and potato and celery salad; beetroot, onion and celery; tomato, walnuts, cabbage or savoy heart chopped up, and sections of an unpeeled apple; artichokes, potatoes, turnip, celery with apples, all these are suggestions which might well be tried. Of course in every case add some fresh lettuce if available, and do not forget the salad dressing.

Salad combinations can be grouped under the stylish heading of *Hors d'œuvre variés*. There is a certain fine art in introducing as many items as possible, and not forgetting on appropriate occasions the blend with extras

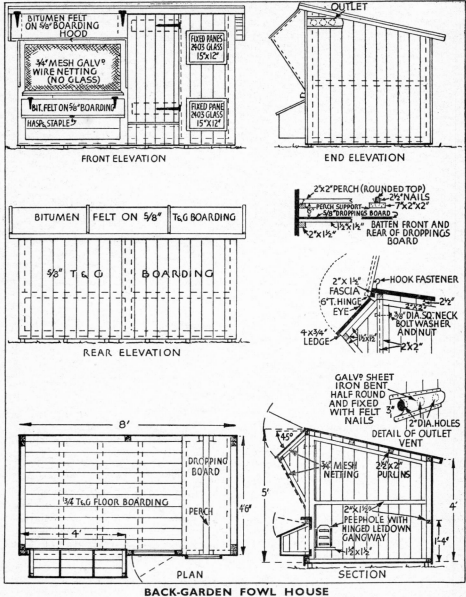

BACK-GARDEN FOWL HOUSE

The working drawings shown comply with the regulations of the housing authorities. The construction is strong and neat and the large amount of open front gives the birds ample fresh air while keeping out any draughts. The object is to obtain the maximum amount of fresh air combined with a perfectly dry floor and litter. The birds roost on the right-hand side of the house as you enter the door, and are surrounded on three sides by a solid wall. The nesting boxes, as will be seen, are placed outside; this is a great saving in floor space, and an extra house can be built on to the side without interfering with the construction.

desired extra house accommodation can be built on, and every experienced poultry keeper will appreciate this point. As the house is planned, it can conveniently be set against an existing wall, so that no space is wasted. The nest boxes are without hinges or other parts that rust can attack. They slide out for cleaning and when in position they are in comparative darkness.

This type of house is one that I can thoroughly recommend to any beginner in poultry keeping, and particularly to the novice who wishes to keep a few backyard layers so that he can be sure of a supply of eggs throughout the year. It is better to start with a small stock, and to practise economy by using up all household scraps, than to attempt to make a " fortune " by investing capital in houses and appliances.

Assuming that a much larger plot of land is available, a semi-intensive house and run might easily be arranged to accommodate about fifty layers. These would have a house 20 ft. by 10 ft., and also a grass run, or an earth or gravel run, in which the hens would be released on favourable days. Or a small house 6 ft. by 8 ft. might take a dozen birds if they have the use of an outdoor run.

There are, in addition, several other ways to house poultry. One is a fold-pen, which is a portable affair that can be moved about the garden each day, so that the birds are always on fresh ground. In rural districts it might be possible for a poultry keeper to rent from a farmer a piece of ground to be utilized in this way.

For all these varying types of houses there is a general rule to guide the selector : only undertake what you can reasonably expect to deal with properly. If your knowledge of poultry keeping is limited to the scattering of grain that you may have done to help a friendly

STANDARD HOUSE FOR EIGHT TO TEN BIRDS

The modern fowl house designed by the *Feathered World*. This can be obtained already machined for bolting together from many of the leading manufacturers, or the handyman can build it from the designs shown on the opposite page. This is large enough to accommodate eight to ten pullets and measures over all 8 ft. by 4 ft. 6 in. by 5 ft. high. The projecting hood, keeps off any driving rain, and slanting netting gives efficient protection.

out both sparrows and mice, and at the same time, confine the fowls, yet allow them plenty of ventilation, and all openings should be netted in this way. It is a good rule for the poultry keeper to remember that birds, like plants, are best grown hardy, that is they respond best to all the ventilation that their constitutions will stand. Windows should only be closed in the very worst weather.

SUN PARLOURS FOR HENS

Another point of importance is that sunlight should be allowed : dirty windows must not be tolerated in the hen house any more than in a private dwelling. A drop or two of glycerine on a soft cloth, used daily, will keep them in good condition if a weekly wash and polish are also practised.

Hens, like humans, have recently been allowed special sun parlours, with good results. These are really wire-floored runs extending along the house front and 2 ft. to 5 ft. in width. They should have the floor of this high enough to allow of droppings being cleared away, or should be provided with a droppings' board. Sides will be of wire netting, and a hinged glass cover or netting cover should also be provided.

Any other arrangement by which hens can be given extra fresh air and sunshine and extra exercise will benefit the birds, and each poultry keeper is advised to exercise his own ingenuity in this matter.

The question of feeding poultry is one that has to be considered from several points of view. First of all it is the food that represents the bulk of the outlay to the backyard poultry keeper. He cannot allow his expenditure on foodstuffs to mount up until the cost of his fresh eggs is as much or more than he would have to pay for them in the shops. He has sufficient expense in obtaining the fowls and keeping up their home. Consequently he feels that any way in which he can reduce expenditure of foodstuffs is useful.

The fewer birds kept, the more purchased food is likely to make a big hole in any possible profit there may be from

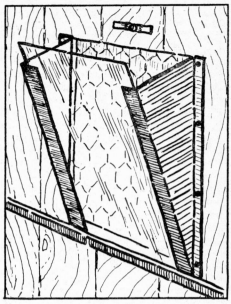

WINDOW DESIGN

The suggestion shown for a window provides the maximum of sunlight and air while protecting the birds from draughts in bad weather.

poultry keeping. However, it is perhaps better that we should first consider the ideal methods of feeding, and then what alterations can be made in these ideal methods without unduly straining the birds or hampering their output.

We have up to now been thinking merely of the poultry houses. When it comes to questions of food, other items have to be thought of, and these may be summed up as follows :—

1. Food troughs.
2. Water supply.
3. Grit box.
4. Dry mash hopper.
5. Dust box.
6. Litter.

Food troughs. A food trough is generally a V-shaped trough, half round or square, raised about 6 in. from the floor. A 2-ft. length does for six fowls.

A very good substitute for the conventional trough sold by stores can be made from an old motor tyre. Cut this in half lengthways, i.e., round the circumference, and it makes two circular troughs. Raise these by nailing them to wooden blocks, and each trough will do for ten fowls.

In these troughs grain or wet mash can be fed to the birds. The troughs should of course be kept quite clean.

Water bucket. A simple device for supplying water is a slatted platform, into which is fitted an ordinary bucket. This platform should be raised from the floor sufficiently to avoid litter being scratched into it. A pan beneath to take the drips is advisable. Both pan and platform can be attached to a wall.

Grit box. Grit is an essential part of birds' food : without it they are unable to digest other foods. A box of grit can generally be attached to a side wall, preferably by the water platform, as the grit is likely then to remain clean.

Greens. Another article of diet for fowls is greenstuff such as cabbages, or root vegetables. It is best for this, too,

WATER BUCKET

This simple arrangement to accommodate water can be fixed to a side wall of the smallest house.

to be supplied at some height from the ground so that it does not get among the litter. Large roots and cabbages can always be spiked on to a nail or hung on the water platform, but it is useful also to have a " miniature hay crib " on the side wall for odd leaves, etc.

Dry mash hopper. If dry mash is fed to fowls in an ordinary open feeding trough, such as described above, the birds have a bad habit of hooking it over the edge of the trough. This is wasteful and insanitary, and dry mash hoppers are therefore generally fitted with a batten lip to prevent this. The hopper can be a simple box type, single or double sided, a small batten being set about 1 in. from the front and 1 in. down from the top, at an angle of 30 degrees. The length of hopper needed is a 2 ft. single-sided hopper for six birds, or larger in proportion to numbers. When these hoppers, or the feeding troughs referred to above, are set in the houses, it is important that light should pass along them, and if there is only one window they should be set end on to it.

All sundriesmen sell other types of hopper, including the true hopper which

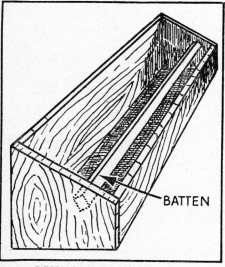

DRY MASH RECEPTACLE

Where dry mash is to be fed a special receptacle will be required to prevent the fowls hooking the mash over the edges of the trough with their beaks. The batten lip set at an angle of 30 degrees in the trough is one of the best methods. The trough can be either single sided as shown in the sketch or double sided.

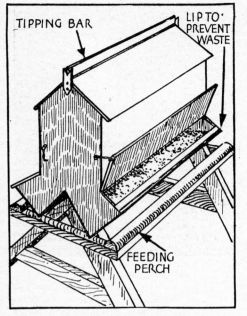

TIPPING BAR

LIP TO·
PREVENT
WASTE

FEEDING
PERCH

DRY MASH HOPPER

A large supply of dry mash is held in this hopper. The lengths required are 1 ft. for six birds, 1½ ft. for ten birds, and 2½ ft. for twenty birds. The mash is fed downwards over a chute from an upper receptacle into the troughs beneath on either side.

pullets, turn down any that are abnormal in any way first. Then turn down any with loose feathers, with ruffled feathers just at the back of the combs, those that crouch, or are " cow hocked," those that carry the tail too low. Pick out then the pullets that seem firm when handled, and have tight feathering, bold prominent eyes, and a satin skin, with round, firm but greasy feeling shanks.

Twisted toes, swollen joints, pendulous crops, are other faults that may be present.

A pullet should lay from the age of six months onwards, and March or April pullets are best for the backyarder who wants eggs in winter. If young chickens are bought instead of ready-to-lay birds, they should be pullet chicks from sex-linked crosses.

Now for details of feeding these newly purchased pullets. The ideal is to give each bird as much as she will eat in a day, and no more. This is in the neighbourhood of 4½ oz. of food per day. The food will be mash and grain. The grain feeds the bird, and the mash produces the eggs, so that the mash is particularly important. House scraps can be included in the mash, and if by chance grain is temporarily unobtainable (as may occur in times of emergency), laying mash alone has to be fed.

SYSTEMS OF FEEDING

The following three alternative systems of feeding pullets for laying are all advocated by the editor of the *Feathered World*.

FIRST SYSTEM

Early morning. Feed ½ oz. of wheat and maize buried in the litter, or oats or barley.

Midday. Layers' mash, made up by one of the firms dealing in poultry foods, mixed to a crumbly moist condition with water or house scraps and vegetable water. Feed in troughs, as much as the birds will clear up in forty-five minutes. For this feed you can use one-third house scraps if available. Such things as plate scrappings, crumbs, rinds and unwanted scraps of cooked vegetables are all good. If necessary, mince these and steep them in boiling water before use. Potato parings, nettles and parings from other roots can be boiled, the water used in the preparation of the mash, and the parings themselves cut up small with a knife before being added.

Evening. Wheat and maize fed in troughs, or oats or barley, as much as the birds will eat. This can be given by artificial light in winter, and if desired the grain can be soaked for twenty-four hours.

SECOND SYSTEM

For those away from home all day.

Early morning. Feed ½ oz. of wheat and maize, or oats and barley in clean litter. Have an open special hopper containing dry mash, i.e., the special laying mash sold by specialist firms. Leave the dry mash hopper open until midday or evening, when kibbled maize and wheat can be fed in the trough—as much as the birds will eat.

THIRD SYSTEM

Give the whole of the grain feed in the morning, and the whole of the mash at night, with green food (if available) at midday.

The backyard poultry keeper is warned against trying to store too much food at a time. Metal bins are best for storage ; a small-size dustbin will hold the food in safety so that mice and rats do not get to it. Twenty-eight pounds each of grain and mash last six hens six weeks and are sufficient to store at one time. Certainly the amount stored by the backyard poultry keeper should not exceed one hundredweight at a time.

As with every hobby or occupation that concerns livestock, it is very important to work to a routine. For one thing, the birds expect it, just as they expect the sun to rise daily. For another, when a routine is once established, the work becomes easier, and as nothing gets neglected, the results are better. Should the owner happen to be called away for a time he is better able to give instructions

to a substitute if he has learnt a satisfactory routine of necessary tasks.

Naturally, there are some things that upset the routine on a large poultry farm—such events as heavy frosts and snows or other troublesome weather, the advent of baby chicks, epidemics of various kinds—but these things should rarely trouble the backyarder. So the work of feeding, cleaning, and generally caring for laying hens can well be reduced to simple rules. Some of the work is daily work, other tasks can be left longer.

Early morning. Scatter half ration of grain in litter. Attend to ventilation. See to the water supply, remembering always to rinse vessels before refilling.

Midday. Feed if necessary (see above systems). Remove droppings in intensive houses. Collect eggs. Give green food, in the rack, suspended in the house, or if the fowls run in the open, give the green food outside, suspended from wooden " gallows." It is better for them to take it from just above their heads, than to trample it among the litter.

Evening. Feed as required. In winter, empty water vessels afterwards. Attend

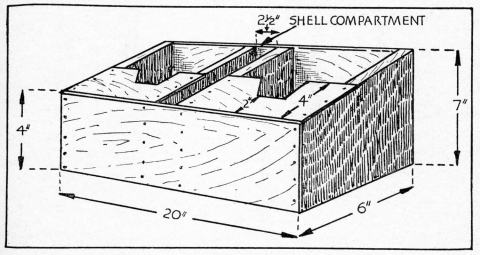

FOOD TROUGH

This food trough prevents wastage by the screening effect of the metal half covers and is sufficient for two birds. The centre compartment provides ample room for oyster shell.

the cause, which may be the hatching date of the birds, the strain, feeding, weather or general living conditions.

Should you wish to know which of your birds is failing to lay, trap-nesting will solve this problem for you. Trap-nesting is merely the practice of trapping the hen in her nest when she lays an egg. By it you can tell immediately which hens are laying, and the quality of their eggs. A trap is made of braided flaps that are rolled up until the hen enters the nest, when she releases them, so that they fall, like a shutter, and trap her in the nest. Any poultry keeper can construct a trap for himself with plywood, laths and some canvas or webbing for the hinges.

BREEDING POULTRY

The next ambitious step from the keeping of a few backyard pullets or hens is breeding. For this the poultry keeper must provide himself with a good cockerel, which should be not less than ten months old when put in the pens with the hens. It is extremely important to choose a good cockerel. Remember that he is the father of every chick born, and it is unwise to use for breeding any bird that has the slightest defect. One cockerel can be mated to ten hens. On larger farms two cockerels will suffice for

Rhode Island Red pullet.

forty hens, but we are not here dealing with large poultry farms.

It is as well to become familiar at the outset with the terms used in this connexion. First crossing signifies the mating of a pure-bred male of one variety to a pure-bred female of another variety. Experiments have shown that in many cases the chicks so reared can be separated definitely into male and female directly they are hatched, which is, of course, an advantage. This is referred to as " sex-linkage," the idea being that the colour of the down on the newly hatched chick is linked with its sex. For instance, if a gold cock of the breeds Rhode Island Red, Buff Rock, Buff Leghorn, etc., is mated with a silver hen of the breeds Light Sussex or White Wyandotte (but not a White Leghorn), some of the chicks will have golden-brown down, and these will prove to be females, while some of them will have creamy-white down, and these will turn out to be males. Other clearly defined characteristics are found to be linked with sex in first crossings of other breeds, though sometimes if the cross is effected the other way round (e.g., a silver cock with gold hen) there is no distinction in the chick down.

Out-crossing means going outside your own run, to some source not related in any way to your own chicks and hens, to obtain a mate of the same variety.

If you decide to go in for breeding, you must choose your times wisely. The best chicks are produced from the middle of February until the end of April. The influence of the male lasts for a week after he has been removed, and the male should be introduced at least a week before eggs are wanted for hatching in spring. In the case of mating during winter only, exceptionally vigorous young cockerels should be used, and they should be introduced a fortnight before eggs are required for hatching. It is necessary to isolate hens for three weeks before introducing fresh cockerels.

Hens selected for breeding should be

Light Sussex pullet.

thoroughly examined. They must not be too fat, for a fat hen is often incapable of producing fertile eggs. If breeders cannot have free range, which is the ideal for them, they must be given plenty of green food, and a special mash should always be mixed for them. This can consist of : five parts (by weight) of wheatings ; two parts bran ; two parts maize ; one part meat meal ; one per cent each cod-liver oil and salt.

Most small poultry keepers prefer to set a broody hen rather than use an incubator. As a matter of fact it is rather better to set two or three broodies at one time, so that if the hatches are bad ones, the chicks can be shared out and one of the broodies dispensed with.

If you decide to set a broody hen and have already obtained fertile eggs, store these large end up in a temperature of forty to fifty degrees until you are ready. When ready to set the bird, find a roomy box, 15 in. square or larger, and cover the bottom with 1-in. mesh wire netting, to keep out rats. Set this nest on the floor over a couple of shovel-fuls of earth. Make a saucer-shaped nest using straw, or if straw is not available, any soft dry material that will completely pack up hollows and corners.

Use dummies in the nest for a day or two, but when the broody shows that she will settle down on the eggs in the

nest, replace the dummies with the eggs, about thirteen in number. Food and water must be given regularly, a handful of maize, and clean water once daily. Leave the hen off the nest ten minutes for this feed at first, and increase to fifteen minutes and then in the third week to twenty minutes. On the nineteenth day chipping of the shells should begin, and the hen should then be left quite undisturbed until the morning of the twenty-second day, when she should have completed the task of hatching.

The health of the broody will be improved if she is kept free from parasites. A dusting of sodium fluoride just before setting will help in this matter. Green food should be available also if she will take it, but not too much should be given. On the tenth day of the hatching period, remove the eggs and

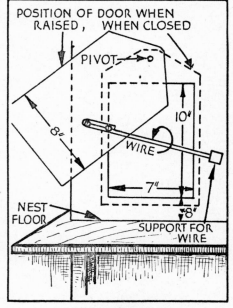

NEST BOX TRAP

Here is another design for a nest box trap, again operated by the fowl. It consists of a small metal door and a projecting length of wire. The wire rests against a small block of wood and is knocked up by the hen in entering. This enables the door to turn on its pivot and completely cover the opening.

the nesting material and just dampen the soil below; then replace the nest and eggs. Apart from this, keep an eye on the eggs, clean them if they become soiled, and remove any breakages.

DAY-OLD CHICKS

A popular way to obtain chicks for rearing is to buy day-old chicks from a large poultry breeder. These can easily be reared by a broody hen if care is taken over their introduction. Wait until the hen has sat on a nest of dummies for a week. A quiet hen, not a pullet, is best for this. Then, when the chicks arrive, keep them cosy and warm until the evening, and then take one chick and place gently beneath the broody's breast. Wait an hour, and after that time, if the hen has "taken" to the chick, give her the others.

To rear chicks with the help of a hen, which is the most convenient way for the amateur without experience, the essentials are a good coop and a small run. The coop is the familiar sloping-roof structure, 21 in. high in front, and a little lower at the back, roughly 2 ft. square (according to the size of the hen and brood) and with slats at the front. Of these slats, which are arranged vertically, one is loose and projects through the roof front, and when raised it allows the hen to pass through. When closed the slats leave only 2-in. spaces, through which the chicks can pass while the hen is confined.

A night shutter is also needed, and this is a wooden affair that is secured by a thumb catch. There is, in addition, a ventilator, usually made by leaving a narrow opening horizontally at the top of the front, this opening being covered with wire netting.

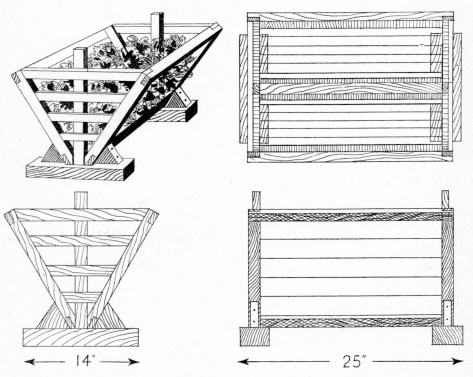

←— 14" —→   ←——— 25" ———→

Construction of handy green food trough, with sections.

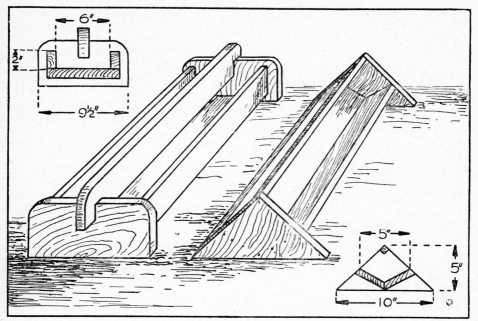

GRIT TROUGHS

One should always keep a supply of two kinds of grit handy inside the house. The alternative troughs shown provide useful receptacles for flint or gravel, oyster shell or limestone grit.

The run is just a small run for the chicks. It fits against the front of the coop, and may be perhaps five or six feet long and the height of the coop shutter. A hinged lid forms the part of the roof that is next to the coop. Two wide boards run the length of the coop and along the end at the base, and so protect the chicks from cold winds. The upper part of end and sides and the remainder of the roof is covered with sparrow-proof netting.

Both the coop and the run are moved daily, and should be used where there is grass if possible.

FEEDING CHICKENS

Other requisites for chick rearing are containers for water and food. A water fountain, which can be arranged by inverting a glass jam jar of water in a pan, and a small wooden trough for food is all that is needed.

To start chicks feeding a little dry food is dropped first on to a flat board, and this is tapped—chicks, like human babies, are very imitative. Chicks do not need any food at all until they are forty-eight hours old, and they eat very little at first. Six feeds daily are given in the first week, each being cleared away after ten minutes. Chick feed and chick mash are the two foods given to the brood, and these will, we hope, be obtainable even in wartime. As it is doubtful whether they will be made up as usual, the poultry farmer will be wise to allow all the green food—i.e., clean short grass—and all the sunlight possible. In this way some of the deficiencies of the wartime foods will be made good.

Normally, chick mash should contain dried milk and cod-liver oil, the latter being a good substitute for sunlight in small back gardens, where direct sunshine is often scarce.

Mash is moistened with water and fed in troughs which are best protected by wire netting, so that the chicks do not walk in the food. An ordinary square or

brown markings, and males with grey or lemon down with black and brown markings.

N.B.—Mating a silver cock with a gold hen produces chicks that cannot be distinguished by the sex down.

3. A black or brown cock—Black or Brown Leghorn or Rhode Island Red—mated with a barred hen—Barred Rock or Cuckoo Leghorn—produces cockerels black with a light patch on the head top, and pullets entirely black on the back of the head.

4. A dark-shanked cock—White Bresse or Silkie—mated with a light-shanked hen—Light Sussex or Wyandotte—produces cockerels that have light shanks and skin at two weeks old, while pullets of the same age have dark shanks.

5. A quick feathering cock, such as White Leghorn, mated with a slow feathering hen — Wyandotte, Rhode Island Red, or Sussex—produces quick feathering pullets and slow feathering cockerels. At a day old the pullets will have feathering extending well beyond the down ; the cockerels show no feathering at all at this age, and no tail until after the sixteenth day.

When special mating of pure-bred stock has not taken place, the poultry keeper may have to wait rather longer to tell the sex of his chicks. Light breeds can, however, be safely separated at a month old and heavy breeds at seven or eight weeks.

You can easily tell the difference if you look for these points in the chicks:—

Light breeds. At one month the combs will be sprouting rapidly on the cockerels, and these birds will have a somewhat cheekier appearance than the pullets. Their tails are longer, their legs long, necks held well up, and their faces red in colour.

The pullets will have smaller combs of yellowish colour, shorter tails, and longer, lower bodies. Their manners at the food table are generally shyer.

Heavy breeds. The cockerels of the heavier breeds are larger, coarser, and with more thickset, heavy bodies than the pullets. Legs are stout but also rather long. The birds are upright in carriage, and stand very erect when alarmed. Some signs of the comb may be visible when the separation of sexes takes place at seven weeks ; backs will be rather bare, or showing pin feathers. The cockerels are always more aggressive and greedy than the pullets.

Pullets of the heavy breeds have small neat heads with practically no comb showing. They are well feathered, specially on wing bows, back and sides of crop. Tails are longish, and well

CHICKENS HATCHING OUT

Chicks just hatching from incubated eggs. Remember to use eggs not more than seven days old and keep the incubator in a room where the temperature does not vary very much. A cellar usually answers quite well for small machines, or even unused living-rooms. Draughty sheds of match boarding should be avoided unless it is possible to line them inside. Earth or concrete floors are quite good but do not select rooms with too much window space as they may admit too much sun heat and cause more variation in the room temperature than is desirable.

formed, bodies long, legs short and rather fine.

Although all the information previously given is designed chiefly for the small " backyard " poultry keeper, it applies equally to those rather more fortunate who can allow their chickens and hens a grass run. I am not writing here for the large poultry farmer who occupies acres of ground, but merely for the home gardener who is prepared to allot a part of his ground to poultry.

THE SUBURBAN GARDENER

Let us consider the position of a suburban gardener who has a plot of ground mainly devoted to the cultivation of ornamental flowers, shrubs, and grass. He may have an allotment elsewhere and there he will be able to cultivate the vegetables required by his small family throughout the year.

It is probably not convenient for fowls to be kept on the allotment, as few allotments are near enough to the house for this to be a reasonable arrangement. He does not want fowls to run riot over the whole of his borders or lawn, nor does he want to spend his few hours of leisure and relaxation gazing at a not too attractive poultry run. Here is a solution.

First make an imaginary end to the garden at a point say 15 ft. from the end wall. Here erect a decorative screen of fine trellis, which can speedily be covered with roses—or even with runner beans, if that seems preferable.

About midway between this trellis and the end wall, build a framework of 5-ft. uprights and top bars, and run a bottom bar of wood along at the ground level. Between each upright (say at 5-ft. distances) fit a framework of wood over which is stretched wire netting ; hinge this at the bottom to the ground bar of wood, and put thumb catches at the top, so that the wired frames can each be laid down on to the soil between the two fences, or raised to close in the fence.

Good turf can be laid, or grass sown in this intervening " run," and the

White Wyandotte pullet.

fowls can be allowed access to it by the simple method of laying down the frames horizontally on the grass. This has the advantage of allowing them access to the grass without their being able to scratch and completely ruin the turf. Further, the appearance of a strip of grass showing through the rose or bean covered trellis is rather more attractive than if a bare patch of earth or ash were all that could be seen.

These trellis and wire frame fences need present very little difficulty to the home carpenter. Posts, as always with garden posts, should be set into concrete so that there is no danger of sudden collapse, and all wood should be treated with creosote. The trellis, which can be of any ornamental pattern, is easily made from ordinary plaster laths dipped into creosote before being nailed to the posts. This is very important. Tight nailing prevents the creosote from covering the whole of the wood, and wood only treated after erection is likely to become rotten at the joints when rains have found their way in.

Grass for poultry can be sown at any time when the soil and weather are warm. Water will be needed in the dry hot weather.

Coarse perennial rye grass is not much use to poultry, and the suburban gardener who wants to sow only a small patch chance an accident occurs at a season when another queen cannot possibly be raised, the hive almost inevitably perishes.

The queen spends her time, when she is a mature adult, laying eggs, one in each cell. If she visits a worker cell she lays a worker egg, that is, a female egg, and if she visits a larger drone cell she lays a male egg which will develop into a drone. The drones are raised purely and simply in order to provide an eligible husband for any young queen that may be hatched out.

So far as one can tell, the queen does not purposely provide a successor, or lay eggs destined to become queens. Queens are raised from ordinary worker eggs, which are removed by the working bees from their small cells to the large, specially constructed queen cells. In these the young larvæ are reared, fed on specially rich food, and brought at last to the stage of adult, unmarried queens.

INSIDE THE HIVE

In the old days, the only way in which the beekeeper could obtain the honey he wanted was by taking it from the hive at the end of summer. This he did in some cases by destroying the bees first, and in others by smoking them out of one hive into another, and then taking the honey from the deserted hive.

What happens now? Let us look at a modern hive and note the general principles of its construction. First there is a lower brood chamber. This corresponds pretty generally to the natural tree home of the bees, except that the wax combs which hang parallel from the roof, and are packed with larvæ and honey and pollen dust, are neatly built into rectangular wooden frames. The bees are induced to build them in this orderly fashion by the simple method of providing the frames, spacing these accurately, allowing 1½ in. exactly from centre to centre of the combs, and by the provision of what is called comb foundation. This is a sheet of wax, already partly stamped out with the hexagonal pattern of the honeycomb. Sheets are

inserted in the centre of the frames, and these frames are then hung parallel, with metal end spacers to space them with real accuracy. Finding their work partly done for them, the bees complete it according to the desire of the beekeeper.

A glance at the detailed measurements and diagrams will show exactly how the frames are hung in the brood chamber. A novice, buying a furnished hive and bees, will always receive the hive before the bees are sent, and he will be wise to make himself quite familiar with all the parts of the hive before beginning any practical work.

It will be seen, for instance, that there are sufficient frames almost to fill the brood chamber. These are not always all required at the outset. A wooden dummy frame is also provided. This can be taken out first to allow one or more frames to be removed easily, and when it is put back, and pressed back as close as it will go to the remaining frames, it leaves no room for the escape of bees beyond the part of the hive allotted to them.

THE BROOD CHAMBER

The brood chamber is the counterpart of the natural bee-home in the tree. No beekeeper ever takes honey from the brood chamber to sell, except in very unusual circumstances : that honey is the bees' own store. It is the other parts of a modern hive which represent the work, and the reward, of the beekeeper.

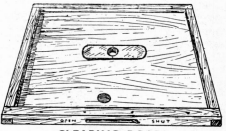

CLEARING BOARD

A clearing board fitted with an escape will prevent bees from returning to comb supers. This is placed in position at midday, but should not be removed until some subsequent evening.

Above the movable frames in which the bees are breeding and storing, the beekeeper lays a sheet of perforated metal, with holes in it large enough to allow for the passage through of the worker bees, but just too small for either drones or the queen bee to pass through. Over this, during the honey-storing months, he sets further wooden frames called " supers." It is in these that the harvest of honey for sale is stored. The modern beekeeper, you will see, does not rob the bees of their necessary provision. He helps them to increased production by providing (*a*) a draught-proof hive, so that they do not have to waste time sealing up cracks to guard against winter winds ; (*b*) sheets of wax foundation that save them a great deal of time and labour ; and (*c*) medical care and attention, with artificial food in seasons of bad weather, and special protective covering in winter. All of this goes to the building up of strong colonies that can store far more honey than they need.

Naturally, in return for his share in maintaining the well-being of the hive, the beekeeper takes the surplus honey.

Several other items are included in the work of the beekeeper. One is the restriction of swarms. The natural tendency of bees living in a flourishing district where food is plentiful, is to raise new queens, and form new colonies. The beekeeper does not necessarily want any increase of stock : one or two hives are all that the small garden can take conveniently. What is important to the beekeeper is that there shall be plenty of surplus honey stored in the few hives he has. So he removes queen cells immediately they are built to prevent queen bees from being hatched. Without surplus queens there can be no setting up of new colonies, and the result is that the bees set themselves to the task of storing the upper chambers of the hive, instead of breaking up the colony to form new homes.

HOW TO BEGIN

These and other tasks of the beekeeper will be described more fully, but meanwhile let us imagine that you have decided to keep bees, that you know nothing, or almost nothing, of their ways, and that you want advice on how to begin.

The best possible first step is to pay a visit to a local beekeeper, and get him to let you stand by while he opens a hive, and manipulates the frames and other gadgets. You can learn more quickly in this way than from books. As that may not be possible, however, you can begin in this way. Place an order for one or two hives with a reputable firm of bee specialists. You will be supplied with a hive corresponding in all its measurements to the one illustrated in our diagram. There are different types of hives, but all have the same internal measurements.

BEEKEEPER'S REQUISITES

It is very important that all your hives should be of exactly the same pattern. At some time you will need to amalgamate two colonies or change over frames from one hive to another, or you may want to change the upper racks from one hive to another. Only the experienced beekeeper knows what a lot of trouble is saved when these fittings are all of standard pattern and can be interchanged freely.

In addition to the hive you need certain other beekeepers' requisites, but as with other hobbies and occupations, I think it advisable to buy most of these only as you feel the need for them. A good

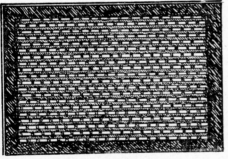

QUEEN EXCLUDER

The queen excluder consists of a sheet of zinc perforated with slots too small for the queen but big enough for the worker bee.

Three types of Old English rabbits.

RABBITS FOR YOUR TABLE

The owner of a small garden can find room for a few rabbits. They breed well in captivity and take up little space, for their natural home is a burrow in the earth, and by nature they are adapted to confined quarters.

There are two ways in which rabbits can be kept :—

(1) In close confinement in a hutch, which can be placed in a shed or outhouse if available.

(2) By what is known as the Morant system. By this method a well-built hutch is constructed, and has attached to it a run, similar to a chicken run, for placing on rough grass or a lawn. The floor of the run is made of wire netting, and the rabbits graze on the grass which comes through the meshes. Both hutch and run are portable. This is certainly the better method, since it increases the health of the animals. During winter some form of protection can be laid over part of the run and a layer of straw on the floor of the hutch, which should be raised from the ground by means of 2-in. battens.

The number of rabbits required to keep a family of four in rabbit meat for say one day a week, would be four does and one buck. The average litter is from four to eight, and a doe in good health will produce at least three litters a year, roughly at the beginning of March, in mid-June and late September. If there are young members of the family, a boy or girl from twelve to fifteen, one of these might well undertake the management of the rabbitry. It should be run on business lines with a double-entry book in which expenses and credits can be entered, the rabbits being charged to assumes that the beekeeper has several colonies, it does not concern the novice.

When a swarm is first hived and has not a great store of honey on which to draw, it should set to work at once gathering supplies. If bad weather prevents this, the swarm may need to be fed artificially : otherwise it may perish. Again, if a colony has not a great store of honey in autumn, and the winter is unduly protracted, it too may perish through starvation unless artificially fed.

Feeding a hive is a simple matter with modern feeding bottles. These allow for syrup to be introduced by means of a bottle inverted over the frame tops. The supply is regulated, and syrup is prevented from escaping by the construction of the feeder.

CANDY FEEDING

An alternative to syrup feeding is feeding by inverting cakes of candy over the frames. The candy is sold in prepared form in glass-topped boxes, so that no difficulty is experienced in its use.

Feeding should never be done when supers are in position, and syrup feeding should only be done when the weather is

It is not proposed to give here details of treatment. The wise beekeeper will in case of trouble call in the county bee expert, in the same way as we call in the doctor for human ailments.

ADULT BEE DISEASES

The disease which is most dreaded is the *Acarine* or *Isle of Wight* disease. If the bees are becoming listless and slack, even on a warm day when they are under ordinary circumstances most active, there is evidently "trouble in the camp." You will see them later unable to rise and the combs will be coated with excreta —all quite unnatural to the scrupulously clean and tidy bee.

Another disease known as *Nosema* is less serious, and the dysentery is less noticeable. Bees will be seen to fly from the hive and then fall on their backs with legs trembling.

Bee paralysis is often caused by mouldy combs or unsealed stores during the winter. Cold winds early in the year will often start this trouble. The bodies of the bees will become shiny and distended, and the wings will tremble. Beekeepers can to a certain extent control this disease by removing mouldy combs, and giving the bees some medicated

Three useful breeds of rabbits to keep, Giant Flemish, White Angora and Small Silver Grey. The pelts of the Giant Flemish and the Silver Grey and the wool of the White Angora are all marketable. The wool is collected from the White Angora by frequent combing.

INDEX